Effective Visual Studio .NET

David Richard Kalkstein DeLoveh

William Sempf

Dan Maharry

Donald Xie

Wrox Press Ltd. ®

Effective Visual Studio .NET

Printing History
Latest Reprint August 2002
First published April 2002

Published by Wrox Press Ltd,
Arden House, 1102 Warwick Road, Acocks Green,
Birmingham, B27 6BH, UK
Printed in the United States
ISBN 1-861006-96-9

Trademark Acknowledgements

Wrox has endeavored to correctly render trademarks for all the companies and products mentioned in this book with the appropriate use of capitals. However, Wrox is unable to guarantee the accuracy of this information.

Credits

Authors
David Richard Kalkstein DeLoveh
William Sempf
Dan Maharry
Donald Xie

Commissioning Editor
Ian Blackham

Technical Editors
Richard Deeson
Devin Lunsford
Robert FE Shaw

Managing Editor
Louay Fatoohi

Project Manager
Emma Batch

Author Agent
Charlotte Smith

Index
Michael Brinkman

Technical Reviewers
Joseph Bustos
Damien Foggon
Slavomir Furman
Mark Horner
Amit Kalani
Johan Normen
Troy Proudfoot
Gavin Smyth

Production Coordinator
Natalie O'Donnell

Illustrations
Sarah Hall
Neil Lote

Cover
Chris Morris

Proof Reader
Chris Smith

About the Authors

David Richard Kalkstein DeLoveh

David Richard Kalkstein DeLoveh is currently a consultant in the Columbus, Ohio area of the US. He specializes in Microsoft data-access technologies with articles published on asptoday.com, 15seconds.com, and developerfusion.com. David loves the work he does and too often makes it his hobby. He can be reached at david@deloveh.com.

I'd first like to thank my wife Heidi who has loved, supported, and encouraged me throughout my endeavors, no matter how time consuming. Thanks to my family and friends for their continuing support.

Thanks to my co-authors for their time and effort to make this book a success. I am especially grateful to them and the employees of Wrox for their support and understanding, as my health became an issue.

I would also like to thank the individuals who have been mentors throughout my career. Thanks to Marc Yabroff who mentored me patiently when I was so junior a developer that my questions were simply ludicrous. Thanks to Robert Patton for being a mentor who helped build my skills in the latest and greatest technology thus opening many doors for me.

David contributed Chapters 1, 2, 3, 4, 11, 12, and 13 to this book.

Bill Sempf

Bill Sempf has spent an inordinate amount of time in the last year writing about .NET. He is a co-author of *Professional ASP.NET Web Services* and *Professional VB.NET*, and a frequent contributor to *TechRepublic*, *Inside Web Development Journal*, and *Intranet Journal*. A Microsoft Certified Professional, Certified Internet Business Strategist, and Certified Internet Webmaster, Bill has developed over one hundred web applications for startups and Fortune 50 companies alike.

Bill began his career in 1985 managing Apple IIe systems for the local library. Since then he has built applications for the likes of Lucent Technologies, Bank One, Nationwide Insurance, and Sears, Roebuck and Co. Currently, Bill is a Senior Consultant at Paros Business Partners in Columbus, Ohio, and an owner of Products Of Innovative New Technology. He can be reached at bill@sempf.net.

Most authors say their thanks in the beginning of the book, but neglect to thank the readers in advance. Thanks. After you read, please do send the authors an e-mail, and let us thank you in person in fact. We put a lot of words on paper, and a lot of code on the screen, to bring this book to you and would like to know what you think. For David and I it was a labor of love, and you would not believe what we went through to do it.

Despite that less-than-inspiring utterance, I want to say a word for all aspiring writers out there. If you have something to say, say it. You may be surprised how many people want to listen.

Also, thanks go out to the friends, family, and clients that have patiently hung around while I ignored them for the last four months. Thanks to Ian and Charlotte at Wrox for their support and tour-guide skills in Oxford – what was that building again, Ian? Thanks to Wrox in general for supporting this book through its trials and tribulations.

I again need to thank Gabrielle for her love and support through this most difficult of projects, which ate a Christmas holiday, a vacation, and countless weekends.

Bill contributed Chapters 5, 6, 7, 8, 10, 15, 16, and the Epilogue to this book.

Dan Maharry

Dan Maharry hails from the South East tip of England but has found himself flung around the globe in the quest for knowledge and, well, a purpose for it all. He's having more luck with the first than the second. For the time being, he is a journeyman freelancer: writing, crewing, and reviewing away – until someone offers him a full time job that is (sic). Get in contact with him on danm@hmobius.com. Feedback and work offers freely accepted.

Dan contributed Chapter 17 to this book, and provided additional material.

Donald Xie

Donald Xie has 14 years experience in enterprise application development for various types of businesses. He is a co-author of *Professional CDO Programming* and a contributing author for a number of books including *C++ Unleashed* and *VB MTS*. Donald – Mack to his friends – currently works as a consulting system architect for the Department of Training in Western Australia, Australia. You can contact him at donald@iinet.net.au.

Mack contributed Chapters 9 and 14 to this book.

Table of Contents

Table of Contents

Table of Contents

Table of Contents

Table of Contents

Table of Contents

Introduction

There have been many books written on .NET – especially new features of .NET. With it being truly object-oriented, language agnostic, and XML Web Service ready; .NET is a formidable developer environment. In fact, many believe that it will significantly change the roadmap for Windows development.

There are few books, however, that are written for developers who use the tools to develop applications. There are many features of .NET that have been the focus of much of the writing on the area what most regular developers need is an honest look at the power of the tool used to work with all of these features. While the intricacies of the Common Language Runtime (CLR) and the definition of Simple Object Access Protocol (SOAP) headers are interesting to some, there are a host of developers that just need to get the job done.

If you are one of those, this book is written for you.

We begin this introduction with a list of **What is in this Book**. This is a quick description of each chapter and section, to give you, the reader, an idea of what we have written about your favorite topics. Second you'll find **What isn't in this Book**. This is probably self-explanatory. Finally, there is a description of **The Unified Example**, a new way to show sample code throughout the book.

What is in this Book

Visual Studio .NET and the New Microsoft Methodology

This book is different, in the fact that it is presenting software born of a new environment that is designed to follow the largest shift in priority that Microsoft developers have ever seen. There have been, as we mentioned, several books written about the .NET Framework, but specifically looking at *how this influences the tools* is a different take. We take this position in this book, and cover:

- ❑ Software as a service
- ❑ Rapid application development on the Server
- ❑ Role-based development
- ❑ Write anywhere, run here

Professional Features

The book is subdivided into sections that cover the different editions of the development environment; in the first section we will cover those main features found in the Professional Edition.

Start Here

In designing this book, we were amazed at the number of things that are just different about the new Visual Studio .NET Environment. *Start Here* is a chapter devoted to all of these things.

First, we will discover that the IDE does a lot more for us than it used to. We will also touch on most of these usable tools, for instance:

- ❑ The Start Page
- ❑ Search Tools
- ❑ Profile
- ❑ The IDE toolboxes
- ❑ Code Viewer

Building Windows Forms

The development of Windows Forms is dramatically different from in VC++ 6.0 or VB 6.0. We will take a developer's look at the way Visual Studio .NET helps with form creation, inheritance, and deployment. Expect information about:

- ❑ The controls
- ❑ Components and references
- ❑ Menus
- ❑ Visual inheritance
- ❑ Accessibility

Web Application Development

For those used to ASP 3.0 and Windows DNA Microsoft has essentially corrected all of the little issues we as web developers have been forced to develop fixes for over the last five years, like hidden action pages and using `Response.Write` for debugging.

Since ASP.NET is based on the Common Language Runtime (CLR), it inherits all of the same language features as regular Windows Applications. Code Behind provides the speed of scripting with the ruggedness of compiled code. In short, web application programming is now largely modeled after the way Visual Basic programmers have been doing things for years. In this chapter, you'll find:

- ❑ Improved Drag-'n'-Drop web application development
- ❑ New tools in your toolbox
- ❑ Server controls
- ❑ Working with ASP.NET and Code Behind

Rapid Application Development for the Server

One of the foundations of the .NET Framework, Rapid Application Development (RAD) on the Server brings the speed of Visual Basic client/server programming to the world of n-tier application development. Rather than creating complex documentation to keep everything straight, and maintaining the registration of hundreds of DLLs, we can code n-tier applications in the RAD style of design. We'll cover:

- ❑ The Server Explorer
- ❑ Object Browser
- ❑ Component Builder
- ❑ .NET Servers
- ❑ The Upgrade Wizard

XML Web Services

This is another major cornerstone of the .NET architecture. We'll cover XML Web Services from the Visual Studio angle, with topics like:

- ❑ The Web Service Project Type
- ❑ Designing services
- ❑ Publishing
- ❑ The Web Service Resource Type
- ❑ Consuming services
- ❑ Discovery

Visual Studio Automation

Along with all this other stuff, it turns out that Visual Studio .NET is a much more extensible tool than previous versions. Two much-needed features have been improved and or added, and Microsoft is encouraging third party providers to produce new features all the time. There is a complete namespace devoted to the IDE, which allows for integration with existing tools. Also, there are some new add-ins we'll discuss. In that spirit, we'll cover the following in this chapter:

❑ Macros

❑ Add-ins

❑ The DTE object

❑ CodeSwap.NET

❑ The VSIP

Mobile Internet ToolKit

It's not how many Wireless Application Protocol webs you've written, it's how many you *should* have written but didn't because the WAP languages are so touchy. This is no longer the case, thanks to the .NET Mobile Internet Toolkit, and its Internet Designer. This easy-to-use Add-In brings true visual integrated development for mobile devices to the .NET Framework. We'll look at:

❑ Requirements

❑ Merging with existing projects

❑ The MIT controls Runtime

❑ The Designer itself

❑ Device Capabilities

❑ Device Adapter Code

Deployment Features

Thanks to the Common Language Runtime (CLR), deployment of n-tier applications and other Windows applications is a different and simpler beast than it once was. Developers have more power and less to do than in Windows DNA. In this chapter, we'll cover the highlights:

❑ Types of projects explained

❑ Microsoft Installer

❑ XCOPY deployment

❑ URL Deployment

❑ Custom Installers

❑ Handling COM+ easily

Crystal Reports

Crystal Reports is finally an embedded Visual Studio tool, and none too soon. Windows and Web Developers alike have been setting aside 25% of their development time to do reports for far too long. With the new integration and partnership between Crystal Decisions and Microsoft comes a host of new features, including:

❑ Tight Web and Windows report integration

❑ Reports as a Web Service

❑ Runtime customization

Debugging

Last but not least in the list of Developer Tools are the new debugging features found in Visual Studio. Without a doubt, Microsoft has added every feature that Win32 programmers have complained about not having for the last five years. Then, we lost the one GOOD feature – Edit and Continue. Rumor has it that this will be in the next release. The chapter will cover:

❑ The New Task List

❑ Run-Time tracing

❑ Break Points on any layer

❑ Drag-'n'-Drop performance monitoring

❑ Functional XML Web Service testing

❑ Remote debugging

Enterprise Developer Features

The Enterprise Developer edition of Visual Studio .NET contains all the features found in the Professional edition but also includes the following features.

Working with Data

Some parts of Visual Studio .NET are difficult to define. The data tools are one of them. There are varying ways to deal with data in Visual Studio .NET, and none of them use Enterprise Manager. Some of these features are only available in the Enterprise Developer edition, but some features are also found in the Professional version. Rather than split them up, we put them all in with Enterprise features.

❑ Data Connectors

❑ Data Designers

❑ XML Designers

Visual SourceSafe

There are a number of current limitations with the Visual SourceSafe, and they are being addressed in version 6.0c. In addition, the Visual Studio .NET has been updated to work with the VSS environment. We'll take a look at the following:

- ❏ New features
- ❏ Updated tools
- ❏ New IDE
- ❏ Pending checkins

Application Center Test

Certainly one of the most fantastic development tools for the average enterprise programmer is the Application Center Test (ACT). This tool allows component developers to look for bottlenecks in the n-tier environment during development, thus supporting the RAD design effort. It is designed to simulate large groups of users by sending multiple HTTP calls through multiple connections to the server. This way, it stresses web servers and middleware then analyzes the results.

We will take a run through creating new tests with ACT, running them against some of the software built in other chapters. We'll look at dynamic testing, authentication, and other testing considerations.

Enterprise Architect Features

The Enterprise Architect edition of Visual Studio .NET contains all the features found in both of the lower level editions and includes the following additional features.

Data Modeling with Fact-Based Design

For architects, Visio's interaction with Visual Studio provides a masterstroke toward the design of distributed applications. We start with data modeling with Visio, and Microsoft's new choice for design – the Object Role Model. This replacement for the Entity Relationship diagram has its plusses and minuses, but the tools that make it happen are entirely a plus for the .NET Enterprise Architect. We'll look at these features:

- ❏ Rule-based Design
- ❏ The Object Role Model (ORM)
- ❏ Designing with Visio
- ❏ Reverse engineering
- ❏ Components of the ORM

Software Design with UML

The second tier of development supported by Visio is the business rule layer. The Unified Modeling Language has long been the choice of structured models for object-oriented development. Now, little of Microsoft has been truly object-oriented for the last 25 years. With the advent of .NET, UML really has a place in the Microsoft world. As one would then imagine, UML modeling of .NET code is also a part of Visual Studio. In this chapter, we'll discuss:

- ❏ The Multipart System Diagram
- ❏ Generating skeleton code
- ❏ Reverse engineering

Enterprise Templates

Enterprise Frameworks are part of the Application Construction Kit, a broad range of technologies developed by Microsoft to deploy enterprise infrastructure. Enterprise Templates are the developer side of this technology – allowing programmers to avoid the blank-slate problem. Together they provide reusable components used by architects to simplify the lives of their developers. Features that we will discuss in some depth include:

- ❑ Unified tracing
- ❑ Task-event correlation
- ❑ Runtime settings
- ❑ Extensibility

What isn't in this Book

The .NET Framework

There is no question that the .NET Framework is going to change the way developers do their work in the Microsoft world. Even developers on different platforms are going to feel the pressure as their suppliers change things due to the marketing pressure applied by the Microsoft marketing juggernaut. Even non-developers will see changes as their software allows for more network operations and provides more machine-to-machine interactivity. .NET will change many, many things.

Although everything in this book is about .NET, this will not be a .NET primer. You won't find a chapter explaining .NET (though we do have a prologue on how the .NET Framework changes the Microsoft methodology).

This is a very fine distinction, but it bears making. What .NET is to COM, Visual Studio .NET is to Visual InterDev and the other software packages by Microsoft circa 1999. You would find COM references in an InterDev book, but little explanation on how COM works. The same is true here. This book won't provide a listing of Framework namespaces, but it will provide a description of various form components that use those namespaces.

For an introduction to the .NET Framework, and how it works, may we suggest *Introducing .NET*, from Wrox (ISBN 1-861004-89-3). This fantastic little book provides both a guide to the frameworks and an overview of the logic of the .NET Framework.

Visual Basic .NET, C#, or Any Other Language

This book's text uses mostly C# in the examples, Microsoft's new .NET specialized language. C# is a fantastic language, fixing many problems in C++ while maintaining the tight, easy to read code structure. It was born and bred for .NET work, and is now an open standard, managed by the ECMA. It is a good language for both academic writing, like this book, and production coding, like what we are all doing every day.

This book is not a C# reference guide. Everything in this book can be done in VB.NET, JScript.NET, and Perl – or any of the 20 odd other .NET languages. In fact, we will focus on visual tools instead of code where we can. This isn't necessarily because it is better to do things that way, but because that is what this book is about – the tools available to Visual Studio users.

You can code everything for a Microsoft Windows program in a text editor if you wish using the .NET Framework. We won't be doing that. In fact, we won't even be showing both ways to do things. If you want to get the job done with Visual Studio, this book is for you. We will use the tools to get the job done.

If you want a language reference, you should look at one of the many, many books on that topic from Wrox. Currently, there are both a Professional and Beginner book for both C# and VB.NET. For more specific topics, look for titles on ADO.NET and ASP.NET in the Programmer's Reference series.

The .NET Servers

The third part of the .NET strategy is the multitude of server software available. Essentially, Microsoft has packaged all of the option packs, add-ons, and toys into stable server batches so that your organizations can build their servers just right. This is a reasonable though expensive strategy, and important to our cause.

Again, though, this book will not cover the installation, configuration, or management of any Microsoft servers. We will often use SQL Server 2000, and will mention BizTalk, Mobile Internet Application Server, and Application Center. In fact, we strongly recommend that readers have SQL Server 2000 installed before reading this book. An installation of Visual Studio will include the developer edition of SQL Server 2000, and this will work for our examples.

For more information on the .NET servers, first look at Microsoft's web page. Their new layout for the .NET information is both easy to use and informative. Next, check out any of these books by Wrox:

- ❏   *Professional BizTalk*, Stephen Mohr and Scott Woodgate (ISBN 1-861003-29-3)

- ❏   *Professional Application Center 2000*, David Sussman et al (ISBN 1-861004-47-8)

- ❏   *Professional SQL Server 2000 Programming*, Rob Vieira (ISBN 1-861004-48-6)

May we also suggest finding a test machine, installing the servers with the 120 day evaluation, and spending a weekend learning them. Since the topics covered by these servers are so specific it is surprisingly easy to see how the software interfaces with existing functionality. We will avoid any examples in this book that require the installation of any specific servers other than SQL Server 2000, but we still advise taking a look at all of them.

This is because of Microsoft's commitment to the componentized model of server creation. One of the major complaints against NT in general was its density; a ton of functionality never used. If you need a web server, you install Windows 2000 and the ASP.NET components, for example. To increase scalability and portability, Microsoft has approached functionality from a divide-and-conquer perspective.

Methodology

Readers will find that this is not a book about how to develop software. While we do our best to design and code in a good Rapid Application Development (RAD) style, please don't take them as examples of the 'right' way to design software. Space considerations and time allowances in writing force us to take shortcuts in our code that most people wouldn't make in a production environment.

As is to be expected, there aren't very many good books out at this time on designing with .NET, but we certainly can recommend several books about designing with UML, and the related process. Anything by Jacobson, Booch, and Rumbaugh would be viewed by most as the first and final word on use of the UML. A good reference/starter book is *Fundamentals of Object-Oriented Design in UML* by Meilir Page-Jones from Addison-Wesley Pub Co; ISBN: 0-201-69946-X.

The Unified Modeling Language

Speaking of UML, another point of clarification should be made about our Architecture chapters. If you plan on using Visio 2002 for the creation of UML static structures for framework code, we suggest familiarity with the UML before you read that section. There is a lot to cover in a small space here, and much has already been written about UML.

If you need a short, excellent work about the language, not the methodology or process, we recommend UML Distilled, Second Edition – a brief guide to the Standard Object Modeling Language, by Martin Fowler and Kendall Scott (2000 ISBN 0-201-65783-X). It provides an essential overview of the six primary diagrams and how to use them, and is only about 200 pages long.

How to Get the Most from this Book

There are software and knowledge requirements for successful progress through this book.

Software

- ❏   The latest build of Visual Studio .NET
- ❏   Microsoft Windows 2000 or later
- ❏   Microsoft SQL Server 2000 and Enterprise Manager

Knowledge

- ❏   You should be familiar with the .NET Framework –we suggest Wrox *Introduction to .NET*
- ❏   Also, a knowledge of C# or another .NET language is assumed – check out *Professional C# .NET*

The Unified Example

Essentially, we have chosen a story line for our sample code. This will accomplish a number of important steps.

- ❏   **The book reads like a book** – Unlike many technical manuals, you should be able to read this book from cover to cover, like a normal book, and the similarity between the examples will provide a running story.
- ❏   **The chapters read like articles** – Each chapter has standalone examples, even though they are based on the same large-scale system.

❑ **A single data model** – You will only need to install one data model on your machine in order to run all the examples in the book.

Our story line is GlobalMarket. This international goods store is upgrading its system from paper and pencil to a digital system backed by .NET. For our examples we have essentially unlimited budgetary controls (a very successful grocery store, this) and a very understanding business owner.

This isn't another database or web-only example, either. This is a complete retail store with POS terminals, a receiving dock, employees, postal mail lists, returns, and damaged inventory – the whole deal. This is an actual store, not just a web site development project. There is a lot to deal with here.

We have chosen a retail store for a number of reasons.

❑ Everyone knows how it works

❑ Lots of different potential sales environments

❑ Ready made data model in Northwind

In addition, retail goods are discrete units of sale, unlike the products of so many service companies. There are distinct roles in a retail store, too, including

❑ Managers

❑ Shipping

❑ Receiving

❑ Cashiers

❑ Technical personnel, like librarians

All of this is good for security models. We have also set up our store in a fantasy environment, so there is no confusion with reality, when it really comes down to it.

This Book Reads like a Book

Undeniably, the most important overall goal of the unified example is to better create a readable book.

The Unified Example was added to this book as part of the effort to create continuity for the book. Since we have one system being built, the hope is that the book will flow from one functional area of the project to another, thus clarifying the migration or new development path from Windows DNA. If the reader can tie a feature to a problem already familiar, our goal is half met.

This may give a prosaic quality to some of the writing in the book. Though individual examples are often creative, the very dry writing in many technical books defies reading from cover to cover.

The Chapters Read like Articles

On the other hand, we understand the Need To Know. Developers buy these books because they have a specific problem that they need solved. Sometimes reading Chapters 1 through 12 is not the answer, but Chapter 13 is just what the doctor ordered. We have a little something for those people too.

Each example is standalone. Readers don't have to run the sample code in Chapters 1 through 12 to get the code in Chapter 13 to work. Everything works like an article one would see on *ASP Today*. Read the text, download the code, run the sample project, compile it to see it work. If you only need to know about add-ins, then you are in luck – we have just the thing.

The corollary to this is that we have a fine sample of .NET code on the Wrox site for the book. This will include examples of how to:

❑ Make web forms with reports

❑ Build windows forms with minimum coding

❑ Write WAP sites

❑ Use Visio to make framework code

A Common Data Model

The final real benefit to GlobalMarket is the common data model. This helps us in two ways.

❑ **The model is largely complete** – we'll use Northwind as a starting point

❑ **We don't have to build something unfamiliar** – Northwind has been much the same since SQL 6.5. We all know how it works.

Since we have a rather complete data model, we don't expect to make too many changes. We will make a few changes, however, so we recommend the reader creates a copy of the Northwind database on their system. After installing Visual Studio (see *Start Here* for more information on installing Visual Studio) you may have to install SQL Client Tools from the 120-day trial version for SQL 2000. Open the SQL Server Enterprise Manager and follow these steps.

Make a working copy of Northwind Database

1. Drill down to Microsoft SQL Servers | SQL Server Group | <MyMachine>\NETSDK, where <MyMachine> is the name of your workstation. This may also be in <LOCAL>\.

2. Open your workstation's listing, and open the Databases folder.

3. Right click on Northwind.

4. Select All Tasks | Backup Database.

5. Set the Name as GlobalMarket in the SQL Server Backup – Northwind dialog.

6. Click the Add... button under destination and add GlobalMarket to the end of the directory location.

7. Click the OK button.

8. Right-click the Databases folder and select New Database...

9. Set the Name as GlobalMarket and leave the rest of the properties default.

10. Click the OK button.

11. Right-click on GlobalMarket database and select Restore Database.

12. Under Parameters, set Show backups of database... to Northwind.

13. Select the GlobalMarket backup set.

14. In the Options tab, select the Force Restore over existing database checkbox.

15. Click the OK button.

16. If there are difficulties, check the SQL Books Online under Backup Database.

That should create a complete copy of the Northwind database with the name GlobalMarket. Make a System DSN on your system also named GlobalMarket, as we will use that in some examples to connect to the database. Adding a DSN is straightforward:

❑ Open the ODBC Data Source Administrator from your Administrative Tools.

❑ Click on the either the User or System tab and select Add...

❑ Select the SQL Server driver and click Finish.

❑ Now enter the name you wish to call the data source, a description if you wish, and the SQL Server you wish to connect to. Now click Next.

❑ You now need to decide how you want to deal with authentication. Select either Windows NT authentication or SQL Server authentication. Click Next.

❑ You now need to select what the default database for this connection is to be. Set this to GlobalMarket. Leave the rest of the settings as default. Click Next.

❑ Leave all settings as default and press Finish.

The Northwind Data Model

As it stands, the Northwind data model is a pretty complete system for a retail store. It handles suppliers, sales, employees, and inventory. We will be adding a few things throughout the book to show examples of the data tools, but base examples will use this model.

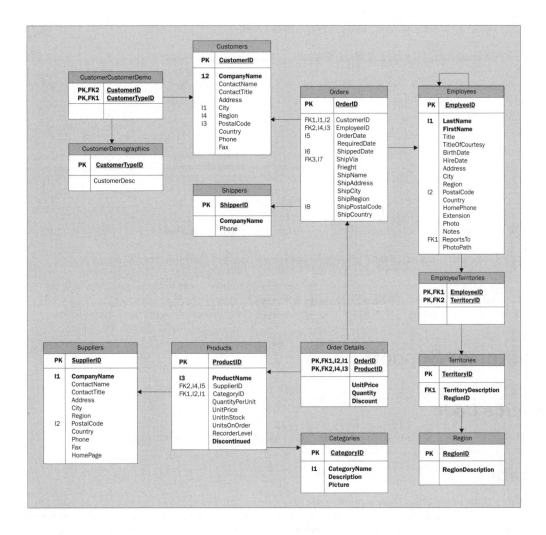

Conventions Used

We have used a number of different styles of text and layout in the book to help differentiate between the different kinds of information. Here are examples of the styles we use and an explanation of what they mean:

Bullets appear indented, with each new bullet marked as follows:

❑ **Important Words** are in a bold type font

❑ Words that appear on the screen in menus like the File or Window are in a similar font to the one that you see on screen

❑ Keys that you press on the keyboard, like *Ctrl* and *Enter*, are in italics

❑ If you see something like, Object, you'll know that it's a filename, object name, or function name

Code in a gray box shows new, important, pertinent code:

```
Dim objMyClass as New MyClass("Hello World")

Debug.WriteLine(objMyClass.ToString)
```

Sometimes you'll see code in a mixture of styles, like this:

```
Dim objVar as Object

objVar = Me

CType(objVar, Form).Text = "New Dialog Title Text"
```

The code with a white background is code we've already looked at and that we don't wish to examine further.

Advice, hints, and background information come in an italicized, indented font like this.

> **Important pieces of information come in boxes like this.**

Customer Support

Source Code

The source code for this book is available for download at http://www.wrox.com.

Errata

We've made every effort to ensure there are no errors in this book. However, to err is human, and we recognize the need to keep you informed of errors as they're spotted and corrected. Errata sheets are available for all our books, at http://www.wrox.com. If you find an error that hasn't already been reported, please let us know.

p2p.wrox.com

For author and peer support, join the SQL Server mailing lists. Our unique system provides **programmer to programmer™ support** on mailing lists, forums, and newsgroups – all *in addition* to our one-to-one e-mail system. Be confident that your query is not just being examined by a support professional, but by the many Wrox authors and other industry experts present on our mailing lists. At p2p.wrox.com, you'll find a number of different lists aimed at SQL Server programmers that will support you, not only while you read this book, but also as you develop your own applications.

Why this System Offers the Best Support

You can choose to join the mailing lists or you can receive them as a weekly digest. If you don't have the time or facility to receive the mailing list, then you can search our online archives. Junk and spam mails are deleted, and your own e-mail address is protected by the unique Lyris system. Any queries about joining or leaving lists, or the lists in general should be sent to listsupport@p2p.wrox.com.

Let's Get Started

We are now ready to get started. We've discussed what this book is about and what is isn't about, and why we've written it. The reader now has a similar data model to that which the authors are using. All there is left to do is to dig in. Let's begin with **The New Microsoft Methodology**.

1

Visual Studio .NET and the New Microsoft Methodology

Introducing .NET

Microsoft asked, "Where do you want to go today?" We developers answered, "Home, preferably before midnight tonight. And this is due tomorrow morning."

This time, Microsoft seems to have delivered.

The New Microsoft methodology is "Do it faster, better, with fewer errors and more maintainability. And do it your way, not ours." The .NET Framework and Visual Studio .NET deliver the ease of use that we have come to expect from Microsoft programming tools.

What is .NET?

.NET is essentially a marketing term that is being used by Microsoft to describe its new approach to software for today's computing environment. Microsoft has a very effective image for explaining this complex idea that it calls 1-3-5.

One Goal

The '1' is for one goal – distributed computing. When we started this whole computing thing, we had servers that shared their power between a number of dumb terminals. The terminals were really just windows into the server, and only a very limited amount of functionality was available to each terminal – certainly no graphics. There just wasn't enough power to go around. This was the Mainframe Era.

With the advent of PCs, we had some pretty smart terminals to hand, but we lacked a good way of getting the information we needed onto them. We were forced to essentially store the data on the server and distribute the logic in terms of application programs, like Microsoft Office. Those were the days of Client/Server.

Then the Internet came along, and with it a whole host of standards. Moving logic from the server to the client and back again, we began to discover how we could allow thousands of clients to use our servers and still enjoy a rich environment – through HTML and the like. More recently, XML Web Services have entered the scene, and have real potential for allowing thousands of clients to easily hook up to our logic.

Though there may have been other technologies that could have driven this along faster, PCs allowed the first step to happen, and HTML and XML are poised to make the second step a reality. Microsoft is pushing for this second step – true distributed computing. Thus – .NET.

Three Objectives

If distributed computing is the goal, what are the objectives? Microsoft names three, this is the '3' in '1-3-5':

❑ Make COM components into XML Web Services the world over

❑ Set up a system to utilize all these new XML Web Services

❑ Build and deploy the application based on these

If you haven't seen a presentation, read a white paper, or run through a demo on XML Web Services, you certainly will soon. This new programming paradigm is making quite a splash. From Microsoft's perspective, any COM component can be turned into an XML Web Service. Since anything can be a COM component, and any other system can potentially use an XML Web Service, this is quite an offering, and it's not so surprising that Microsoft is excited.

As well as cross-platform compatibility, the other big plus that Microsoft sees in the Web Service model is that it would enable it to put in place a new software deployment strategy. There is a feeling – or fear – that many office products have pretty much reached the maximum level of required sophistication, and customers will no longer see the need to keep upgrading. So, if Microsoft can provide software as a service rather than a package, it would constitute a much more enduring revenue source. It would also mean that customers that make more use of the software would pay more. Conversely, if a user only uses a package say, once a year, they will pay significantly less than someone who uses it every hour. Plus, subscriptions are better for cash flow – revenues wouldn't be tied in to releases of new revisions, the software would be continually updated, and cash flow would be constant.

Five Actions

The '5' represents the five key technologies envisaged to implement these objectives:

- ❑ Tools for the programmers

- ❑ Enterprise servers

- ❑ XML Web Services

- ❑ Smart devices

- ❑ An enhanced user experience

We are looking at the first of these today – Visual Studio .NET and the .NET Framework SDK being the first of the developer tools to support Microsoft's goal. Rather than talk about it here, we'll let the reader draw conclusions after reading the rest of the book.

Enterprise servers consist of platforms like Windows 2000 and the Windows .NET server family, and functional servers like BizTalk and Internet Application Server. They will be the backbone for the third action, the proliferation of a base set of XML Web Services. The first two of these are Passport and .NET My Services (NMS), giving us a framework for further development.

The last two, smart devices and the enhanced user experience, are also tied together, and the best example I have seen so far was at the XP launch, when Microsoft's Steve Ballmer showed a video of a family using .NET technologies. They were at the zoo, touring with the aid of a map on the kids' mobile phone. Then MS Messenger popped up to tell them automatically that a friend was nearby (literally nearby, perhaps looking at the monkeys) and they swapped messages, and arranged to meet up and grab a bite to eat.

The demonstration continued to show the family at home, taking a group picture, and the camera automatically and wirelessly uploaded the picture to the family album. The grandparents in their home were automatically informed on their TV that the new picture was available, and they used a handheld PC to send the picture to the digital picture frame in the next room.

Of course, this was a concept demonstration, but the technology it is based upon is all there now, although it is not likely to enter into widespread use for some time yet. Really, the user experience is the result of the combination of all the first four technologies, but it's also logical to group it with the device itself, because that is how the user perceives it.

The 1-3-5 vision can be expressed diagrammatically as a pyramid:

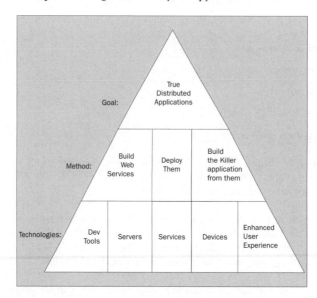

The .NET Framework

While the business reasoning interests us as programmers, we really want – and need – to get to the root of it all. The .NET Framework describes that pretty well. Three things in particular define our path into the world of .NET:

- ❏ The .NET Framework
- ❏ The Framework SDK
- ❏ Visual Studio .NET

We'll describe the .NET Framework below, and the SDK is the programming model that makes it all work. We'll rely on that SDK a lot throughout this book, but we'll mostly focus on the integrated development environment that will allow us to build all of these goodies – Visual Studio .NET.

The .NET Framework provides the structure that lets it all work together – meaning everything from USB ports to web pages. Microsoft accomplishes this feat with two key elements, the CLR and the BCL.

Common Language Runtime (CLR)

The CLR has two roles. Firstly, at design time, it gives developers a quicker, better, easier path to creating powerful applications:

- ❏ Lifetime management
- ❏ Strong type naming
- ❏ Exception handling
- ❏ Dynamic binding

Secondly, it provides services at run-time, which include:

- ❏ Integration

- ❏ Security enforcement

- ❏ Memory control

- ❏ Process integration

- ❏ Thread management

Base Class Library (BCL)

The most fundamental of the base class libraries, BCL provides services that we've previously had to get by accessing the operating system directly, such as:

- ❏ Input/Output

- ❏ String manipulation

- ❏ Security management

- ❏ Network communications

- ❏ Thread management

- ❏ Text management

Some of this functionality was available through one control or another, but now we directly get it from the BCL no matter what language we are using. This is one of the principal reductions of overhead for all of .NET.

There are more libraries that support network communications and data access. ADO.NET, ASP.NET, and the XML namespaces are generally considered part of the BCL.

A Unified Model

This library is important because .NET isn't just Web Services, and it isn't just C#. It's a new way to do an old job – that of writing software for Windows. Everything is new – data, graphics, network, device drivers, the lot.

Developers in general tend to see things in a very granular way, and a shift to a new programming model becomes a series of deployments, training classes, support problems, and headaches.

Potentially, Microsoft's .NET vision is a whole new way to do business. It means that the systems in our network can share logic regardless of operating system. It means development of 'Windows software' isn't immediately restricted by language and architecture choice – because language is not an issue and there is only one architecture.

This has significant benefits for us. Aside from the fact that this will create more work for us developers, it gives us an ability to reuse like never before. If we have a useful, or perhaps just plain large, COBOL routine, that's no problem. .NET speaks COBOL. Want to wrap up a legacy MTS application for your Solaris box to make use of? Again, no problem, because .NET provides XML Web Services.

So this becomes important. We'll see going forward that it is easy too. In working for a year with .NET, I can say that things just kind of slide together like never before. To that point, let's look at the evolution of Visual Studio.

Visual Studio Transformed

This change in architecture has prompted a change in programming tools. Firstly, since we have only one architecture, we have only one tool. People ask "What about FoxPro?" but in reality the need for FoxPro is gone, because what we could do with FoxPro – maintain flat databases – is not included in the Framework. However, it can be coded against using the .NET Framework SDK, which is used by Visual Studio .NET.

The same can be said for any other technology in the Microsoft Development toolkit. Even as basic a distinction as VB versus InterDev can be made. We don't need two tools anymore, because of the single architecture.

The .NET Border

Before .NET, we had a raft of tools that had evolved over time. As Microsoft grew over twenty-five years, the tools needed to develop solutions for Microsoft environments grew alongside. The development tools always slightly trailed behind the thinking behind the architecture. Whether it was the invention of Windows, or the inclusion of IE, the tools were never quite there. They were always almost like an afterthought.

After .NET, the development tools are a part of the plan from day one. As we saw above, the tools to do the job are one of the five actions that Microsoft considers essential to the push towards its new vision. One platform for one architecture – that is the goal, and it has been achieved. From the distributed application point of view, everything from SQL stored procedures to JavaScript client-side code can be done in one place – Visual Studio .NET.

In fact, we don't need Visual Studio at all. One of the best proofs for the convergence of the platforms is the fact that Notepad can do everything Visual Studio can do. Try to write a Visual Basic 6 application in Notepad one day – it's not possible, but there's nothing to stop our writing a Visual Basic .NET application in Notepad, though:

```
' The System namespace contains the Console class
Imports System

' Module is like a class for this application
Public Module modmain
   ' Standalone application requires a Main()
   Sub Main()
     ' Write text to the console
     Console.WriteLine ("We did this without an IDE!")
   End Sub
End Module
```

We can then compile this on the command line, using the vbc.exe tool.

A New Methodology for a New Architecture

This convergence of architecture means a change in methodology, because there are now much better ways to do the same old things. Consider these points:

❑   **DCOM is dead.** XML Web Services are the way any two systems that don't share operating systems should now communicate. Every significant piece of logic written in the .NET world should ideally have a SOAP access point built-in – there just isn't any excuse not to.

❑ **ADO.NET is asynchronous by design.** The data schema for the .NET style recordset – called a dataset – is stored in the project as an XSD.

❑ **All languages support a** `try...catch...finally` **structured error handling scheme.** Gone is the complex error handling with `goto` on statements, although the error objects sitting in your existing projects may still be useful.

❑ **ASP.NET is a compiled language.** When ASP.NET pages are created for Web Forms applications, a secondary file is created to contain with the functional code – the **code-behind** page. This is compiled into a DLL by the ASP engine when first required.

❑ **DLL Hell is frozen over.** XCopy deployment has brought an end to Component Manager in Windows 2000 and MTS in Windows NT4. The new `EnterpriseServices` namespace handles things like just-in-time (JIT) activation now.

Essentially, these changes do not alter the basic concept of n-tier, or distributed computing. The concepts are still the same; it's just the design that is different. Some will take this author to task for equating methodology with design, but there is a difference between design in terms of actually putting words on the page and design in terms of thought patterns. We need to think about solutions a little differently under .NET in order to effectively use the tools and the Framework.

Distributed Applications

Let's take an application that hasn't changed much and look at how we can apply some new ways of thinking to its design. We'll use a distributed n-tier application for this example because it is a rather ubiquitous type, and it highlights some of the new decisions that have to be made.

Under Windows DNA

Windows DNA is the term that describes the component architecture for development under ASP 3, COM+, and SQL Server 7. Most, if not all, of us would have used a three-tier model when creating distributed applications under Windows DNA.

Three-tier in Brief

A three-tier system is one that has presentation components, business logic and data access physically running on different platforms. Web applications are perfect for three-tier architecture, as the presentation layer is necessarily separate, and the business and data components can be divided up much like a client-server application.

The benefit to a three-tier system is twofold. The modularity of a good three-tier design allows for the removal or replacement of a particular component without affecting the functionality of the rest of the application. Secondly, separation of the business logic from the database allows for load balancing in highly scalable systems.

The bottom line is that three-tier transactional systems are replacing the reams of COBOL code that prop up the world economy. If you want to have an impact – you need to understand three-tier systems.

The Three Steps Methodology

In 2000, myself, Mike Gallaugher, Doug McDowell, and I of Paros Business Partners defined what we named the Three Steps Methodology for building distributed applications. There are quite literally three steps to comprehensively designing a transactional system:

1. Abstract your data model or database with data objects.

2. Abstract your web page events with methods in business objects.

3. Diagram the connections between the business layer and the data layer.

Of course, if that were all there is to it, Rocky Lhotka wouldn't have written all of those great books on the subject! There are some tricks to abstracting data and business logic through the use of objects. You then have to match up the objects, which requires some knowledge of UML. Finally, you need to decide on an architecture, and actually code the things.

Under .NET

Not much has changed about the Three Steps methodology in the new world. All that's really different are the conceptual tools in our toolbox:

- ❑ Design in UML ability
- ❑ XML Dataset support
- ❑ Easy creation of XML Web Services
- ❑ Object access to Windows services
- ❑ Device mobility

These just represent some of the new functionality that may influence the reader's methodology for their particular programming problem – I feel that these most directly influence the methodology around the design of distributed applications.

> **Basically, what we are saying is this: there are many new ways to solve your problems, and they work better than the old ways. Keep this in mind as you go on.**

Design in UML

Documentation is always a problem in small and medium sized projects. The project is easy to get your hands around, and the team understands what is happening, so no one writes it down. Then something goes wrong, and someone leaves, and suddenly the project is 40% over budget.

Another problem is the whole object-oriented thing. We distributed application developers are mostly functional programmers, and thinking in namespaces and classes isn't really what we are all about.

Using the Unified Modeling Language to design our applications, however, can solve both these problems, and it is certainly a paradigm shift. UML has actually been around for a while, but it matters more now because the arena we play in is only now truly object-oriented.

How does it solve the documentation problem and the object-oriented thing at the same time? In general, we wouldn't document small projects because it doesn't add any obvious value. And we don't code in an object-oriented style because we design in a functional style. But with Visio and UML, we can turn a diagram straight into code. For instance, the UML for a tool we will build later in the book is shown below:

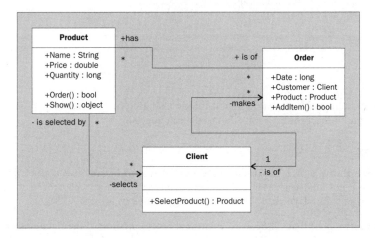

What's interesting is that, in four clicks, we can turn it into this skeleton code:

```
public class Product
{

    public string Name;
    public double Price;
    public long Quantity;
    private System.Collections.ArrayList selects;

    public bool Order()
    {
    }

    public object Show()
    {
    }

}

public class Client
{

    private System.Collections.ArrayList makes;

    public Product SelectProduct()
    {

    }
}
```

```
public class Order
{

  public long Date;
  public Client Customer;
  public System.Collections.ArrayList Product;
  private Client isof;

  public bool AddItem()
  {
  }
}
```

We have solved both problems with a methodology change. The tool has helped us with our OO programming, and it has brought real value to documentation.

XML Datasets

Recordsets were always a problem in the Windows DNA world. They had a custom binary format, were big and slow, and not relational. We find ourselves returning arrays of recordsets to the client to get the data we need from a data layer call – not a tool for good design.

XML datasets solve all of that. They are a relational representation of the data, controlled by an XML Schema. Imagine how nice this is. Firstly, we have a system by which we can pass relational data with a known schema to our application. Secondly, we can communicate with other applications nicely.

Take this diagram, for instance. We couldn't have even represented this in a recordset easily before ADO.NET:

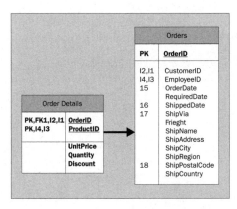

Also, we most certainly couldn't have shown you the code behind the recordset, but we certainly can look at the dataset:

```
<?xml version="1.0" standalone="yes" ?>
<xs:schema id="DataSet1" targetNamespace="http://www.tempuri.org/DataSet1.xsd"
xmlns:mstns="http://www.tempuri.org/DataSet1.xsd"
xmlns="http://www.tempuri.org/DataSet1.xsd"
xmlns:xs="http://www.w3.org/2001/XMLSchema" xmlns:msdata="urn:schemas-microsoft-
com:xml-msdata" attributeFormDefault="qualified" elementFormDefault="qualified">
```

```xml
<xs:element name="DataSet1" msdata:IsDataSet="true">
  <xs:complexType>
    <xs:choice maxOccurs="unbounded">
      <xs:element name="Order_x0020_Details">
        <xs:complexType>
          <xs:sequence>
            <xs:element name="OrderID" type="xs:int" />
            <xs:element name="ProductID" type="xs:int" />
            <xs:element name="UnitPrice" type="xs:decimal" />
            <xs:element name="Quantity" type="xs:short" />
            <xs:element name="Discount" type="xs:float" />
          </xs:sequence>
        </xs:complexType>
      </xs:element>
      <xs:element name="Orders">
        <xs:complexType>
          <xs:sequence>
            <xs:element name="OrderID" msdata:ReadOnly="true"
             msdata:AutoIncrement="true" type="xs:int" />
            <xs:element name="CustomerID" type="xs:string"
             minOccurs="0" />
            <xs:element name="EmployeeID" type="xs:int"
             minOccurs="0" />
            <xs:element name="OrderDate" type="xs:dateTime"
             minOccurs="0" />
            <xs:element name="RequiredDate" type="xs:dateTime"
             minOccurs="0" />
            <xs:element name="ShippedDate" type="xs:dateTime"
             minOccurs="0" />
            <xs:element name="ShipVia" type="xs:int"
             minOccurs="0" />
            <xs:element name="Freight" type="xs:decimal"
             minOccurs="0" />
            <xs:element name="ShipName" type="xs:string"
             minOccurs="0" />
            <xs:element name="ShipAddress" type="xs:string"
             minOccurs="0" />
            <xs:element name="ShipCity" type="xs:string"
             minOccurs="0" />
            <xs:element name="ShipRegion" type="xs:string"
             minOccurs="0" />
            <xs:element name="ShipPostalCode" type="xs:string"
             minOccurs="0" />
            <xs:element name="ShipCountry" type="xs:string"
             minOccurs="0" />
          </xs:sequence>
        </xs:complexType>
      </xs:element>
    </xs:choice>
  </xs:complexType>
  <xs:unique name="Constraint1" msdata:PrimaryKey="true">
    <xs:selector xpath=".//mstns:Order_x0020_Details" />
    <xs:field xpath="mstns:OrderID" />
    <xs:field xpath="mstns:ProductID" />
```

```
        </xs:unique>
        <xs:unique name="Orders_Constraint1"
          msdata:ConstraintName="Constraint1" msdata:PrimaryKey="true">
          <xs:selector xpath=".//mstns:Orders" />
          <xs:field xpath="mstns:OrderID" />
        </xs:unique>
      </xs:element>
   </xs:schema>
```

The dataset, combined with XML Web Services, gives us a whole new way to communicate within an application, and outside the boundary as well.

XML Web Services

We have all heard the marketing spiel surrounding XML Web Services. They:

❑ Use HTTP as a transport allowing remote method requests to pass through enterprise firewalls and through various network protocols.

❑ Support the use of the Secure Sockets Layer (SSL) protocol for security, as well as standard web authentication techniques to better match existing standards.

❑ Are not tied to a particular component technology or object calling convention. As a result, programs written in any language, using any component model, and running on any operating system, can access XML Web Services if SOAP is an intrinsic protocol.

We already mentioned that combined with the dataset they will make a large difference inside and outside the enterprise, and they will. Chapter 6 contains an extensive piece that shows just how easy it is to create powerful Web Services in Visual Studio .NET.

Object Access to Windows Services

Creating an application fully integrated with the operating system used to be the preserve of Unix and C++ Windows programmers. Not any more. With the .NET Framework, we can all access every part of the OS, and even use a graphical interface.

A large part of this is due to the System.Diagnostics namespace, which gives us access to five of the most important components for the stability and scalability of our applications:

❑ **EventLog component** – gives us access to the three default eventlogs on a read basis, plus ability to write our own

❑ **Process class** – provides access to monitor system process across the network

❑ **PerformanceCounter component** – does just want it sounds like – we can access system counters, and build our own

❑ **Trace class** – allows us to attach instrumentation to release builds

❑ **Debug class** – allows more robust trace functionality without impacting release size

The impact on methodology here is a nod toward scalability and stability. With this enhanced view into the operating system, we can have the application respond better to failure, and also have it better tell us what is wrong. It is a change in the way we think about stability and scalability in the Microsoft environment.

Device Mobility

If we would have thought about not using component services, this should change our minds. In Windows DNA, we talked a lot about the DLL files being used for more than one user interface, but really all we were talking about was Windows Applications and ASP Applications.

Now there is so much more at stake. Phones, PDAs, and even TV sets enter the mix. How can we be ready for all of this? By designing for these eventualities. We must alter the methodology for the reality of building global logic, and a wide diversity of user interfaces.

The device mobility of form components in .NET makes this easier than ever before. These components don't create strange little black boxes that we can't decipher, and that only work on Microsoft clients, either. These controls are inheritable: modifiable objects that automatically produce usable code for the client side depending on the client device in use.

For more about the device mobility features of Visual Studio .NET, see Chapter 8, *Mobile Internet ToolKit*. It might just change your mind about separating logic and the user interface.

The New Mantra

OK, so a lot is new, and you must be wondering how we should think about this stuff, from a method perspective. What are the new corporate buzzwords? How do we sell it? Well, here is the New Mantra.

Software as a Service

The impact of XML Web Services cannot be overstated. Trust us; we have tried, as has Microsoft, to overstate the importance of this new tool. The ability to connect the logic of two computers, from anywhere, to anywhere, independent of the platform, is very profound.

Microsoft has not overlooked this technology in the tools developed for our use. Visual Studio .NET is specifically designed to readily take advantage of this new W3C standard. At long last, Microsoft developers have been given the opportunity to use the Internet for something other than a fancy bulletin board.

Part of the New .NET Strategy

XML Web Services are actually an integral part of the new .NET strategy – to a fault. In fact, I can say that I spend much of my time convincing people that Visual Studio is used for more that just creation of .NET Web Services. Microsoft has oversold this facility a little, and many upper management types now have the impression that this is all that it's about.

Microsoft supports standards to a greater extent in the .NET Framework than ever before, but it isn't being completely altruistic about all of this. There are two products that are designed to help all of us make a little money, and take advantage of the open XML Web Service standard – called SOAP – as well. They are .NET My Services (formerly Hailstorm) and Passport.

.NET My Services and Passport are – as mentioned earlier – going to be one of the building blocks of the goal around which .NET is focused – Microsoft's vision of some kind of distributed application utopia(!). They provide a pre-built set of tools on which we can build distributed network appliances using the Smart Devices, which also form a part of the strategy. They are in fact a vital piece of the puzzle.

Rapid Application Development on the Server

We discussed this functionally above, in discussing the development of distributed applications. There is also an entire chapter later in the book on the topic. This concept is so strong, and so regularly overlooked recently, that it requires some more explanation.

Rapid Application Development (RAD) is a pretty simple concept. Essentially, it is a design methodology that says that instead of documentation, we should create prototypes to design our application. This way, we get testable betas earlier, we get something functioning in front of senior management, and we get the user interface in front of real users at the first stage.

For ten years, Microsoft Visual Basic has been providing this design model for Windows platforms – in a client/server environment. We have been able to build forms for Windows – and before that, for DOS – using an easy, drag-and-drop programming interface. Not that it gets around coding entirely of course, but it does reduce the need significantly.

In the last five years, the designs have swung to distributed, component-based software. This was due partly to the Internet, and partly to object-oriented languages like C++ gaining popularity. Whatever the reason, VB programmers – all 2.2 million of them – needed to create DLL files and deploy them using servers that were not running the actual user interface, and install databases... well, you get the picture. There is panic.

So, the architects went to work. There are now several good, solid processes for writing component architecture in Visual Basic. The problem is that most of them are not all that good. We VB programmers are RAD programmers at heart. We like property panels, and visual tools. Perhaps not all of us fall into that category, but many do. We just want more bang for our buck.

Drag 'n' Drop DLL

So Visual Studio .NET – with help from the .NET Framework – has solved this problem. Creation of DLLs for use in distributed applications is now a visual process. More to the point – the visual tools produce better code than we would. If we don't like the code it creates for whatever reason, we can change it around through inheritance until we do like it.

A Missing Slogan?

Although Microsoft was really pushing the RAD for the Server slogan in the Beta 1 announcements, it was strangely missing from DevDays and the Launch Event. That may just be because it is misunderstood by some – hence the extensive amount of information on the subject throughout the book. It is an important concept, because it changes the way we build components, and that changes the designs, which in turn changes the methodology.

Role-Based Development

Role-Based Development (RBD) is at the heart of the New Microsoft Methodology. The existence of an Architect in a Microsoft development pool has, until .NET, been something of a documentation position. With Visual Studio .NET, the architect will never need change their hat.

Visual Studio Versions

Since this book is divided by Visual Studio .NET version, it would be a good idea to discuss what the three primary versions offer before we go any further.

Visual Studio .NET Professional

Professional is made for the single developer in a small organization, or consultant perhaps. It is not designed to work in an enterprise as much as on a single machine. The core features only are included:

❑ The IDE

❑ The Compact Framework

❑ VB, C#, and C++

❑ Web, Windows, and Service development templates

Visual Studio .NET Enterprise Developer

Enterprise Developer is the appropriate version for the majority of programmers in large organizations. It includes the features of Professional, plus:

❑ Developer editions of the server software

❑ SourceSafe

❑ Application Center Test

❑ The data tools

❑ Enterprise Frameworks execution

Visual Studio .NET Enterprise Architect

Architect is the complete version of the software. It is designed for team leaders and system analysts who need to visually model software, and control the access of other developers. To the tools of Enterprise Developer it adds:

❑ Template authoring

❑ Biztalk

❑ Software and data modeling with Visio

Enterprise Frameworks

Enterprise templates contain two key components: the initial project structure, or template project, and the policy that is associated with the project. The template project is the solution for the blank-slate problem.

Using templates, an architect can create an application starting point that includes reusable components, projects, and solutions, which developers can use to code a system. Combined with the `System.Web.UI` namespace, along with others, we have a powerful set of solutions to provide to the development team.

The policy component associated with a template project provides the solution to the full-slate problem – that of having toomuch information to choose from. An architect can specify which technologies should be used, as well as which technologies should not be used, so that developers can choose from a narrower list of appropriate options at any given time during the development of an application.

Visual Design

There are two very handy visual tools available for the design stage of application development.

ORM

Object Role Modeling (ORM) provides a conceptual, easy-to-understand method of modeling data. The ORM methodology is based on three key principles:

❑ **Simplicity** – Data is modeled in the most elementary form

❑ **Communicability** – Database structures are described using language that can be easily understood

❑ **Accuracy** – A correctly normalized diagram is created based on the database itself

Typically, a modeler develops an information model by gathering requirements from people who are familiar with the application but are not skilled data modelers. The modeler must be able to communicate data structures at a conceptual level in terms that the non-technical business expert can understand. The modeler must also analyze the information in simple units and work with sample populations. ORM is specifically designed to improve this kind of communication.

UML

On the software side, Visual Studio .NET supports Visio for Enterprise Architects in the creation of Unified Modeling Language diagrams describing .NET systems. This is of benefit to those who are serious about their architecture – UML is not for the faint of heart. With the partial integration of Visio, however, the architect's is no longer a code-free position.

With Visio and Visual Studio .NET, architects can create diagrams to specify the application architecture and business requirements as well as communicate these across their teams. Business analysts, architects, developers, and others who want to perform analysis and design tasks to enhance communication and increase the productivity of their development teams can take advantage of this – and not just for the .NET world. Microsoft has honed the UML tools from the Visio 2000 version, but it still handles VB 6 and C++ templates.

The Last Stage

Visual Studio .NET provides some useful tools for the final stages of development, before an application is ready for deployment.

Testing

Application Center Test (ACT), a new feature integrated with Visual Studio .NET, enables developers to gather performance metrics and perform functional testing of XML Web Services and applications within the Visual Studio .NET development environment.

ACT provides sophisticated scripting capabilities, so developers can analyze relative performance by simulating many simultaneous page requests to an XML Web Service or application. This helps developers design faster, more stable XML Web Services and applications.

Deployment

Deployment presents a challenge for both the developers of an application and the network administrators who must install and maintain it. The developer often has to make assumptions about where and how the components of distributed applications will be installed; the administrator must deal with issues ranging from version conflicts to dependencies.

Visual Studio .NET mitigates the difficulty of deployment by offering new tools for deployment, simplifying the process for both the developer and the administrator. The aim of Visual Studio deployment is to transport solutions of any size or makeup from a development platform to multiple target platforms in a single step. The following are just a few of the features of deployment in Visual Studio .NET:

❑ Deployment is fully integrated as a part of every solution, not an add-on

❑ Users can deploy to Web servers such as Internet Information Server, non-Web servers, traditional media such as CDs or any combination of the three – all in a single step

❑ Solutions for debugging can be deployed across multiple machines

❑ The .NET Framework, including installer classes, is fully supported

❑ The Zero Administration initiative for Windows, including side-by-side installation and application publishing, is supported

The Full Picture

All of these tools go to define the roles of developers in the world of application development with Visual Studio .NET. It is so much easier to decide who is doing what when there is some control. Now that deployment doesn't require walking over to the server and logging in, the team lead of the development group can carry out their job without being babysat by the system administration team.

Role Based development isn't a requirement in small, single-user applications. Once we get into larger and larger distributed applications, though, one rogue coder can make the project much more difficult. A few well-defined positions on the team can really improve the speed and accuracy of the coding – and that's what it is all about.

Write Anywhere, Run Here

The .NET Framework enables developers to use any programming language, and applications written in different programming languages can integrate deeply and seamlessly with each other, enabling current development skills to go forward without retraining. At the bottom level, all languages are translated into Intermediate Language (IL), a sort of bytecode for the Framework.

Objects written on top of the .NET Framework can integrate with each other regardless of the language in which they were created, because they are built on top of a common type system. The multilanguage integration of the .NET Framework includes:

❑ Calling methods on other objects

❑ Inheriting implementations from other objects

❑ Passing instances of a class to other objects

❑ Using a single debugger across multiple objects

❑ Trapping errors from other objects

Cross-language integration is useful in several scenarios. For example, development projects gain access to a larger skills base – project managers can choose developers skilled in any programming language and place them together on the same team. Alternately, developers writing components for a distributed web application will find it helpful to know that no matter what language they choose to write their components in, those components can interact closely with each other and with components supplied by other developers. Also, we probably all agree that some languages are better for data access, while others are better for presentation layers. Since all languages lead to the Framework, we can program in the language of choice as needed.

When we say language of choice, we mean it. Below is a selection of the languages available for the Framework:

- COBOL
- Component Pascal
- Dyalog APL
- Eiffel
- Fortran
- Mercury
- Mondrian
- Oberon
- Pascal
- Perl
- Python
- RPG
- Scheme
- SmallScript and Smalltalk
- Standard ML

To be totally honest, Visual Studio currently complains if we code in anything other than C#, C++, Visual Basic .NET or Jscript.NET. That isn't the point though – Enterprise Frameworks can be used to make a COBOL programmer feel as comfortable as a VB programmer – IntelliSense and all.

Summary

All this boils down to the reality that actually designing applications hasn't changed much. They still have databases, components, and a user interface. If there were a single way of summing up the new Microsoft methodology, it would be to say that it gives us *options*, lots of options.

Many developers in other languages using other architectures have rightfully argued that the Microsoft platform is too riddled with prison bars – restricting the programmer from doing things the way they want to do things. That isn't true any more, frankly. No matter the language, no matter the device, we have access to everything the operating system can do.

So, before we move on to the book proper, and start playing, we should dust off that Design Protocol handbook for Microsoft applications and reconsider. Reconsider the strict guidelines for the way problems are solved. Reconsider the loose guidelines surrounding the roles in the development teams.

After we've considered those changes, though, we must move on and learn all about the amazing new piece of software, Microsoft Visual Studio .NET.

2

Start Here

Be it small task or large, ten lines of code or a thousand, it will always be the case that knowing your way around the Visual Studio .NET interface will help you write and debug your code faster than if you don't. There are quite a few differences between this IDE and that of VS 6.0, most noticeably that the component pieces of this latest incarnation – Visual C#, Visual Basic .NET, Visual C++ .NET, and so on – all use the same interface rather than variations on a theme.

In this chapter then, we'll take our first steps with Visual Studio .NET, looking at:

❑   The Visual Studio .NET Start Page and its links to Studio's online community and support network

❑   The various windows and tools that make up the IDE and their function

We'll also take a brief look at two of the most basic concepts in Visual Studio – projects and solutions.

The Start Page

Once you've installed Visual Studio .NET and run it for the first time, the first thing you'll see is Studio's customizable Start Page surrounded by menus and tool windows.

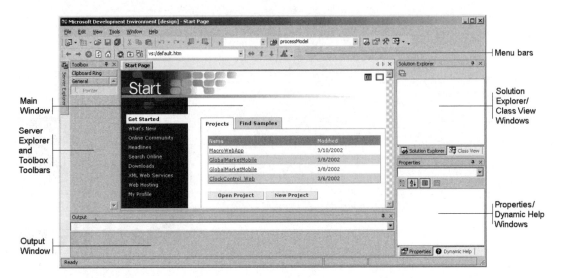

The Start Page provides quick access to many of the tasks you'll be performing on a daily basis and is also the foundation for the online community and support system Microsoft has enhanced and is emphasizing with this release of the product.

We'll get to the tool windows surrounding the Start Page in the next section.

Visual Studio .NET is actually running an instance of Internet Explorer 6.0 to display the Start Page and its associated pages. Try clicking through the titles on the left with IE working offline and you'll see the message 'This feature requires that you have connected to the internet previously or are currently online.' for all but Get Started and My Profile unless you've already worked through them while online. In this case, these pages will have been stored in IE's cache and you'll see the last version of them you downloaded (provided they're still in the cache.) Quite a few pieces of Visual Studio .NET do depend on your copy of IE (Netscape Navigator and Opera won't do here) being up to date and online. Don't worry if you forget though – Visual Studio will tell you when this is the case.

Note the two icons in the top right hand corner of the Start Page. The left hand button lets you determine whether any links in the Start Page will reuse the window showing the Start Page to display the new pages or will open a new window. The right hand button determines whether or not the Start Page will be shown at startup. If you do decide to switch it off, you can open it by choosing Show Start Page from the Help menu.

Get Started

The Get Started page has two tabs, Projects and Find Samples. Projects displays the names of the most recent projects opened and the date they were last modified. Note that we'll look at projects in the next section, but suffice to say for now that they are the smallest useful grouping of files to a developer, comprising the source file for a single (small) application.

When you open the project files they are marked as being modified by default, so this more accurately tells you when they were last opened, not when you changed the files. The two buttons at the bottom, Open Project and New Project, do exactly what they say. The Projects tab provides an easy way to get started or resume projects, but if you prefer, the same options are available on the File menu.

The Find Samples tab is used to locate sample code from the MSDN documentation and MSDN online samples.

The Samples Profile dropdown helps you to narrow the samples to languages you are familiar with. In this case we will use Visual C# Developer. The Filter by box allows you to narrow your search by Keyword or Type. When you select Keyword a textbox is displayed allowing you to enter the words to match. If you select Type, the textbox is replaced with a dropdown box to select a topic.

When a search is performed the results are grouped into two sections, Help Samples and Online Samples. The Help Samples are what was found in the MSDN Library supplied with Visual Studio .NET. The Online Samples are the samples found in the MSDN online samples database. The results are displayed as a list of links under each section heading.

Visual Studio .NET Online

In keeping with the .NET initiative, which is very much an online effort filled with web services, distributed applications, and multi-various end-user devices, Microsoft is making it much easier for us to get hold of information online that we may have not had the inkling to check before or simply didn't realize existed in the first place. The middle seven tabs all make use of IE embedded into Visual Studio to grab information from microsoft.com and make it readily available as follows.

The **What's New** page keeps you up to date with any new developments made to make Visual Studio .NET an easier, more powerful tool to use. These are broadly divided into three categories. Technology informs you of new service packs for visual studio and new plug-ins that have appeared on the market. Training Events contains links to talks about the technology and training events, and finally Tips and Walkthroughs links to useful information for shortcut tips and general walkthroughs. This information is geared to toward the new user of Visual Studio .NET.

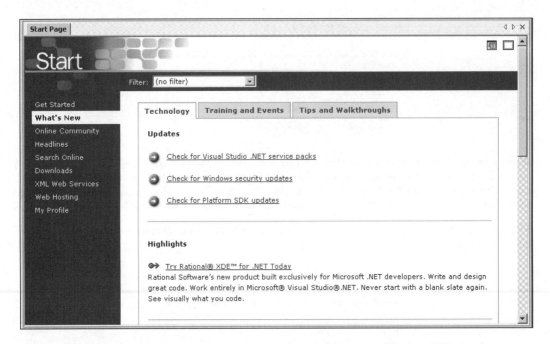

The **Online Community** page helps keep you in touch with other Visual Studio .NET developers, providing links to code-share web sites, Microsoft newsgroups, technical chat sessions and online seminars with experts, and a catalog of downloadable components you may add to your own work. You may also specify content you don't want to see using a simple filter control at the top of the page.

The **Headlines** page provides links to specific content on the MSDN web site about programming for the .NET Framework. It is broadly divided into the latest news and announcements, programming on the .NET Framework itself, working with XML web services, and using Visual Studio .NET through all stages of the software lifecycle in order to develop an application. This page will likely change often as is the wish of the MSDN site in response to public demand.

The **Search Online** page provides a simple way to search the MSDN Online Library without leaving the IDE. Although this may not be a necessary feature, it can be nicer than having all the clutter that is displayed when you go to the MSDN online search page. When this pane is displayed the Filter box is hidden. To perform a search, enter keywords into the textbox and click Go. The results will be placed below and paged in groups of ten up to 100 results. If you click Advanced, you will be taken to the search page on Microsoft's site.

The **Downloads** page gives you direct access to the free samples and password-guarded MSDN subscriber downloads that Microsoft makes available from time to time. The MSDN subscriber tab also includes links to the monthly highlight from the MSDN site.

The **XML Web Services** page allows you to search the online (UDDI) directories for XML Web Services and once found, incorporate them into your own projects. It also provides the means to register your own production-quality web services with the same online directories.

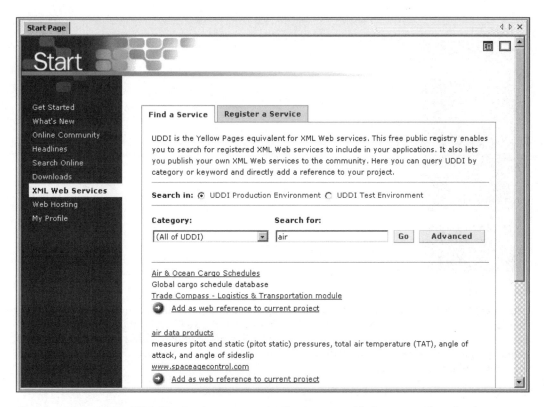

Last but not least, the **Web Hosting** page contains information and links to providers that have partnered with Microsoft to provide hosting for .NET applications and XML web services. These are divided into Premier Providers, which can give you high availability access to the complete range of .NET enterprise servers, and Additional Providers that offer general access to database services based on .NET Enterprise servers. All these companies provide all the support necessary for running .NET-based XML Web Services. Finally on this page, you can also access an FAQ on .NET web hosting.

My Profile

One of the most useful initial setup and configuration tools in Visual Studio .NET is the **My Profile** page under the Start Page. If you've used a previous version of Visual Studio before, this will help make Visual Studio .NET look and feel closer to the environment you're used to. If you're new to VS, then experimenting with the different arrangements that My Profile allows is a good start to getting this complex IDE into the configuration that will best suit you.

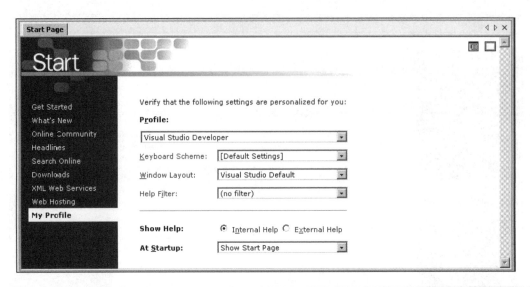

The Profile drop-down box allows you to choose the type of developer you are. This will adjust the Keyboard Scheme, Window Layout, and Help Filter located directly below, and adjusts the IDE to the changes. For instance, if you choose Visual C++ Developer, the keyboard will be adjusted to the scheme used in previous versions of Visual C++. The Solution Explorer, Class View, and Resource View windows will be tab-docked on the left. Just below these the Properties and Dynamic Help windows will also be tab docked.

Solutions and Projects

Before we have a look at the different windows surrounding the Start Page, we need to have a quick look at the concepts of projects and solutions, two things you'll deal with every day you work with Visual Studio .NET. We've already seen that the Start Page enquires of you whether when you load to start a new project, or load one already in progress, so let's start with that.

Invariably as you continue to work with .NET, the applications you build will consist of more than one file – perhaps several C# class files, an icon or two, an ASP.NET page or a Windows form, and so on. Visual Studio .NET lets us define a **project** as a container that holds all of the files that when compiled will contribute towards our final executable file, DLL, or web site. Thus when we open a project in Visual Studio .NET, all the files we've created so far towards our goal will also be made available should we need to access them.

Visual Studio .NET also makes life easy for us by auto-generating the files we'll most likely need in our project when we first create it. As you'll see if you try to create a new project by clicking on the New Project button in the Start Page or File | New | Project, Visual Studio defines close to fifty different types of project in the New Project dialog box for you to choose from according to your needs. Each of these generates a different set of files to start with according to the templates Microsoft has predefined. We'll see at the end of the book how we can create our own project templates, but that's getting ahead of ourselves.

The contents of the majority of the windows surrounding the main one are determined by the project (or file) you have opened at the time so let's create one for the first (but not the last) time. Bring up the **New Project** dialog box if it isn't still in view and select **Visual C# Projects** in the left hand pane and **Windows Application** in the right. This will create us the basis for a simple Windows Form-based project much like the ones Visual Basic users loved and Visual C++ users got tired of quite rapidly.

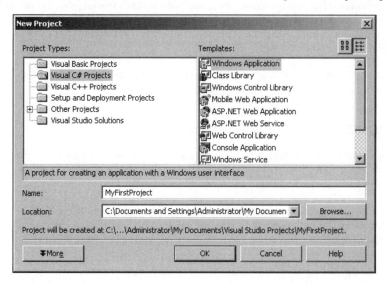

This dialog also lets us choose a name for our project and a location for saving it. The default name, `WindowsApplication1`, is pretty bland, so change it to `MyFirstProject`, and let the location stay at the default. Press **OK**. All being well, Visual Studio will work a few things out behind the scenes for a couple of seconds, generate a few files, display an empty Windows Form in the main window and populate some of the surrounding windows with information. That was easy wasn't it?

Before we go on, it's here you should note that in creating a new project, we have *also* created a new solution. A solution is a container representing a larger development. It can contain more than one project reflecting the fact that as development tasks grow, several smaller projects may be thought of collectively as a solution to the overall task. For example, in a classic 3-tier development, an application is split into the user interface, business logic, and data access tiers. The Visual Studio solution for the whole development might well contain a project for each of these tiers.

> **Visual Basic 6 users should note that Visual Studio .NET contains an upgrade wizard that opens VB 6 projects, converts them into either unmanaged COM code or .NET applications, and generates a report saying whether or not all went to plan. To activate it, simply try to open the project in Visual Studio .NET.**

As we work through the book, we'll see what files each type of project generates and what they're for. Right now, however, it's on to the support windows as promised.

Windows

There are two types of window in Visual Studio .NET. The Start Page, the form window, and the many code pages that will inevitably be created and displayed in the centre of the IDE are called **document windows**. A document window may show either the code you are working on, or, if you are working on something with a user interface – a WinForm like the one we just created or a web page – the designer for the visual representation of that page. There are quite a few different types of visual designer for us to use, we will discover more of these in Chapter 3.

The second type of window – the **tool window** – is what we'll look at now. Each of these has a specific function to aid the development and debugging of your solutions and projects.

Tool Windows

Although they're not all immediately available to you and their use not immediately clear, there are in fact eighteen different tool windows in VS .NET. All bar one can be opened and closed from the View menu. The eighteenth, Dynamic Help, can be found in the Help menu.

Now we won't cover all eighteen in this chapter. A few simply aren't relevant until we get into deeper topics like customizing Visual Studio with macros, using Visual SourceSafe, and debugging, so we'll leave those until later on. We will cover those that are immediately useful, however.

Solution Explorer

One of the first tool windows to get yourself familiar with is the Solution Explorer. Here you'll see a hierarchical listing of all the projects that your current solution contains and the files within each of those projects. Double-clicking on a container icon will either show or hide its contents and double clicking on a file will open a document window for that file. For our newly created project, the solution Explorer will look like this.

The icons above the tree view represent the most common user options for the selected file and change according to the file selected. With `form1.cs` selected for example, the icons from left to right represent View Code, View Designer, Refresh, Show All Files, and Properties. Hovering your cursor over the icon will trigger a tooltip after a few seconds if you're not sure what they do, and you can get a full set of options for the file rather than the most common ones, by right-clicking on the file and choosing an option from the context menu that appears.

The solution explorer also tells us a few more useful pieces of information about our solution if we know what to look for.

- ❑ Files can be part of a solution, but not part of a project. These will be shown directly under the solution. A container called **Miscellaneous Files** may also appear in the window, the contents of which are files that are not part of either project or solution. For example, a file containing useful code snippets to reuse.

- ❑ If the name of a project is in bold (as above), it is the **active project** in the solution. That is, when we compile, build, and run our solution it is this project that will run initially. Any other projects in the solution will run only when called from this active one.

- ❑ Filenames suffixed with a red exclamation mark in Solution Explorer denote that while the file is still part of the solution, it has been moved or deleted by someone outside of Visual Studio .NET, which cannot now find it.

- ❑ Files with grayed-out icons denote that these files have been excluded from a project or solution and will not be included when it is compiled and built.

Server Explorer

The other 'explorer' window to familiarize yourself with is the Server Explorer. Here you'll find a hierarchical view of each of the servers available on your network and of the data connections you've set up so far with Visual Studio.

The **Data Connections** tree is populated by the many or few connections you have made to databases on the various servers in your network. Each node under the root of the tree represents a connection to a single database. The above screenshot, for example, shows that we have established the details of a connection to the master database of our local SQL Server Desktop Edition that comes as part of Visual Studio .NET .NET. We now have access to the elements of that database that already exist and via the context menu (right-clicking on the item) for each element, we can add new ones without leaving the IDE. We'll revisit data connections in Chapter 12, *Working with Data.*

The **Servers** tree meanwhile lists the available database servers and specific server management resources – Event Viewer, Performance Counters, Message Queues, and Services – for each Windows server on the network. From here you may check the databases available to make connections to and keep tabs on your various machines as you would if you were using the Microsoft Management Console.

The icons above the tree view do not change with the selection of an item as they do in the Solution Explorer. The same four – Refresh tree view, Stop refresh, Add new data connection, and Add new server – remain constant at all times.

The real power of this window is not as a management tool, however. When designing a form, dragging a data connection, performance counter, or service onto the form automatically generates the code behind the form for you and the other elements on the form to access and make use of it. Trust me, it's a godsend.

Class View

Those of you who have used previous versions of Visual Studio will recognize the Class View window as unchanged and still present. For those of you new to this version, the Class View window is another hierarchical tree view representing an alternative view of the solution as a whole. Instead of files and resources, the Class View shows the projects in the solution as a collection of the classes and class members that are declared within them. Even our first project has a few things declared in it from the start, as you can see:

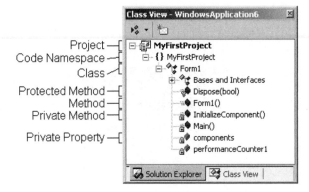

The Class View uses many different icons in its tree view to denote exactly what type of class member or class container each particular branch refers to. Although you can't see it, the icons for basic class members are also color-coded; methods are purple, fields light blue, and properties (not shown here) white rather than various hues of gray as you'll see in the book. If you're not familiar with what an icon represents or cannot remember how a particular class or class member was declared you can:

❑ Hover your cursor over the entry in the tree and a tooltip will appear containing the member's declaration

❑ Double-click the entry and the code file containing that particular class will appear in a document window open at the point where the item is declared

As with the other tool windows, right-clicking on any item will bring up a context menu allowing you to view the file containing its definition, the file containing the call to it (the reference), or its definition as given by the object browser, which we'll meet later. The Quick Find Symbol option will also run a search through the files in the project and return a list of definitions and references to it.

The Class View can get messy pretty quickly. In .NET, everything is an object derived from the System.Object class – even the form in our project, albeit fourteen levels down. With the vast number of classes and members to deal with then, Visual Studio .NET offers you five ways to sort Class View into a set of items you can navigate. Four options are available via the icons above the tree in the window and via the context menu.

❏ **Sort Alphabetically**: orders the members of a class alphabetically

❏ **Sort By Type**: groups class members into methods, fields, properties, and events first and then sorts those subgroups alphabetically

❏ **Sort By Access**: orders class members by their access property – public, private, protected – and then alphabetically

❏ **Group By Type**: emphasizes the sort by type options by creating virtual folders for each type of item in a container and placing that type of item within (see below)

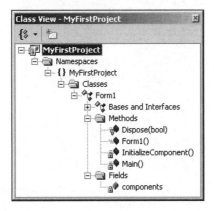

The final option to make some sense out of a busy class view window is to create a folder for your own purpose using the second icon in the class view toolbar and drag copies of classes and class members into this folder for easy reference. For example, we could create a folder for the definitions we most commonly use and populate it accordingly.

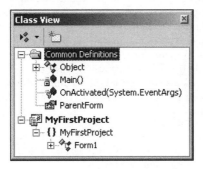

Note that dragging icons to a new folder will not change where your code is declared or alter it in any way – it simply copies the reference to it.

Toolbox

Used in conjunction with a form's designer, which we mentioned above and will look at in much more detail in the next chapter, the toolbox window is probably the most useful in Visual Studio .NET. Make sure you can see the toolbox window and do a simple experiment. First of all, if it's not already open and visible, open the form designer for our simple project. If you closed it, double-click on `form1.cs` in the solution explorer, or if it's open but hidden in the main window, click on the tab labeled Form1.cs [Design]. Now look at the toolbar. You will see the Toolbox looking something like this.

Now double-click the form in the designer to reveal the code that underlies the form. Note that the Toolbox becomes almost completely empty. The toolbox contains a dynamically updated collection of controls and components (invisible controls) that are valid for use with the document that is currently active. So, when you make the form designer active, the toolbox will adjust to show the components and controls that are used with this type of project.

What are components and controls? That's really for the next chapter to go into detail about, but to give you a clue, bring the form designer for `form1.cs` into view again, then select and drag a Button control from the Windows Forms list in the Toolbox onto your form. A button will appear on your form and if you switch to the form's code page, you'll see that the appropriate code for the button has been generated here as well. In this way, you can design the look of complete user interfaces for your solutions without writing a single line of code simply by dragging whichever controls you want onto your forms. The toolbox is flexible as well in that once comfortable with the way things work you can download or create your own controls and add them to the toolbox for future use.

As you can see from the screenshot above, the controls in the toolbox are divided into various categories according to what they would be used for. If there are more controls available in a category than can be shown in the toolbox, you can scroll through the full list by hitting the black arrows or selecting the toolbox and using your mouse's scroll wheel.

By default, the toolbox for a basic installation of Visual Studio .NET comes with the following category tabs, which you can see at the same time, by right-clicking on the toolbox and selecting Show All Tabs:

❑ General – A catch-all tab for components not falling into the other categories, we can also add our own custom items

❑ Clipboard Ring – Stores a list of the most recent text items copied or cut onto the clipboard

❑ HTML – Controls used for creating web forms

❑ Components – Contains some components from the .NET Framework and some third-party controls

❑ Windows Forms – Controls used only in the development of Windows Forms

❑ Web Forms – Controls used only in the development of web forms

❑ Dialog Editor – Controls designed for creation of dialog boxes and forms

❑ XML Schema – Controls used when working with XML Schemas or ADO.NET DataSets in XML Schema view

❑ Data – Components relating to data access such as the DataSet or SQLCommand

You might see extra tabs here depending on what you've chosen to install and what edition of Visual Studio .NET you have. For example, a Crystal Reports tab will appear if you have installed Crystal Reports with your copy of the IDE.

Customizing the Toolbox

The display of these tabs and their items can be controlled to a highly granular level. Tabs can be ordered to your liking. We prefer to keep the tabs we use most often at the top while you may like them sorted alphabetically. To adjust placement in the list, right-click a tab and select Move Up or Move Down from the context menu or drag the tab to its new position. Items within the tabs can be reordered the same way. You can also reorder the items in a tab alphabetically by right-clicking the tab and selecting Sort Items Alphabetically. Items can be moved between tabs by cutting and pasting or dragging and dropping. Unwanted items, excluding the Pointer, can be removed by right-clicking them and selecting Delete from the context menu. Removal of tabs is done by right-clicking the name section of the tab and choosing Delete Tab. The General tab and Clipboard Ring cannot be removed.

By default, items are displayed as labeled lists (as in the screenshot above) and a check mark is shown next to the List View option of the context menu. This setting is on a per tab basis. If you click the List View option in the toolbox's context menu to remove the checkmark, the items will be displayed as compact icons. This view displays the icons for the items without their text.

You may find that certain icons are easy enough to recognize without text or that some tabs are too large for effective use of labeled lists. On the other hand, look at the icon view of the Windows Form tab above. How many would you remember straightaway?

The names given to the tabs and their items are yours to change with the exception of the Pointer item, which cannot be altered. For example, you can change the General tab to be labeled Conglomerate. You can also change the Label item to be named LabelPlain because it distinguishes it better from the LinkLabel. Both these operations are done by right-clicking the item you want renamed and selecting Rename from the context menu.

Working with items in the toolbox is important, but more important is how we add items to work with. The Customize Toolbox dialog, shown below, gives us control over the items in the toolbox.

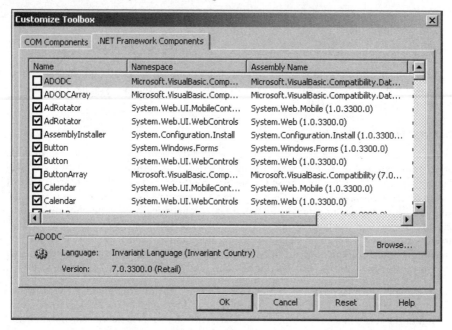

To access the Customize Toolbox dialog choose Customize Toolbox... from the Tools menu or right-click the Toolbox and choose the Customize Toolbox ... option. Although the name implies that the primary purpose of the dialog is to customize the Toolbox itself, actually it's to select and deselect items that will be displayed in it. This can be performed by checking and unchecking the COM and .NET Framework Components on their respective tabs. Your changes are not committed until you click OK. If the component you're looking for is not found in the list you can click Browse to find and add it. By clicking the Reset button all of the tabs and their components will be restored to their original setup.

Properties Window

Like the Toolbox, the Properties window allows you to change the code behind a form, a web page, and so on, without needing to actually write a line of code. Most useful when you're working with in a designer document window, the properties window automatically updates itself with a list of the properties (or events) for the element of the page – form, control, image, and so on – that is currently selected. For example, bring up the designer window for the form in our little project and you'll see the properties window populate itself with a very long set of properties as shown opposite:

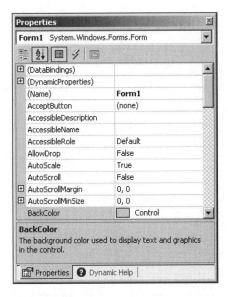

There's a great deal of information here, so let's walk through what's on offer starting at the top and working our way down.

- ❏ The drop-down list at the top of the box contains a list of all the items in the current designer that can be accessed and altered. These are listed alphabetically by name and beside each name is the .NET object type of the item. Our empty form then is listed as **Form1 System.Windows.Forms.Form**. If you drag controls from the toolbox onto the form you'll find entries for them appear here as well.

- ❏ The icons under the dropdown determine what will be shown here and how. From left to right, you can choose to view an item's events or properties grouped by category (shown overleaf) or alphabetically (the default view shown above). The next two toggle between a view of the item's properties and its events. A third, visible only using VC++, toggles to a list of all Windows messages. The last item will give you access to a project's configuration properties when selected in Solution Explorer or Class View.

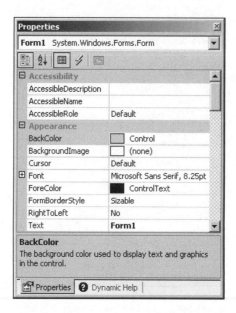

❑ The main area of the properties window displays the item's properties\events\messages and their current value, if any. You may change the value by clicking on the box opposite the property name, and either choosing from the drop-down menu of choices or typing a value straight in. If an ellipsis button (...) is displayed at the end of the value property then you'll make your choice using a dialog box that will appear when you click on it.

When an expansion icon (+ or –) is displayed next to a property, you can expand and access multiple values underneath it. For example, the Font property in the screenshot above can be expanded to reveal properties for font name, size, unit of width, boldness, and so on.

❑ Finally, the textbox under the property selection area gives a user-friendly description of the property you've selected in case you don't understand what it does.

Working with properties in this window is fairly straightforward – you just select a property and change its value. If you've chosen to make use of it to add events to the form you're designing, however, you need to change tack slightly. In order to add a reaction to an event on your form or web page, you can do any of:

❑ Add the code directly in the code window and it will be displayed in the properties\events window accordingly

❑ Double-click the name of the event that you wish to add and Visual Studio .NET will create the stub for the event and take you to edit the code

❑ Enter the name of an existing function to be used for this event

Note that while the properties window becomes inactive when working directly with programming languages, it does work with markup languages such as HTML, reflecting the possible attributes and their values as the cursor is placed within the tag. In fact, it seems to work with any XML file whose schema Visual Studio .NET can access and parse. Likewise, this window will show properties for items selected in the solution explorer and a few of the other tool windows we regularly make use of.

Resource View

The Resource View window harks back to days of using Visual C++ 6 or earlier when, in order to create a windowed application, you would have to include a resource file containing non-compiled code such as cursor images and icons the application would use. The Resource View then allows those of you who need to revisit old C++ applications to navigate through these resource files and see what lies within. It works in exactly the same way as the previous version, presenting the resources in a tree view grouped by type of resource.

C# and Visual Basic .NET users will not need to use this window.

Task List

Once you've gone beyond creating trivial routines to get a hang of the language you're learning and start developing good-sized applications, one of the things you'll inevitably need to do is to keep track of the things you have still to do and the ideas you have for improvement along the way. The task list is the place to do it and Visual Studio even helps by placing system messages for the developer here as well.

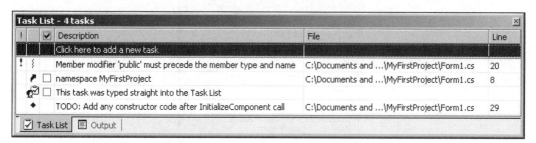

In fact, quite a few different types of message can be found here. In the order they appear in the screenshot above, they are

- ❏ Warnings that Visual Studio will add if its IntelliSense detects a syntactic error in your code, telling you what it might be and where it thinks it is located.

- ❏ Bookmarks to a specific line of code you create by right-clicking the line of code in the document window and choosing Add Task List Shortcut.

- ❏ Notes written straight into the task list.

- ❏ Comments written in the code prefixed with // TODO instead of the usual //. These comments will be copied into the task list verbatim.

Two other types of error message will be displayed here should they occur.

❑ If you're building an application based on an Enterprise Template (see Chapter 17) and a piece of code disobeys the template policy, an error saying as much will be shown here

❑ Should you compile and build your code and errors occur at build time, you'll find the build error messages here in the task list

Double-clicking on any item in the task list will activate a document window containing the relevant code open to the specific line of code the task/error message is attached to for your convenience. If you're getting lost in the number of tasks, notes, and errors you've got in this window, you can also customize the view on this list. Right-clicking anywhere in the task list and bringing up its context menu will give you access to the Show Tasks and Sort By viewfinders. The former allows you to specify which types of message of the six named above you wish to look at (singularly or together) and the latter allows you to sort those messages in view by column (priority, category, checked/unchecked, description, and file.

One last note here. If you do get build errors when you try to make your project, the task list will by default show only those errors. If you still have other messages, you can retrieve them again by bringing up the context menu and choosing either Previous View or an option from the Show Tasks view filter.

Dynamic Help

One last window to make a swift but careful note of is the Dynamic Help window.

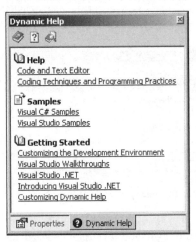

The default view, shown above, dynamically updates itself with hyperlinks to help files relevant to the item, window, or codeword currently selected. The easiest way to come to grips with it is experimentation. Just click onto different areas of the Visual Studio IDE and see the different hyperlinks appear. Each grouping has a slightly different context related to that selected item. Clicking on a hyperlink will open a new document window in the IDE containing that particular help topic.

The three icons at the top of the window offer you the traditional Windows Help-style access to the full set of Visual Studio .NET help files. From left to right, they give you access to the help contents subject tree, the keyword index, and a search page to check the help files for phrases and words that may not be present in the other two. Each of these is useful depending on the context of your query. Indeed, if you're just starting out, the Dynamic Help window will become your friend very quickly.

Designing Your Own Window Layout

We saw earlier on that we could change the layout of our development environment by choosing one of five presets from a drop-down box in the My Profile section of the Visual Studio Start Page. As you may have already realized though, it's not particularly difficult to create a layout to our own tastes.

Laying Out Document Windows

As we've seen, the document windows we create for the files we open take up all the space not used by tool windows or the menu bars. As multiple windows are created they are placed on top of one another, each distinguished by a tab with its name (and mode) on it. By default, Visual Studio uses a single, horizontal **tab group** to make each document window available, but we can add more as we wish, either horizontal or vertical though not both at the same time, to create a split window effect. This can come in handy when the code we need to reference is split across separate files. It can also be helpful when trying to look at multiple forms to ensure they share a consistent look and feel.

For example, in the screenshot below, a new vertical tab group allows us to work on both the design and code behind of our form at the same time.

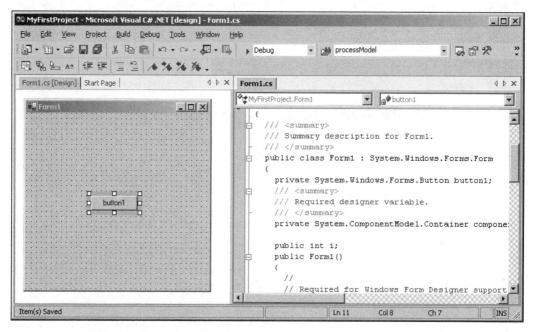

To start a new tab group in Visual Studio .NET:

1. Select a document in a tab group that has multiple open document windows

2. From the Window menu select New Horizontal Tab Group or New Vertical Tab Group.

The order of tabs in a tab group can be rearranged by dragging them. Dragging tabs can also move them between groups. The main restriction on creating tab groups is that they can only be created in one direction. Remember, you cannot create both horizontal and vertical tab groups at the same time.

MDI Mode vs. Tabbed Windows

If you've used previous versions of Visual Studio, you'll recall that rather than being herded together in a tab group, documents were each given their own window, which coud be maximized, minimized, or arranged as the developer wanted. This option is available to Visual Studio .NET users as well if required.

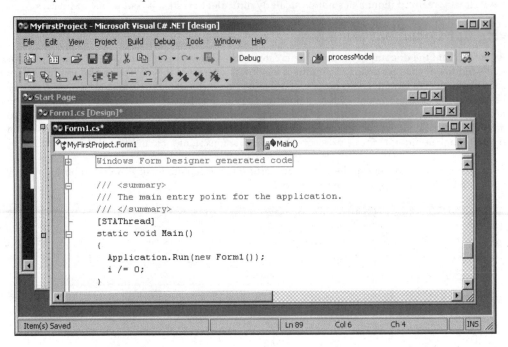

To work with this configuration,

1. Navigate to Tools | Options.

2. In the resulting dialog box, select the Environment | General pane from the left hand side pane, and select MDI Environment at the top.

3. Visual Studio .NET will tell you it must be restarted before MDI Mode can be used. Click OK, then close and restart Visual Studio .NET.

To change back from MDI mode to using tab groups, follow those instructions again, but select Tabbed Documents from the Environment | General box rather than MDI Environment.

Laying Out Tool Windows

There are a more ways to have your tool windows act and fill the screen than there are for document windows. The first thing to do though is to make sure we have the windows we want actually on screen. If you need to make a window available, either select it from the View (or Help) menu or use its keyboard shortcut.

If you want to cose a window from view:

❑ Click on the close icon

❑ Click on the window, and then choose Hide from the Window menu

❑ Right-click on the window and choose Hide from the context menu

You might want to consider having available all the tool windows mentioned earlier at least initially. It's easier to figure out if you never use a window rather than trying to figure out which window you need but can't see.

Floating Tool Windows

All tool windows have three 'layout modes' dockable which is the default; floating; and neither of the above. The second of these, floating, is the easiest to demonstrate in that it makes a tool window behave like any other application running Windows, rather than as a piece of Visual Studio. To put a tool window in float mode, do either of:

❑ Right-click the window and select Floating

❑ Select the window and choose Floating from the Window menu

Whichever you choose, you'll see the window detach itself from the Visual Studio .NET IDE window, free to drag around the screen to wherever you want it to be. We did exaggerate ever so slightly by saying that the window is like those of all other applications, however. A floating window in Studio's case has only a close button and no maximize or minimize functionality. This is still tied in with Studio itself and all floating windows will minimize and reappear when Studio does. As the mode name would suggest, if you now maximize the Studio window, you'll see that the tool window continues to float on top of its parent application.

Dockable Tool Windows

The default state for a tool window is dockable, which means that like any other window, you can select and drag it around your screen like a floating window. But when your cursor reaches an inside edge of the Visual Studio .NET IDE window, you'll see a ghosted outline in the IDE suggesting that the window could be attached to the IDE again.

Note that you can also keep a tool window from docking by holding down Ctrl while moving it. Or, if you need it docked immediately, you can dock a tool window immediately by double-clicking its title bar.

The Floating option tells a window to immediately detach if docked. If already floating, this option will keep the tool window from docking.

To better use the space available tool windows can also be **tab docked**. This is when multiple tool windows share the same display area but have tabs at the bottom for selecting them. The following screenshots show the Server Explorer and Solution Explorer docked in the picture on the left and tab docked in the picture on the right.

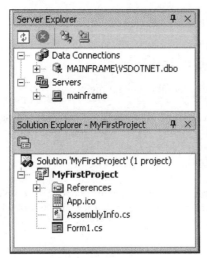

To tab-dock a window with another one, pick it up and drag it so your cursor is in a corner of the window you want it to share space with. The ghost outline we saw earlier will encompass the target window and you can let go your mouse button, et voilà. If you drag the tab-docked window anywhere, you'll now take both windows with you. To un-tab-dock a window, double-click its tab.

Auto Hide

The Auto Hide option is new in Visual Studio .NET and is applicable only to windows that are docked in the Visual Studio .NET IDE window. Making a tool window auto-hide means that when not being used, the window 'minimizes' itself to the edge of the IDE which it was docked to. It can then be brought back into view by hovering the cursor over its tab.

There are several ways to make a docked window-auto hide:

❑   Right-click on the window and select Auto Hide from the context menu.

❑   Select the window and choose Auto Hide from the Window menu

❑   Left-click the 'Pin' icon next to the window's close button

Note that the Pin icon will change from vertical to horizontal signifying the window is now in auto-hide mode. You can also make every tool window auto-hide at once by selecting any one tool window and then Auto Hide All from the Window menu.

When you build up a number of tool windows on any one side the tabs will cover the descriptions, or may be scrolled off the screen. To view a full list, right-click in any part of the tab area they use and a list will be displayed.

None of the Above

The last layout option occurs when a tool window is not set to be Dockable or Floating. This will cause a tool window to be placed in the tab group and act like a document window. That's it for our laying out the IDE to our satisfaction.

Miscellaneous Items

Before we start working with Windows Forms in Chapter 3, there are a couple more features of Visual Studio .NET that are handy to know about – IntelliSense and the IDE options control panel.

IntelliSense

IntelliSense is an auto-completion feature much like the one found in Microsoft's Office suite, only instead of proffering the correct spelling for the word it thinks you're spelling, it proffers a list of namespace, class, class member, and so on, names that you might be trying to use.

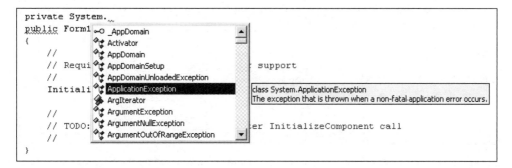

In the example above, we've opened the code behind `form1.cs` and started to declare a new private variable. As we type the period after `System`, IntelliSense realizes we're going to be writing an object type and proffers a alphabetized list of the valid names we could use here. If I scroll down the list with cursor keys, a tooltip appears with a fullname of the class and its short description.

The list that IntelliSense offers is dynamically generated, which means that if we typed one or two more letters of the class name into the page, it will refine itself down to six or seven valid possibilities, which are then easy to select (double-click) from. This is an invaluable time-saving feature and puts paid to the cost of a lot of debugging for syntax errors and looking up the right name for a class or something in your project.

Environmental Controls

Not quite as drastic as it sounds, Visual Studio has a set of options that allow us to control the way in which the IDE itself operates. Indeed, we've already been there once, experimenting between tabbed windows and MDI Mode. To find the dialog, choose Options from the Tools menu.

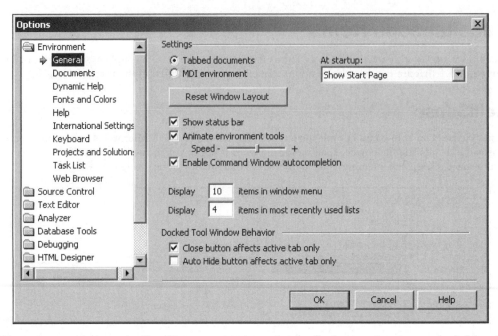

The various controls can be found in ten categories under the Environment option on the left hand side pane as follows:

❑ The General tab controls the options over the presentation of the windows in the IDE

❑ The Documents tab looks after the interaction in certain circumstances between Studio and various project files

❑ The Dynamic Help tab allows us to control what will be shown in the Dynamic Help Tool window

❑ Fonts and Colors allows us to define the font style being used at any point while using Visual Studio .NET

❑ The Help tab allows us to define the language of the help files being used and the collection of help files to be searched when required

❑ International Settings lets us define the language we are working in

❑ Keyboard lets us set up our own system of keyboard shortcuts within Visual Studio or choose one of the pre-installed systems that mimic old versions of Visual Studio

❑ Projects and Solutions lets us define the default save directory for our projects and solutions and several options relating to how Visual Studio reacts to us building our solutions

❑ Task List allows us to define the behavior of the Task List window with a bit more clarity

❑ Web Browser lets us set the Start Page and search options for the web browser (Internet Explorer) integrated into Studio

Only the General tab has a reset button, so do be careful when you change these options. It may be awkward to change them all.

Summary

In this chapter, we've got ourselves comfortable with Visual Studio the IDE, and the notion of projects and solutions. We've discovered the two types of window the IDE makes a distinction between – document and tool – and how to lay them out for our own convenience. We've also seen where the settings panel is for the IDE as a whole and what you can do with it. Last but not least, we've also checked out the IntelliSense functionality and look forward to using it in the next chapter when we start working with Windows Form projects.

3

Building Windows Forms

Building desktop applications in Visual Studio has changed radically with the switch from Visual Studio 6.0 to Visual Studio .NET. With the advent of the common language runtime, the rapid development of desktop-based, client-side applications is now a reality regardless of the language you work in. The underlying classes for forms-based applications in the .NET Framework are the same whether you use VB.NET, C#, Visual C++.NET, or any of the other languages that have been ported to .NET. It's a far cry from the gulf that separate Visual Basic's dominance over Visual C++ and the MFC library in the days when COM was required for making calls into the Win32 library.

Whether or not you agree with the statement that everything should be web-based these days, it's still true that Windows Forms (WinForms)-based applications are very much used and created every day. Microsoft knows that and has improved its support for WinForms in Visual Studio .NET with some very cool new features (visual inheritance, ease of use in any language, extra controls) and some useful updates to the existing feature set.

In this chapter then, we'll take a look at WinForms and tour through the significant features for WinForms-related projects in Visual Studio .NET. Specifically, we will:

❑   See how a WinForm project works

❑   Look at the different controls in the toolbox to add to your forms

❑   Investigate the tools to make designing your form that much easier

❑   Work through a simple WinForms application from start to finish

First though, let's look a little more at WinForms in general.

The Power of Windows Forms

WinForms were a revolutionary advance when they first appeared on the scene. If you've ever attempted to create a rich user interface for an application without the benefit of a visual tool like Visual Studio, you'll know all about the coding horrors required to bring up a window and populate it with a few buttons and a menu. In successive incarnations of Visual Studio, however, the ease with which we can create SDI or MDI client-side applications, explorer-like applications, MMC snap-ins, games, and front ends for large systems has increased as Microsoft has reacted to the requirements of its developers and continued to add new features to an already feature-rich development toolbox. We've already alluded to the equal support for .NET languages – VC++ developers will be relieved to see the back of MFC and the headaches that went with form design while VB developers will be happy to find they now have the power and low-level access to develop things such as fast graphics-based games that used to be the preserve of Assembly and C++ developers.

One of the aims of the .NET Framework was to include high-level support for visual designers and tools, and this has certainly been achieved with WinForms. Visual Studio .NET includes a WinForms designer for adding controls to your form supported by utilities for designing your controls, components, menus, and icons. A further set of resource editors are available for VC++.NET developers to include non-executable content in their applications. Backwards compatibility with past COM-based applications has not been ignored either: one of the .NET class libraries is dedicated to COM Interoperability in a .NET scenario.

Underneath the design, Visual Studio .NET gives us a high level of control over every aspect of our WinForms, both visually and programmatically, allowing us to take total control over the user experience if need be. We can work with printers, registries, display options, system resources, and so on. User rights can be restricted very precisely at every level of a WinForms application to control user's progress through processes in a very specific manner. Visual Studio's highly interactive wizards and customization features can really make difficult tasks simple for the developer. For example, the new feature called visual inheritance means that visual controls on a WinForm inherit their container's visual properties unless told otherwise, saving us a lot of tedious setting of properties. Another allows us to incorporate Print functionality into our WinForm applications at (almost) the touch of a button.

WinForms can be standalone or part of a larger whole, connected up to database and/or internet-centric applications. In the former case, the data controls that can be added to a WinForm provide a fast and straightforward way of sorting, paging, grouping, and presenting the data they contain. The connections to the data sources that provide that data can also be treated as invisible controls to add to a form with the added bonus that data consistency will be tightly maintained by default if you use them. In the latter case, we can create WinForm front ends that tie into Internet-based applications through the Web Services they expose – a new approach to development available only now thanks to .NET.

The last consideration to take into account when considering whether to use the WinForms model is "no-touch" deployment. Later versions of Internet Explorer can be used to access and host .NET applications from a URL. Unless you have a very accommodating IT department or very helpful interns, you want to avoid having to roll out a new version of an application every time a minor bug is fixed or some small feature added. "No-touch" deployment means that as soon as you update the application on the server, users will automatically start using the updated code when they next request the application. We will look at this further in Chapter 9, *Deployment Features*.

Developing WinForms in Visual Studio .NET

Visual Studio .NET is an incredibly powerful tool for creating WinForms applications. You can write in any of a multitude of languages – you can even use a language that you've devised yourself. Arranging and organizing items on a form is intuitive, very customizable, and surprisingly fast. IntelliSense and context-sensitive help are real boons for the developer that can seriously cut down the time we need to spend getting accustomed to new usage and syntax. User interface designers sometimes say that the best programs are the ones you never notice. We can't say development of WinForms with Visual Studio .NET has been that way for us – every time we use it we find new features that are so helpful they take us off-guard!

The best way to explore any new programming tool is to knuckle down and start getting our hands dirty with some actual coding. So let's begin by creating a new WinForms project to play with. When we've seen what there is to see, we'll start again and create a simple but useful application to pull together what we have learned.

Creating a WinForms Project

Load up Visual Studio and from the Start Page click New Project. The New Project dialog box will appear:

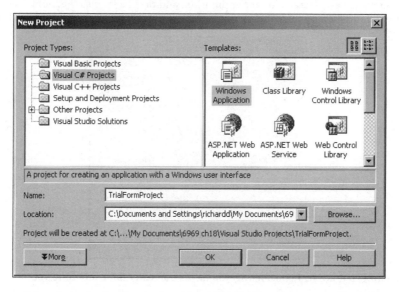

We'll be using C# code in this book, so select Visual C# Projects from the left hand list. In the Templates pane on the right of the dialog, click Windows Application, and then change the name in the Name box underneath to TrialFormProject and hit OK. Visual Studio .NET will go ahead and create a new solution containing our WinForms project, as you can see in Solution Explorer. If it looks familiar, that's because it is the same type of project we created in Chapter 2 and so Visual Studio has created all the same files to get us started:

A Windows Application project is a standard WinForms application template, providing the minimum required files and plumbing to run such an application. To show this, hit Debug | Start, or *F5*, at this point. Visual Studio builds our form project according to the information given in Assemblyinfo.cs, which sets out some basic features of our application, and then as long as the build succeeds, will go on to run it. A window will appear, with nothing in it apart from maximize, minimize, and close buttons:

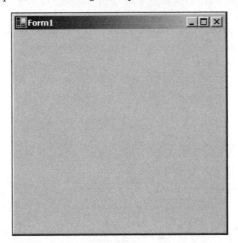

Not very exciting, but not bad considering you haven't actually done anything yet.

There is one other project type in Visual Studio .NET, the Windows Control Library project, which also uses forms by default. However, this is a project for creating new controls to put on forms in other projects, and we'll come back to it later.

The Contents of our Project

At this initial point, four items are visible in Solution Explorer for our WinForms project:

❑   App.ico: The icon associated with the executable file created when you build your project. Visual Studio has a built-in icon editor you can use if you'd like to change it from the default, which we'll see later.

❑ Assemblyinfo.cs: Contains the metadata info (such as name, version, culture, private key) for the assemblies that will be built for this project.

❑ Form1.cs: Our initial form that we'll build upon.

❑ A set of references to the .NET class libraries that give our form the necessary functionality to work (System, System.Drawing and System.Windows.Forms) and to house the various controls we can add to it (System.Data and System.XML)

We'll look again at icons and references later in the chapter. For the meantime, let's get back to our form and take a quick look at how the code behind it all works.

Our project does in fact contain several files in addition to these, however, and we can see them by clicking the Show All Files *button at the top of Solution Explorer. As it is the above files that constitute the bulk of the application logic, we need not worry about the others at this point.*

How a Form Works

One of the many debugging features provided by Visual Studio .NET is the ability to run through the code in an application line by line to check whether the flow is what we intended. Of course, we haven't changed anything with our WinForm yet, and so we aren't likely to dig out any bugs with this method, but it provides a handy insight into how a form works (debugging is covered in detail in Chapter 11). So then, let's **step into** the application by pressing *F11*, choosing Step Into from the Debug menu, or clicking the Step Into button on the Debug toolbar if we have that visible.

All WinForms applications attempt to start up at the line highlighted below within the special Main function declared in the code for Form1.cs:

```
/// <summary>
/// The main entry point for the application.
/// </summary>
[STAThread]
static void Main()
{
    Application.Run(new Form1());
}
```

It contains a single call to create and run a new instance of Form1, and we can step into that process if we press *F11* again. First of all, the Form's global scope member variables are set up. Note that, because variables can be assigned values at declaration, such lines are treated as executable code that can be stepped through and even have breakpoints set. At this early stage in the Form's life, this section just sets the single components variable to null.

Press *F11* again and we find ourselves inside the constructor for Form1. Like the Main function, this contains only one call to begin with – to the InitializeComponent function hidden inside the autogenerated code in Form1.cs. At the moment, all it does is create a new container (that is, our form window), set its size and title bar text, and then return. As we add controls, wire up events, and change properties on our Form, Visual Studio adds corresponding code inside this method to initialize them appropriately.

> Note that all the designers in Visual Studio .NET are full two-way tools. That is, if we add a control to a form, the designer will add the corresponding code to the code for the form. Similarly, if you add the code yourself, the designer will add the corresponding control to the design view of the form. There is no hidden code that we cannot get at when creating our applications.

Pressing *F11* a further five times will get the form on screen, and the application now sits in the background waiting for events to occur. Now because we've not added anything, there are no events being monitored, so the only thing we can do is close it and see what happens. Actually, not a lot. When the form closes, we simply come to the end of the `Main` function. Pressing *F11* one more time takes us out of 'Run' mode for the application and back to the form in 'Design' mode, as indicated by the Visual Studio .NET title bar. Notice that Visual Studio did not step through the `Dispose` method, which is only called internally by the .NET garbage collector when the form is closed ('falls out of scope') and its resources are to be reclaimed by the system. This would occur if our form were a part of a larger application and it was closed while the 'parent' application continued to run. The garbage collector would eventually spot that the form was no longer being used and call its `Dispose` method to reclaim its resources.

Therefore, a simple WinForm is dependent on two key routines, the application's `Main` function, which tells it to create a new form for display, and the `InitializeComponent` routine that initially sets up the form and its contents. Every function and event handler we later add to the code behind our form will take effect once `InitializeComponent` has run and the form is active.

Our form may be active but it doesn't do too much at the moment, so let's look at some of the many and varied controls we can add to our empty form.

The Toolbox

As we saw in Chapter 2, the Toolbox window presents us with a context-sensitive collection of controls and components that we can add to various applications simply by dragging the icon representing the desired control onto the appropriate area of the designer. When we do this, Visual Studio .NET automatically generates the appropriate code to initialize that control on the form and adds it to the code behind the form. Once you've finished designing it, you can then go into the code and add events and business logic as we'll see later on.

With a WinForm active in a document window, the toolbox gives us access to three groups of controls: Data, Components, and Windows Forms. The first two contain sets of components (controls that are invisible on the form) that perform 'behind the scenes' work for us, setting up connections and queries for databases, message queues, event logs, and so on. The latter contains mostly visible controls, which represent the typical items on a form that you might expect to find in Windows these days. (Note that the above screenshot shows the Toolbox items sorted alphabetically, using the option from the context menu, as this often makes it easier to quickly locate a particular control.)

Using the WinForms Designer

We've alluded to the form designer since the middle of the last chapter and now it's time to start putting what we know into practice. In this section, we'll look at how to use the designer to create and perfect your form's user interface using the `TrialFormProject` that we created earlier. In particular, we'll look at:

- ❑ How to change the visual properties of controls
- ❑ How to align the controls on the form with each other
- ❑ How to define the tab order for the form
- ❑ How to deal with a user resizing the form window

Let's start by bringing up the form designer for `Form1` in our `TrialFormProject`. If it's not already open, open the project and double-click Form1.cs in Solution Explorer to see the form in Design view. Now, let's add some controls and experiment. Drag two buttons, a checkbox, a combo box, a label, and a radio button onto your form. It doesn't matter where as we'll tidy them up in a minute. At this point, it's enough to note that when you do place a control on the form, it aligns itself with the grid marked out on the floor. If you don't like where you've put it, you can of course pick it up and drag it to another place on the form as you wish.

If at any time, you want to have a look at the code the designer is generating as you add controls to the form, right-click Form1.cs in Solution Explorer and select View Code.

Here's what our form looks like to start with:

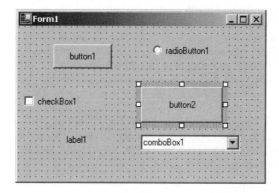

Don't be afraid to experiment with other controls and resizing both form and controls. If you want to add several of the same control to the form, try holding the *Ctrl* key down as you left-click it in the Toolbox, and then clicking on the form where you want that control to appear. Also notice that when an element is selected, a ghost outline with eight control points surrounds it (as shown for Button2 on the previous page). Dragging a control point around will resize that element as required.

Each item on a form also has a context menu (right-click) with four useful options:

❑   If the controls on our form are overlapping, we can choose to have it display on top of the other controls intersecting with it (Bring to Front) or to have it displayed underneath the other controls (Send to Back).

❑   If the form's controls are no longer aligned to the grid, Align to Grid will move the top left corner of the selected control to the nearest grid point and the rest of the control with it.

❑   Lock controls freezes the position of all the controls currently on the form. Selecting a control once we've selected this option will show it with a solid outline rather than the ghost one we saw earlier. Note that this does **not** mean that any new controls added to the form are locked.

If you drag an invisible control (component) onto the form, it is placed in what's known as the **component tray** at the bottom of the designer window. Because they have no visual aspect to them, controls placed in the tray can't be moved, but can be selected, and have their properties changed using the Properties window just like any other control.

For example, try dragging a printPreviewDialog from the toolbox onto the form. You'll see the component tray appear and the print dialog icon in that. Selecting and deleting the dialog will also hide the tray.

Changing a Form Control's Properties

Changing a control's properties is as easy as selecting the control on the form and changing the appropriate box in the Properties window. Just as code is generated when a control is added to the form, changing properties either by adjusting the form or by editing in the Properties window causes changes in the code, and vice versa. Indeed, you may have already noticed this as you've added to and resized element on our test form – every visible control has Size and Location properties reflecting its (x,y) co-ordinates, and its width and height. Every control also has a Locked property mirroring the Lock Controls option in the context menu we saw earlier.

The properties to change for the most obvious effects are those governing the text and font of the controls on the form – Text, Forecolor, and Font. The Font property itself consists of nine values governing font type, size, boldness, italics, and so on, though oddly its color is left for the separate ForeColor property. As its name suggests, the Text property sets the text associated with the control on the form.

For example, with our trial form, we've changed the form's Text property to Trial Form Project and played about a bit with the properties of the other controls. Note that as the radio button below demonstrates, we do need to match the size of the control with its contents to avoid truncation. A 36pt font here simply doesn't fit:

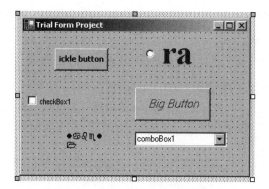

If you wish to alter some or all of the controls on your form together, you have several options rather than selecting and altering each individually.

- ❑ You can select the form itself and set new default values for the controls it hosts. If a control hasn't already had that property explicitly altered, it will inherit the new values given from the form. Any controls you add to the form will also inherit these new default values.

- ❑ You can select multiple controls at once by *Shift*-clicking or *Ctrl*-clicking on each in turn and changing any common properties for them all the Properties window.

In the form example then, I've set two form defaults and altered three controls directly by multi-selecting them and changing their `Backcolor` property to **ActiveCaptionText**. In addition, we've set the `RightToLeft` property for the form to **Yes**, so that, by inheritance, all the controls will now align from right to left, unless we should change it for any controls explicitly:

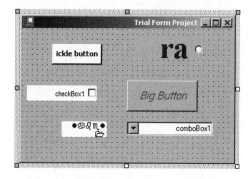

Six other properties you might like to experiment with are `TextAlign`, `Image`, `BackgroundImage`, `FlatStyle`, `Cursor`, and `Visible`. The first three are fairly self-explanatory, but the remaining two need a short sentence each:

- ❑ `FlatStyle` lets us specify the way a button looks when (not) pressed.

- ❑ `Cursor` lets us determine the look of our cursor when it passes over a control.

Ironically, the `Visible` property is not reflected visibly in the form designer. This property specifies whether or not the control is hidden from the user or not.

In this section, we've not tried to cover every single available property of every available control as that would not make for a very readable or useable chapter. We've just focused on enough to get started with setting up a form, so that you can go on, and find out about the others as you need them, or through experimentation at your leisure.

Arranging Controls on a Form

A lot of the groundwork to give a form a consistent feel can be done away from the Properties window, using the Format menu on the top Visual Studio .NET menu bar. Here we find a good number of options for visual consistency:

We've already seen how Lock Controls and the Bring to Front and Send to Back options in the Order submenu work. The others depend on multiple controls being selected that we wish to arrange similarly, and then selecting the relevant menu item. Setting a consistent spacing between controls can be accomplished by selecting the options in the Horizontal Spacing and Vertical Spacing sub-menus and controls can also be made the same width, height, or both using the options under Make Same Size.

Let's take one particular example and tidy up our somewhat messy form by arranging the controls into two more clearly defined columns as shown:

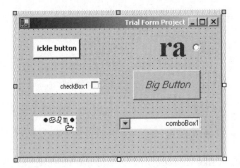

Your form will probably not have exactly the controls shown above, but you'll get the idea as we explain the steps followed. First, select the leftmost controls, choose Format | Align | Lefts, and drag them together off any other controls if necessary. Next, select the remaining controls, and choose Format | Align | Rights. We've also leveled the three rows of controls with each other by selecting the top, middle and bottom rows and selecting Format | Align | Tops, Middles, and Bottoms respectively. It's all quite painless and self-explanatory, just like the Center in Form options that center a selected group of controls either horizontally or vertically.

One useful thing to note when arranging a set of multi-selected controls like this is that the last control to be added to the multi-select group has the 'focus' of the group, as indicated by the eight points around that control appearing as solid black, rather than white as for the other controls. It is with the control with the focus that all others are aligned, and we can change which control has the focus in a given group by simply left clicking on the appropriate control.

Note that all the options found in the Format menu have corresponding buttons in the Layout toolbar, which by default is docked to the top of the Visual Studio .NET window:

Tab Order

Setting the TabIndex of each control on a form was one of the more frustrating tasks when creating Windows Forms applications in previous incarnations of Visual Studio. For newcomers, this defines the order in which controls are switched to when the user presses the *Tab* key. In the old days, if we added a new control when the tab order had already been set, we could end up having to go back and select each control in turn to change its tab order using the Properties window. Not any more, and we can now view the tab order for all controls on the form together by choosing Tab Order from the View menu. This displays the current order for each control as a small numbered box in the upper left corner of the control:

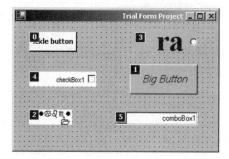

The initial tab order reflects the order in which the controls were added. Altering the order in Visual Studio .NET is as easy as clicking on the controls in the order they are to receive tab focus. As they are clicked, the number will change to show the new TabIndex, and the box containing the number changes to take on a white background with dark lettering:

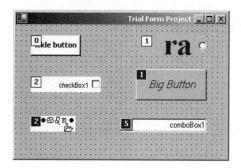

When all controls have been assigned a new tab order, all numbering returns to the original dark background with white lettering. When you're done configuring the tab order, hit View | Tab Order again to return to the standard view.

Form Resizing

More annoying in previous versions of Visual Studio even than resetting the tab order for your form was writing resize code for it. If you're not familiar with this, resize code is what a developer writes to keep controls placed and sized appropriately when the user changes a form's size, and is a task that many developers complain about. To address this, a few new properties have been created for controls to minimize the amount of resize code required.

Now it's not in the nature of the controls we've already got on our sample form to resize at all, so we will use a DataGrid to demonstrate this idea. Drag one from the toolbox onto the form. Again, we're only experimenting with the forms designer here so there's no need to worry about how messy your form looks. Feel free to move or even delete the controls we've put on so far – we won't be using them again.

First, the Anchor property. This property determines which sides of the control should be kept at the same distance from the corresponding sides of the containing control. It defaults to Top, Left for a DataGrid. The following shot shows how the Anchor property appears when you click the 'down' arrow next to it in the Properties window:

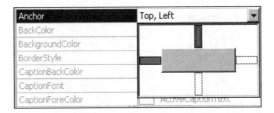

To see it in action, change the Anchor property of the DataGrid to Top, Left, Right. Now build and run the application by pressing *F5*. Resize the form from the bottom right side. The DataGrid will stretch with the form so that its left and right sides remain the same distance from the Form's edges. Note that the Anchor property relates to its container, which is not always the form. If the control were inside a Panel object, its Anchor would be with respect to the Panel's borders.

Another property related to Anchor is Dock. The Dock property defines what side, if any, is **attached** to the parent container. You can choose to dock to any side, all (by clicking the center panel), or none:

Dock	None ▼
Enabled	
FlatMode	
Font	
ForeColor	
GridLineColor	
GridLineStyle	
HeaderBackColor	None

Docking the DataGrid to all sides will fill the entire form. If our Anchor properties were in conflict with our Dock selection, Visual Studio gives precedence to the property set last.

The MinimumSize and MaximumSize properties can also be useful in limiting the amount of resize code. As you can guess, they set upper and lower bounds for a form's size. No longer do we need to write code to check new size values to ensure a form stays within certain limits.

Visual Inheritance

Before we move away from the form designer, there's one more handy and powerful feature for WinForms developers that is new to Visual Studio .NET: visual inheritance. We've already seen when working with fonts that a control will inherit its default values from the form or control that contains it and this is one consequence of this new feature.

The real power of visual inheritance, however, comes when you realize that this simple principle extends to generating entire forms that inherit their initial layout and contents from a single base form. To demonstrate this in action, let's take our TrialFormProject form and create a form that inherits from it. Make sure that the project build is up-to-date, by either running the project, or selecting Build | Build Solution. Right-click on the project name in Solution Explorer (making sure to be in Design mode first) and choose Add | Add New Item. This will bring up the Add New Item dialog. Scroll the templates pane on the right, choose Inherited Form, and click Open. Visual Studio will display the Inheritance Picker listing forms in the project that we can inherit from. Select Form1 and click OK:

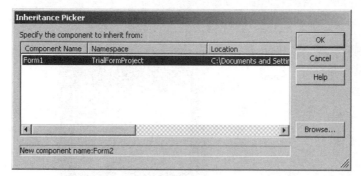

The new form, Form2, is added to the project and opened in the designer:

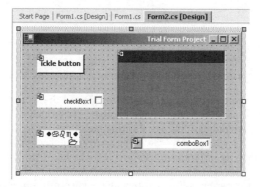

As you can see, Form2 looks just like Form1, even down to having the same text in the title bar and the data grid anchored to three sides of the form. The small icon in the top left corner of each control indicates that they are inherited and that we cannot make changes to them on this form. However, if we now make changes to Form1, then Form2 would reflect these changes as soon as we rebuild.

There are plenty more new tricks and techniques introduced with Visual Studio .NET that simplify the creation of Windows Forms, and we've tried to illustrate the more useful ones here. For a fuller investigation, have a look at *Professional Windows Forms*, from Wrox Press (ISBN 1-861005-54-7). We'll now move on to look at Visual Studio's integral icon editor.

The Icon Editor

As we saw at the top of the chapter, one of the four items automatically generated in our project is `app.ico`. This is the icon that will be used for the executable file created for our WinForms application. If you open your `My Documents\Visual Studio Projects\TrialFormProject\bin\Debug` folder in Windows Explorer, you'll find the file `TrialFormProject.exe` and an icon file, called `app.ico`.

If you want to change this from the default generic application icon, Visual Studio .NET has a built-in graphics editor that can be invoked by just double-clicking an image file in Solution Explorer, including icon types:

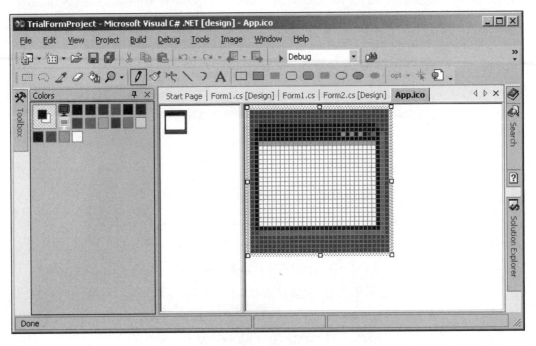

When the editor opens, as seen in the above screenshot, we see the Colors palette, an "actual size" view of our icon, a close-up view, and the Image Editor toolbar. We can adjust these two views to any of the sizes available. By default, the pane on the left has no magnification – that is 1x – and the pane on the right has 8x magnification. To change this, select the pane to alter, click the down arrow next to the magnify icon, and select the size you require. You have a choice of 1x, 2x, 6x, and 8x.

Note that the palette only shows the colors that our image currently supports. To use more colors, we can change the image type by selecting Image | New Image Type, which brings up a list of common choices. We can also create our own format by clicking Custom:

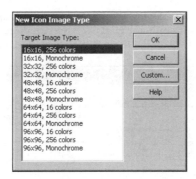

Although the Visual Studio .NET image editor is nothing fancy, it can work with GIFs, JPEGs, cursors, icons, and standard bitmaps to get the job done without having to get your graphics department on the case. Of course, you may well be like us, with no drawing skills so you may decide to palm it off on someone else anyway. For minor alterations though, the image editor will usually be adequate.

Adding References to Your Form

One more thing to look at before we tackle a small WinForms application is the references to various .NET class libraries that our project contains. In order to write code that makes use of a class located in another project, be that COM or .NET-based, the project must contain a reference to it in Solution Explorer, and the actual file must declare the reference to the class with a using statement at the top of the code. Form1.cs, for example, contains five of these. Adding a reference to your project couldn't be easier. Right-click on the References folder for your project in Solution Explorer and select Add Reference to bring up this dialog:

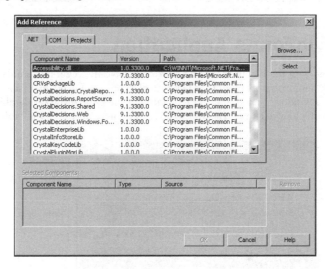

The first two tabs let you select .NET and COM library references, and the last allows you to reference other projects contained within the current solution. Alternatively, click Browse to add a reference to a file directly.

The other kind of reference we can add, the Web Reference, opens up the dialog shown next, which lets us either search through Microsoft's online UDDI Web Service directory to locate an appropriate third-party Web Service, to enter the URL of the desired Web Service directly:

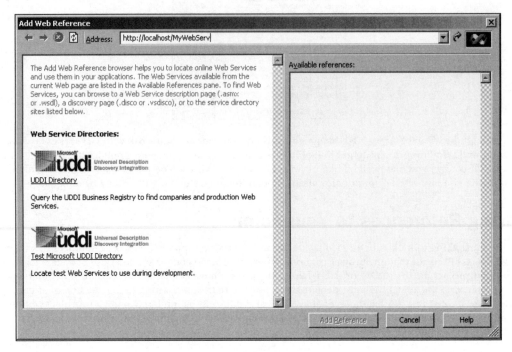

A Sample WinForms Application

Now that we're done with the layout ideas and shortcuts, it's time to get our hands a bit dirty and write a basic application to demonstrate some other features of Windows Forms in Visual Studio .NET. The application itself is a window onto the Shippers table of the GlobalMarket database and will allow you to view, update, create, and delete entries in the table. You may also save the table as an XML file.

In order to set this application up, we'll:

- ❏ Create a new WinForm project
- ❏ Add the items around the rim of the window – status bar, toolbar, and menu
- ❏ Populate the menu
- ❏ Add a datagrid to the main section of the window and hook it up to an OLE DB connection to the `Shippers` table.
- ❏ Add a dozen or so lines of code to the code behind the form to wire up the menus.

Note that this last task is the only time we'll actually need to write any code. Such is the power of WinForms in .NET that we can do everything else simply by manipulating controls, components, and their properties.

Let's begin by starting a new project. Close down `TrialFormProject` with **File | Close Solution** and save any work you've done. Bring up the **Add New Project** dialog box as we did before and select another Visual C# Windows Application project. Change its name to `ShippersMaintenance` and press **OK**.

With the files generated as expected, let's change a few things about the form itself before we add anything. First, the name of the file holding our form's code. In Solution Explorer, right-click the `Form1.cs` file, choose **Rename**, and type `ShipperForm.cs`. It's important to be aware that doing this changes the file name to `ShipperForm.cs`, but the form itself is still called `Form1`. The reason is that the file `ShipperForm.cs` is the code file *behind* the form. It has the definitions for the form inside, but the file name doesn't define its type. With that distinction made, we'll go ahead and actually change the `Name` (property) of the form from `Form1` to `frmShippers` and finally the text displayed in the form's title bar by changing the `Text` property to **Shipper Maintenance**.

We won't set any default properties on the form for the controls to inherit here but feel free to experiment as always.

Setting Up a Status Bar

The first item we're adding to our form is the status bar to be found at the bottom of the form. Drag a `StatusBar` control from the Toolbox onto the form and change its `Name` property to **sbrShippersBottom**. Note that it will appear at the bottom of the form by default.

As you may have noticed from the screenshot of the application in full swing, the status bar has two panels. The left displays the number of records in the table and the right the co-ordinates of the cell you've currently selected. To configure the panels for the status bar, click the ellipsis button (...) displayed when you select the `Panels` collection property. This displays the **StatusBarPanel Collection Editor** dialog. Click the **Add** button to create a new panel. The new panel will be selected in the left pane and its properties displayed in the right. The number that appears in left pane before the panel name denotes the `Index` value of that panel in the `StatusBar`:

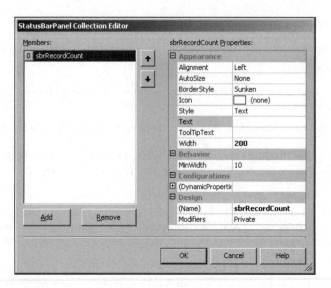

This type of two-paned interface is used for manipulating most control collections. Before moving on, we want to point out something that can save you time when using the collection editor. The list in the left pane is a standard multi-select box. We can select multiple items in the left pane, and see the options that can be configured together for the selected group in the right-hand pane. Since most of our application uses small collections of various controls, this won't be all that useful here, but when developing a large application it can be very convenient.

Click Add again to create a second panel, which will have an index of 1. Now, configure both panels' properties as follows:

Panel	Name Property	Text Property	Width Property
Panel[0]	sbrRecordCount	*blank*	200
Panel[1]	sbrDataGridLocation	*blank*	200

The Text properties are blank because we will populate them programmatically. Click OK when you're finished but note that the panels you've just set up will not appear initially in the form designer because the status bar is not configured for panels by default, and the Text property of the StatusBar is displayed instead of its Panels. To display the panels, select the status bar on the form, and change the ShowPanels property to True.

Adding a Toolbar

Next, we'll add the ToolBar to the top of our form and create the two buttons that populate it. Drag a ToolBar control onto the form and change the Name property of the ToolBar to tbrTop. By default toolbars dock themselves to the top of a form, so no need to worry about that. The icons for the buttons are simply 32x32 GIFs that we drew previously, and can be found in the code download as UpdateDB.gif and RefreshDB.gif.

To get them onto the toolbar, we need to set up an `ImageList` control that the toolbar can then reference and pull the graphics from. Drag an `ImageList` control from the Toolbox onto the form and set its `Name` property to **imlToolBarButtons**. The image list itself has no UI so it appears in the component tray under the form.

To add items to the `ImageList`, click the ellipsis button of the `Images` property to display the Image Collection Editor. When you click the **Add** button, you will be prompted with the standard Windows Open dialog allowing you to browse to find the images you want: `UpdateDB.gif` and `RefreshDB.gif` in this case. When complete, the Image Collection Editor will look like this:

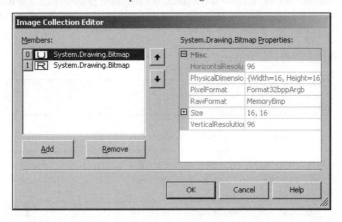

Click **OK** to close the editor. Select the `ToolBar`, `tbrTop`. In the Properties Window, click the down arrow by the `ImageList` property, and select **imlToolBarButtons**. Doing this makes all of the items in the `ImageList` available to the `ToolBar` buttons that we shall add.

Let's now add the buttons. Click the ellipsis button in the `Buttons` property of `tbrTop` to bring up the buttons' collection editor. Click **Add** to create a new button, which will appear in the left hand pane with its properties in the right as usual. Set the `Name` property to **tbbUpdateDB**, and the `Text` property to **Update DB**. Click the down arrow of the `ImageIndex` property to see the icons contained by `imlToolBarButtons`, and select the icon for this button:

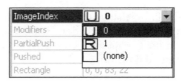

The last property to set is the button's `Style`, which determines what a button does or how it acts. It can take one of the following values:

❑ **PushButton** – (default) A standard three-dimensional button, like the **OK** button in informational dialog boxes.

❑ **ToggleButton** – A button that toggles between sunken and flush when clicked. Buttons in Microsoft Word such as the **Bold** button act in this way.

❑ **Separator** – A line or space, depending on the `ToolBar`'s `Appearance` property, that serves to separate items. As an example, Microsoft Word uses thin lines as a separator to group together buttons with related functions.

❑ DropDownButton – A button that displays a menu or other window when clicked. Buttons like this are often used for font size and type selections.

For this button, we will select the default option of PushButton.

Add another button and set its Name property to **tbbSeparator1**. As the name implies, this will be a separator between our buttons, and hence we only need to set its Style property to **Separator**.

We need to add one last button. Create the button, set its Name property to **tbbRefreshData**, the Text property to **Refresh Data**, and choose the appropriate icon for the ImageIndex property. When finished, click **OK** to close the collection editor.

Our toolbar should currently look like this:

It looks all right, but since we have just two buttons, we could perhaps use the space a little better. To improve things, set the TextAlign property of tbrTop to **Right**. This will move the text from underneath the icons to their right, completing our toolbar setup, and set the Appearance property to **Flat** to give the buttons and the ToolBar a flattened look.

Adding a Menu

Just about all professional-grade applications make use of menus these days and ours will be no different. The toolbox contains two types of menu to add to your form – **Context** and **Main**. Context menus are those that pop up when we right-click a control and list actions appropriate to that control in that context. Form menus, called MainMenus in Visual Studio .NET, are the menus that appear as a bar along the top of an application window and the type that we're using here.

Drag a MainMenu control onto the form, change the Name property to **mnuMain**, and set the Menu property of the *form* to **mnuMain** if it hasn't already done it automatically. Like the ImageList control, the MainMenu will be displayed in the Component Tray but the space for the menu will be added and the contents of the form will be shifted downward.

You'll see that in the space for the Menu is a small box with **Type Here** written on it. To add our menu options, we simply type the option names straight into this box. We want to add a file menu first, called File, so type **&File** and press return. You'll see that the &F has been replaced by an underlined F and that there are now two more **Type Here** boxes to the right and below. You can add menu items to the File menu, or a new menu altogether, by typing in the respective boxes. As you might suspect, the underline indicates the 'hotkey' to press in combination with *Alt* to select that particular menu option.

Our application will have a menu set that uses the layout shown opposite. The Name property of each menu item appears in parentheses and should be set accordingly. Don't forget to use the ampersand to enable the hotkeys:

&File (mnuFile)
   Save &as XML (mnuSaveAsXML)
   E&xit (mnuExit)

&Help (mnuHelp)
   &About (mnuAbout)

When finished select the `mnuAbout` item. In the Properties window, select the `Shortcut` property, click the down arrow, and choose **CtrlShiftA** from the dropdown. Also ensure that the `ShowShortcut` property is set to **True**.

Adding Dialog Boxes

Dialog boxes, like menus, are also commonplace and the Toolbox contains seven standard types of dialog that can be attached to your form as needed:

- ❑   `ColorDialog` – A (custom) color picker dialog

- ❑   `FontDialog` – Dialog that lists all the fonts installed on the machine

- ❑   `OpenFileDialog` – Standard dialog for selecting and opening a file

- ❑   `PageSetupDialog` – Standard dialog for setting the size of the page that will be printed on

- ❑   `PrintDialog` – Standard dialog for starting a print session

- ❑   `PrintPreviewDialog` – Standard dialog for displaying a preview of a printed document

- ❑   `SaveFileDialog` – Standard dialog for choosing a location and name for a file to be saved

Dialogs are invisible controls so they'll appear in your component tray and they need to be attached to a button or menu item to invoke them as appropriate. If you need to create a dialog other than one of the above seven, you must create that dialog on another form first and then attach it to your original as required. We'll cover this scenario briefly in the next section when we create an **About** dialog for **Shipper Maintenance**.

Right now, we'll set up a `SaveFileDialog`, which we'll attach to our **Save as XML** menu option later on. Drag one from the toolbox onto our form (where it appears in the component tray) and set the following properties for it:

Property	Value
Name	sfdXML
DefaultExt	xml
FileName	*blank*
Filter	*blank*
InitialDirectory	*blank*
Title	Save XML File as...

We'll add the code for the `Click` event of the `mnuSaveAsXML` item that will pop up this **Save** dialog once we've created the `DataSet` to save the XML from.

Adding an Additional Form to the Project

A WinForms project is not restricted to just one form. An About dialog here, a clipboard there, and they soon add up. Like the prefabricated dialogs, all they require is a means for them to appear (and a little design of their own of course).

Being proud of our work, we'll add an About dialog to our Shipper Maintenance application. The toolbox doesn't have one ready made that we can just drag across though, so we'll have to create one using a blank form. First, we'll add the new form by right-clicking the project in Solution Explorer, and choosing Add | Add Windows Form from the context menu.

This brings up the Add New Item dialog with Windows Form selected in the right-hand Templates pane. Enter a name of About.cs, click Open and the new form will appear in the Designer. Change the Name property to frmAbout and the Text property to Shippers Maintenance.

The only functionality we need for this form is an OK button to close it. Drag a new button onto the form, change its Name to btnOK and its Text property to OK. Double-click the button in the Designer to bring up the code editor with the skeleton code created for the btnOK_Click event. We only need to add a single line of code that will close the form when the button is clicked:

```
private void btnOK_Click(object sender, System.EventArgs e)
{
    this.Close();
}
```

You can add other controls to the form if you wish. Here, we have added a pair of Label boxes with some suitably inane text:

Note that to make the labels and button nicely lined up, we can use the alignment buttons on the Layout toolbar as mentioned earlier. Select them all, and choose Align Centers, Center Horizontally, and then Center Vertically. Not all dialogs and support forms will be this simple to construct of course, but the principle of attaching them to your main application window (that is, form) remains the same.

Adding a Data Grid

With our `ToolBar` and `StatusBar` configured, we'll now move on to add and set up the `DataGrid` that we'll use to display information from the GlobalMarket database. Drag a `DataGrid` control from the Windows Forms tab of the toolbox onto the center of the form and change its `Name` property to dgShippers.

We'd like the grid to completely fill the space in the form not already covered by the controls we've added to date, so we'll make use of the `Anchor` and `Dock` properties we saw earlier to ensure that design feature remains true even if the form is resized. So then, set the `DataGrid`'s `Dock` property to Fill and its `Anchor` property to Top, Bottom, Left, Right.

To be sure your `Anchor` is configured properly, run the application and try resizing the form to check that the `DataGrid` continues to occupy the whole form.

The Data Retrieval Objects

Switch back to `ShipperForm.cs` in Design view and we'll link up the appropriate data to the `DataGrid`. Drag an `OleDbDataAdapter` from the Data tab of the toolbox onto the form. It will be placed in the Component Tray, and the Data Adapter Configuration Wizard will launch. It starts with a standard Welcome screen, so click Next to continue.

At the next screen, the wizard allows us to choose a preexisting connection or create a new one. Since we have not yet created a connection, the dropdown will be blank, so we need to click the New Connection... button. This launches the Data Link Properties dialog. On the Provider tab, select Microsoft OLE DB Provider for SQL Server, and click Next. We now progress to the Connection tab. Enter the server name, the user authentication information (if you're logged in as a user with access rights to the SQL database, you'll be able to simply use Windows integrated security here), and select the GlobalMarket database. The dialog should look something like this:

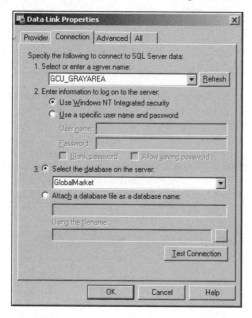

Click **OK** to close the dialog and return to the wizard. The connection we've just created now appears in the dropdown, and the **Next** button is enabled. You may be wondering why we have chosen to connect to a SQL Server database using the OLE DB data controls when we can get better performance with the tailor-made SQL Server data controls. The reason is that OLE DB means we can connect to both SQL and the Access versions of the GlobalMarket database, and will make things easier should we later wish to connect to the Access version. Click **Next** to continue:

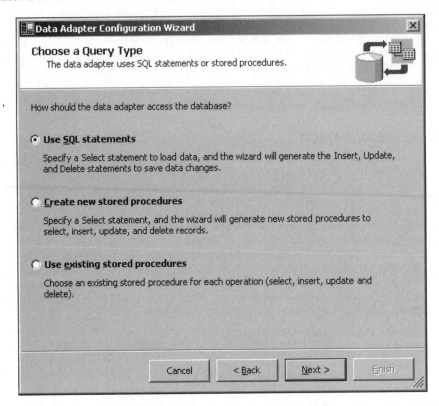

The wizard now requires us to specify how the DataAdapter is to access data. In this case all three options are available. When an Access database is used, the second two options are grayed out because stored procedures are not available in Access. Leave the default option of Use SQL Statements set, and click **Next**.

We must now enter the SQL statement that retrieves the information we require from the database. Because the SQL statement we are using is so simple, typing it in makes the most sense. If we were using a more complex query, we might decide to develop it graphically using Visual Studio .NET's Query Builder, which is covered briefly in Chapter 5. Here though, simply enter the following SQL statement in the text box:

```
SELECT ShipperID, CompanyName, Phone FROM Shippers
```

Click the **Advanced Options** button to see the **Advanced SQL Generation Options** dialog settings. In this dialog three options appear, which are all checked by default. The first, **Generate Insert, Update and Delete statements**, determines whether corresponding INSERT, UPDATE, and DELETE statements should be created, which can save a significant amount of time. The second option, **Use optimistic concurrency**, decides if UPDATE and DELETE statements should be modified to prevent concurrency conflicts. The last option, **Refresh the DataSet**, specifies whether, after UPDATEs and INSERTs are performed, the DataSet is to retrieve new values that may have been generated by the SQL operations, such as identities, calculated values, and default values. In our case, identities will be created on INSERT, and this will retrieve them for us. Leave all three options checked, and click **OK** to close the dialog:

After the dialog closes, we return to the **Generate the SQL Statements** screen. Click **Next** to move on to the final screen of the wizard, **View Wizard Results**. Assuming all is well, it will show a message saying the DataAdapter was configured successfully, followed by the details of how it was configured. Click the **Finish** button to complete the wizard.

When the wizard completes it does a lot of work for us. It starts by creating and adding the oleDbConnection object, placing it in the Component Tray of the form. If we examine the Properties window for the DataAdapter, we can see that the wizard has created and assigned the oleDbCommands for SELECT, INSERT, UPDATE, and DELETE:

Now that we have the DataAdapter configured, we need a DataSet. Although we could create a DataSet by adding it to the form and configuring it, it's often better to create a typed data set, as that will allow us to use IntelliSense on it. Right-click oleDbDataAdapter1 in the Component Tray, and choose the **Generate DataSet** option:

We'll now see the Generate Dataset dialog. Select the New option and enter a name of dsShippers. In the middle pane of the dialog, the Shippers table will be listed and checked. If we had created other queries with the wizard, they would be displayed here also. The Add this dataset to the designer option will be checked, meaning Visual Studio .NET should display the DataSet in the Component Tray when created. Click OK to close the dialog, and Visual Studio .NET will create and instantiate the dsShippers DataSet as dsShippers1 in the Component Tray. If you look in Solution Explorer, you'll see that the XML Schema (XSD) file dsShippers.xsd has also been generated and added to the project.

Binding Data to the Grid

With the DataSet configured and populated, we are almost complete. We have yet to link up the dgShippers DataGrid to the DataSet. We do this by setting the DataSource property of dgShippers to dsShippers1. Next, set the DataMember property to Shippers. The DataGrid now has a source for the data it is to display; however, it will not implicitly populate the DataSet. We need to do this ourselves, and the best place would be inside the frmShippers_Load event that fires when the form is first loaded. We can double-click on a blank area of the form in the Designer to create the event signature, but as we've filled up our form with the DataGrid and other controls, we'll need to double-click on the title bar. Add the code shown below to the event handler:

```
private void frmShippers_Load(object sender, System.EventArgs e)
{
    this.oleDbDataAdapter1.Fill(dsShippers1, "Shippers");
    this.UpdateTotalRecordsPanelDisplay();
}
```

The UpdateTotalRecordsPanelDisplay function that we call above updates the record count information in the StatusBar we've created, and consists of the following code:

```
private void UpdateTotalRecordsPanelDisplay()
{
    this.sbrShippersBottom.Panels[0].Text = "DataSet Record Count = " +
    dsShippers1.Tables["Shippers"].Rows.Count;
}
```

With this function in place, the form is able to retrieve the data using our SQL statement. Now, we shall add code to display the current coordinates in the DataGrid in the second panel of the StatusBar. We can do this in the CurrentCellChanged event for the DataGrid. We can't double-click on the DataGrid in the Designer though, as this would create the event handler for the Navigate event. Instead, we need to select the DataGrid in the Designer, and open the Properties window. Click the Events button that appears at the top of the Properties window, and shows an image of a lightning bolt. Find the entry for CurrentCellChanged in the left-hand column. Double-click it to create the handler's signature, and add this code:

```
private void dgShippers_CurrentCellChanged(object sender, System.EventArgs e)
{
    this.sbrShippersBottom.Panels[1].Text = "Current Cell = " +
    this.dgShippers.CurrentCell.ColumnNumber + "," +
    this.dgShippers.CurrentCell.RowNumber;
}
```

When finished with the About form, the visual setting up of the application is complete. We have yet to wire up the menu options such as Help | About to make this form appear, but we'll come back to that task later.

Wiring the Grid to the Toolbar

Create a handler for the `ButtonClick` event of the `tbrTop` ToolBar, by double-clicking on it in the Designer. Add this code to take the appropriate action based on the index of the button clicked:

```
private void tbrTop_ButtonClick(object sender, System.Windows.Forms
    .ToolBarButtonClickEventArgs e)
{
    switch (tbrTop.Buttons.IndexOf(e.Button))
    {
        case 0:
            oleDbDataAdapter1.Update(dsShippers1,"Shippers");
            this.UpdateTotalRecordsPanelDisplay();
            break;

        case 2:
            this.dsShippers1.Clear();
            this.oleDbDataAdapter1.Fill (dsShippers1, "Shippers");
            this.dgShippers.Refresh();
            this.UpdateTotalRecordsPanelDisplay();
            break;
    }
}
```

Wiring the Grid to the Menus

The last task we have to deal with is to wire up the menu items appropriately. We'll start with File | Exit, so go to that option in the menu editor in the Designer, and double-click to create the `Click` event for `mnuExit`. Add the highlighted code below as the method body:

```
private void mnuExit_Click(object sender, System.EventArgs e)
{
    this.Close();
}
```

Add an event handler for the Save As XML option of our menu next, with the following code:

```
private void mnuSaveAsXML_Click(object sender, System.EventArgs e)
{
    DialogResult XMLDialogResult = sfdXML.ShowDialog();
    if(XMLDialogResult == DialogResult.OK)
    {
        dsShippers1.WriteXml(sfdXML.FileName);
    }
}
```

This will save the XML file to the location specified by the user in the `SaveFileDialog`. The last menu option to wire up is Help | About. Create the handler as before, and add this code:

```
private void mnuAbout_Click(object sender, System.EventArgs e)
{
    frmAbout AboutForm = new frmAbout();
    AboutForm.ShowDialog(this);
}
```

Final Touches

At last, we're finally ready to run our form. Choose Debug | Start or hit *F5* to get the application up and running and take a minute to test out some of the features we've built into it, such as the About form and the toolbar buttons. Check out the *Ctrl-Shift-A* shortcut we set for the About box too. Try changing some values, clicking updateDB, and then check they've been stored correctly by hitting Refresh Data. Verify that the DataGrid position and number of records are correctly displayed at any time in the StatusBar.

Overall it doesn't look too bad, but with some extra steps it can look and work a little better. For a start, we can set the MinimumSize property of frmShippers to 200, 200 to prevent the user crushing the form down to an unusable size. Next, right-click the DataGrid and choose Auto Format from the context menu. The Auto Format dialog that appears lists several pre-configured layouts that can be applied to the grid and shows us a preview of the selected scheme. Choose one that you like, and click OK.

Next, set the CaptionText property of the DataGrid to Shippers. Finally, set the DataGrid's PreferrredColumnWidth property to 120 so that all the data will be viewable without needing to resize the columns. Rerun the project to see the effect of these changes.

Summary

The world of Windows Forms has matured a lot since the first form design tools back in the early nineties, and Visual Studio .NET must surely represent the premier IDE for the rapid development of windowed applications and their interfaces. It's especially welcome for non-VB developers who can now work with forms with all the speed and grace that was previously only afforded to Basic programmers. In the space of a few pages, we've knocked together a very functional front end for the Shippers table that allows us to easily view and change data.

In this chapter, we've really only covered the very basics of working with Windows Forms applications to get comfortable with the various pieces of the IDE – toolbox, form designer, Properties window, Component Tray – so you can go on and experiment on your own. We touched on the various visual aspects of forms that we can control and built a small application to demonstrate a practical approach to working with controls and components.

We leave WinForms now to look at their Companions in crime, Web Forms. These are based on the same concept and rapid construction methodology but based on a web page rather than a Windows form. If you'd like to go into more detail with WinForms specifically, check out the MSDN documentation included with Visual Studio .NET. We will cover more controls and components in depth throughout the book that will apply here as well, but you should also check out Wrox Press's *Professional Windows Forms*, (ISBN 1-861005-54-7).

4

Web Application Development

It's not too often in the development world that the way something works is scrapped and completely revamped between versions. Usually changes are made that will have the least affect on backwards compatibility while still rendering large benefits. As we are sure you have heard by now, this is not the case with Visual Studio and the .NET Framework. By bucking the trend, Microsoft has been able to cut out or resolve a large number of the problems that the development community has been up in arms about for a long time.

When talking about web applications, perhaps the first such problem that comes to mind is "spaghetti" code. The ASP scriptlets that must be scattered liberally among static HTML in order to create a usefully interactive page do not offer a nice clean separation of presentation and logic making such pages slow to develop, and very hard to maintain. Furthermore, the development model used for ASP web applications is not an event-driven one like that used for standalone applications. Without a direct connection between events on the client and events on the server, it can be difficult to handle actions the user requests in traditional ASP. To respond to a button clicked on the client on the server, code must be written on the server to link up the users' actions to the handler. Sometimes even client-side code is needed in addition.

Another big hurdle that we as developers must overcome is to create ASP pages that will work consistently in different browsers and browser versions. Even if we set minimum requirements for an application, such as compliance with HTML 4, it can still be difficult to create code that works in browsers from different vendors. We can easily find ourselves distracted from the true priorities as we fiddle around attempting to achieve compatibility across browsers and versions.

In this chapter, we will look at and use the answers to these and many other problems developers are faced with in web development. Note that, throughout the chapter, ASP will only be used to describe versions prior to .NET. For .NET Active Server Pages, the term ASP.NET will be used.

The Power of Visual Studio Arrives in Web-Land

If you've worked through the previous chapter, you'll have realized what a powerful tool Visual Studio .NET is for creating flexible desktop applications very rapidly. So what does it bring to web application development? As it happens, the improvements that .NET offers web application development are arguably the most wide-ranging, maybe because this arena is still so early in its evolution.

To see just how much has changed, let's walk through the development of a simple ASP.NET web application.

1. Choose File | New | Project from the menu, or click the New Project button on the toolbar or Start Page.

2. When the New Project dialog appears, select Visual C# Projects in the left pane, and ASP.NET Web Application in the right.

3. Change the directory in the Location box to WebApplicationIntro:

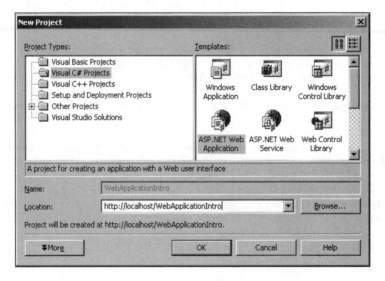

4. Click OK.

The New Project dialog will disappear and the server will be contacted to create the project. Here, we're creating our project on the local machine (that is, the one currently running Visual Studio .NET), but we can create the project on any accessible machine by replacing localhost above with the name of the target computer. We will of course require sufficient rights to create the project on the machine we specify.

The new project is created with some references already set up, and a handful of files are generated as we can see in Solution Explorer:

Here is a brief description of each file:

File Name	Description
AssemblyInfo.cs	Contains the information about the assembly such as version and culture.
Global.asax	Handles application-level events and can be used to set application- and session-level variables.
Web.config	Contains configuration information for the project in XML format.
WebApplication.vsdisco	An XML file used for discovery of XML Web Services in the project. We look at Web Services in more detail in Chapter 6.
WebForm1.aspx	A new Web Form for our project.

This list assumes you have not clicked the Show All Files button. If you have, additional files are shown which will be covered shortly.

The Web Form Designer

Visual Studio's central pane will be displaying the Web Form created by default for the application, WebForm1.aspx in the Web Form Designer:

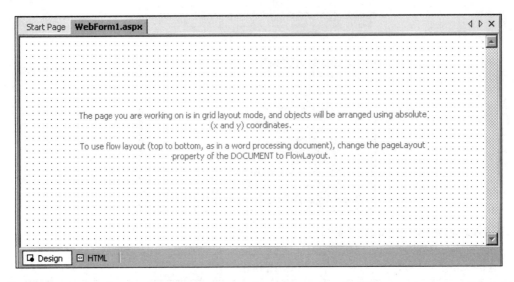

Notice the displayed text stating that the form is in grid layout mode. There are two ways of designing a Web Form in Visual Studio .NET. **Grid layout mode** uses absolute positioning to place elements on the form in a very similar way to how controls are placed for a WinForms application. We simply drag the item from the Toolbox, and place it wherever we wish on the Web Form. The other option, **flow layout mode**, is the more standard way of placing items on a web page, where a new item appears either immediately to the right of the previous control, or directly below it, depending on whether the items are inline or block-level elements.

At the bottom of the designer are two buttons, Design and HTML. Design mode is the mode currently displayed and reflects how the Web Form will eventually appear in a browser. Clicking HTML brings up a view that shows the HTML that has been generated by Visual Studio .NET to produce the layout in the Design view:

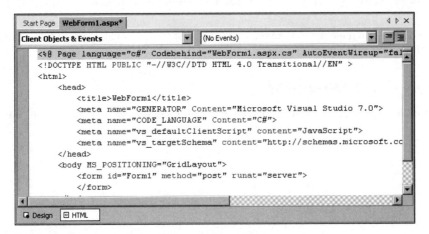

This is the standard HTML that Visual Studio .NET produces for a new Web Form. You can see in the above screenshot that Visual Studio has added an HTML <form> element to our page:

```
<form id="Form1" method="post" runat="server">
</form>
```

Viewstate

When the page is sent to the client, values representing the current state of the page's controls are persisted in a hidden form field by the mechanism of viewstate. This field is then sent along with the page as it is posted between server and client, and is used to reload fields with the appropriate values so that controls can maintain state. In order to use a hidden form field to persist these values, an HTML form is required. Even before we've added anything to our page, a small amount of information is still stored in the viewstate, and hence the <form> element in the page's HTML code.

To see the current viewstate for our page:

1. Right-click the project in Solution Explorer and select Build.

2. Right-click WebForm1.aspx in Solution Explorer and click View in Browser.

3. When the page is displayed, right-click it and click View Source.

You will see the HTML form shown below, which defines the hidden form field called __VIEWSTATE that stores viewstate:

```
<form name="Form1" method="post" action="WebForm1.aspx" id="Form1">
  <input type="hidden" name="__VIEWSTATE" value="dDwtMTI3OTMzNDM4NDs7Pg=="/>
</form>
```

Viewstate is a very useful feature that takes the legwork out of preserving the state of controls on a web page when it posts back to the server so we may re-display it as it was. It can also reduce the number of round-trips to the server, as we don't need to get values for dropdowns and grids from the database. A note of caution is in order here though. Because this requires the state data to be passed between client and server, this can have a detrimental effect on performance if you use controls that have very large amounts of data.

Using AutoComplete in HTML Mode

Shut down the Browser and the View Source views. But while we're looking at the HTML side of things, let's have a quick look at one of the ways that statement auto-completion has improved in Visual Studio .NET. Open the HTML view for WebForm1.aspx, and place the cursor inside the <form> element. When typing in tags and properties, we now get a list to choose from when the less-than sign (<) is typed to start an HTML tag:

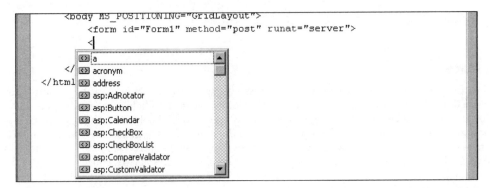

As we continue typing, the list narrows down to highlight the closest possible available keyword:

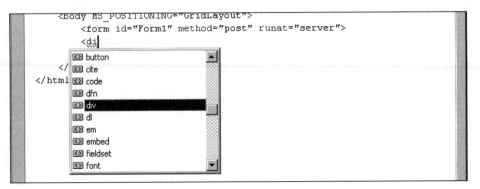

When we've typed in enough for the correct item to appear, we can press the *Space Bar* to complete the tag name, insert a space, and open up a new list showing the properties that element supports:

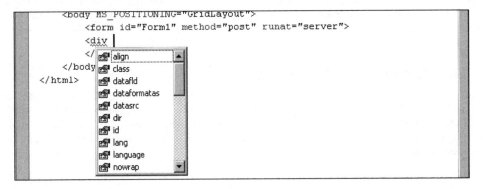

When we type the greater than sign (>) to close the tag, Visual Studio .NET automatically adds the corresponding closing tag:

```
<body MS_POSITIONING="GridLayout">
    <form id="Form1" method="post" runat="server">
        <div align="center">|</div>
        </form>
    </body>
</html>
```

If we are pretty certain of what we want to create, it is sometimes simpler to enter HTML directly like this. The AutoComplete feature of Visual Studio .NET's IntelliSense, along with the color-coding it applies to various elements, can really make such tasks much more approachable.

Features like this are configured using the Options dialog. To access the options dialog from the menu bar, select Tools | Options. When the Options dialog appears, select Text Editor and its sub-item HTML/XML in the left pane to display a list of option pages:

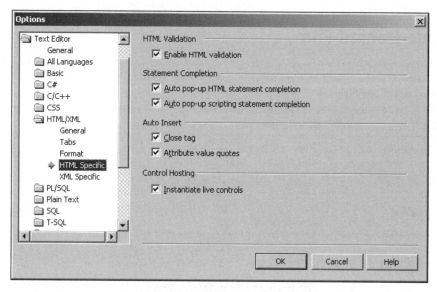

The above screenshot shows the HTML Specific property page. One option that we find stylistically preferable is to check Attribute value quotes. This tells Visual Studio to include quotes around attributes such as align (as used in the previous example). This can also enhance compatibility with protocols like XHTML.

This doesn't change code that has already been added, but affects any future additions or changes. Let's continue working with the above <div> tag. The tag already has an align property set, so now let's add a title property. Our code currently looks like this:

```
<div align="center"></div>
```

Place the cursor in the opening <div> tag just before the greater than sign and insert a space character. Now invoke List Members either from the menu bar by Edit | IntelliSense | List Members, or by using the *Ctrl+J* shortcut. A list of properties and events will now appear that we can choose as before.

99

If we had only part of the word typed and wanted to finish it or see a list of the possible words in that context, we can use the "Complete Word" feature. Select Edit | IntelliSense | Complete Word or hit *Alt+Right Arrow*. When the correct item is located press *Enter*. These IntelliSense features work in most text scenarios such as code or XML and Style Sheet editing.

Don't forget of course that adding and changing properties for HTML elements can be performed equally well using the Properties Window. Visual Studio .NET offers three ways of selecting the control to alter:

1. Select the control in the designer while in Design mode

2. Place the cursor within the tag in HTML mode

3. Select it from the drop-down list of controls at the top of the Properties window

The Code-Behind File

As mentioned earlier we can now do a lot to get rid of spaghetti code for our application. When a Web Form is created within Visual Studio three files are created. For the Web Form above, `WebForm1.aspx`, the files are:

File Name	Description
WebForm1.aspx	Contains the HTML for the form. This is directly displayed when we selected the HTML tab in the designer previously.
WebForm1.aspx.cs	Contains the code for Web Form.
WebForm1.aspx.resx	Resource file that stores localization information and other data in XML format.

To see these, click the Show All Files button ( ) in Server Explorer:

So far we have been viewing the way the `WebForm1.aspx` file appears in the designer. To view the code that *lies behind* this form, perform one of the following sequences of steps:

❑   Right-click in the Designer, in either the HTML or Design view, and select View Code.

❑   Right-click the `WebForm1.aspx` file in Solution Explorer and choose View Code.

❑ Double-click the `WebForm1.aspx.cs` file in Solution Explorer.

Visual Studio starts all code-behind files for Web Forms with the same standard skeletal structure, as shown below. Note that the region labeled **Web Form Designer generated code** has been expanded:

```
using System;
using System.Collections;
using System.ComponentModel;
using System.Data;
using System.Drawing;
using System.Web;
using System.Web.SessionState;
using System.Web.UI;
using System.Web.UI.WebControls;
using System.Web.UI.HtmlControls;

namespace WebApplicationIntro
{
  /// <summary>
  /// Summary description for WebForm1.
  /// </summary>
  public class WebForm1 : System.Web.UI.Page
  {
    private void Page_Load(object sender, System.EventArgs e)
    {
      // Put user code to initialize the page here
    }

    #region Web Form Designer generated code
    override protected void OnInit(EventArgs e)
    {
      //
      // CODEGEN: This call is required by the ASP.NET Web Form Designer.
      //
      InitializeComponent();
      base.OnInit(e);
    }

    /// <summary>
    /// Required method for Designer support - do not modify
    /// the contents of this method with the code editor.
    /// </summary>
    private void InitializeComponent()
    {
      this.Load += new System.EventHandler(this.Page_Load);
    }
    #endregion
  }
}
```

The necessary namespaces have been imported into the page with various `using` statements, and a blank `Page_Load()` event handler has been created. The page is also set with a namespace taken from the project name.

Code-behind files – declared in the ASPX file – define classes that power the controls on .NET Web Forms. These classes consist of event handlers and other functional logic we want included on the page. In classic ASP, we have HTML pages with inline scripts scattered throughout, which are parsed and interpreted server-side. New HTML code is generated to replace these script sections. With the ASP.NET Page Framework, the state of affairs is somewhat different. The entire Web Forms page is in effect an executable program running on the server that dynamically generates the required HTML page as output and sends it to the browser whenever the web form is requested. This "executable" page is compiled the first time it is accessed, and so subsequent hits will be fulfilled much more quickly.

This subdivision of code and presentation allows for greater flexibility. The graphic designer responsible for the overall look of a page will probably not be concerned with the page's associated code, but in traditional ASP it is often difficult to alter the look without wreaking havoc on the code. When using Visual InterDev, trying to do anything on the Design tab after code was inserted into the page was often a problem, but one that doesn't exist in Visual Studio .NET. With ASP.NET, as long as the controls don't substantially change in functionality, the code won't care, and a designer is free to rearrange them and redesign them as they wish.

Server Controls and HTML Controls

If you have made much use of a Visual InterDev, the precursor to Visual Studio .NET, you might be familiar with the Design Time Controls it provides. At first glance they seem like a good idea as they allow us to drag controls straight onto our page. Problems arose however when these were used in an application that needed to scale. They were also very taxing and slow on the client, and thus were generally looked down upon.

The controls provided in ASP.NET are quite different, and offer flexibility, speed, and intelligence. Since they execute server-side, the client won't know the difference and are hence much more independent of the client's capabilities. They are smart enough to know what type of client is requesting the page and will tailor the response according to the make and version of browser that is accessing the page. Another wonderful advantage of these is that they are not magic. They are simply controls written for use in ASP.NET. Microsoft has provided a good handful of controls to use ranging from a data grid to a radio button. With their open nature expect to see component manufactures to provide a plethora of them. These controls are provided on the Web Forms tab of the Toolbox.

Since we don't always want to use these powerful controls, the HTML tab of the Toolbox offers simple HTML controls that we're used to in ASP. As standard HTML controls, these do not tailor their output for the requesting client nor do they require any server-side processing.

The controls are one of the ways the .NET Framework has brought development on the Web closer to how we currently develop for the desktop. Let's take a brief look at some of the ASP.NET controls available in the Web Forms tab of the Toolbox. Note that we're able to rearrange the order they appear in the Toolbox by simple drag-and-drop.

❏ The **Pointer** is the default tool, and can only be used to select existing controls on a Web Form.

❏ The **Label** is used when one would use `Response.Write` in an ASP 3.0 application to write text to the screen. Since it is a server control, we get an ID to refer to it, and can change the font of text on the server side.

❏ The **TextBox** and **ListBox** are form elements that can be bound to data elements. Like the `Label`, they have an ID and can also be subject to a `Bind` method with a dataset or datareader.

❏ The **RadioButton** and **RadioButtonList** can also be bound like the `TextBox` and `ListBox`, and, but they act much more like the Visual Basic elements of the same name, either individually or in a control array. The list is used when we need to only allow a single selection in a list, and can also be bound to a list of data.

❏ The **Table** and **DataGrid** are an interesting comparison. We have much greater cell-by-cell control over the `Table` control, but the `DataGrid` can easily be bound to a variety of data structures, as we'll see in the example below.

❏ The **HyperLink** and **LinkButton** are the primary server side navigational tools. They allow modification of the displayed text or linked URL through server-side code.

❏ The **Button** and **ImageButton** provide the mechanism for posting information from the client. As in the example below, in ASP.NET most posting occurs back to the same page (called a **postback**), and we use the `Page.IsPostBack` property to determine how the page is to be interpreted.

❏ The validator controls, of which **CustomValidator** is a member, provide client-side validation appropriate to the viewing browser.

Putting It All Together

The power of Visual Studio is best shown by example, so without further ado, we will create an application that pulls together a simple list of all customers in the Customers table, and offers basic sorting functionality.

We will assume for these examples that you have already set up the GlobalMarket database as described during the *Introduction*.

We will start by adding a new Web Form to the project we already have open. From the menu bar, select File | Add New Item, or right-click the project in Solution Explorer and choose Add Web Form:

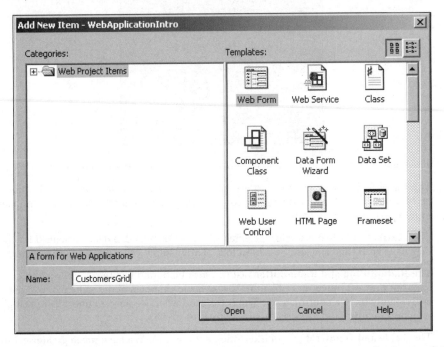

Making sure that Web Form is selected in the right-hand pane, enter the name CustomersGrid, and click Open. The Web Form is created and displayed in the Designer. We'll display data from the GlobalMarket database on this page, so we need to set up a connection to the relevant table.

Connecting to SQL

Open Server Explorer (*Ctrl+Alt+S*), and expand the Data Connections node until you come to the tables of the GlobalMarket database:

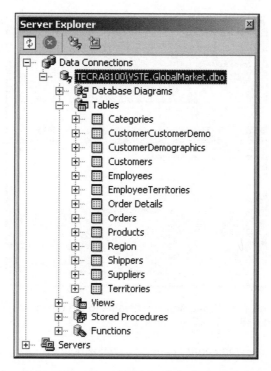

Visual Studio .NET has a neat drag-and-drop method for setting up a connection to a SQL table. Drag the **Customers** table straight onto the form, and a connection object called `sqlConnection1` and a SQL `DataAdapter` called `sqlDataAdapter1` are created and added to the Component Tray:

DataSets and DataGrids

Select `sqlDataAdapter1` in the Component Tray, right-click it, and choose **Generate Dataset**. When the **Generate Dataset** dialog appears, select the **New** radio button and enter **dsCustomers** as the `DataSet` name. Ensure the **Customers** table is checked in the list below:

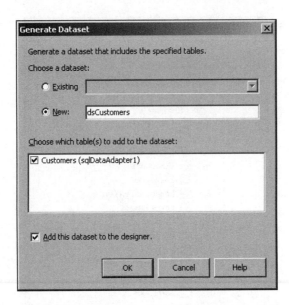

Click **OK** to create the `DataSet`. If the **Add this dataset to the designer** checkbox was checked, the new dataset will be displayed in the Component Tray.

Drag a `DataGrid` from the **Web Forms** tab of the Toolbox onto the form near the top left edge:

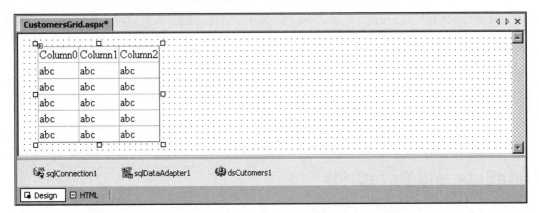

Right-click on the `DataGrid` in the Designer, and select **Property Builder**. Alternatively, click the **Property Builder** link that appears at the bottom of the Properties window for the `DataGrid`. The Property Builder dialog can be used to configure many aspects of a `DataGrid` control. With the **General** group selected in the left-hand pane, choose **dsCutomers1** from the **DataSource** drop down, and **Customers** in the **DataMember** drop down. Also check the **Allow sorting** option in the **Behavior** section at the bottom of this page:

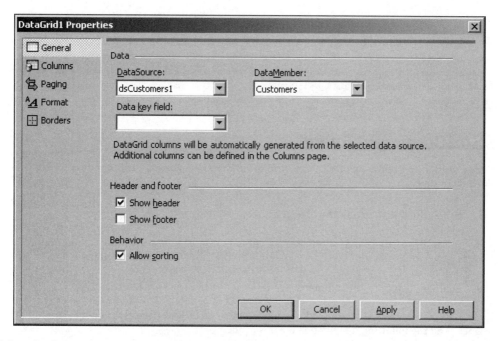

Select the **Columns** group in the left-hand pane. Make sure the **Create columns automatically at run time** check box is not checked. In the **Available columns** list box in the **Column list** section, expand the top **Data Fields** item. Select the **(All Fields)** option that appears underneath and click the right arrow to add each column of the **Customers** table to the **Selected Columns** list on the right.

We'll also set the **Sort Expression** option that appears on this page to sort the data in the `DataGrid` on the `CompanyName`, `Contact Name`, `City`, `Region`, `Postal Code`, and `Country` columns. Select each of these fields in turn in the **Selected Columns** list box, and enter the column name in the **Sort Expression** box.

Return to the **General** screen, and set the **DataSource** drop down to **(Unbound)** removing the association between the `DataSet` and the `DataGrid`.

What we have done may seem a little pointless at first because we first set a data source and then removed it after altering the columns. The only reason for doing this is that by assigning the `DataSet` a data source, we populate the **Available Columns** list. If we didn't do this, we'd have to type each column name in manually, a tedious and error-prone prospect. It might just be acceptable if we're only working with a couple of columns, but here we're using eleven!

Click **OK** to commit the changes and return to the Designer. The column headings for the columns that have a **Sort Expression** set will appear as hyperlinks. When we finally run our application, the user will be able to click these to sort the `DataGrid` by that column:

CustomerID	CompanyName	ContactName	ContactTitle	Address	City	Region	PostalCode	Country	Phone	Fax
Databound	Databound	Databound	Databound	Databound	Databound	Databound	Databound	Databound	Databound	Databound
Databound	Databound	Databound	Databound	Databound	Databound	Databound	Databound	Databound	Databound	Databound
Databound	Databound	Databound	Databound	Databound	Databound	Databound	Databound	Databound	Databound	Databound
Databound	Databound	Databound	Databound	Databound	Databound	Databound	Databound	Databound	Databound	Databound
Databound	Databound	Databound	Databound	Databound	Databound	Databound	Databound	Databound	Databound	Databound

The SortCommand Event

Next we need to respond to the `SortCommand` event that fires when the column headers are clicked. Follow these steps:

1. Select the `DataGrid` in the Designer.

2. In the Properties window, click the **Events** button (the one with the 'lightening bolt' image) to display the event associated with the currently selected control.

3. Double-click the **SortCommand** event, or select it and press *Enter*.

Visual Studio will create an event handler called `DataGrid1_SortCommand` and display it in the code Designer. Add the following line of code for this event:

```
private void DataGrid1_SortCommand(object source, System.Web.UI
  .WebControls.DataGridSortCommandEventArgs e)
{
    BindDataWithSorting(e.SortExpression);
}
```

We also need to call the `BindDataWithSorting` method from the `Page_Load` event to perform the initial binding. Add the highlighted code below:

```
private void Page_Load(object sender, System.EventArgs e)
{
  if(!Page.IsPostBack)
  {
    BindDataWithSorting("");
  }
}
```

As you see, all this does is call the custom function `BindDataWithSorting()` with an empty string as the only parameter. The empty parameter indicates that no particular sorting is to be applied, as we shall see when we come to this function shortly.

The following code constitutes the `BindDataWithSorting` method:

```
private void BindDataWithSorting(string strSort)
{
    sqlDataAdapter1.Fill(dsCustomers1, "Customers");
```

```
DataView dvCustomers = dsCustomers1.Tables["Customers"].DefaultView;

if(strSort.Trim() != "")
{
  dvCustomers.Sort = strSort;
}

DataGrid1.DataSource = dvCustomers;
DataGrid1.DataBind();

ViewState.Add("DataGridSort", strSort);
}
```

This code will populate the DataSet, create a DataView from it, and if requested apply a sort before binding it to the DataGrid for display on the web form. The last line uses the viewstate for the page to save the sort value. We will be using this value later when we implement functionality to delete records.

This will be enough to see to our results. Since we do not need debugging, we can use *Ctrl+F5* to start the project. Right-click on the CustomersGrid.aspx from the Solution Explorer and select **Set As Start Page**. The output will look something like this:

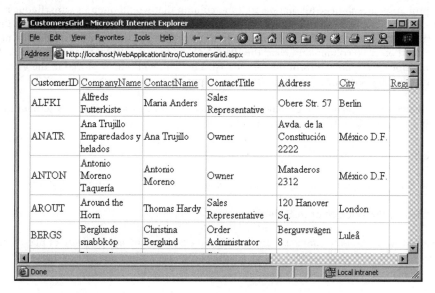

Using the column header links, we can re-sort the table according to a specific column. This isn't much to look at so far, but it's fairly functional and has required very little work.

A Little Bit of Polish

We can make it look a little better by applying a standard format to the DataGrid. Right-click the grid in the Forms Designer and select **Auto Format**. Choose a scheme you find suitable from the left-hand box. Note that the box on the right shows a preview of the currently selected scheme. In this case, we have chosen **Professional 2**:

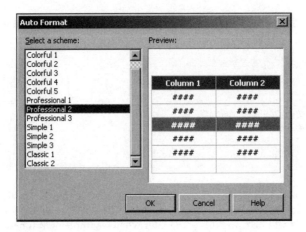

Once you click **OK**, the template will be applied to the grid in the designer. This is a quick and easy way to apply a nice look to a `DataGrid`.

Currently our list is useful, but a little large. The problem is that we are displaying every column when the user probably doesn't need all that detail. One column that would often be superfluous might be the `CustomerID` column. We can hide that column by reopening the Property Builder for the `DataGrid` and selecting the **Columns** tab in the list on the left. In the **Selected Columns** list box that now appears, select the `CustomerID` column and clear the **Visible** check box. Note that this hides the `CustomersID` column, but does *not* remove it from the `DataGrid`. The field will remain stored in the viewstate for the `DataGrid` allowing certain properties of the page to persist between page calls.

While we have the Property Builder dialog open, let's also set the grid to display alternate rows with a background color of silver to improve readability.

1. Click the **Format** tab.

2. In the **Objects** list box, expand the **Items** group, and select **Alternating Items**.

3. Change the **Back color** to **Silver**.

Now click **OK** to commit the changes, and run the project to see the current state of play. The `CustomerID` column is now hidden, and every other row has a silver colored background:

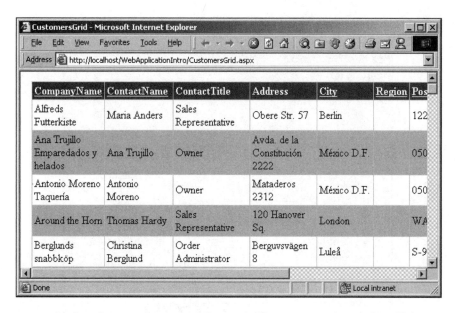

Our page now displays the records quite neatly, much like a report-style interface. If that was all we wanted, then it would probably preferable to use Crystal Reports, described in Chapter 10. However, we shall now move on to add an ability to delete, add, and edit records.

Adding and Editing Data

For the add and edit functionality, we will create a second page. It is possible to edit data using the `DataGrid` directly, but we won't for two reasons. Firstly, the grid has the potential to become very large and if data is entered incorrectly, a lot of page reloads could result. Secondly, the validation controls that we'll use have functionality that displays better on a separate page. Creation of this page requires a number of extra steps, but it will be time well spent in order to end up with a form the way we want.

Start by adding a new Web Form as we did before, but this time named `AddEditCustomer.aspx`. When the page appears, in Grid Layout mode, right-click on the blank form, choose **Properties,** and change the `pageLayout` property to **FlowLayout.** We'll now add a new table by the following steps:

1. From the menu bar select **Table | Insert | Table** to display the **Insert Table** dialog.

2. Set the `Rows` property to 15

3. Set the `Columns` property to 2

4. Set the `Width` property to **600** (should already be set to pixels)

5. Set the `Border size` property to **0**

When the dialog looks like that shown below, click OK to create the table:

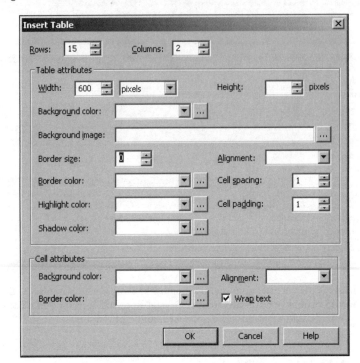

Notice that the table is displayed with a border even through we set the border property to zero. This is in fact a feature of the Visual Studio IDE to assist the developer, and when the project is run, the user will not see a border. In fact, this is a setting that can be changed, but we find it very useful to see borders while in the designer because without them, the form appears to be blank, making it difficult to place new items correctly. However, it can be useful to turn them off in order to get a more accurate indication of how the final page will appear to the user. You'll need to follow these steps:

1. From the menu bar select Tools | Options

2. Select the HTML Designer folder in the box on the left when the Options dialog appears

3. Select the Display page within the HTML Designer folder

4. Under the Display Options section, uncheck Show borders for borderless elements

The general flow of our page will start with the page title at the top, field names will appear in the left-hand columns of the table, with form elements in the right-hand columns, and action buttons appearing at the bottom right.

Cascading Style Sheets in ASP.NET

An effective way to create a consistent feel for a page is to use a style sheet, which we can apply to all pages of our site so that related elements are rendered similarly. To add a style sheet to our project:

1. In Solution Explorer, right-click the project and select Add | Add New Item

2. With Web Project Items selected in the Categories pane, select Style Sheet in the Templates pane

3. Enter the name you want to give your style sheet in the Name text box. We'll call ours SiteStyles.css

4. Click Open

Visual Studio will immediately display the CSS Outline window on the left, with the style sheet open in the code editor window on the right:

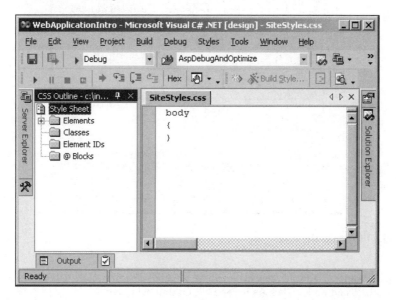

Those readers who have tried using the Visual Studio 6 style sheet editor will be relived to hear that the one included with Visual Studio .NET is better in many ways. I searched around for a better editor that could be used with the older Visual Studio, but never really found one that met my requirements for ease of editing in both visual and text modes. In the end, I chose to edit solely with Notepad, which isn't the ideal solution as it requires a thorough knowledge of CSS syntax.

The CSS editor in Visual Studio .NET has a fairly simple visual editor, but also includes text editing with IntelliSense and AutoComplete.

Creating a New CSS Class

The tree view in the CSS Outline also makes style sheets easy to manage. Let's start by creating a CSS class visually, that we'll then apply to the page title.

1. Right-click in either the CSS Outline window or the text editor window, and select Add Style Rule.

2. When the dialog appears, click the Class name radio button

3. Enter PageTitle in the Class name text box,

4. Click the right arrow to add the style to the Style rule hierarchy list box

5. The dialog should now look like this:

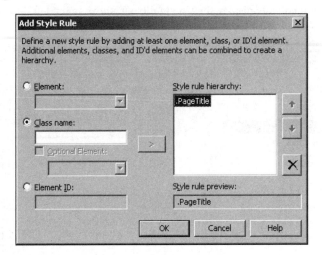

6. Click OK to add the class.

The dialog will disappear and the new class will be created. The new class will appear in the text editor, and it will also be listed under Classes in the CSS Outline window:

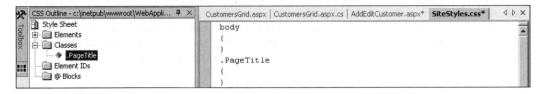

The Style Builder

The new class does not have any styles defined by default. We can define a style by choosing **Build Style** from the context menu that appears when we either right-click on .**PageTitle** in the CSS Outline window, or right-click inside the .`PageTitle` definition in the text editor. Use the following process to create style definitions using the Style Builder dialog:

1. The **Font** tab is selected by default, which allows us to specify how text with the given CSS style rule is to be rendered. Click the **Specific** radio button within the **Size** section, and enter **18** in the text box, and set the drop down to **pt**, indicating the measurement is to use the traditional printer's point. Other units include further traditional publishing measures, such as **pc**, **em**, and **ex**, percentage values for the relative sizing of text, and standard size units, such as **mm**, **cm**, and **in** (inches).

2. Next, select the **Absolute** radio button in the **Bold** section, and choose **Bold** in the drop down

3. Change to the **Text** tab, where we can set properties to define how text within an individual line should appear

4. Under **Alignment**, change the **Horizontal** drop down to **Centered**

5. Click **OK** to commit the changes

The CSS syntax has been generated according to the options we've just set, and can be seen in the `PageTitle` class within the code editor. The CSS style name, such as **text-align**, is displayed in red while the style value, such as **center**, will be displayed in blue:

```
.PageTitle
{
    font-weight: bold;
    font-size: 18pt;
    text-align: center;
}
```

Adding Style Rules Directly

The creation and definition of classes visually with the Style Builder is useful when you don't know the style names and values you want, or if you wish to preview how text will appear with certain settings. If on the other hand, you have a fairly concrete idea of which styles you wish to create, using the text editor to enter them directly can be a lot quicker, and IntelliSense means we don't need to know the exact spelling of style names and values. To demonstrate, we'll now add a CSS class called `FieldDescriptions`. Start by typing .**FieldDescriptions{** and press *Enter*. Visual Studio responds by formatting the entry and displaying a list of styles to choose from:

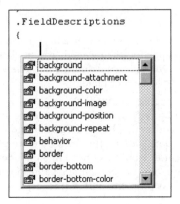

AutoComplete works here just as it does in other areas of Visual Studio. As you type, the list focuses down until the style name you wish to add is highlighted, and you can press *Enter* to complete it. A similar process happens when you type the colon (:) after the style name: Visual Studio displays a brief tool tip about the style, and brings up a list of selected values that you may choose from.

Using the code editor and AutoComplete, add the following style:

```
text-align:left;
```

Don't forget the semicolon at the end of the style, because if you do, Visual Studio may think you've made a mistake or that you plan to add more to the value on the next line, which can have confusing effects for IntelliSense.

Using either the code editor or the Style Builder dialog, add the remaining properties highlighted below to complete the style sheet:

```
body
{
   text-align:center;
}
.PageTitle
{
   font-weight: bold;
   font-size: 18pt;
   text-align: center;
}
.FieldDescriptions
{
   text-align:left;
   font-size: 12pt;
}
.ActionButtons
{
   font-size: 10pt;
   background-color: Silver;
}
```

When the style sheet is complete, save and close it.

You might expect Visual Studio .NET to have a nice drag-and-drop way of associating our style sheet to a page, and you'd be right. Open the `AddEditCustomer.aspx` page in the Designer, and drag the style sheet from Solution Explorer onto the page. You'll notice the table centers itself on the page when you do this, thanks to the `text-align: center` rule we've set for the page body. Click the HTML tab at the bottom of the Designer, and you'll see that Visual Studio has added the following HTML tag to the `<HEAD>` section to attach the style sheet:

```
<LINK href="SiteStyles.css" type="text/css" rel="stylesheet">
```

Setting the Table

We now need to set up our form. Place the cursor in one of the top cells of the table while in Design view, and choose Table | Select | Row to highlight the top row of the table. Right-click that row, and choose Merge Cells. Do the same for the last row of the table. Set the `align` property of the `<TD>` for the first row to `center` and that of the `<TD>` for the bottom row to `right` (place the cursor in the appropriate row in the Designer, and open the Properties window by pressing *F4*). From the Web Forms tab of the Toolbox, drag a label into the top row of the table, and set the following properties:

Property Name	Value
ID	lblPageTitle
CssClass	PageTitle
Text	*blank*

Note the `CssClass` property, which specifies the CSS style rule that should be applied to the currently selected control. Also, note that we're clearing the `Text` property for the label because we will be changing it dynamically through code.

Next, add a cancel link by dragging a `HyperLink` control onto the bottom row of the table. Set its properties as follows:

Property Name	Value
ID	hlnkCancel
CssClass	ActionButtons
Text	Cancel
NavigateURL	CustomersGrid.aspx

Now, drag a `LinkButton` onto the last row of the table. Place a few spaces between it and the Cancel hyperlink by typing directly into the editor, but make sure to keep them on the same line. Set the following properties for the link button:

Property Name	Value
ID	lbtnAddEdit
CssClass	ActionButtons
Text	*blank*

Like `lblPageTitle`, the `lbtnAddEdit` button will have its `Text` property set programmatically, according to whether the user is currently adding or editing a record.

As mentioned earlier, the two main columns of the grid are going to contain a description of each field in the database table followed by that field's current value. Place a `TextBox` inside 11 of the cells in the right-most column of the table. We will name these according to the column names in the table, and set other properties appropriately. Open the **GlobalMarket** database in Server Explorer, right-click the `Customers` table, and choose **Design Table** to bring up the following display Only for the enterprise version of VS.NET. Use SQL Server Enterprise Manager for lower versions of VS.NET:

Column Name	Data Type	Length	Allow Nulls
CustomerID	nchar	5	
CompanyName	nvarchar	40	
ContactName	nvarchar	30	✓
ContactTitle	nvarchar	30	✓
Address	nvarchar	60	✓
City	nvarchar	15	✓
Region	nvarchar	15	✓
PostalCode	nvarchar	10	✓
Country	nvarchar	15	✓
Phone	nvarchar	24	✓
Fax	nvarchar	24	✓

We can now set the `ID` and `MaxLength` properties of each of the 11 text boxes to the values given under **Column Name** and **Length** above. Each text box is named after the associated column, prefixed with `txt` (`txtPostalCode` for instance). Although this is quite a laborious task, it can be made easier by selecting the column names from the above view in Visual Studio, and copying and pasting them over to the Properties window of the relevant text box. If you do this, you'll find it even easier if you choose **Window | New Vertical Tab Group** from the menu, allowing you to have the Properties window open while you also view the database table.

Lastly, set the `Columns` property to **30** for all the text boxes. This is not required, but it helps to give the form a consistent look. The best way is to multi-select all the text boxes, and use the Properties window to adjust the `Columns` property for all of them in a single swoop.

In the left-hand column of the table, add descriptions for each field by simply placing the cursor and typing. When complete, the form will look something like this:

[lblPageTitle]	
Customer ID	
Company Name	
Contact Name	
Contact Title	
Address	
City	
Region	
Postal Code	
Country	
Phone	
Fax	
	Cancel [lbtnAddEdit]

Differentiating Between Adding and Editing

We need to add code to the Page_Load() event to initialize the page depending on whether the user is editing existing data, or inserting a new record. We'll decide this using a separate method called GetCustomerDetails(), which examines the query string to see if a valid customer ID has passed in, representing the record to modify. If that is not the case, the method returns false to indicate that the user wishes to add a new record. If we do have a valid ID, GetCustomerDetails() will retrieve that customer's details with a SQL SELECT query, use them to populate the textboxes on the page, and return true:

```
private void Page_Load(object sender, System.EventArgs e)
{
  if (!Page.IsPostBack)
  {
    if(GetCustomerDetails()) // ...then we are updating existing details
    {
      lblPageTitle.Text = "Edit Customer";
      txtCustomerID.ReadOnly = true;
      lbtnAddEdit.Text = "Update";
    }
    else // ...otherwise we are adding a new customer
    {
      lblPageTitle.Text = "Add Customer";
      lbtnAddEdit.Text = "Add";
    }
  }
}

// Determine if we are adding or editing
```

```
private bool GetCustomerDetails()
{
  string strCustomerID = "";

  if (Request.QueryString.Count > 0)
  {
    // Trim the CustomerId taken from the querystring
    strCustomerID = Request.QueryString["CustomerID"].Trim();

    if(!(6 > strCustomerID.Length && strCustomerID.Length > 1))
    {
      return false;
    }
  }
  else
  {
    return false;
  }

  string strSQLTemp = "SELECT CustomerID, CompanyName, ContactName," +
   "ContactTitle, Address, City, Region, PostalCode, Country, Phone, Fax" +
   "FROM Customers WHERE CustomerID = '" + strCustomerID + "'";

  SqlCommand cmdCommand = new SqlCommand(strSQLTemp, sqlConnection1);

  sqlConnection1.Open();

  SqlDataReader drDataReader;
  drDataReader = cmdCommand.ExecuteReader(CommandBehavior.CloseConnection);

  if (drDataReader.Read())
  {
    txtCustomerID.Text = drDataReader.GetValue(0).ToString();
    txtCompanyName.Text = drDataReader.GetValue(1).ToString();
    txtContactName.Text = drDataReader.GetValue(2).ToString();
    txtContactTitle.Text = drDataReader.GetValue(3).ToString();
    txtAddress.Text = drDataReader.GetValue(4).ToString();
    txtCity.Text = drDataReader.GetValue(5).ToString();
    txtRegion.Text = drDataReader.GetValue(6).ToString();
    txtPostalCode.Text = drDataReader.GetValue(7).ToString();
    txtCountry.Text = drDataReader.GetValue(8).ToString();
    txtPhone.Text = drDataReader.GetValue(9).ToString();
    txtFax.Text = drDataReader.GetValue(10).ToString();

    drDataReader.Close();
    return true;
  }
  else
  {
    drDataReader.Close();
    return false;
  }
}
```

Next we need to add code to handle the retrieval and update/insert for the customer records. Since the page doesn't have a connection to the database yet, drag a `SqlConnection` control from the **Data** tab of the Toolbox onto the form. Set the `ConnectionString` property to point to the **GlobalMarket** database. Open up the `AddEditCustomer.aspx.cs` code file, and add a `using` statement for `System.Data.SqlClient` to the top of the file, then add these new methods:

```
private void AddCustomerRecord()
{
   string strSQLTemp = "INSERT INTO Customers(CustomerID, CompanyName, " +
                "ContactName, ContactTitle, Address, City, Region, " +
                "PostalCode, Country, Phone, Fax) " +
                "VALUES('" + txtCustomerID.Text + "'," +
                "'" + txtCompanyName.Text + "'," +
                "'" + txtContactName.Text + "'," +
                "'" + txtContactTitle.Text + "'," +
                "'" + txtAddress.Text + "'," +
                "'" + txtCity.Text + "'," +
                "'" + txtRegion.Text + "'," +
                "'" + txtPostalCode.Text + "'," +
                "'" + txtCountry.Text + "'," +
                "'" + txtPhone.Text + "'," +
                "'" + txtFax.Text + "')";

   ExecNonQuery(strSQLTemp);
}

private void UpdateCustomerRecord()
{
   string strSQLTemp = "UPDATE Customers SET CompanyName = '"
      + txtCompanyName.Text + "', ContactName = '" + txtContactName.Text
      + "', ContactTitle = '" + txtContactTitle.Text + "'," + "Address = '"
      + txtAddress.Text + "', City = '" + txtCity.Text + "'," + "Region = '"
      + txtRegion.Text + "', PostalCode = '" + txtPostalCode.Text + "',"
      + "Country = '" + txtCountry.Text + "'," + "Phone = '" + txtPhone.Text
      + "', Fax = '" + txtFax.Text + "' WHERE CustomerID = '"
      + txtCustomerID.Text + "'";

   ExecNonQuery(strSQLTemp);
}

private void ExecNonQuery(string strSQL)
{
   SqlCommand cmdCommand = new SqlCommand(strSQL, sqlConnection1);

   sqlConnection1.Open();
   cmdCommand.CommandType = CommandType.Text;
   cmdCommand.ExecuteNonQuery();

   sqlConnection1.Close();
}
```

Wiring up the Button

We now need to link up the events for the link button at the bottom of the table. Add a click event handler by double-clicking on it in Design view, and adding the following code:

```
private void lbtnAddEdit_Click(object sender, System.EventArgs e)
{
    if(lbtnAddEdit.Text.ToString() == "Update")
    {
        UpdateCustomerRecord();
    }
    else
    {
        AddCustomerRecord();
    }
    Response.Redirect("CustomersGrid.aspx");
}
```

Testing the Sub-Page

Our new page is now functional enough to test. Right-click it in Solution Explorer and select **Set As Start Page**. Now run the project by pressing *F5*. The window will launch showing the form ready to add a new record. The `lblPageTitle` will read **Add Customer** and `lbtnAddEdit` will read **Add**. None of the text boxes will contain values:

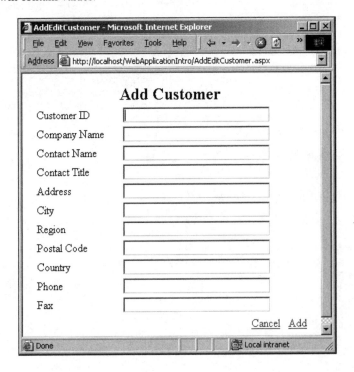

Enter valid data into the text boxes and click **Add**. The record should be added and the browser redirected to the `CusomersGrid.aspx` list page, where we can check that the new customer is listed. Click the back button to return to `AddEditCustomer.aspx`. Append a querystring to the URL shown in your browser's **Address** box with this value: `?CustomerID = ANATR`, and hit *Enter*. The page should reload and display the appropriate data for that customer in the text boxes:

Note that the `lblPageTitle` reads **Edit Customer** and `lbtnAddEdit` shows **Update**. Check to ensure that the **CustomerID** text box is read-only.

The Data Validation Controls

Now we've got everything working as it should, we're ready to move on to add validation. The .NET Framework provides controls that allow for very strict validation to be applied.

We will use a couple of Required Field Validator controls to make the `CustomerID` and `CompanyName` fields obligatory. From the **Web Forms** tab of the Toolbox, place a `RequiredFieldValidator` control to the right of each of the `CustomerID` and `CompanyName` text boxes. Select both controls together, and set the following properties:

Property Name	Value
Display	Dynamic
Text	*

Next, use the `ControlToValidate` property list box for each control to associate it with the required text box. Also set the `ErrorMessage` property for each validator control to a meaningful message to indicate that a value for that field must be entered. Remember however that these messages will be displayed separately from the control in a `ValidationSummary` control that we'll add next. The asterisk (*) will be shown next to the control to indicate the text boxes that messages apply to.

To create a space for the `ValidationSummary` control, we'll insert a new row at the top of the table, by placing the cursor in the top row and choosing Table | Insert | Rows Below from the menu. Select the new row, right-click, and choose Merge Cells. Again from the Web Forms tab, drag a `ValidationSummary` control from the Toolbox to the new row. Set the `align` property for the row containing the `ValidationSummary` control to center.

The Document Outline Window

Before we test out our work, let's take a look at the Document Outline window, using the View | Other Windows | Document Outline menu option, or by hitting *Ctrl-Alt-T*. The following is a subsection of what it shows us for the `AddEditCustomer.aspx` page:

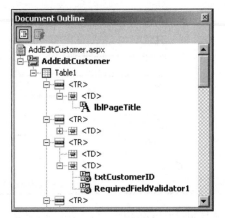

The Document Outline window shows the HTML elements and scripts on our page using a treeview interface. It can really come into its own when dealing with very long pages, as we can select items in the Document Outline to jump to them in the Designer.

So now let's fire up our application again. Make sure `AddEditCustomer.aspx` is still set as the start page, and run the project using *F5*. Your browser will launch showing the form ready to add a new record. Without entering any details, click the Add link button. The validation will display the error messages we set for the text boxes in the Validation Summary, while an asterisk ("*") appears next to both affected text boxes:

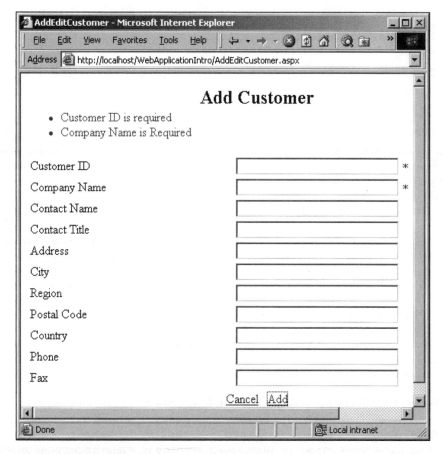

If we now correct the errors by entering values for the affected fields, the asterisks will disappear, but the error messages will remain until we click **Add** again.

To test the functionality for an edit scenario, change the URL to include a querystring of ?CustomerID=ANATR. The page will reload with the values for that customer in the text boxes. Delete the text from the CompanyName text box and click **Add**. The page should show the appropriate error message and place an asterisk against the CompanyName text box.

Linking to the Main Page

We now need to link the pages together so the page to add and edit data can be accessed from the main page. Last of all, we'll add functionality for deleting records. Reopen the CustomersGrid.aspx form, and drag the SiteStyles.css style sheet onto it to create an association. Add a HyperLink control above the DataGrid and set the following properties:

Property Name	Value
ID	lnkAdd
CssClass	ActionButtons
NavigateUrl	AddEditCustomer.aspx
Text	Add New Customer

This takes care of setting up the Add link, so let's move on to add the edit and delete functionality. The best way to do this is to add two columns to the grid where we can place buttons for deleting or editing that record. Follow these steps:

1. Open the Property Builder for the DataGrid and change to the **Columns** tab

2. In the **Available Columns** list, select the **Button Column** item and click the button marked with an arrow that lies between the two list boxes to add it to the **Selected Columns** list

3. Change the **Text** and **Command name** properties for this column to **Edit**

4. Next, expand the **Button Column** node

5. Select the **Delete** item that now appears, and add it to the **Selected Columns** list also

6. Click **OK** to commit these changes

The new columns will show up on the right-hand side of the DataGrid in the Designer:

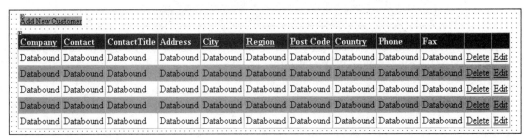

The ItemCommand Event

Now we will add the code to interpret and respond to the action the user requests. Open the **Events** view in the Properties window, and double-click on the **ItemCommand** event to create and set up an appropriate event handler for the DataGrid:

```
private void DataGrid1_ItemCommand(object source, System.Web.UI.WebControls
  .DataGridCommandEventArgs e)
{
    string CustomerID = e.Item.Cells[0].Text;

    switch (e.CommandName){
```

```
     case "Edit":
       Response.Redirect("AddEditCustomer.aspx?CustomerID=" + CustomerID);
       break;
     case "Delete":

       string strSQLTemp = "DELETE FROM CUSTOMERS WHERE CustomerID = '"
                           + CustomerID + "'";

       SqlCommand cmdCommand = new SqlCommand(strSQLTemp, sqlConnection1);

       sqlConnection1.Open();
       cmdCommand.CommandType = CommandType.Text;
       cmdCommand.ExecuteNonQuery();

       sqlConnection1.Close();

       BindDataWithSorting(ViewState["DataGridSort"].ToString());

       break;
   }
 }
```

This code will interpret the button pressed and retrieve the associated `CustomerID`. The need to retrieve the `CustomerID` is the reason why we have not turned off viewstate for the grid. In a production environment for a list this large, you would probably not want to use viewstate unless adding and editing data within the grid. It was used here predominantly to demonstrate viewstate.

Run the application now, and check that when the Edit button is pressed, we are redirected to `AddEditCustomer.aspx` with the appropriate `CustomerID` given in the querystring. Also check that when the Delete button is pressed, the SQL statement to remove the specified customer is executed correctly, and the records are then reloaded into the data grid using the sort setting held in viewstate.

Summary

We can now run our application and maintain the list of customers. Are you impressed? Should you be? We hope that this example has succeeded in highlighting several of the usability improvements that Visual Studio .NET brings to web application development, namely:

❑   No plumbing code needed to reload values between posts

❑   Event-driven programming

❑   Separation of presentation logic and HTML – no spaghetti code

❑   Drag-and-drop control placement

Visual Studio .NET provides even better IntelliSense support than ever before. Thanks to innovations like code behind and grid layout mode, Visual Studio .NET allows us to lay out controls on our web applications the same way as for desktop applications. Wizards abound to help you through many common tasks.

Things such as the Property Builder allow us to quickly and easily configure the `DataGrid` control. The ability to select multiple controls and alter certain properties once to change all of them can save a lot of time and aggravation. Visual Studio .NET automatically adds many of the required references and code for declaring and initializing our page and its controls, and it makes excellent use of drag and drop to make tasks such as associating a style sheet with a page very intuitive.

As you continue to develop .NET web applications, you'll find that Visual Studio .NET quickly becomes a rock-solid tool that you'll wonder how you ever did without.

5

Rapid Application Development for the Server

Introduction

Rapid Application Development (RAD) is more than a buzzword – productivity is foremost in the minds of anyone building development tools these days, and with good reason. If you can do the same thing in 1000 hours with Product A that you can do in 2000 hours in Product B, guess who will make money? Hardware today has dropped to such a low price level that by far the largest factor in the overall efficiency of any IT project is the man-hours spent on it. To the chagrin of old-school programmers everywhere, no longer is efficient use of memory or processor time the overriding priority in the design of production applications.

Visual Studio .NET brings true Rapid Application Development to the server, and we'll talk about why exactly this is so important in a second.

There are four main features that facilitate this server-side RAD:

- ❑ The Server Explorer
- ❑ The Object Browser
- ❑ The Component Designer
- ❑ The Property Window

We'll dig into how these tools combine to take the pain out of developing server-side business logic components for the Microsoft platform, and how we can modify our existing code and methodology for the new environment. We will then look at how we could take a customer request from requirement to product with just the RAD tools.

The Strategy

There is a lot to methodology. Though we discussed it initially in Chapter 1, let's review where we were, and where we are now.

When RAD was Radical

When Microsoft introduced Visual Basic in 1990, it wasn't really suited to complex programming problems. In fact, it fell foul of 'real' programmers, because of its perceived simplicity. Programming just wasn't that easy, they cried, so this must not be a very good way to do things.

Microsoft's marketing team recognized this problem, and so they cunningly stapled Visual Basic to the coattails of a new design methodology starting to make the rounds, called Rapid Application Development. Essentially, Microsoft wanted people to see Visual Basic as a RAD tool, and **that** was a masterstroke.

In a related vein, Computer Aided Software Engineering (CASE) is a theory of design that promotes the use of computers to help design computer programs. Since Visual Basic had these design time controls that allowed quick programs to be built like Lego toys, it was essentially an alternative to developing with a CASE tool, and Microsoft pushed it as such.

In the world of Client-Server, that was fine. We could put together a little application with an Access back end, then install it on the user's machine. Everyone was happy. In 1996, though, Netscape turned everything around with the Intranet White Paper. In this paper, Netscape introduced the concept of using the Web internally within a business to allow common applications to run on a number of platforms – essentially replacing the Green Screen.

Suddenly, people realized that we could be writing applications with this different architecture. The business-to-business movement started. The scalability, stability, and security of these web servers was suddenly a big deal. And where was Visual Basic?

People had been building ActiveX controls, OCXs, DLLs, or COM components to do their business logic in these little client-server applications. So why not use them in Internet applications too?

And at first, it was a great idea. Then the problems started. All of the Internet stuff for VB was an add-in, an afterthought. Developers had to hand control everything – the various servers, services, and processes. DLL hell raised its ugly head. In short, it was bad. But it was all we had.

Where RAD is Now

At present, the need is for a tool that allows us to:

❑   See all the resources available on (corporate) networks

❑   Modify the properties of instances of these services

- ❑ Contact related servers and services, like databases and message queues
- ❑ Quickly review the objects in the architecture

Though some of these tools exist in some places, the Microsoft architecture just didn't think that way all the time. Or that used to be true. Now, we have .NET.

The architecture is really object-oriented. So when we browse an object structure it really means something. The servers are interacting, so we really can tell them to do something programmatically. And products like Crystal Reports (http://www.crystaldecisions.com/products/crystalreports/) and Microsoft Message Queue (http://www.microsoft.com/msmq/), are providing interactive objects that speak to Visual Studio.

We now go from dragging a grid to the screen, and interacting with it, to dragging a mail server to the screen and interacting with it.

Why RAD was Bad for Server Development

Simply put, when building client applications, we use pre-built objects that we can drag around and manipulate on screen. Take a textbox – we can drag it, resize it, and set the Name property.

The last time you created a server interaction DLL, did you even look at the design screen? Visual Basic doesn't even offer one. – there are no visual elements at all. It's all code. Most people close their toolboxes on their default screen configuration.

Now, server elements, like tables in a database, message queues, and FTP servers can be manipulated as visual elements. Sure, we still use code to manipulate them – they don't have visual interfaces. But the property window recognizes them and the Object Browser thinks that they are accessible. It's different.

The Tools

As we mentioned before, we have four tools, each with its own part to play:

- ❑ The Server Explorer
- ❑ The Object Browser
- ❑ The Component Designer
- ❑ The Property Window

Server Explorer

The Server Explorer is a sort of Microsoft Management console that allows developers to see all available server resources on any network server. In effect, it takes the MMC into the world of the middle-tier developer.

You can use Server Explorer to view and manipulate data links, database connections, and system resources on any server to which you have network access. Need an instance of the ASP.NET Requests Rejected PerfMon counter? No problem. Need to intercept an eventlog message sent to the print log? It's right there in VS.NET for us to view or use in our programs:

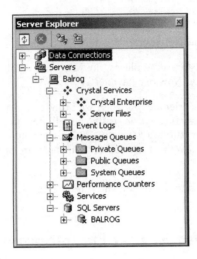

As one can see, each category of tool appears as a top-level item. There can be a number of these, and we won't go over every one. We will look at:

❑ SQL Servers

❑ Services

❑ Data Connections

❑ Performance Counters

❑ Message Queues

❑ Event Logs

Products like Crystal Reports will have their own top-level item, and should be covered in the product documentation. We'll cover the concepts here, and the idea should hold true for middle-tier development with any of the tools.

SQL Servers

The SQL Server explorer is where many RAD server developers will spend their time. The days of switching back and forth to Enterprise Manager are gone. The SQL Server Explorer gives us access to everything Enterprise Manager does – at least from a developer's perspective.

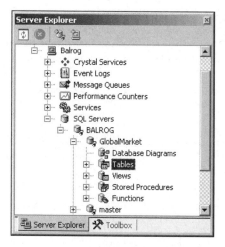

The tables and views create `SqlConnection` and `SqlDataAdapter` objects, with properties specifying the object. Developers can further create a `DataSet` by right-clicking on a `SqlDataAdapter`. Another option when working with a Server Explorer-generated `SqlDataAdapter` is using the Data Adapter Wizard.

To access the data adapter wizard from an existing `SqlDataAdapter`, right-click and select **Configure Data Adapter** The wizard then allows you to:

❑ Select an existing data connection, or create a new one

❑ Determine how the adapter is to access the database

❑ Specify the information to get from the database as part of the adapter

❑ Determine what to name the statements used to interface with the data (update, delete, insert, and select)

The Data Adapter even allows us to specify that stored procedures be created rather than using inline SQL. After specifying the use of the `SELECT` statement to get information from the database the wizard interpolates some pretty impressive SQL code to generate the procedures. Note that all four statements (`UPDATE`, `DELETE`, `INSERT`, and `SELECT`) are generated with unique names that we specify. Here is some generated `SELECT` code, for example:

```
IF EXISTS (SELECT * FROM sysobjects WHERE name = 'NewSelectCommand'
    AND user_name(uid) = 'dbo')
  DROP PROCEDURE [dbo].[NewSelectCommand];
GO


CREATE PROCEDURE [dbo].[NewSelectCommand]
AS
  SET NOCOUNT ON;
  SELECT CustomerID, CustomerTypeID FROM CustomerCustomerDemo;
GO
```

On the visual side of things, the properties of a table or field are readily viewable in the Properties window, which we'll discuss in more detail later.

Stored procedures can also be dragged into the component tray – the lower area of the designer where non-visual components are placed – for drag-and-drop access through the IDE. A stored procedure creates an instance of the SqlCommand class. For instance, dragging the SalesByYear procedure out of the globalMarket Stored Procedure folder causes the following code to be generated:

```
this.SalesByYear.CommandText = "dbo.[Sales by Year]";
this.SalesByYear.CommandType = System.Data.CommandType.StoredProcedure;
this.SalesByYear.Connection = this.sqlConnection1;
this.SalesByYear.Parameters.Add(new
   System.Data.SqlClient.SqlParameter("@RETURN_VALUE",
   System.Data.SqlDbType.Int, 4, System.Data.ParameterDirection.ReturnValue,
   false, ((System.Byte)(10)), ((System.Byte)(0)), "",
   System.Data.DataRowVersion.Current, null));
this.SalesByYear.Parameters.Add(new
   System.Data.SqlClient.SqlParameter("@Beginning_Date",
System.Data.SqlDbType.DateTime, 8));
this.SalesByYear.Parameters.Add(new
   System.Data.SqlClient.SqlParameter("@Ending_Date",
   System.Data.SqlDbType.DateTime, 8));
```

Perhaps slightly more convoluted than we would write it by hand, but certainly not bad for a RAD tool. It is certainly better than a hidden batch of compiled code, or a dependence on a group of included server-side JavaScript.

Services

The Services Server Control essentially gives us visual access to the System.ServiceProcess.ServiceController object. We can actually drag an instance of a service controller, like the MSFTP service on a Windows 2000 Server in our network, onto the project and access it visually and programmatically. A whole host of properties are available to us through the Properties window, including the name of the instance, and also:

- ❑ CanPauseAndContinue
- ❑ CanShutdown
- ❑ CanStop
- ❑ Container
- ❑ DependentServices
- ❑ DesignMode
- ❑ DisplayName
- ❑ Events
- ❑ MachineName
- ❑ ServiceName
- ❑ ServicesDependedOn
- ❑ ServiceType
- ❑ Site
- ❑ Status

The Server Explorer shows us the state of the services through use of VCR-like icons to indicated whether started (green triangle), stopped (red square), or paused (two orange dashes):

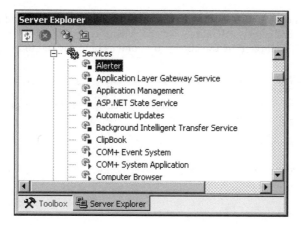

The Properties window gives us access to the instance name, the service we are managing in that instance, the machine name, and other information.

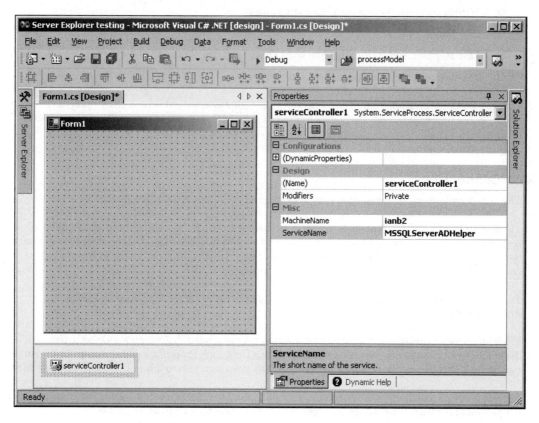

Remember, that it is just an instance of the `ServiceController`. If we need two services at the same time, we would need two instances with two names.

As with other drag-and-drop tools in Visual Studio, all that is happening is that references are being added to our code. There is no magic here – we could hand-code all of this if we wish. For instance, here is the code that is generated by the above components being added to our project:

```
public class Form1 : System.Windows.Forms.Form
{
  private System.ServiceProcess.ServiceController serviceController1;
  private System.ComponentModel.Container components = null;

  public Form1()
  {
    InitializeComponent();
  }
{...}
}
```

This kind of functionality lends itself to a number of possible uses, including but not limited to:

❑ Writing our own service controller application

❑ Checking for the state of a service before using it

❑ Easy stopping and starting for low-level changes during an install

❑ The `ExecuteCommand()` method lets us execute a custom command to the service

Creating a SQL Server function inside your development environment is now child's play, as is creating tables, stored procedures, and direct data editing. It's the SQL Functions that really are impressive, though. SQL Functions can be dragged onto the designer to appear instantly as corresponding `SqlCommands` instances, just as for Stored Procedures.

Data Connections

The Data Connections icon provides easy access to the Data Link Properties dialog.

There are a number of different ways to link to a database in .NET. We're not going to talk about all of them here, because this isn't a book about ADO.NET, but from a RAD perspective, the key is to visualize the data connections in a comprehensive yet compact way. Having access to all the different kinds of data connections for a project in one visual interface is the key.

To access the Data Link Properties dialog, right-click on the Data Connections icon and select Add Connection

While in previous versions of Visual Studio, it wasn't recommended that we create DSNs in the development environments, now it is encouraged. The Data Link Properties dialog assumes we want to connect to a SQL Server, but clicking the provider tab gives us access to a list of installed data providers.

There are even a few more interesting connectors, like the Microsoft Project 9.0 OLE DB connector. Select the provider type from the Provider tab, and then click the All tab to edit other details:

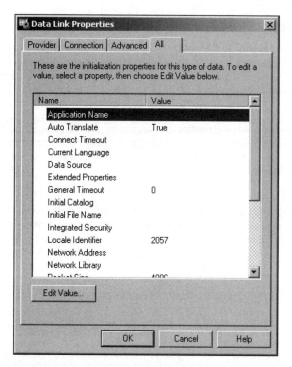

If we choose a random project file from our local hard drive, and enter it in the flagged Project Name property, we have a whole new way of handling our project files from within Visual Studio:

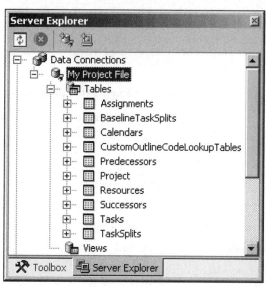

All of these tables act in a similar manner to SQL Server tables – we can view the data, edit properties, and in general get in touch with the environment. Check out the *SQL Servers* section in this chapter and Chapter 12 *Working with Data* for more on this.

Performance Counters

Another of the nice visual features of Windows Servers is the performance monitor (PerfMon), software that reads continuous performance and error-tracking data produced by all of the system's hardware and software services. Everything from ASP.NET cache to the temperature of the processor is often available from the performance monitor. Most of us view it from PerfMon, the neat little graphing tool that comes with Windows Servers. Few of us think of it as a development tool.

The fact is, if we could track every aspect of our programs' function using the performance counter, wouldn't we? No more writing the number of corrupt images to a field commented out in HTML. We can now easily write performance information to a custom counter and leave it in – forever out of the user's way, but available to us as needed.

Another interesting facet of this is system tracking, which could be an essential part of our maintenance applications. Imagine a desktop application that is smart enough to know when the rest of the system is taxed, and reduces its own needs in response. Or a server application that automatically carries out a cleanup after a certain kind of error. Watching the properties of the performance counters makes it all possible:

Dragging an existing performance counter onto the component tray produces the familiar icon, and creates the underlying code that calls and configures the `System.Diagnostics.PerformanceCounter` object with properties set to set the instance to the counter chosen.

```
this.performanceCounter1 = new System.Diagnostics.PerformanceCounter();
((System.ComponentModel.ISupportInitialize)(this.performanceCounter1)).BeginInit()
;
this.performanceCounter1.CategoryName = "ASP.NET";
this.performanceCounter1.CounterName = "Application Restarts";
this.performanceCounter1.MachineName = "Balrog";
```

The instance of `performanceCounter1` gives us access to the properties of the class, including:

- ❏   `CategoryName` – the category name for this instance of counter, like ASP.NET or Memory.

- ❏   `Container` – inherited from component

- ❏   `CounterHelp` – gets the description

- ❏   `CounterName` – gets or sets the name of the counter, like `Request Wait Time`

- ❏   `CounterType` – gets the type of counter for the instance, like `Continuous` or `Instance`

- ❏   `InstanceName` – the name of the instance, like `performanceCounter1`

- ❏   `MachineName` – the PC name being watched

- ❏   `RawValue` – the uncalculated value of the counter

- ❏   `ReadOnly` – true for system counters, `false` for our custom counters

- ❏   `Site` – inherited from component

To get into the really interesting stuff, we have to make custom counters for our namespace. This is an amazingly simple endeavor, never requiring us to leave Visual Studio:

1. In Server Explorer, right-click on **Performance Counters** and select **Create New Category**.

2. Set the **Category Name** to `GlobalMarket`.

3. Click the **New** button.

4. Name the counter `Errors`.

5. Set the **Type** to `NumberOfItems32`.

6. Click **OK**.

7. From the **Server Explorer**, drag the new Errors counter you just created onto the designer.

8. Right-click on the `performanceCounter1` and select **Properties**.

9. Set the **InstanceName** to `Errors`.

10. Set the **Readonly** attribute to `False`. We'll now have the following generated code:

```
private void InitializeComponent()
{
  this.performanceCounter1 = new System.Diagnostics.PerformanceCounter();

((System.ComponentModel.ISupportInitialize)(this.performanceCounter1)).BeginInit()
;
  //
  // performanceCounter1
  //
  this.performanceCounter1.CategoryName = "GlobalMarket";
  this.performanceCounter1.CounterName = "Advertiser";
  this.performanceCounter1.InstanceName = "errors";
  this.performanceCounter1.MachineName = "draco";
  this.performanceCounter1.ReadOnly = false;


((System.ComponentModel.ISupportInitialize)(this.performanceCounter1)).EndInit();

}
```

It is a simple operation to use the `performanceCounter1.Increment()` method then to increment the value. After setting up a new counter, we can right-click and select **Add Installer**, which creates the C# code needed to install the counter on the computer running the software. This is the code, for instance, that would install the counter on an installation server:

```
using System;
using System.Collections;
using System.ComponentModel;
```

```
using System.Configuration.Install;

namespace Server_Explorer_testing
{
  [RunInstaller(true)]
  public class ProjectInstaller : System.Configuration.Install.Installer
  {
    private System.Diagnostics.PerformanceCounterInstaller
      performanceCounterInstaller1;
    private System.ComponentModel.Container components = null;

    public ProjectInstaller()
    {
      InitializeComponent();
    }

    private void InitializeComponent()
    {
      this.performanceCounterInstaller1 = new
        System.Diagnostics.PerformanceCounterInstaller();
      this.performanceCounterInstaller1.CategoryHelp = "None";
      this.performanceCounterInstaller1.CategoryName = "GlobalMarket";
      this.performanceCounterInstaller1.Counters.AddRange
        (new System.Diagnostics.CounterCreationData[] {
      this.Installers.AddRange(new System.Configuration.Install.Installer[] {
    }
  }
}
```

Event Logs

Event logs offer the same features as performance counters – ease of responding to events or logging your own. Doing this in Visual Basic 6 was a hassle, requiring all kinds of hacks. Now with the RAD tools, it's a drag, drop-'n' code kind of operation. Dragging the application, security, or system log onto the design window generates the following methods and properties in a single stroke of the mouse (note that even this is not the complete list!):

Properties:

❑ EnableRaisingEvents

❑ Entries

❑ Log

❑ LogDisplayName

❑ MachineName

❑ Source

❑ SynchronizingObject

Methods:

- ❏ Clear
- ❏ CreateEventSource
- ❏ Delete
- ❏ DeleteEventSource
- ❏ EndInit
- ❏ Exists
- ❏ GetEventLogs
- ❏ LogNameFromSourceName
- ❏ Send
- ❏ SourceExists
- ❏ WriteEntry

MSMQ

We don't want to get into a discussion of message queuing in depth here – there just isn't space. Suffice it to say that we can easily create components to run on a server that watch a message queue, and react when there is a message. For more information on MSMQ, check out http://www.microsoft.com/msmq/.

A possible use of this would be in a fax server. When a client places an order, the application generates a fax document, which is then dropped in a queue using the built-in Send method. The fax server is a component on another machine that checks for messages every 5 seconds say. When one arrives, it passes it on to the fax transmitter.

Message queuing in .NET is easier than making a recordset in Windows DNA. Even without the Server Explorer, it's a four-line accomplishment, and with the Server Explorer, it's even easier. The following picture shows how simple it is:

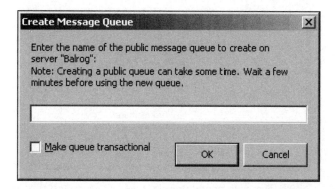

Right-click on Public Queues in the Server Explorer and select Create Queue... Now type in the name of the message queue you want to create and click OK. Keep in mind that workgroups can't manage public queues – non-domains systems will pass errors if you try to view, edit, or make new public queues.

Let's go ahead and right-click on the **Private Queues** folder and select **Create Queue**. Name the queue `TestMessageQueue`:

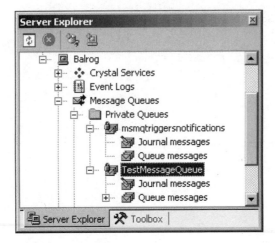

Now drag the new queue onto the designer. From here on it's code. To add a message to our queue, we need to add the following code to an appropriate event:

```
messageQueue1.Send("Hello World","Test Message");
```

This clearly isn't what you might call complex code. What it does is to place the information in a waiting area, for another program to pick up when it is ready. Essential for stable scalable systems, message queuing is an essential addition to the distributed application designer toolset.

We can invoke the `Send` method a few times by attaching it to the event handler for a button, and we can then view the independent messages in the queue using Server Explorer:

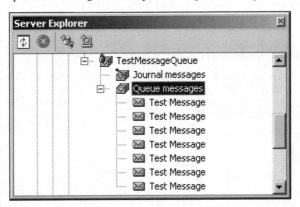

Here is the code for a quick form with two buttons that we can use to test this:

```
private void button1_Click(object sender, System.EventArgs e)
{
  messageQueue1.Send("Hello World","Test Message");
}
```

```
private void button2_Click(object sender, System.EventArgs e)
{
   System.Messaging.Message myMessage = messageQueue1.Receive();
   label1.Text = myMessage.Body.ToString();
}
```

Property Window

The Properties window was covered in some depth in Chapter 2 as a fundamental piece of the Visual Studio .NET development environment. It has another significant use in rapid server development, however. Since an instance of anything, including tables, messages, and event logs, is considered an object, they all have properties. Click on one of the messages in the previous message queue and open the Properties window:

All of the properties of the message instance are found here, in one place. Now, click on the messageQueue1 icon in the component tray, and look at the property browser.

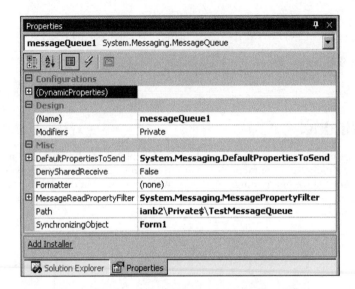

That's a lot of space to explain a simple concept, but it's important. The first icon is the instance of the message – in other words, this particular message. The second image is the queue class we have programmatically instantiated – it has settable properties and events to handle. The Properties window provides an interface to both.

Object Browser

The Object Browser allows us to examine the members of objects in any .NET construct. Since everything is an object in .NET languages, we can look at everything – namespaces, classes, structures, interfaces, types, enums, and so on.

The Object Browser is not a new feature, and not much has changed about the browser itself, but we can see so much more because of the true object orientation of the .NET Framework.

You can launch the Object Browser by pressing *Ctrl+Alt+J* or selecting it from the View | Other Windows menu. It appears similar to the code view or designer. The left pane describes a hierarchal breakdown of the Framework, including namespaces in the current project, and the right pane shows members (properties, methods, events, variables, constants, enum items) of the selected object:

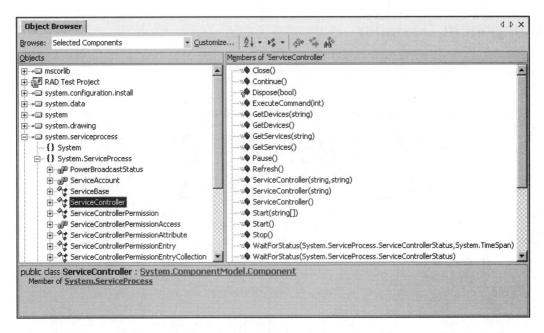

Playing with this is the best way to learn, but we will take a look at some of the more salient points, here:

- ❑ Clicking any object will give the little summary at the bottom panel.

- ❑ Right-clicking on a member will allow you to copy the statement appearing in the bottom panel and paste it into your code.

- ❑ Right-clicking on any symbol and selecting **Quick Find Symbol** will show similar members. Here are the results from the `System.Messaging.AccessControlEntry.Trustee` property.

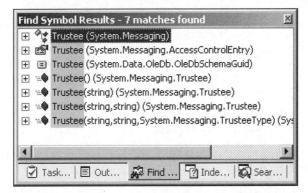

This is a great reference tool, but what does it really do for us in terms of RAD for the Server? In a large-scale project, for example, a corporate environment, the Object Browser gives a very necessary roadmap. With .NET – where everything is inherited from a base class – the ability to research your surrounding code is a requirement. And remember – our code shows up in there too, so custom or third-party namespaces will appear as well.

Component Designer

This is a new feature, drag-and-drop component processing. This designer is similar to the component tray found in Windows Forms projects, or the designer for XML Web Services.

To use the component designer, add a new component to your project, from Project | Add Component. The component type will be highlighted in the right-hand pane:

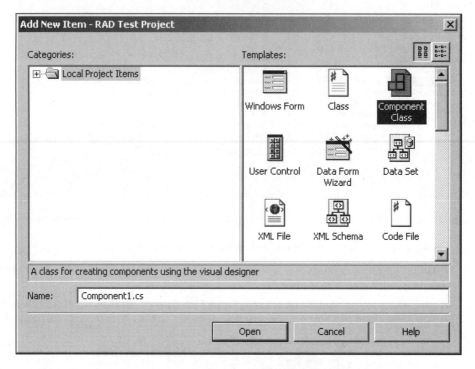

After we add a new component, we can drop resources from the Server Explorer into the designer, and start to wire them together using the Property Explorer. Hopefully, you're now starting to get the picture of how all of this works together.

The GlobalMarket Example

In a structured client environment, we would probably hand-code some parts of the application that in this example we use visual tools to generate.

Here's the business case. The IT Manager decided that security is suddenly an issue for the GlobalMarket application, and that a user authentication system must be implemented. The requirements are as follows:

❑ User identities must be stored in the database

❑ A user must log on to the system in order to user it

❑   A user is logged on until they log themselves off

❑   Logging on and off is a page-level implementation issue

❑   The system has to track logons and logoffs

To start open a new Windows Application project; we can use it for testing the class. First, we need a table, so open up Server Explorer open the local machine, and select **SQL Servers | <Server> | GlobalMarket**. Then right-click on the Tables icon and select **New Table**.

The New Table dialog works just like the feature of the same name in Enterprise Manager, except we can use it in Visual Studio now. Set up a table with four fields:

Column Name	Data Type	Length
UserId	int	4
UserName	varchar	12
Password	varchar	12
LoggedOn	bit	1

Also set the UserId field as the identity column of the table, so that it will automatically number for us. Finally, right-click on the UserId row and set it as the Primary Key. Save the table as Users. The finished product should look something like this:

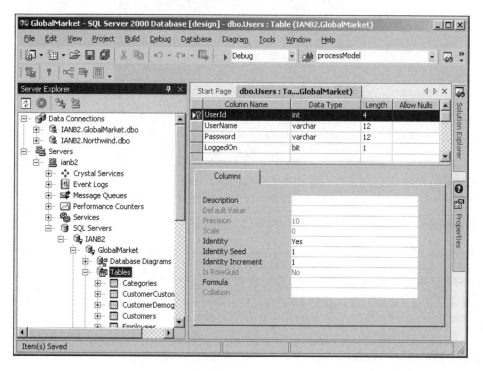

Now we have a table, let's enter some test data. Double-click on the new table in Server Explorer to open the grid in design view. The table schema opens up in the designer:

UserId	UserName	Password	LoggedOn
1	bsempf	pass1	0
2	drkdeloveh	pass2	0
3	iblackham	pass3	0

We will need a new data connection, so right-click on the Data Connections icon and Add Connection. This brings us to the Data Link dialog, where we can select the GlobalMarket database for our server:

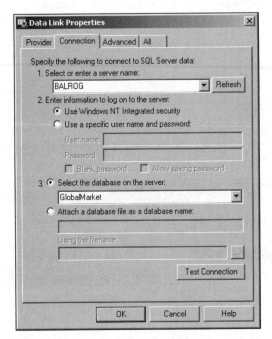

Once the connection has been made, drill down into that data connection, and drag an instance of the Users table onto the designer. This will create two visual objects, as we've seen before – the sqlConnection and sqlDataAdapter. Refer to Chapter 12 for more on using connection and data adapter objects.

In the design window select the sqlDataApater1 object, right-click and select Configure Data Adapter. If the wizard option doesn't appear, the objects are probably both selected in the designer, and the context sensitive menu is giving only the common options.

In the wizard, make sure the data adapter is configured to use the connection we made above, then in the second step configure it to generate new stored procedures for us.

As we discussed previously, the next step gets the field name for the SELECT statement, which will be used to make the rest of the statements. The default will be fine here:

```
SELECT UserId, UserName, Password, LoggedOn
FROM Users
```

We will then name the procedures. Everyone has their own strategy when naming stored procedures for the four major types, but we'll use:

```
upUsers_Select
upUsers_Insert
upUsers_Update
upUsers_Delete
```

From this screen, we can set a few options, preview the create scripts, and click Finish. When we go back and check the Server Explorer, we can see that the stored procedures have been created for us. Below is the SQL UPDATE statement, as created by the Adapter Wizard:

```
ALTER PROCEDURE dbo.upUsers_Update
(
  @UserName varchar(12),
  @Password varchar(12),
  @LoggedOn bit,
  @Original_UserId int,
  @Original_LoggedOn bit,
  @Original_Password varchar(12),
  @Original_UserName varchar(12),
  @UserId int
)
AS

SET NOCOUNT OFF;

UPDATE Users
SET UserName = @UserName,
    Password = @Password,
    LoggedOn = @LoggedOn

WHERE (UserId = @Original_UserId)
AND   (LoggedOn = @Original_LoggedOn)
AND   (Password = @Original_Password)
AND   (UserName = @Original_UserName);

SELECT UserId,
    UserName,
    Password,
    LoggedOn

FROM Users

WHERE (UserId = @UserId)
```

One thing this didn't do for us was generate a stored procedure in the SELECT statement that does what we really need – get a user by their UserId. We can double-click on the upUsers_Select procedure in Server Explorer, then select all the code in the blue box, right-click and in the context menu select Design SQL. The SQL Designer will then appear; to add the filter add the following code to the procedure:

```
WHERE (UserId = @UserId)
```

Your screen should then look like the following:

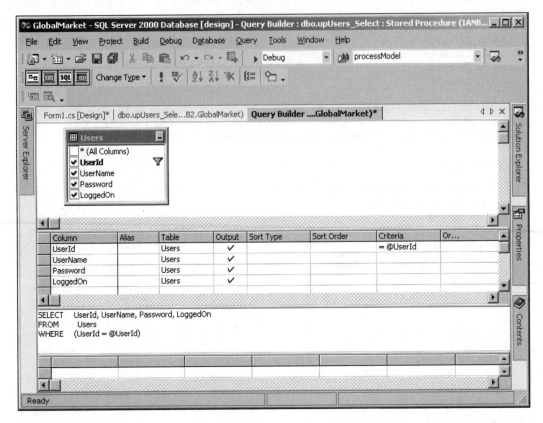

So there is our data layer, and we haven't written a single line of code ourselves. We still need to make a useful middleware component out of all this, however. Given the requirements, we are probably looking at a user class that's something like this:

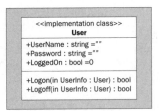

The logon method will get information out of the database to ensure that the username and password are correct. If they are, the `LoggedOn` property in the database will be set. Also, logons will cause an event to be logged in the event log, which we have yet to add to the system.

The `Logoff` method will essentially do the same in reverse: set the `LoggedOn` property to 0 in the database, and log an event. Both methods should make sure that the user is not already set to the state we are aiming for.

In order to move forward then, we'll need to get an instance of the event log rolling. As we talked about above, drag an instance of the Application log from the Server Explorer into the designer for the component. Select the object, then look at its properties in the Properties window:

Set the `Source` property to UserMaintenance – it should be blank when we first instantiate the object, but we want to be able to see who left the log when the time comes.

And with that, we have all the tools we need right in our hand. All that is left is the hard part (in this kind of example, anyway) – writing the code that makes it all happen. In fact, we could use Visio 2002 Enterprise Architect to produce the template code to get us started if we wished. In the EA edition of Visual Studio .NET, open the Visio document in the samples area, and get the properties of the sole class found in the document. The Code Generation Options tab offers a Preview Code option, which gives us the skeleton code we need to get the project started. It sets up required properties, including SQL objects for accessing the database, and also blank `Logon` and `Logoff` methods ready for us to complete, like this:

```
public bool Logon(User UserInfo)
{
  //
  //TODO:
  // Verify the user in the database
  // Make an event log entry
  // Set the user's Logged On property to 1
  //
}
```

Summary

Server-side RAD in Visual Studio .NET is a very large topic, and we've not really had the space available in this chapter to do it justice. Indeed, the subject of creating server components using the new RAD tools merits an entire book. Such a book is in fact in the pipeline, and it will examine the complete process in detail. However, we have been able to look at a number of very useful tools during this chapter, which will without doubt help make the life of the middle-tier developer that much more straightforward.

These tools include:

- Data Connection tools
- Server Explorer, including:

    MSMQ

    Event viewer

    SQL Servers

    Performance Counters

    Services

- The Property Window
- Object Browser
- Component Designer

To illustrate some key concepts, we used a simple example, which avoided heavy code in order to show how powerful server-side RAD can be in VS.NET. If you haven't already done so, read through Chapter 1 for further information on the Microsoft view of RAD on the server as well. There is some worthwhile insight there into the reasons behind Microsoft's decision to build this aspect of VS.NET the way it is.

6

XML Web Services

XML Web Services are undeniably one of the cornerstones to the .NET strategy for Microsoft and a fundamental application architecture for distributed Internet applications in future. Network operations have long been a weakness in Microsoft development languages, and the .NET Framework goes a long way toward changing that. The standardized interface of XML Web Services goes the rest of the way.

In this chapter, we will discuss how XML Web Services fit into the Microsoft strategy with a discussion of the *Two Sides to This Issue*, namely **building** and **consuming services**. We will then proceed into a section called *Building Services* getting into the details of:

❑ The XML Web Service project type

❑ The Design View for XML Web Services

❑ The Code View for XML Web Services

❑ Discovery and hosting

❑ An example Web Service: our simple Advertising service

After that we'll move into the implementation of *Consuming Services*. This is a very simple operation with Visual Studio .NET, to the relief of anyone who is used to SOAP Toolkit 2.0. We'll look at some details of:

❑ The Web Reference

❑ Auto-compiling a proxy

❑ Accessing an XML Web service with a form

Finally, in *Tying It All Together* we'll look at why Visual Studio .NET is so good with XML Web Services, and how Microsoft expects them to be used in day-to-day programming with Visual Studio.

Two Sides to This Issue

A Web Service is a group of components, packaged together for use in a common framework throughout a network. The diagram below shows how both internal and external Web Services provide access to information through standard Internet Protocols via a WSDL contract – an XML description of the service. This provides for a very wide variety of potential uses by developers of Internet and Enterprise applications alike.

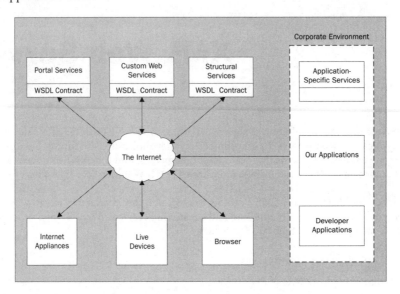

This simple concept does so little to describe the revolution that is taking place where XML meets HTTP, with SOAP. Web Services are going to be the heart of the next generation of systems architecture. Here's a taste of why:

❑ **Architecture-neutral**. Web Services don't depend on a proprietary wire format, schema description, or discovery standard.

❑ **Ubiquitous**. Any operating system or application that supports SOAP can support XML Web Services.with ASP.Net.

❑ **Simple**. Creating Web Services is easy and quick. The data schema is human-readable. Any language can participate.

❑ **Interoperable**. Since the Web Services all use the same standards, they can all speak to one another. This allows us to build application architectures that could not be built before.

Building Services

We build XML Web Services for three reasons:

❑ To expose functionality or information to customers, over the Internet

❑ To expose internal business logic over a secure network for the use by our partners

❑ To expose internal business logic over the Local Area Network for the use of internal systems

For the Internet

In the .NET Framework, XML Web Services are an extension of the `System.Web` namespace, similar to ASP.NET. For the rest of the world, though, XML Web Services are a platform-agnostic, remote method invocation structure that allows a blind eye to be turned to the technology of the provider. For Visual Studio .NET users, this means that logic programmed using the .NET Frameworks can be used by anyone willing to pay.

Microsoft is banking on this reality with **.NET My Services**. Fortunately, it is willing to share the pot, and XML Web Services are very easy to create and expose using Visual Studio .NET. We can easily use existing .NET Frameworks classes, like ADO.NET, and expose the data to a consumer of our service. We can also write custom functionality using the languages of .NET and expose the logic.

All of this is remarkably easy to implement with Visual Studio .NET. Once the program is written, exposing portions of the logic using XML Web Services is a straightforward operation.

For Our Partners

The Business-to-Business (B2B) craze didn't pan out in the stock market, but it is booming behind the scenes. Businesses are intercommunicating more than ever before, and XML has become a huge part of it. Formats like Electronic Business XML (ebXML), providing EDI-like data structures, and SOAP, providing platform-agnostic message passing, are fueling the growth of inter-company communication like nothing before. Even without complex EDI-like systems, businesses can profit from the sharing of business data and logic on a case-by-case basis.

Our Advertising service can function in that capacity. Based on login, for instance, we can provide more in-depth information to our partners, like our cost and internal item number for a book. In this way, we are reusing important business logic, and sharing it to a series of clients. The partners don't have to be on the same platform as GlobalMarket, namely .NET, and they will have access to logic and data formerly only available to internal programs.

For Our Company

The use of XML Web Services within the Local Area Network shouldn't be overlooked. Though it is somewhat outside the scope of the book, services between platforms can be of extreme benefit to most organizations. In addition, providing access to internal logic from our public web presence is often of use, as in one of our examples below. Finally, commonly-used logic can be provided internally as an XML Web Service rather than a component for ease of use.

Many organizations have an outdated database sitting around supplying human resources data, inventory information, or other important business information. Since XML Web Services are supported by so many vendors, including Sun, IBM, and others, we can often (though not always) expose logic that is usable by Visual Studio .NET in the form of a Web Reference. The cost savings involved here are, as one could imagine, tremendous.

Consuming Services

Microsoft's Web Reference is a new take on the old Visual Basic 6 References dialog. It allows the easy addition of Web Service proxies to our projects, described in more detail below. We will be referencing two kinds of services.

- ❑ External services, using the World Wide Web
- ❑ Internal services, locally hosted

External Services

Publicly available XML Web Service usage is already booming. Technology companies and individuals are publishing services that do things they are interested in. This time, businesses are getting involved sooner, but just as quietly. Already, a quick search of Universal Description, Discovery, and Integration services comes up with an imposing list of available services, like:

- ❑ Chat Services
- ❑ Credit Card Services
- ❑ Conversion Services (financial or otherwise)
- ❑ Shipping calculations
- ❑ Translators (Even VB.NET to C#!)
- ❑ Network Management
- ❑ News Headlines

Many of these services are available for free, some for a per-use charge. All of them are functional services ready for a production environment. Companies like SalCentral are already providing Yahoo-like search engines and Component Source-like brokerages.

Microsoft has made it very easy for us as developers to utilize these services. The Proxy environment, described below, allows us to read a Web Service Description Language document like a DLL file. We can then use a hosted service at runtime just as if we had downloaded a component from a site and installed it on our local server.

Internal Services

The creation of a component for internal use is quite a simple matter; consuming it is even simpler. Microsoft has provided, in Visual Studio .NET, a button that shows all services in easy reach for addition to your project.

What this does is provide a reference-like service to our developers in an architecturally controlled environment. Alternatively, it can create a much simpler environment for a single developer. Use of internally created services within a project streamlines communication between systems, and the simple discovery mechanism we will discuss below will make this process much simpler.

Let's turn our attention to the Visual Studio environment and look at how it can help us to build some services.

Building Services

In this section we'll build our Advertising service, and along the way check out the ways we can use Visual Studio to our advantage. We'll look at Web Service projects and discuss discovery and hosting before writing the code and listing our service, ready for it to be consumed.

XML Web Service Projects

The XML Web Service project type is our path to the simple creation of Web Services with Visual Studio .NET. As with other project types, it creates the needed files, sets up the web project, and makes registry entries that let the Visual Studio and Windows know that the project is available. With Web Services, this is particularly important because of discovery, the system used by the operating system to determine what services are available in a given web.

ASP .NET Web Service

To add a new XML Web Service to your solution, select File | New Project... and click on the ASP .NET Web Service icon shown above. Change the name of the solution on your local machine by changing the URL in the Location textbox. Visual Studio will create a new web project for you. Note that this is different from adding a web reference to an application!

Requires IIS

XML Web Services require a web server. The .NET Framework does most of the work for you, creating the Web Service Description Language (WSDL) files used by consumers dynamically, but this requires that IIS be installed on your machine. Windows 2000 Server installs IIS by default, and Professional requires that you set the Internet Services when you install the OS. They can be installed afterwards through Add/Remove Programs on the Windows Control Panel. You need to install IIS first, and then VS .NET – if not, it's not guaranteed that the two will integrate correctly.

Visual Studio .NET refers to an XML Web Service project by its URL. This can create some interesting problems depending on the setup of your development environment. We recommend that you develop XML Web Services on your local machine and publish them to the staging or production server on completion. All projects in this chapter will be referred to with the HTTP://localhost/ URI because of this situation.

Files Created

Visual Studio will create five files for you on the generation of a new XML Web Service using ASP.NET:

- ❑   `AssemblyInfo.cs` (or .vb)
- ❑   `Global.asax`
- ❑   `Web.config`
- ❑   `<projectname>.vsdisco` where `<projectname>` is the name you gave the Web Service in the Location textbox
- ❑   `Service1.asmx`

The first three files are unchanged as for a normal web project. The last two are discussed below.

ASMX

ASMX files are the special format used by the .NET Framework to delineate Web Service files. The code created automatically by the designer looks something like the following.

```
using System;
using System.Collections;
using System.ComponentModel;
using System.Data;
using System.Diagnostics;
using System.Web;
using System.Web.Services;

namespace ProductLookup
{
  /// <summary>
  /// Summary description for Service1.
  /// </summary>
  public class Service1 : System.Web.Services.WebService
  {
    public Service1()
    {
      //CODEGEN: This call is required by the ASP.NET Web Services Designer
      InitializeComponent();
    }
```

```
    #region Component Designer generated code

    //Required by the Web Services Designer
    private IContainer components = null;

    /// <summary>
    /// Required method for Designer support - do not modify
    /// the contents of this method with the code editor.
    /// </summary>
    private void InitializeComponent()
    {
    }

    /// <summary>
    /// Clean up any resources being used.
    /// </summary>
    protected override void Dispose( bool disposing )
    {
      if(disposing && components != null)
      {
        components.Dispose();
      }
      base.Dispose(disposing);
    }

    #endregion

  // WEB SERVICE EXAMPLE
  // The HelloWorld() example service returns the string Hello World
  // To build, uncomment the following lines then save and build the project
  // To test this web service, press F5

//     [WebMethod]
//     public string HelloWorld()
//     {
//         return "Hello World";
//     }
  }
}
```

Visual Studio gives us a new namespace defined with the same name as the project. As we'll see, unless you rename this file you must refer to classes within this namespace using this generic filename. For the sake of simplicity, we'll use the generic Service1 file name throughout the examples. We have named our project ProductLookup because that is the example we'll be building below.

Here's an interesting caveat. Notice that the default class above is the same name as our default page name. If we rename the page, however, the class does not rename as expected. The same is true with the class – it does not change the name of the page. We will be renaming our class later to make the naming clearer, but the filename will remain Service1.asmx. The namespace for the project was set to the name of the project we gave during the File | New Project process (ProductLookup).

In the examples, we'll refer to Web Service files using the ASMX file extension. This gives us the ability to automatically generate the WSDL file for the service by using the ?WSDL query string after we have built the project.

http://localhost/ProductLookup/Service1.asmx?wsdl

This gives us a look at the empty WSDL file.

```
<?xml version="1.0" encoding="utf-8" ?>
<definitions xmlns:s="http://www.w3.org/2001/XMLSchema"
xmlns:http="http://schemas.xmlsoap.org/wsdl/http/"
xmlns:mime="http://schemas.xmlsoap.org/wsdl/mime/"
xmlns:tm="http://microsoft.com/wsdl/mime/textMatching/"
xmlns:soap="http://schemas.xmlsoap.org/wsdl/soap/"
xmlns:soapenc="http://schemas.xmlsoap.org/soap/encoding/"
xmlns:tns="http://tempuri.org/"
targetNamespace="http://tempuri.org/"
xmlns="http://schemas.xmlsoap.org/wsdl/">
    <types />
    <service name="Service1" />
</definitions>
```

This file uses all of the default settings for WSDL, which we have access to through the
System.Web.Services namespace. In the course of our example below we'll add a custom XML namespace
and other settings. For the purposes of this demo, rename the Service1.asmx page to Products.asmx. The
default namespace (tempuri.org) can stay the same, since we don't have an actual one.

VDisco

The VDisco file is the special discovery file used by Microsoft to define XML Web Services using
ASP.NET. By default, it enables Dynamic Discovery – probably the best option for most simple XML
Web Services. It simply allows searching systems to look at all files indexed automatically by IIS,
excluding those created expressly by FrontPage Server Extensions.

```
<?xml version="1.0" encoding="utf-8" ?>
<dynamicDiscovery xmlns="urn:schemas-dynamicdiscovery:disco.2000-03-17">
    <exclude path="_vti_cnf" />
    <exclude path="_vti_pvt" />
    <exclude path="_vti_log" />
    <exclude path="_vti_script" />
    <exclude path="_vti_txt" />
    <exclude path="Web References" />
</dynamicDiscovery>
```

Discovery is a complex part of the overall XML Web Services picture. We'll discuss it below, in terms
of Discovery and Hosting.

Design View

As with other projects in Visual Studio, the user is initially presented with a Design View page upon
creation of a new XML Web Service.

Not a Visual Interface

XML Web Services are not visual components – they are code components. In both development and consumption of services developers will be creating namespaces, classes, and methods and not forms or visual controls. However, Microsoft has provided a design view for certain drag-and-drop operations.

For most XML Web Services using ASP.NET, however, we will be writing actual managed code, not using the components. Components that depend on a user's manipulation of their visual interface are not useful to us. Data controls and access to certain machine-specific components are the exception, including:

❑   The Error Provider

❑   Performance Counters

❑   The Event Log

❑   Crystal Reports

❑   SQL Connections and Providers

❑   Components from Server Explorer

Add Components

For instance, let's add a data connection the visual way. Open the Server Explorer and drill down to the GlobalMarket database we created in the *Introduction*. Find the `Products` table and drag it onto the Design view. After a short processing time, the Design view will look like this:

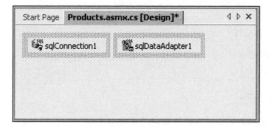

This in itself is not very useful to us. The managed code, in C#, is quite useful to us. If we right-click on the components above and look at the included property pages, we'll find that the parameters of various classes and functions added are editable, as seen here:

As we'll see below, the code is much more useful.

The Code-Behind

Adding these two objects to our page includes the code for a `SqlDataAdapter`, a `SqlConnection` and four `SqlCommands` to our XML Web Service, including the basics:

- ❑   `sqlSelectCommand1`
- ❑   `sqlInsertCommand1`
- ❑   `sqlUpdateCommand1`
- ❑   `sqlDeleteCommand1`

These methods are callable by code in our Web Service now, though generated by a 'visual' element. Essentially we have used a drag-and-drop element to auto-generate some code for us to use in our hand-coded classes.

Code View

We can check out the code behind our Web Service by clicking on the View Code button. The Code View screen is where we will maintain and edit most of the Web Services we will create. As stated before, XML Web Services using ASP.NET are not visual components; they are functional components, like COM components in Windows DNA. They will provide classes, methods, properties, and events we will use in other applications with visual elements.

For instance, let's look at the code generated by the table we dragged onto the Design View. Within the code generated above, we now find in the Code View six private defined objects.

```
private System.Data.SqlClient.SqlCommand sqlSelectCommand1;
private System.Data.SqlClient.SqlCommand sqlInsertCommand1;
```

```
private System.Data.SqlClient.SqlCommand sqlUpdateCommand1;
private System.Data.SqlClient.SqlCommand sqlDeleteCommand1;
private System.Data.SqlClient.SqlConnection sqlConnection1;
private System.Data.SqlClient.SqlDataAdapter sqlDataAdapter1;
```

These functions are defined below in the **Component Designer generated code** section. For instance, the `sqlSelectCommand1`, as defined in the `InitializeComponent()` event, looks like this:

```
this.sqlSelectCommand1.CommandText = "SELECT ProductID, ProductName, " +
"SupplierID, CategoryID, QuantityPerUnit, UnitPrice, UnitsInStock, " +
"UnitsOnOrder, ReorderLevel, Discontinued FROM Products";

this.sqlSelectCommand1.Connection = this.sqlConnection1;
```

Useful code, generated by a visual component? This is a big change from the Visual Studio 6 package, where even the simplest code from visual designers often had to be edited by hand to make it useful.

Necessary Parts

This generated code will not stop us from having to code most of the XML Web Service by hand. There are several new and necessary parts of the code that need hand-coding for both C# and Visual Basic .NET.

First, all XML Web Services must implement the `System.Web.Services` namespace. This is added by default by the project generator, along with the useful `System.Web` namespace. The `System.Web.Services` namespace lets us define the next necessary part – the class.

The class file that implements the XML Web Service must inherit from the `System.Web.Services.WebService` class (this is automatically generated by the project generator).

```
[WebService] public class Service1 : System.Web.Services.WebService
```

This exposes the `?WSDL` query string via IIS, and provides for several useful options, like transaction participation. It also notifies the ASP.NET page framework that the class is available for SOAP calls. In short – it is a requirement for creating a Web Service. All public methods within the class are available for exposure as methods for the Web Service.

The last necessary part is that all methods that should be exposed as services need to implement the `WebService` property. In the `HelloWorld` example in the sample code, it looks like this:

```
[WebMethod] public string HelloWorld()
```

Essentially one could take an existing block of code, add the `System.Web.Services` namespace, have the class inherit the `System.Web.Services.WebService` class and add the `WebMethod` attribute to the method declaration in order to make a web service. It's that simple. The other parts of the code, while important, are covered earlier in the book, in Chapter 3.

Discovery and Hosting

In order to use a Web Service, you need to be able to find it. For that, we need something called 'discovery'.

What is Discovery?

Web Service **discovery** is the process of locating and interrogating Web Service descriptions. It is through the discovery process that Web Service clients learn that a Web Service exists, what its capabilities are, and how to properly interact with it.

One way to enable discovery is to use applications that look for services. In order to implement this, Visual Studio puts a <projectname>.vsdisco document in the Web Service directory – a file that an application can look for that enables the discovery of the Web Services present in that directory, or on that machine. This is known as Dynamic Discovery, ands is the most used discovery format. Alternatively, we can mark each particular service we would like to enable, known as Static Discovery.

The vsdisco file will be all we need to know about discovery for ninety-nine percent of all our Web Service projects. Either the projects will be for internal use, or they will be advertised through traditional material and the WSDL file will be made available. Still, it is an important concept in XML Web Services, and is used by one of the more important features of the global XML Web Service community, UDDI.

UDDI

The Universal Description, Discovery, and Integration Project is basically group of web-based registries similar to DNS servers, where businesses provide descriptions of their Web Services in terms of an XML file with "white", "yellow", and "green" pages. The white pages include information about businesses' names, addresses, phone numbers, and where to find the service. The yellow pages contain business listings based on the types of the businesses and include binding information, and the green pages contain information indicating the services each business offers and also include the technical specification of the service.

UDDI takes an approach that relies upon a distributed registry of businesses and their service descriptions implemented in a common XML format. That schema is very long, but all the information is available at http://www.uddi.org.

One-Click Hosting

Discovery lets the robots find us, and UDDI is the search portal for services. Now we have to host the service if we want the public to use it. XML Web Services using ASP.NET must be hosted on Windows 2000 or above using the .NET Framework. Your workstation may be one of these, but to allow public access to the service, or to put it on a production environment, we must host it, like any other web project.

One of the great new features of the Start Page in VS .NET is Web Hosting, which allows the programmer to host a web application or web service with just a few clicks. Go to the Start Page in the Visual Studio .NET browser, and click in the Web Hosting tab. At time of writing, five services were offering free hosting for XML Web Services using ASP.NET:

- ❑ Brinkster
- ❑ EraServer

- ❏ Hostbasket

- ❏ Innerhost

- ❏ Protier

Old-Fashioned Hosting

Of course, there is always the more traditional web hosting, with your local ISP, or in the corporate server farm. Microsoft has done away with the old FrontPage Publish Web, and all that is left is the Copy function. Only certain files are needed to host an XML Web service using ASP.NET:

- ❏ The ASMX files

- ❏ The VSDISCO files

- ❏ The web.config file

- ❏ The \Bin directory and its contents.

We can copy the project with the **Copy Project** button on the Solution Explorer; this gives you the option to use either file share or FrontPage Server Extensions to move the files. For publishing a service, use the **Only files needed to run this solution** option that is selected by default.

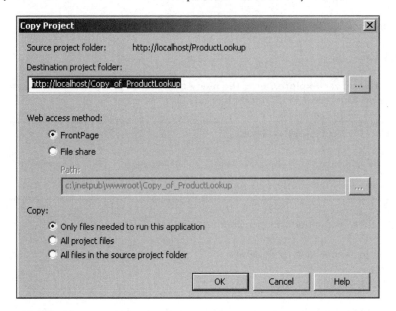

The Advertising Service

Say *Epicurious* or some other fine foods magazine wants to pull advertising information off our database system at GlobalMarket for use on its print or electronic content. Problem – it has a 100% Macintosh environment. What do we do? We provide it with XML containing the information it needs to use XML Web Services with ASP.NET.

What we want to do is provide the consumer with a list of categories we want to advertise, with some marketing text and an image. This they can format however they see fit. Then we want to increment a performance counter to see how everything is doing.

Get the Components We Need

1. Make a new ASP.NET Web Service project with the name Advertiser.

2. In design view, drag the Categories table onto the screen like we did above with the Products table.

3. Select the sqlDataAdapter1 then right-click and select Generate Dataset...

4. Check Add this dataset to designer and click OK.

5. In Server Explorer, right-click on Performance Counters and select Create New Category.

6. Set the Category Name to GlobalMarket.

7. Click New and under Name enter Advertiser.

8. Set the Type to CountPerTimeInterval32.

9. Click OK.

10. From the Server Explorer, drag the new Advertiser counter you just created onto the designer. The screen should look like this:

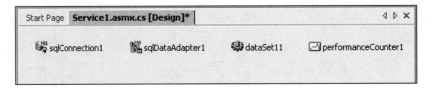

11. Right-click on the performanceCounter1 and select Properties.

12. Set the InstanceName to TotalHits.

13. Set the ReadOnly attribute to False.

Click on View Code in the Solution Explorer. We have instantiated every component we will need for the service without writing a single line of code, or having to remember what any of those objects are called. Yet unlike Visual InterDev, there are no compiled ActiveX controls that we can't see. If we open the Component Designer generated code region, we find that we could have hand-coded the whole thing.

We now have to hand-code the meat of the service.

Write Some Code

Let's start with something simple, to make sure our objects are configured correctly, and that we have our server set up. Uncomment the Hello World code:

```
[WebMethod]
public string HelloWorld()
{
    return "Hello World";
}
```

There will be some other code in the method, but it will compile invisibly to a Web Service consumer. Right-click on the `Service1.asmx` file and select **Build and Browse**. We should get the IIS test screen for XML Web Services:

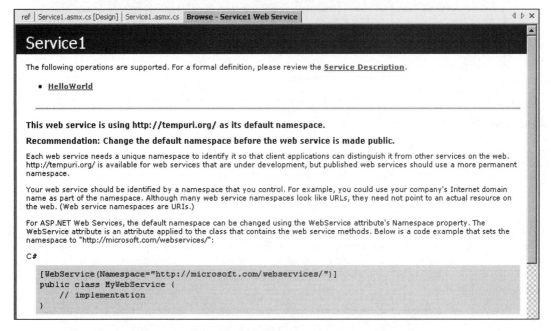

Two things come right to view. First, there is no descriptive text about the service – it is just there, for consumers to view. No idea is provided on what is does. Of course, the name isn't right either, so we'll take one step at a time. Also, there is a huge disclaimer about the tempuri (pronounced Temp URI, like a temporary Universal Resource Indicator) domain. We can change that too. The most important thing is that with this screen, we have shown that our database, web server, and objects are all set up properly.

Set Up the Template

Next we should add the code that sets up our service so that it looks right, even if it doesn't do anything yet. Appearances matter, you know. We need to add parameters to the `WebService` and `WebMethod` parameters that the project generator added to the class and method. While we're at it, we'll rename the class and method to something more appropriate than `Service1` and `HelloWorld()`:

```
[WebService(Description="Access to the GlobalMarket Advertiser",
    Namespace="http://Localhost")]
public class PublicAccess : System.Web.Services.WebService
```

```
[WebMethod(Description="Gets a random category from the database")]
public string GetAdvertising()
```

Remember to rename the initialize method that was also named Service1 by the Designer when we added the draggable components. If we forget, the compiler will remind us. Anyway, with those changes (after hitting the refresh button) we have something that looks more like what we are going to need:

PublicAccess

Access to the GlobalMarket Advertiser

The following operations are supported. For a formal definition, please review the **Service Description**.

- **GetAdvertising**
  Gets a random category from the database

Add the Functionality

There is some functionality we need to add:

❑   Return the information needed to make an advertisement for GlobalMarket

❑   Record the fact that an advertisement was distributed

To get started, we'll need to add the output parameters that will contain the data we want to pass for the advertisement. The requirements document states that we need to pass a type of product and a description of that type of product, for a general advertisement. The consumer is going to add it to our logo for a nice changing ad on their pages. When they implement this service, an example would look something like this.

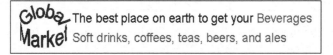

We will send them part of this dynamically, which includes Categories.CategoryName and Categories.Description. To implement this, we will just return a concatenated string of the Category Name and the Description.

To do this, we need to get the information in question, for which we'll use the sqlConnection we added to the design above. We'll use the DataSet and DataAdapter set up by the designer, but ignore most of the commands for this system. Thanks to the designer, though, the adapter already knows that it is associated with the Categories table – we could change that in the designer if needed, or at the code level. After making these changes, our WebMethod now looks like this:

```
[WebMethod(Description="Gets a random category from the database")]
public string GetAdvertising()
{

    //Fill the dataset
    sqlDataAdapter1.Fill(dataSet1);

    //Get a random number
    int ourRandomSeed = DateTime.Now.Second;
    int tblRowCount = dataSet1.Tables["Categories"].Rows.Count;
    int RandomRow = new Random(ourRandomSeed).Next(tblRowCount);

    //Get the values we need
    object [] arrValues = dataSet1.Tables["Categories"].Rows[RandomRow].ItemArray;

    //Make our advertising line
    return arrValues[1].ToString() + ", including " +
arrValues[2].ToString();

}
```

We are using few of the controls originally created for this page, and we haven't snuck in the counter yet. Nonetheless, we have a data-aware method here with a minimum of coding, and it works quite well.

In the code above, we start with the DataSet defined in the **Designer Generated Code** section. We'll use the Fill method of the DataAdapter to get data from the Categories table. This places a copy of the table in the object, which we can manipulate at the atomic level. We are using the dataset because we can easily specify a row.

Next we need to insert randomness into this. This not the best example of a random number generator, as we will discover when we view the service, but it does the job here. First we get a seed using the system clock. Then we get the number of rows in the table, for the upper limit of the random number. Finally, we use the System.Random object to give us a number bounded by the row count.

Our next step is to fill a variable array with the contents of the row we need. Using the Rows.ItemArray method, we have the option to write directly to an array in ADO.NET. It's a slick system. So now we have a one-dimensional array containing the text in the row of choice.

The last step is to get the text from the array cells, and build the single line of text we'll pass to the consumer. This can be added to the logo graphic to build an ad bar.

Let's right-click on the Service1.asmx file, **Build and Browse**, and see what it looks like. Go ahead and click on the method name once we get there, and we'll see something like this.

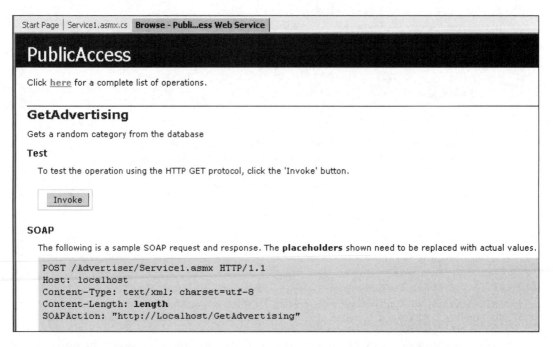

There are no text fields on the test screen because there are no input parameters on the method. Another piece of information that is of use is the SOAP information on the screen. This is extremely helpful to those who wish to consume this method with more code-intensive tools, like SOAP::Lite or Soap Toolkit 2.0.

If we click the Invoke button, we get a sample of the XML string with our text line that would be the response from the service.

Tack On the Counter

The last task we have to accomplish is to have the counter increment in the performance monitor every time the service is hit. This is a one-line endeavor.

```
//Increment the counter
performanceCounter1.IncrementBy(1);
```

For this example, we can drop that piece of code anywhere in the method. After we Build and Browse again, then go to the Performance Counter again, we see that the count has been incremented by one.

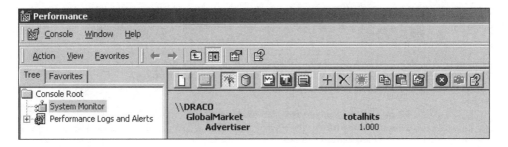

One-Click Hosting

For the sake of example, let's host this service on our public (and free) Brinkster account. Of course, not everything will work, because we don't have a database there, or access to the performance counter, but it is a good exercise. Another caveat – the hosting pages on the VS Start page are dynamic pages, and may have changed since the book was published. All of the deployment features, though, work the same here as they will on a corporate web server.

Go to the Start page in Visual Studio, and click on Web Hosting. On the Hosting page, click on the Hosting Services tab, and if everything remains the same, Brinkster (and other services) should offer an Upload Directly to your <provider> Account link. Click on that, and we are at the Login page of the service of our choice.

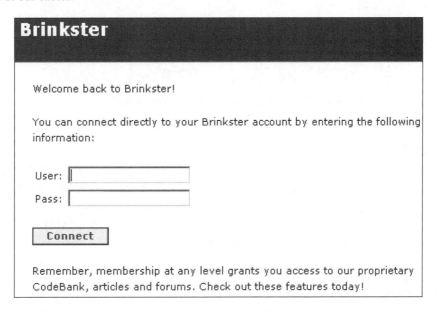

Log in with the information used when signing up, and we have the option to upload any of the web projects currently on our project. Click on the project in question and click the Upload button.

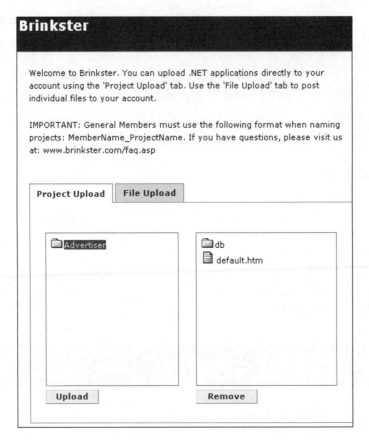

We can then surf to the service using the URL to our account, plus the project name and the file name.

Listing Our Service

In the XML Web Services tab of the Start page, there is a link to the Microsoft UDDI server. This will allow others using XML Web service development software to find and use our service after it is hosted publicly.

To use the UDDI service at Microsoft, we need to register with our Microsoft Passport, and jump through a few other hoops. After that, however, it is a simple matter to pass the WSDL link to the UDDI server and provide some other pertinent information.

Consuming Services

The second half of XML Web Service with ASP.NET and Visual Studio .NET is the consuming of services. This is, if possible, even easier than the creation of services. WSDL files for services are compiled into a binary proxy, similar to a DLL file, and referenced in a similar manner as well.

We will take a look at the options available to add references to local and remote services, and then look at the proxy itself and what is happening behind the scenes. Then we will build the ad our client will be building with the Web Service we just created.

Web References

The Add Web Reference... command is our path into the world of consuming XML Web Services. We'll start by adding a new ASP.NET Web Application to our `Advertiser` project.

1. Right-click on the `Advertiser` solution and select **Add | New Project** ...

2. Click the ASP.NET Web Application icon.

3. Rename the project in the **Location** bar to `AdServer`.

4. Click **OK**.

We notice right away that there is a **References** folder for .NET namespaces referenced in our project. We'll need to add a **Web References** folder to that, using one of two methods.

Add a Local Service

To add a Web Reference, right-click on the project and select **Add Web Reference...** For most development initiatives, we'll be adding local services. Microsoft has made this easy on us, with the **Add Web Reference** dialog:

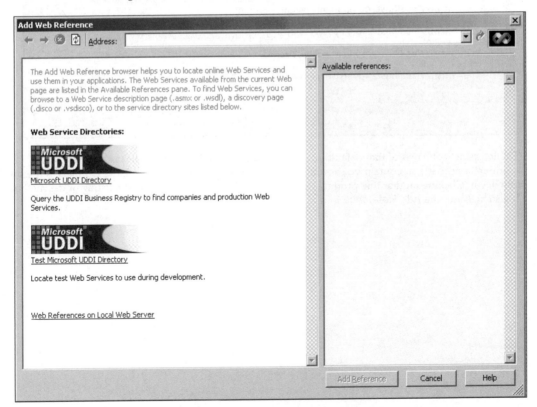

We have a choice here to use Universal Description and Discovery, type in a URL manually, or use the little link on the bottom of the page, **Web References on Local Web Server**. This checks into the `default.vdisco` in the root of the local server, to see about existing ASMX files in that directory or any below it.

The left pane is the text of that default `vdisco` file, and the right contains clickable links to the subdirectories that also contain `vdisco` files. On my local system, the `Advertiser` project is the third one down. Clicking on that link produces the `vdisco` file for that service, and a listing of the methods. It also activates the **Add Reference** button.

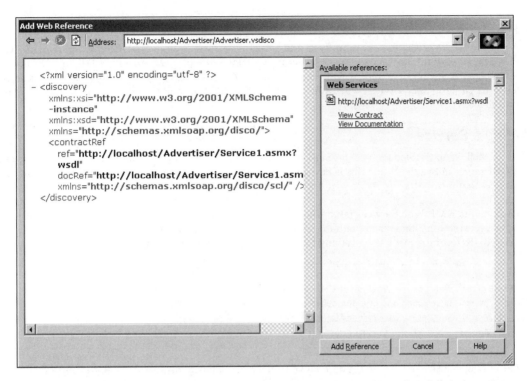

From here, we can look at the WSDL of the service by clicking on the View Contract link, or the documentation we put in the `WebService` and `WebMethod` parameters. Also, we can click the Add Web Reference button and add the service to the references in the `AdServer` project. That's what we'll do. After we add the reference, the project looks like this:

Add a Remote Service

As we saw, there is also the opportunity to add a remote service through UDDI or by typing in a URL. Play around with this, by clicking on the Microsoft UDDI and typing 'Microsoft', 'IBM', or 'HP' into the search box. A few services appear with similar results to what we saw working with local services. If you have the path to a real service's wsdl file – say from Xmethods or SalCentral, type in the address and give that a try.

Finding a Service

In the XML Web Services tab of the Start page, Microsoft has provided a simple search function for the UDDI server in Seattle. While this is far from complete, it can provide a starting point for referencing services in our projects.

Click on the XML Web Services tab in Start Here, then on the Find a Service tab at the top of the page. A search function is there, and the user can select a category of service, and a search term if desired. (In testing, I just left everything blank and clicked Go to get a fair number of services.)

EightBall
The EightBall Web Service simulates the well-known eight ball toy we've all come to know and love. It does so by randomly selecting one of a number of standard answers from an XML file.
http://www.gotdotnet.com/playground/services/EightBall/eightballws.asmx
 Add as web reference to current project

Each example provides a link to the descriptive UDDI entry, a link to the service itself, and a link that actually adds a Web Reference to the project. On adding a reference to the EightBall service, we find that it is just as functional as if it were a local service, due to the proxy added to our development machine.

The Proxy

When we add a web reference, the .NET Framework is compiling a DLL file around the information contained in the WSDL of the service we are consuming. This allows us to talk to the service just as if it were any other class file in the Framework.

Once the proxy is compiled, we can right-click on the web reference and update the information within by selecting Update Web Reference. This actually gets a fresh copy of the WSDL from the service, and recompiles the proxy.

ASMX vs. the WSDL File

A major point of confusion with cross-platform services is the WSDL file. When organizations like SalCentral or Xmethods or UDDI request documentation on our services for publishing, they ask for the WSDL file. This file is an XML representation of the methods within the service, and can be used to build consuming code in any platform.

Microsoft doesn't explicitly use WSDL files – instead, it depends on the .NET Framework and ASP.NET to represent the service, and only generate the WSDL on request. As mentioned above, we can add ?WSDL to the end of the URL to our services, and view the WSDL explicitly. If someone were to ask for the WDSL to one of our published services, that is what we would do.

How Microsoft Meets the Rest of the World

So while the other third-party tools for building XML Web Services, including Microsoft's SOAP Toolkit 2.0, actually generate WSDL, ASP.NET does not. This is a marked difference from the rest of the world, but does not preclude interaction at all.

Services that expect the WSDL just need to use the ?WSDL query string to get the WSDL from our services, and we can easily use WSDL to generate proxies – in fact that is what is required to generate them, and what is being used behind the scenes even with ASP.NET services consumed by .NET applications.

Build an Ad Using the Advertiser XML Web Service

Let's see how simple this really is. In the AdServer web application we created above, open the WebForm1.aspx file, and change the pageLayout property to FlowLayout. Then go into the HTML by clicking on the HTML tab at the bottom of the page, and slip a new table in there. In the table, we'll place a Label server control.

```
<table width="300">
  <TR>
    <td>
       <asp:Label id="Label1" runat="server" Width="300px"
Height="100px">Label</asp:Label>
    </td>
  </TR>
</table>
```

That looks like this in Design view:

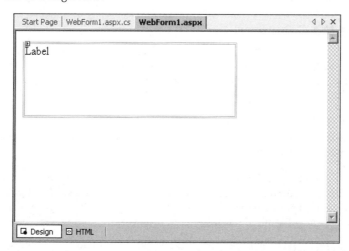

In the code-behind, viewable by clicking on the **View Code** button on the Solution Explorer, we'll add two lines of code to get the text out of the service we referenced above. It goes in the Page_Load event.

```
private void Page_Load(object sender, System.EventArgs e)
{
    localhost.PublicAccess WsAdvertiser = new localhost.PublicAccess();
```

```
      this.Label1.Text = WsAdvertiser.GetAdvertising();
   }
```

That's it, folks. Right-click on the `WebForm1.aspx` file and **Build and Browse**, and our ad is shaping up. Just add some formatting and a logo, and we have it all together.

| Accessing an XML... in Managed Code | WebForm1.aspx.cs | WebForm1.aspx | **Browse - WebForm1** |

Beverages, including Soft drinks, coffees, teas, beers, and ales

Tying It All Together

Now that we have the model for Web Services, we have to ask: Why? Why is Microsoft making such a big deal out of this? What is the point? And why with all that Visual Studio does well, is XML Web Services marketed at such a push?

Why Microsoft is Pushing This

There are three main reasons that Microsoft is pushing the XML Web Service model. Bill Gates (OK, he's not the only one...) has a new way of looking at things; it's a great way to make money; and it fixes a major flaw in the Microsoft model.

The Network is the Computer

In *Business @ the Speed of Thought*, Bill Gates intoned an oft-repeated phrase – the network is the computer. By this he means that sharing of information should not be like it is now. We e-mail, we use CDs and floppies, we FTP files around. This is reminiscent of the flat-file days of computing, and programming has passed it by. Until SOAP and XML Web Services, there wasn't a model to represent this.

Now, however, the **logic** is what is being shared, in a model much more like programming itself. Web services allow servers to expose a piece of themselves, and give clients, partners, and friends access to the very code that makes them function.

This is a crucial new model to follow in this time of decreasing returns on our technology dollar. For years, every small step in computing showed huge gains in productivity. That curve is sloping off, and we need to make up for that somehow. XML Web Services give us the opportunity to increase the power of a given system yet again, but using shared resources of other servers in a manageable way.

New Model for Selling

'Software as a Service' is another of Bill Gates' big pushes, and with good reason. Software competition is fierce, and pirating is at an all-time high. Two new models for selling have the potential to turn that around.

.NET My Services

.NET My Services is a set of XML Web Services that make it easier to integrate the 'silos' of information that exist today. It puts users in control of their own data and information, protecting personal information and providing a new level of ease of use and personalization, according to Microsoft. From the developer's perspective, it provides a platform-agnostic method of accessing this information about our users.

Since this system is subscription based, there is continuing revenue for both Microsoft and developers using and reselling the services. Unlike software that must be revved to generate more income, .NET My Services, and other XML Web services, provide a continuing stream of cash.

Activation

In further use of XML Web Services, Microsoft has produced a private service that accepts the registration of its software from a single machine. This allows the tracking of keys to the software, and prevents pirating the best way – with a database. This is a model that others are sure to follow.

Distributed Computing Always an MS Weakness

As anyone that has tried to use DCOM to do anything interesting already knows, distributed computing has been a weakness of Microsoft from the start. The operating systems are designed for PCs and nothing more, unlike Unix – evolved from the ground up to be more of a network OS.

XML Web Services provide Microsoft with the opportunity to not only join the rest of the world in networking, but also to shore up its own internal network programming. Even .NET Remoting, the replacement for DCOM, uses SOAP for some things.

Visual Studio .NET Can Handle It

To make its point in stellar fashion, Microsoft has made using XML Web Services – as we have seen – extremely easy with Visual Studio .NET. The moral of the story? Use it early and often.

Building WSDL files into compiled proxies is not an original idea, but certainly turned the tide for service usability in Visual Studio .NET. Since programmers can access services like all other referenced classes, they will do just that – access them. With Microsoft soon planning to release a number of services for subscription access, making them easy to use is a good financial and technological decision.

The design tools handle services well. The example pointed this out best – we implemented the Advertiser service with two lines of code – for real. Not two lines with a bunch of other stuff. Two real lines of code were added. And since it is like any other method, the Designer handles it without a lurch. It is really quite impressive. The goal was to make XML Web Services easy to build and implement, and it has been reached.

Summary

It seems as if we have covered a lot in a little space, but really there were two main topics:

- ❏   Building XML Web Services
- ❏   Consuming XML Web Services

In the chapter, we also covered a few other interesting topics, such as:

❑   Discovery

❑   Hosting

❑   Proxies

❑   WSDL

❑   File Types

❑   A little Strategy

For more information on Web Services in general – even outside Visual Studio – keep an eye on the hosting services, like Xmethods (www.xmethods.com) and SalCentral (http://www.salcentral.com), as well as the MSDN site (msdn.microsoft.com) and Wrox's Web Architect site at www.webarchitects.com.

7

Visual Studio Automation

The lack of a macro language for Visual Studio 6 was one of the largest shortcomings of the platform for many professional developers. Although we could use Visual Basic's Add-in functionality, it was awkward and not terribly powerful. Generally, the best way to code functionality to, say, repetitively edit a block of text, was to copy it over to TextPad or another text editor with macro capabilities.

Even with the Add-in Project type of Visual Basic 6, creation of true Add-ins for the Visual Studio 6 suite was very demanding. Add-ins were hard to create and even harder to debug. The problems lay in the fact that there wasn't a good object model surrounding the Visual IDE – it was almost like an afterthought, and never really worked all that well.

There was also very little help for those who wanted to create decent Add-ins. Many companies create Add-ins every day that don't follow any standards, and have no-one to turn to for assistance or standardization help, short of Microsoft technical support, that is.

Thankfully, these problems have been solved with the advent of Visual Studio .NET. The following three features have been added, which, when mixed together, create an exciting brew of customization for the IDE:

- ❑ There is a macro recorder which allows us to customize without writing any code if we so wish. We can even define shortcut keys and add new buttons to the toolbars.

- ❑ The IDE has a namespace in the .NET Framework (the DTE namespace, described below) allowing us to write add-ins and wizards to truly tailor our experience.

- ❑ The Visual Studio Integration Program (VSIP) provides the support third-party developers need to be successful with deeply integrated customization.

This is an exciting topic, and we'd be hard pressed to cover everything in just one chapter, so we'll concentrate on the following key aspects:

❑   The Macro recorder

❑   The Macro IDE, featuring Visual Studio for Applications

❑   The Design Time Environment namespace which accesses the inner workings of the Visual Studio IDE

❑   Building Add-ins from scratch, and from macros

❑   Visual Studio Integration Program

Macros

Macros are in essence single commands that comprise a sequence of sub-commands, actions, or keystrokes. In Visual Studio .NET, they are saved as a regular text file with a .vsmacros extension deep inside the VS.NET directory tree. The language that powers the macros may only be VB.NET, but it provides complete access to the automation model. However, the real benefits of macros come when they are recorded. Since they are so often used to replicate repetitive actions, we only need to perform the action once for the recorder, and then have it available forever after with a single key.

We'll look here at recording a macro, and then how it may be edited in the source code editor – probably the most common way of building macros. We can of course just record the full macro, or write one from scratch too, but most find this way quite useful.

Recording a Macro

Open Visual Studio .NET, and create an Empty Web Project called MacroWebApp. Add an HTML page by right-clicking in Solution Explorer and choosing **Add | Add HTML Page**. Select the **Tools | Macros | Record Temporary Macro** menu item or press *Ctrl+Shift+R* to activate the macro recorder, which appears as a dockable toolbar:

We are now in record mode, and all our actions are being recorded. In the status bar at the bottom of Visual Studio, the little record icon spins away to indicate this:

Click stop for now, and let's set up a little scenario to help us format HTML. First, in **Tools | Options | Text Editor | HTML/XML | HTML Specific**, turn off **Auto Insert Close Tag** which would otherwise add the closing tag in the wrong place for the macro that we're going to create. Don't forget though to turn this setting back on after the example. Then, using HTML view on the new page, enter a list of items in the body, as shown:

```
<!DOCTYPE HTML PUBLIC "-//W3C//DTD HTML 4.0 Transitional//EN">
<html>
  <head>
    <title>TestMacro</title>
```

```
    </head>
    <body MS_POSITIONING="FlowLayout">
      <UL>
        List item 1
        List item 2
        List item 3
        List item 4
      </UL>
    </body>
  </html>
```

Now place the cursor in front of the first list item. Restart the recorder with *Ctrl+Shift+R* and follow these steps:

❑   Add a list item tag before the first list item, by typing <LI>

❑   Press the **End** button on your keyboard to go to the end of the line

❑   Add the closing list item tag by typing </LI>

❑   Press the down arrow followed by the **Home** key, to place the cursor at the beginning of the next item

❑   Press the **Stop** button on the recorder

We now have this short sequence held in the buffer as a "temporary macro". Press *Ctrl+Shift+P* three times to run the macro and add opening and closing unordered list tags to create a list:

```
<!DOCTYPE HTML PUBLIC "-//W3C//DTD HTML 4.0 Transitional//EN">
<html>
  <head>
    <title>TestMacro</title>
    <meta name="vs_defaultClientScript" content="JavaScript">
    <meta name="GENERATOR" content="Microsoft Visual Studio.NET 7.0">
    <meta name="ProgId" content="VisualStudio.HTML">
    <meta name="Originator" content="Microsoft Visual Studio.NET 7.0">
  </head>
  <body MS_POSITIONING="FlowLayout">
    <UL>
      <LI>List item 1</LI>
      <LI>List item 2</LI>
      <LI>List item 3</LI>
      <LI>List item 4</LI>
    </UL>
  </body>
</html>
```

This feature has been present in many other IDEs for donkey's years, and at last it has finally been added to Visual Studio.

The Macro GUI

Press *Alt+F8* to bring up the Macro Explorer:

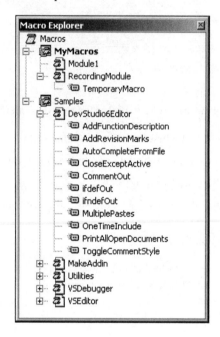

There are two main folders of macros here, **MyMacros,** which is the namespace for our custom macros and the temporary macros, and the **Samples,** which are a set of very helpful prebuilt macros. We'll talk more about these later.

The **MyMacros** folder contains two class files, the blank `Module1` and `RecordingModule`, which contains the macro we just recorded as the `TemporaryMacro` subroutine. Double-click on `RecordingModule` to bring up the Macro IDE.

The Macro IDE

The IDE for macro development is VS.NET's baby sibling, Visual Studio for Applications (the same macro recorder found in Microsoft Office):

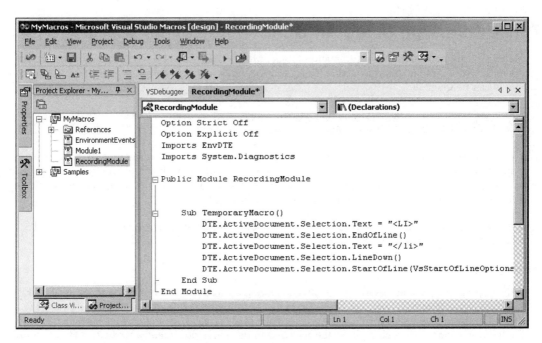

Here we can see the code that has been automatically generated for our macro:

```
Option Strict Off
Option Explicit Off
Imports EnvDTE
Imports System.Diagnostics

Public Module RecordingModule

  Sub TemporaryMacro()
    DTE.ActiveDocument.Selection.Text = "<LI>"
    DTE.ActiveDocument.Selection.EndOfLine()
    DTE.ActiveDocument.Selection.Text = "</li>"
    DTE.ActiveDocument.Selection.LineDown()
    DTE.ActiveDocument.Selection.StartOfLine(vsStartOfLineOptions.
    vsStartOfLineOptionsFirstText)
  End Sub

End Module
```

Although macros use Script for the .NET Framework, the only supported language at this time is Visual Basic .NET – perhaps in the future we will get the option to use JScript.NET or C#. For now though, those other CLR languages are not supported in the Macro IDE. So, RecordingModule is the default module used by the macro recorder, and the temporary macro is always called TemporaryMacro. We can rename our macro quite simply, by either clicking on it to enter edit mode, or by right-clicking and choosing **Rename**. We can then enter the new name, say MakeAList; it will show up as a runnable macro in the Macro Explorer, and when we next create a temporary macro, it will not be overwritten.

The Automation Object in Brief

Macros mostly make use of the Automation Object Model contained in the DTE namespace – though the entire .NET Framework is available if necessary. A figure giving a comprehensive overview of the model can be found at:

http://msdn.microsoft.com/library/default.asp?url=/library/en-us/vsintro7/html/
    vxgrfautomationobjectmodelchart.asp

The Automation Object Model gives us the Design Time Environment, represented by a namespace called EnvDTE, and the DTE object. This is a relatively straightforward block of functionality which gives access to everything in the development tool. Let's now look at a selection of the properties available on a DTE object. The complete list can be found at the following URL:

http://msdn.microsoft.com/library/default.asp?url=/library/en-us/vsintro7/html/
    vxmscdteobjectpropertiesmethodsevents.asp

ActiveDocument

This property provides access to the selected document in the project currently open in the VS.NET IDE. We generally assume that the user wants to run a macro at the point where the cursor is located in the active document. The Selection object gives access to any currently selected text, as in the following example which replaces the selection in the active document with the text Hello World:

```
Sub TestActiveDocument()
   DTE.ActiveDocument.Selection.Text = "Hello World"
End Sub
```

In a production environment, we may wish to add error handling to cater for the case that no text is selected, but for our own macros, that's not usually necessary of course.

ActiveSolutionProjects

This property is simply an array of all of the projects in the current solution. This example pops up a message box displaying the number of projects in the current solution:

```
Sub ActiveSolutionProjectsCount()
   Dim OurProjects As System.Array
   OurProjects = DTE.ActiveSolutionProjects()
   If OurProjects.Length > 0 Then
      MsgBox(OurProjects.Length & " Project(s) in Solution")
   Else
      MsgBox("No Projects Found")
   End If
End Sub
```

We can also use this property to add new files to a particular project in the background.

ActiveWindow

This returns a `Window` object representing the currently active window if there is one, the top-most window if no others are active, or `Nothing` if there are no windows. The `Window` object is a very powerful tool that we can use to carry out numerous useful tasks. Refer to the section later on the `Windows collection` for information.

AddIns

This gets a collection of all of the add-ins now loaded, be they `DTE.AddIns` (all add-ins installed and available), or `Solution.AddIns` (just those presently running in the solution).

CommandBars

The `CommandBars` property returns a reference to the `CommandBar` object, which is actually a Microsoft Office object, found in `mso.dll`. The `CommandBar` comprises one or more `Commands`, described next. The commands are also found in the DTE.

Commands

All of the commands, found in the `CommandBars` or `Menus` properties, are available as `Command` objects in the `Commands` collection. We can add to menus, execute commands, or make our own new toolbars with the `Command` objects. We get hold of the `Commands` collection through the `Commands` property of the `DTE` object. The following code outputs the first ten commands:

```
Sub CommandsExample()
  Dim x As Integer
  Dim ourCommand As Command
  Dim commandText As String

  commandText = "Here are the first 10 commands:" & ControlChars.Lf

  For x = 1 To 10
    ourCommand = DTE.Commands.Item(x)
    commandText = commandText & ourCommand.Name & ControlChars.Lf
  Next

  MsgBox(commandText)
End Sub
```

Documents

In the same vein, the `Documents` property returns a collection of the documents that are open in the environment. Documents have a whole host of methods and properties, including `Redo` and `Undo`, `Save` and `Close`, `Path` and `Kind`, and a ton of others. It is very useful for object builders, as we shall see in the main example. The next example cycles through all open documents, saving any that are in a modified state:

```
Sub SaveAllDocuments()
  Dim ourDocument As Integer

  For ourDocument = 1 To DTE.Documents.Count
```

```
      If Not DTE.Documents.Item(ourDocument).Saved Then
        DTE.Documents.Item(ourDocument).Save()
      End If
    Next ourDocument

  End Sub
```

Events

The Events class allows us to respond to some of the events that occur in the Visual Studio IDE.

Properties

The Properties object returns a collection representing the settings in the Options dialog under the Tools menu:

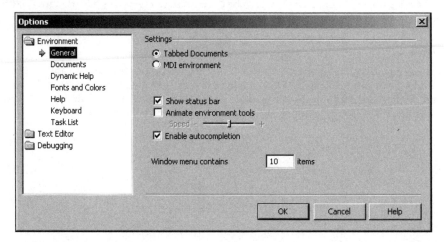

These values are subdivided into categories, so one has to reference by category then subcategory, as in this example, which displays all the available properties of this object:

```
Sub PropertiesExample()

  Dim x As Integer
  Dim ourProperty As [Property]
  Dim propertyText As String

  For Each ourProperty In DTE.Properties("Environment", "General")
    propertyText = commandText & ourProperty.Name.ToString() & ControlChars.Lf
  Next

  MsgBox(propertyText)

End Sub
```

The property names that this short piece of code outputs are fairly self-explanatory, and it's not hard to deduce which settings in the Options they refer to. Not all options in the Options dialog are available through the DTE namespace however, so some experimentation is necessary.

SelectedItems

The `SelectedItems` property returns a context-sensitive collection of the items selected in a particular environment.

❑ In the Task List, a call to the `DTE.SelectedItems` property returns a collection of tasks

❑ In Solution Explorer, a call to the `DTE.SelectedItems` property returns a collection of all selected files and folders

Solution

The `Solution` property, which returns the related open `Solution` object, is used extensively in working with add-ins. We'll look more at this functionality later. Generically, the object gives us control over the basic controls that a solution offers: open, save, close, and the like.

```
Sub CloseIfOpen()

  If DTE.Solution.IsOpen Then
    DTE.Solution.Close()
  End If

End Sub
```

SourceControl

This addition is a masterstroke. The true object orientation of the .NET Framework gives us underlying access to the programs supporting Visual Studio .NET (as long as those programs themselves support the Framework). Among those programs are source control systems. This property returns a source control object that gives us control over the basic functionality of Visual Source Safe (VSS, discussed in Chapter 13) and other compliant source control programs.

```
Sub CheckOutItem(ByVal ourFileName As String)

  If DTE.SourceControl.IsItemUnderSCC(ourFileName) Then
    If DTE.SourceControl.IsItemCheckedOut(ourFileName) Then
      DTE.SourceControl.CheckOutItem(ourFileName)
    End If
  End If

End Sub
```

SuppressUI

This is a simple Boolean value that determines whether or not the user interface should be shown during the execution of a macro or script.

```
Sub RunWithSuppressUI()
    'Turn off the suppression of the UI so the UI becomes visible
    DTE.SuppressUI = False
    'Run the method in question
    OurSampleMethod()
    'Turn suppression back on
    DTE.SuppressUI = True
End Sub
```

Windows

The Windows property returns a collection of Window objects. This is reminiscent of the Window object in DHTML as supported by JavaScript. We have control of a host of properties of each open window, including:

❑ AutoHides – Sets or returns whether the window is able to be hidden

❑ Caption – Returns a string representing the title of the window

❑ Collection – Returns the collection containing the object supporting this property

❑ ContextAttributes – Gets the ContextAttibutes collection for the window

❑ Document – Returns the Document object associated with the window, if one exists

❑ DTE – Returns the top-level extensibility object

❑ Height – Sets or returns a value indicating the dimensions of the window in pixels

❑ IsFloating – Sets or returns whether the window is a tool window, not able to be docked

❑ Kind – Returns a GUID indicating the kind or type of the object

❑ Left – Sets or returns the distance between the internal left edge of an object and the left edge of its container

❑ Linkable – Sets or returns a Boolean indicating whether the window can be docked with other windows

❑ LinkedWindowFrame – Returns a Window object representing the window frame containing the window

❑ LinkedWindows – Returns a collection of all linked windows contained in the linked window frame

❑ Object – Returns an interface or object that can be accessed at runtime by name

❑ ObjectKind – Returns the type of the Window.Object object, which is a GUID representing the tool contained in the window

❑ Project – Returns the Project object associated with the window

❑ ProjectItem – returns the ProjectItem.Object associated with the window

❑ Selection – Returns an object representing the current selection on the object if the window's owner has an automation object for the selection

❑   `Top` – Sets or returns the distance between the internal top edge of an object and the top edge of its container

❑   `Visible` – Sets or returns the visibility of a window

❑   `Width` – returns the width of the window in twips. A twip is a printing unit, and is 1/20 of a point. This means that it is normally 1/1440", but it can be varied to scale an image.

❑   `WindowState` – Sets or returns the state of the window, whether it is minimized, normal, and so on

A Macro Example

A great use of a macro is to generate frequently used code. Taking a text document, and inserting company-specific include statements, references to style sheets, and paragraph markings to create an HTML page is a good example. Another is the automatic generation of objects according to a specific scheme.

The ASPX Page Generator

We'll now move on to an example that uses a macro as a web page generator for the GlobalMarket web site. The blank page rule states that if we begin development with a blank page, the chance of coding errors triples under a normal programming environment. The macro that we will produce will help mitigate this problem by gathering information about the environment and then generating a page template for us.

For this example, we'll stay fairly simple. There is a lot of information that a macro could gather, but doesn't apply to the GlobalMarket scenario. Therefore, we'll restrict the macro's interaction with the user to just getting the filename for now, and it will then generate a text page using that name with the standard company text on it. Something like this can be done using Enterprise Frameworks or even just the Page Templates, but macros are much more extensible, which is often invaluable later.

To sum up, we need a macro that:

❑   Gets a filename from the user

❑   Generates a new ASPX file

❑   Puts the company approved text in the file

❑   Saves the file

❑   Returns control to the user

Building the ASPX Macro

Everyone will find their own zone of comfort with macros. Some will always just want to code. Some will prefer to use the macro recorder to create macros. Most will probably find the best to be somewhere between the two, recording some actions to start with, and then fine-tuning in the macro IDE.

Towards that end, we'll use a little of both methods. Generating a new file in the right place requires some quite obscure code, so we'll use the macro recorder to start with, and then edit it to accept the filename from the user.

On the other hand, adding the required text to the page is not the kind of thing you want to be doing with a macro recorder, so we will open up the macro file and add the commands by hand for that.

Using the Recorder

Before we begin, we'll need a new ASPX project set up on a web server in Visual Studio .NET. Then, use *Ctrl+Alt+R* to start the macro recorder.

With the recorder running, create a new ASPX file by right-clicking on the project in Solution Explorer and selecting Add | New Web Form.

Set the name of the new form to TestForm.aspx, choose Open, and select the new form. Now stop the recorder by clicking on the Stop button on the recorder console. Bring up the Macro Explorer (*Alt+F8*) and open the macro code file by double-clicking the Temporary Macro icon in the Macro Explorer. The code should look something like this:

```
Sub TemporaryMacro()
  DTE.Windows.Item(Constants.vsWindowKindSolutionExplorer).Activate()
  DTE.ActiveWindow.Object.GetItem("MacroWebApp\MacroWebApp").Select( _
  vsUISelectionType.vsUISelectionTypeSelect)
  DTE.ItemOperations.AddNewItem("Web Project Items\Web Form", "TestForm.aspx")
End Sub
```

As before, we now need to move the code from the temporary macro to somewhere it can be kept. Right-click on the MyMacros category in the Macro Explorer and select New Module from the context menu.

Name the new module ComponentGenerator, and click Open. Copy the code from the temporary macro into the new module, and rename the TemporaryMacro method to WebPageGenerator. We end up with something like this:

```
Imports EnvDTE
Imports System.Diagnostics

Public Module ComponentGenerator

  Sub WebPageGenerator()
    DTE.Windows.Item(Constants.vsWindowKindSolutionExplorer).Activate()
    DTE.ActiveWindow.Object.GetItem("MacroWebApp\MacroWebApp").Select( _
    vsUISelectionType.vsUISelectionTypeSelect)
    DTE.ItemOperations.AddNewItem("Web Project Items\Web Form", "TestForm.aspx")
  End Sub

End Module
```

Now we need to add some code to this macro to get the filename, and to write the text to the web file we'll create.

Using the Macro IDE

The Macro IDE is used to enter or edit macro code. In this case, we need to:

❑ Get the name of the new file from the user

❑ Write the custom text into the new file

Let's start with getting the name of the file. We'll just use an `InputBox` for that – a component that can be found in the Script for the .NET Framework, just as it was part of Visual Basic for Applications before it. Add a few lines of code as shown below to get the filename, and then replace the `"TestForm.aspx"` string in the second parameter of the `AddNewItem` method with the variable name:

```
Sub WebPageGenerator()
  Dim strFileName As String

  Do
    'Get the name of the data connection from the user
    strFileName = InputBox("What is the name of your new GlobalMarket form?", _
    "Name web form")
    If (strFileName = "") Then
      MsgBox("You must enter a name for the web form")
    End If
  Loop While (strFileName = "")

  'Add a new file to the project
  DTE.Windows.Item(Constants.vsWindowKindSolutionExplorer).Activate()
  DTE.ActiveWindow.Object.GetItem("MacroWebApp\MacroWebApp").Select( _
    vsUISelectionType.vsUISelectionTypeSelect)
  DTE.ItemOperations.AddNewItem("Web Project Items\Web Form", strFileName)

End Sub
```

Now run the macro to see the `InputBox`, and how it adds the new file:

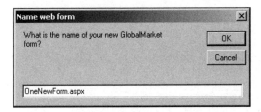

After creating the file, the filename, which we keep in a variable (but could obtain from the object model) and the created date are to be added as comments within the existing HTML of the new `.aspx` file:

```
Sub WebFormGenerator()
  Dim strFileName As String

  Do
    'Get the name of the data connection from the user
    strFileName = InputBox("What is the name of your new GlobalMarket form?", _
    "Name web form")
    If (strFileName = "") Then
      MsgBox("You must enter a name for the web form")
    End If
  Loop While (strFileName = "")

  'Add a new file to the project
  DTE.Windows.Item(Constants.vsWindowKindSolutionExplorer).Activate()
```

199

```
DTE.ActiveWindow.Object.GetItem("MacroWebApp\MacroWebApp").Select( _
    vsUISelectionType.vsUISelectionTypeSelect)
DTE.ItemOperations.AddNewItem("Web Project Items\Web Form", strFileName)
```

```
'Insert the standard company comments
DTE.ActiveDocument.Selection.LineDown(False, 10)
DTE.ActiveDocument.Selection.Text = "        <!--Filename : " & strFileName & "-->"
DTE.ActiveDocument.Selection.NewLine()
DTE.ActiveDocument.Selection.Text = "<!--Date Created : " & Now() & "-->"
DTE.ActiveDocument.Selection.NewLine()

'Save the document
DTE.ActiveDocument.Save()
```

```
End Sub
```

In order for this to work properly, we need to have the Tools | Options | HTML Designer > General | Start Web Forms Pages option in Visual Studio set to HTML View. This is unfortunately not one of the properties accessible through the object model, so we need to do it by hand. Upon running the macro, the new form will be set up with the following HTML:

```
<%@ Page language="c#" Codebehind="AnotherNewForm.aspx.cs" AutoEventWireup="false"
Inherits="MacroWebApp.AnotherNewForm" %>
<!DOCTYPE HTML PUBLIC "-//W3C//DTD HTML 4.0 Transitional//EN" >

<html>
  <head>
    <title>OneNewForm</title>
    <meta name="GENERATOR" Content="Microsoft Visual Studio 7.0">
    <meta name="CODE_LANGUAGE" Content="C#">
    <meta name=vs_defaultClientScript content="JavaScript">
    <meta name=vs_targetSchema
      content="http://schemas.microsoft.com/intellisense/ie5">
    <!--Filename : OneNewForm.aspx-->
    <!--Date Created : 2/5/2002 9:17:09 PM-->
  </head>
  <body MS_POSITIONING="GridLayout">

    <form id="AnotherNewForm" method="post" runat="server">

    </form>

  </body>
</html>
```

Add-ins

On the surface, .NET add-ins are not much different from those found in Visual InterDev or Visual Basic 6.0. They are compiled DLLs that provide added functionality to an application, based on an object model – it's quite possible to distribute such add-ins for sale. In function, they are very similar to macros as described above.

Add-ins can be used to generate new functionality for Visual Studio .NET, or to encapsulate proprietary business logic used internally or for sale. Component generators, text manipulation, and documentation filters are all suitable applications for the add-in approach.

To start a new add-in, create a new Visual Studio .NET Add-in project with the File | New | Project | Other Projects | Extensibility Projects menu item. We'll call our add-in OurAddin:

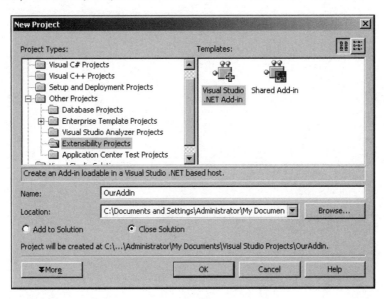

When we now click OK, the Extensibility Wizard fires up, and asks the series of questions below to determine how to set up the base template for the add-in project:

❑   What language are we developing in?

❑   What hosts are we using?

❑   What is the name of the new Add-in?

❑   What options would we like?
    (In our example, select the option of adding a UI for the user to interact with our add-in.)

❑   What message would we like in the About Box?

On completion, the template code for our add-in is created. Since we are not actually using the Script for the .NET Framework language, we have a choice of languages available, and the eventual add-in will be a compiled library file, rather than a runtime script. The Add-in Wizard will then generate several methods, properties and events, most of which are blank, as this abridged listing shows:

```
namespace OurAddin
{
  using System;
  using Microsoft.Office.Core;
  using Extensibility;
  using System.Runtime.InteropServices;
  using EnvDTE;
```

```
[GuidAttribute("B026AC4B-C239-45BD-83A3-D6CEEC7C173F"),
              ProgId("OurAddin.Connect")]
public class Connect : Object, Extensibility.IDTExtensibility2, IDTCommandTarget
{
  public Connect()
  {
  }

  .
  .
  .

  public void OnDisconnection(Extensibility.ext_DisconnectMode disconnectMode,
                             ref System.Array custom)
  {
  }

  public void OnAddInsUpdate(ref System.Array custom)
  {
  }

  public void OnStartupComplete(ref System.Array custom)
  {
  }

  public void OnBeginShutdown(ref System.Array custom)
  {
  }

  public void QueryStatus(string commandName, EnvDTE.vsCommandStatusTextWanted
        neededText, ref EnvDTE.vsCommandStatus status, ref object commandText)
  {
    if(neededText == EnvDTE.vsCommandStatusTextWanted
                  .vsCommandStatusTextWantedNone)
    {
      if(commandName == "OurAddin.Connect.OurAddin")
      {
        status = (vsCommandStatus)vsCommandStatus.vsCommandStatusSupported |
              vsCommandStatus.vsCommandStatusEnabled;
      }
    }
  }

  .
  .
  .

  }
}
```

As we can see, the add-in, which needs to be registered in the registry in order to be accessible, has already been assigned a class ID and indeed loaded in the registry. In fact, near the top of the generated source code it warns us:

```
When run, the Add-in wizard prepared the registry for the Add-in.
At a later time, if the Add-in becomes unavailable for reasons such as:
 1) You moved this project to a computer other than which it was originally
created on.
 2) You chose 'Yes' when presented with a message asking if you wish to remove the
Add-in.
 3) Registry corruption.
you will need to re-register the Add-in by building the OurAddin project
by right clicking the project in the Solution Explorer, then choosing install.
```

The Add-ins Model

The template above provides a peek into the add-in model. The environment supports a number of methods which act as event handlers for the add-in itself. This is, of course, in addition to whatever code we need to add to provide the required functionality. The methods are:

❑   Connect – This is the constructor

❑   OnConnection – Inherited from the IDTExtensibility2 interface – handles the event thrown when the add-in is loaded (regardless of how it is loaded)

❑   OnDisconnection – Same as above, but for unloading

❑   OnAddInsUpdate – Implements the IDTExtensibility2 interface again, but only supports changes to the AddIns collection

❑   OnStartupComplete – Handles the host application finishing the load of the AddIn

❑   OnBeginShutdown – The reverse of the above, occurs before the shutdown

❑   QueryStatus – Inherited from IDTCommandTarget, called when the availability is changed

❑   Exec – Called when a command is invoked

Fortunately, Microsoft has provided a great way for us to see all of this in action, the MakeAddinFromMacroProj macro. If we follow a few simple rules, we can change our macros into AddIns as needed, and get a good example of the structure of an add-in in the process.

Making an Add-in from a Macro

In order to use the MakeAddinFromMacroProj macro, we need to meet these criteria:

❑   The open project must be an add-in project (such as the one created above)

❑   The project must be in Visual Basic .NET – this is the only language supported at this time

❑   The Tools Menu option must be checked in the wizard

If all of these are true, we can generate add-ins from our macros. The MakeAddinFromMacroProj command – in the MakeAddin module of the Samples macro project –just requires the name of the Macro Project in order to make the change.

Working with Add-ins

The Add-in Wizard created two projects for us as part of the new solution: the add-in component itself, and the Setup deployment project.

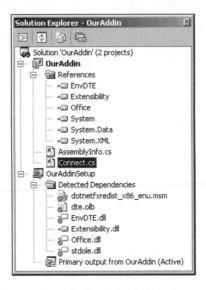

As discussed in Chapter 9, the *Deployment Features* chapter, the Primary Output File System Editor allows us to move necessary files into the user's machine upon install. Only the Extensibility DLL, containing the EnvDTE namespace, is currently included. You can find this information by right-clicking on the **OurAddinSetup** project in Solution Explorer, and choosing View | File system:

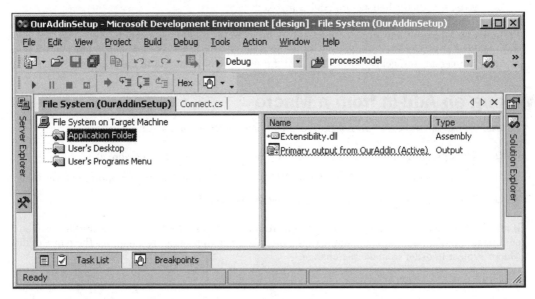

In order to work with an add-in, the configuration project must be built, and then installed. Building this project moves the necessary libraries to a usable area of the project (similar to XCopy deployment for web applications), and installing allows us to reregister the class. Once the build is complete, right-click on the `OurAddinSetup` project and select Install – a wizard assists with the installation procedure.

Creating code for an add-in is similar to any other project (apart from the initial template wizard that is). We can use Windows Forms, component files, and data access to create our solution. It should be noted that the extensibility model is completely available to the add-ins, and hence the ability to transfer macros.

For instance, we can recreate the Web Builder Macro above as an add-in with very little effort. Of course, should we decide to use a Visual Basic project, we could create the add-in from the macro itself, but it would be quite simple to add a form file to this project with the input box details, then put the DTE code in the Submit button.

CodeSwap

CodeSwap is a remarkable example of an XML Web Service and an add-in combined. It is a very simple concept, with a flawless execution. Essentially, CodeSwap is an add-in that provides access to an online database that stores code snippets using a web service. Download it from http://www.vscodeswap.NET/.

Installing CodeSwap

After downloading and installing the CodeSwap add-in, we can right-click on a piece of code, and choose the new Publish Code Snippet option. If we select this, that code is added to our list of published snippets, along with a short description. The snippet is logged in a remote database, managed by Vertigo:

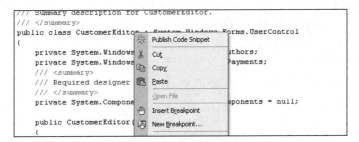

Accessing Others' Code with CodeSwap

When looking for code, we can access the online CodeSwap service from our PC using the Web Service. We specify criteria to search under, and any relevant results are returned:

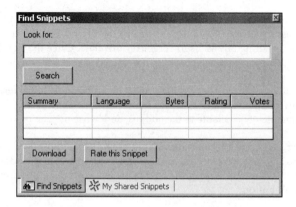

Returned snippets can then be inserted directly into the source code on-screen.

CodeSwap is a neat little peer-to-peer application that makes use of the Menu control of the DTE, combined with XML Web Services. Aside from that, though, it is pretty simple. It is left as an exercise for the reader to see if they can top the exploits of the Vertigo team and develop an add-in as original as CodeSwap!

Visual Studio Integration Program

The Visual Studio Integration Program is Microsoft's way of retaining some control over packages created for the highly extensible Visual Studio .NET IDE. The most powerful part of this program is the deep, thorough integration with the Visual Studio IDE that one just can't get with add-ins. The program provides, for a fee, these three things:

❑ Technical Resources – Technical support and advance previews of forthcoming SDKs, along with some rich tools for add-in development

❑ Co-marketing – Marketing support, the ability to add logos to the Visual Studio Splash Screen, and permission to use the Visual Studio .NET logo.

❑ Communications – Private newsgroups

In exchange, Microsoft is looking for help with three things in particular:

❑ New languages compatible with the .NET Framework

❑ New software lifecycle development tools

❑ Line-of-business solutions for vertical and horizontal markets

The Benefits of the Program

This program is of interest to the average developer for several reasons. If we wanted to really market our GlobalMarket Web Page Builder, VSIP would be the place to turn to first. On the other hand, should we decide to buy a web page builder rather than create our own, a VSIP partner would be a good place to start. This is the new model for Microsoft's business partnering strategy.

The reader might have noticed that the Visual Studio for Applications (VSA) add-in is conspicuously missing form this book, with the exception of some mention in the context of the Macro IDE. There is a good reason for this. This new business model is *very* new, and the VSA interface is one of the first pieces of software integrated with the model. As such a new model, the lines of communication can be rather shaky to those who are not already members of VSIP.

It will more than likely be a viable business model eventually, and it's worth keeping an eye on – it's the way of the future for Microsoft. Further information can be found at:

- ❑ http://msdn.microsoft.com/vstudio/vsip/
- ❑ http://msdn.microsoft.com/vstudio/vsip/vsi/default.asp
- ❑ http://msdn.microsoft.com/vstudio/vsip/vsi/vsiindepth.doc

Summary

The Visual Studio Automation environment wins the voting for the 'Most Likely to Be a Cool Book of its Own' prize out of all of the chapters in this book. It is a large, rich model bristling with tools, and it was not easy to cover in so few pages.

We looked at macros, the Macro IDE, and the recorder. These tools work together to at last offer us that which, until now, has been a mainstay of every development environment except Visual Studio – the ability to quickly automate repetitive tasks.

We also took a brief look at the EnvDTE namespace, where the Visual Studio .NET IDE is exposed for our programming delight. This set of development components provides even more control than the add-in modules for VB 6, and they are available to the macros, and will be accessible to Office and other applications as well.

From there, we moved on to the add-ins and the Add-in Wizard. Similar to the Visual Basic 6 Add-in Wizard, we have easy access to a template that exposes the inner workings of the menus and structure of the Visual Studio environment. Coupled with the DTE objects and support for Web Services, ADO.NET, and Windows Forms, we have carte blanche in creating new and flexible functionality for Visual Studio .NET's IDE.

We looked very briefly at CodeSwap, a cool third-party add-in that allows us to share code with fellow programmers. Though not available for the final release of VS.NET as yet, it is useful not only for its own functionality, but for the potential it shows us that the world of add-in development and VSIP membership has.

We finished up by looking at Microsoft's new Visual Studio Integration Program, or VSIP, the new way Microsoft has devised for working with partners. Though still sketchy at press time, this has great promise for further integration of products and third-party partners into the Visual Studio fold.

8

Mobile Internet Toolkit

The mobile device market is currently a hotbed of technological advances as each manufacturer tries to consolidate its position in a very competitive marketplace. As well as increasingly sophisticated mobile phone handsets being introduced from Nokia, HP, and a host of smaller firms, the market for PDAs is reaching critical mass. Heavy competition between Microsoft's Pocket PC platform, Palm's operating system, and Symbian's EPOC OS is pushing and pulling the developers of corporate software all over the map. While Palm is fairly easy to develop for, very few developers are really using it for hard-core Internet or intranet applications. Pocket PCs are even easier to develop for, but the user base is smaller, so that if a company wishes to use that technology, it'll generally end up having to purchase devices for their employees to use.

Part of the allure of .NET is its promise of solving the problem of developing effective applications that will run effectively on any of these various devices. The Framework is able to offer such an ambitious feature thanks to the Server Controls technology that has been introduced. They provide the means for easily creating applications that support multiple devices, just as we can create applications for multiple web browsers. The mobile device returns certain server variables which tell ASP.NET what type of code that device can render.

This all adds up to much easier device development, especially when Visual Studio .NET is used as the development platform. Once the Mobile Internet Toolkit is installed, it allows for cross-device web applications using Server Controls to be created as simply as any other type of project. The Smart Device Extensions allow for compiled applications to be written in a variety of languages for several devices. What's more, all of this takes place in .NET's visual development environment with all the benefits of drag-and-drop, IntelliSense, and so on.

What this Chapter Covers

Both the Mobile Internet Toolkit (MIT) and the Smart Device Extensions (SDE) come as separate downloads from Microsoft's MSDN web site. We'll start with some general information about the add-ons, including:

❑   Installation

❑   An overview of MIT

❑   An description of SDE

❑   Third-party viewers

Once we've looked at a little of the background, we will get stuck into the meat of the toolkits. Since the Smart Device Extensions are in a very early beta stage at the time of writing, we'll not spend as much time on it as on the MIT. We'll take a look some of the many labor-saving features it offers before moving on to the details of the various components of the toolkit, namely:

❑   The Mobile Internet Controls Runtime

❑   The Mobile Internet Designer

❑   Device Capabilities

❑   Device Adapter Code

❑   Templates

❑   Device Filters

❑   Help Documentation

We'll then move on to Smart Device Extensions, paying particular attention to the similarities it shows to Windows Forms, regarding graphic manipulation and the like. SDE is not equivalent to the MIT, and they can be used in concert.

Finally, we'll get into a useful example, and create an employee directory for the GlobalMarket database. To make things a little more fun, the application will let us look at how to view each employee's calendar, call them from the directory, and other interesting features.

Getting Started

Before we delve into the world of developing .NET mobile applications, there are three essential components that we need to add to our Visual Studio .NET installation. Let's set these up now, and then we can take an overview of the features they offer.

Installation of the Mobile Internet Toolkit

The Mobile Internet Toolkit is a Software Development Kit (SDK) that lets us quickly create Internet applications for mobile devices like cell phones and PDAs. We'll need IIS and the ASP.NET libraries installed locally in order to create applications that use the MIT. This is because the MIT creates web sites for mobile devices – not compiled applications. It assumes:

❑ The device is capable of displaying WAP, cHTML, or HTML

❑ It is connected to a network

❑ The application will be served from a Windows Server

To download the toolkit, navigate to http://msdn.microsoft.com/ in your browser, and use the options displayed on the left of the window to go to Downloads | Software Development Kits | Mobile Internet Toolkit | MMIT Version 1.0. Alternatively, you can go straight to that page by typing the URL http://download.microsoft.com/download/VisualStudioNET/Install/RC/NT45XP/EN-US/MobileIT.exe into your browser.

The version you download must match the Visual Studio version that you wish to use it with, so if you have Visual Studio .NET 1.0, you'll need the package indicated above. Installation proceeds like most other Microsoft downloads. You must agree to the license agreement before you download, and choose to either save the executable or run it directly from your browser. Just select the Complete setup option – there is little that is not needed.

Mobile Web Applications are very closely related to standard ASP.NET applications in that they use the ASP.NET libraries and server controls. They are created and set up so they can be accessed by a browser – specifically a mobile browser – hence they are hosted by IIS and are classed as web applications.

When we install the MIT, we also install the Mobile Quickstart guide that contains information about the SDK. The Quickstart can be found by entering the location below in a browser:

http://localhost/mobilequickstart/

Installing the Smart Device Extensions

Microsoft plans to supply the Smart Device Extensions as part of Visual Studio .NET as soon as they are finalized, which should be some time in mid-2002. If you have a version that dates from before then, you will need to install the SDE separately.

The Smart Device Extensions enable the creation of standalone applications for cell phones and other smart devices. The .NET Compact Framework effectively allows us to create Windows Forms applications on these devices, and also lets our applications easily access XML Web Services. The namespaces and classes it uses are very similar to the equivalent PC versions of the Framework, and it shares the same language-agnostic attitude to application development. In essence, the SDE lets us develop compiled applications for mobile devices in a very similar fashion to developing for PCs.

Once again, go for the full install, because everything is more or less mandatory for the correct functioning of the software. After installation, we have access to several new kinds of project in the New Project dialog:

❑ Pocket PC Application

❑ Pocket PC Class Library

❑ Pocket PC Control Library

❑ Windows CE Application

❑ Mobile Phone Application

The Pocket PC project types, due to the richer environment of such devices, can create new DLLs and build device drivers as well as regular executable applications. The other types – Windows CE and Mobile Phone – support only modest applications. Currently, Palm applications cannot be built with the .NET Framework and SDE, although Palm devices may access Mobile Internet Toolkit applications, if they have a wireless modem and a web browser installed of course.

Since SDE applications are still rather specialized in nature, and rely on beta software, we won't concern ourselves too much with them here. We'll take a shot at building a simple application to sample the tools it provides, but the topic is large enough to fill a book in its own right.

There's one other thing we should mention about the SDE install. When we installed the SDE, we already had the MIT on our system, and once the SDE had been set up, the MIT documentation seemed to vanish from Visual Studio's help system. This will hopefully be one of the problems that Microsoft will resolve before the final SDE release, but it may be worth installing the two in a different order until then.

The .NET Compact Framework

The .NET Compact Framework is the run-time library that a device needs in order to run SDE applications. While there are other advanced uses for the Compact Framework, this is its primary purpose, and the Framework generally installs it onto a device automatically during the installation of an application.

Our First Mobile Web Application

By far the best feature of both the MIT and the SDE is their integration with Visual Studio. Aside from the language integration mentioned above, all the major features of Visual Studio are available to these SDKs, including:

- ❑ Integrated development environment
- ❑ Rich toolbox and designer
- ❑ Drag-and-drop server and user controls
- ❑ Automatic deployment

When Visual Studio is first launched after installing the MIT, a new MME icon appears on the splash screen, and the help files will now include information on the toolkit. If we now choose to create a new project, we'll see a new **Mobile Web Application** option on offer:

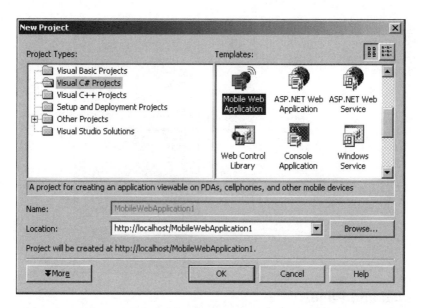

Go ahead and create a mobile web application project, using the default settings as shown above. The project will be created with a default page already set up and open in the Mobile Form Designer. The project layout is very similar to an ASP.NET project.

As with other .NET applications, we can drag controls from the Toolbox to create the functionality we require.

There are a few important differences in the way forms and controls work with mobile applications, so let's stop here a moment to cover some important ground.

Mobile Forms and Panels

Forms and panels are container objects. Like Visual Basic tab dialogs and panels, they contain other objects that the application can use. Forms and panels are referenced by identification names, like DHTML controls, and may be shown or hidden, more like Windows Forms applications than traditional web applications. Unlike with standard ASP.NET applications, a page can be represented by more than one form – think of mobile forms as pages within a page, similar to cards in a WAP deck. Communication between these pages of forms is easy too, just as with Windows Forms.

Here are a few facts about mobile forms that you'll need to remember:

❑ The first form on a given page is shown by default when the device navigates to that page.

❑ All pages must have at least one form.

❑ All controls (except style sheets) must exist on a form, or within another control on a form.

❑ Some devices may paginate long forms. The form keeps track of the current page (in the PageCount property) and throws a Paginated event when the page is changed.

Adding Controls to our Page

Open up the Toolbox, and drag a Form control onto the Designer. Next, drag a couple of Panel controls, and place them inside the new form. The page should now look something like this:

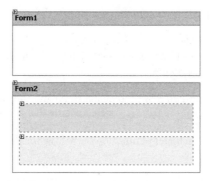

We can click the HTML button at the bottom of the Designer to see the code that has been produced to create this page on a client. We only need to concern ourselves with the contents of the <body> element of the page. For this basic example, the code it contains is very close to what we'd expect for an equivalent ASP.NET application:

```
<body Xmlns:mobile="http://schemas.microsoft.com/Mobile/WebForm">
  <mobile:Form id="Form1" runat="server"></mobile:Form>
  <mobile:Form id="Form2" runat="server">
    <mobile:Panel id="Panel1" runat="server" BackColor="#FFE0C0">
    </mobile:Panel>
    <mobile:Panel id="Panel2" runat="server" BackColor="#FFFFC0">
    </mobile:Panel>
  </mobile:Form>
</body>
```

Notice that we have two forms on a single ASPX page; the lower form containing two panels. When coding a mobile application, panels are a very effective way of organizing controls. They can be used to:

❑ Show or hide certain groups of controls

❑ Dynamically create or remove controls within a sub-form container

❑ Control pagination

We'll discover more of the various features of forms and panels as we look at the other types of controls. Before we continue with our journey into the world of .NET mobile web design however, we need a way of viewing how our pages will appear on a typical mobile device.

Testing Mobile Applications

To test MIT and SDE applications, we must either run them on a mobile platform or use mobile simulators on a desktop machine. The Microsoft Mobile Explorer (MME) is a very capable simulator that will be sufficient for our purposes. When creating production applications, however, I would strongly recommend testing on as wide a range of simulators (or ideally the actual devices themselves) as possible. You will find that your application's appearance and functionality will vary greatly as ASP.NET automatically tailors it for the capabilities of the device in use.

Version 3.0 of the MME was used for the examples in this chapter. To download it, go to the URL overleaf, and click the Microsoft Mobile Explorer Toolkit link:

http://msdn.microsoft.com/vstudio/device/mitdefault.asp

The MME is a nice functional microbrowser that emulates a device that accepts WAP or HTML. The installation is very straightforward. Go for the default setup, which installs both a standalone emulator and an integrated Visual Studio emulator.

The standalone microbrowser has two main screens: a status monitor for debugging and the device image itself. The image comes in three flavors – a rich model like a PDA (called XP), a rich cell phone (called **Large**), and a normal cell phone (called **Small**). Use the **View** menu to switch between formats. For this chapter, we can use the rich cell phone, shown below, for most examples:

❑ Keypad input is simulated by clicking the mouse on the appropriate button, or using the PC keyboard.

❑ The browser emulates a touch-sensitive device, and clicking on an on-screen link mimics the action of a stylus.

❑ As well as the on-screen and keypad controls, a toolbar above the phone image itself offers **Back**, **Home**, **Refresh**, and **Stop** buttons for convenience while testing.

❑ Within Visual Studio, the integrated emulator works in very much the same manner. Visual Studio .NET can be set to use the MME for all web project debugging, or on a page-by-page basis. As we shall see later, the latter approach is often preferable (unless we intend to develop solely mobile applications).

When developing a mobile ASP.NET application, right-click on the `.aspx` file in Solution Explorer, and select **Browse With** to use the MME browser with that page. Several options will appear – chose the Microsoft Mobile Explorer emulator. If the MME browser is set to default, it will remain as default for all ASPX pages, so be careful of that. If there are a lot of mobile pages to be built, however, that may be the best option.

The MME does integrate well with Visual Studio, but there are plenty of other mobile emulators available of course. The following are some of those that have been tested with the MIT:

❑ i-Homepage Master 2 (502i)

❑ Ericsson R380

❑ Microsoft Mobile Explorer 2.01

❑ Microsoft Mobile Explorer 3.0 (HTML)

❑ Microsoft Pocket Internet Explorer 2000 (4.01)

- ❑ Openwave UP.Browser 3.3.1
- ❑ Nokia 7110
- ❑ Openwave UP.Browser 4.1
- ❑ Openwave UP.Browser 3.2

To get a copy of the Windows CE emulator for evaluating how the server controls function in a richer mobile environment, you can download and install the Embedded VB Toolkit from Microsoft, although it is a 305 MB download. You can access this tool at http://www.microsoft.com/mobile/downloads/emvt30.asp, but check your Visual Studio disks because Microsoft may well decide to include the Windows CE debugging environment in a later version of the SDE.

Multiple Device Support

The Mobile Internet Toolkit has been tested on a very wide variety of mobile devices, and the list is growing all the time. At the time of writing, the Toolkit support has been tested on over 150 devices, including models from Nokia, NEC, RIM (makers of the Blackberry unit), and many others. For a full list of currently supported devices, check out http://msdn.microsoft.com/vstudio/device/mitdevices.asp. Do be aware that this list is for MIT online services only – the list of devices tested with compiled SDE applications is much smaller. This is mainly because testing is hindered by the fact that the .NET Compact Framework must be recompiled for each platform, similarly to the Java Virtual Machine. Currently, Visual Studio .NET users have the option of developing Windows Forms applications for the following Operating system only:

- ❑ Pocket PC 2002
- ❑ Windows CE
- ❑ Mobile Phone (Nokia 3330)

However, Microsoft is forging alliances with Mitsubishi, Lucent, and Qualcomm to bring the .NET Compact Framework to a mobile phone near you. Most of the HTML applications we can write will work on any phone – only the advanced functionality needs the .NET CF.

Write-once Web Applications

The Mobile Internet Toolkit provides developers with well-designed server controls that automatically tailor their output so that they are rendered on a given mobile browser with as rich an interface as that particular browser supports. The mobile browser is automatically sent a variant of each server control placed on a Mobile Web Form such that the control will display as close to the original design as possible, and provide the basic functionality required from that control in the context of that mobile web application.

Many developers working with WAP (Wireless Application Protocol) pages complain about a host of inconsistencies in the way individual devices render the WAP markup, in a similar way to how regular web browsers from different vendors can sometimes render the same page differently. While this issue hasn't evaporated entirely, the server controls provided with the MIT do make the developer's job considerably simpler.

The server controls use the user agent information that mobile browsers pass to the server – just as a regular web browser does – to generate HTML or WAP code that contains as many features as a particular device can handle. It is this mechanism that enables the .NET programmer to create a mobile web application knowing that a very wide range of devices will be able to successfully, and meaningfully, access it.

Customizability and Extensibility

The Mobile Web Form controls are really just regular ASP.NET server controls in disguise. Because of this, we can change the output they produce, modify them (perhaps to add support for a new device), or create new controls entirely from scratch.

Also, as .NET is truly object-oriented, we can extend existing controls through inheritance and polymorphism to create custom controls for an application. As with ASP.NET, the .NET mobile tools open up endless opportunities for new and sophisticated mobile web pages – and more to the point, without a huge effort required by the developer.

Mobile Internet Controls Runtime

The Mobile Internet Controls runtime is an addition to the .NET Framework that supports mobile devices. It consists of the controls, elements, classes, and elements that make up the programming model.

Mobile Internet Designer

The Mobile Internet Designer extends the Visual Studio environment to take advantage of the special server controls created for mobile devices. It consists primarily of the mobile web project type that we have already started, along with several categories of server controls.

The List Control

List controls are useful for navigation and data displays. They are similar to the HTML <UL> or <OL> objects, but do not have default bullets or numbers. Adding numbers or bullets can be achieved through the Decoration property.

Drag a List control onto the first form of our mobile project. Switch to the HTML view, and we find a new <Mobile:List> element within the pre-existing <Mobile:Form>. Typing directly into the HTML editor, add three <Item> tags within the <List> control, like this:

```
<mobile:Form id="Form1" runat="server">
  <mobile:List id="List1" runat="server">
    <Item Text="First Form"></Item>
    <Item Text="Second Form"></Item>
    <Item Text="Third Form"></Item>
  </mobile:List>
</mobile:Form>
```

Just as with other types of projects, IntelliSense is available when in HTML view for a mobile page, prompting us with possible options when we type a start tag character (<). This behavior – just like that of regular ASP.NET server controls – is found throughout the Toolkit. When we switch back to the Design view, we can see the effects of our changes in the List control:

Alternatively, we can add list items by right-clicking the list control in Design view, and selecting **Property Builder**, or by clicking the ellipsis button (...) next to the **Items** property in the Properties window, to bring up this dialog:

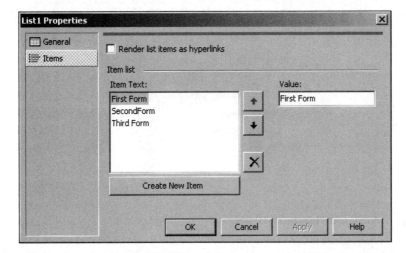

Adding items in this way is a simple matter of clicking the **Create New Item** button, and typing in the text to display for that item. Visual Studio .NET will automatically insert this text in the **Value** box, but you can of course change it if is inappropriate.

List controls are often used for presenting several navigation options, so let's set up ours for this purpose. Double-click on the list control on `Form1` in Design view to add a new `ItemCommand` event handler, and open the code editor for the code-behind file for our mobile form. The cursor will be positioned within the new empty `List1_ItemCommand` handler, which catches clicks on items in our list. We'll add a C# `switch` statement to activate the correct form according to the list item clicked:

```
private void List1_ItemCommand(object sender,
  System.Web.UI.MobileControls.ListCommandEventArgs e)
{
    switch (e.ListItem.Text)
    {
      case "First Form":
          ActiveForm = Form1;
          break;
      case "Second Form":
          ActiveForm = Form2;
          break;
      case "Third Form":
```

```
        ActiveForm = Form3;
        break;
    default:
        throw(new Exception("Fell through the switch!!"));
    }
}
```

The last thing to do before we can run this page is to add the third form, which should have the default name of `Form3`. We can then select **Build | Build Solution** from the menu to compile and build `MobileWebApplication1`. When that completes successfully, right-click on `MobileWebForm1.aspx` in Solution Explorer, and select **Browse With | Microsoft Mobile Explorer Emulator**. MME will open, navigate to our page, and after a short delay while ASP.NET compiles our page, our list is displayed, ready for use as a hyperlink menu:

Populating a List from a Database

List controls are also good data handlers. Add another list control onto `Form3`. Next, drag the **Employees** table from the Server Explorer (under *your local SQL Server name* | NETSDK | GlobalMarket | Tables) onto the page. Right-click on the `sqlDataAdapter1` object that will appear in the Component Tray at the bottom of the Designer, select **Generate DataSet**, and leaving the defaults set, click **OK** on the dialog. Now select the `List` control on `Form3` (it should be called `List2`), and open the Properties window. Click the **Categorized** button on the left side of the mini Properties toolbar, and scroll down to the **Data** grouping:

Set the properties as shown above, but start by setting the `DataSource` property to the name of the data set we just generated using the dropdown. That causes the other property dropdowns in this grouping to be populated, making the job of selecting the appropriate values much easier. All we now need to do is populate the dataset, and bind the data to the list control. The best time to do this is within the `Page_Load` event which fires when the page is first accessed in a given user session:

```
private void Page_Load(object sender, System.EventArgs e)
{
  if (!IsPostBack)
  {
    // Populate the DataSet
    sqlDataAdapter1.Fill(dataSet11);
    // Bind the list, already set to use dataSet11, to the new data
    List2.DataBind();
  }
}
```

Now re-run the project, using the **Browse With** option again, and navigate to the third form. Hey presto, a nice list of all the employee names from the database!

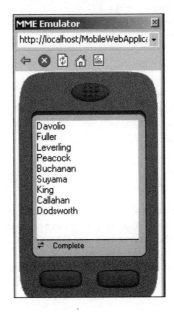

Accepting User Input

The controls provided by the MIT to collect input from users, known as input controls, include the following:

Control Name	Description
TextBox	Provides an area for the user to enter data by typing on their keypad. Equivalent to the regular ASP.NET TextBox control.
SelectionList	Allows the user to select one of several options. Roughly equivalent to the regular ListBox control, but used for navigation.
Command	Allows the user to choose an on-screen option. Equivalent to the standard Button control.

Drag one of each onto the first panel of Form2, just to see how they look:

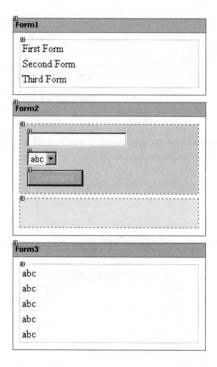

These three inputs function remarkably similar to their equivalents in Web Forms applications. They can be data bound, they can react to events, and they have very similar properties to other server controls. Add a regular Label to the second panel of Form2, and let's see how the input controls work.

The SelectionList control can be databound using the Properties window in just the same way as the List control. Go ahead and bind it to the DataSet we made for our list on Form1, except set it to display the last name, and have a value of the first name:

Then add the following databinding code to the Page_Load event for the page, right after the code we already added to bind the List control of Form3:

```
private void Page_Load(object sender, System.EventArgs e)
{
  if (!IsPostBack)
  {
    sqlDataAdapter1.Fill(dataSet11);
    List2.DataBind();
    SelectionList1.DataBind();
  }
}
```

Start up the application as before, and go to the second form. We can see the selection list of last names rendered on the page, along with the first name set as the value field of the selected item in the list, as we will demonstrate when we add the code for the command button.

Input boxes are input boxes – nothing new here, we can just take the value that such objects contain and use it within code as we wish, just like we do in Web and Windows Forms.

That leaves us with the Command control, which can handle click events by passing information between forms, if we wish. Similar to a DHTML environment, where we have strict control over divisions on a page, with the MIT we have very fine-grained control over the forms on a mobile web page. If the form content needs to be processed by the server, we need to support the post back of the form information, just as we would in an ASP.NET page – use of the Form.IsPostBack property in the Form_Load.

In our case, though, we just want to change the value of the Label control (which should have the default ID of Label1) to reflect the contents of the other two input controls on the form. Add a click event handler for the Command object by double-clicking it on the Designer. It needs to contain the following code to make the label change value when we click the command button:

```
private void Command1_Click(object sender, System.EventArgs e)
{
  Label1.Text = TextBox1.Text + " " + SelectionList1.Selection.Value;
}
```

Fire up the page now, and try tinkering with the textbox and selection list controls to see the effects when the command button is clicked:

There are some advanced options for the input controls that are worth a mention. For example, if we want multiple selections, we can't of course use *Ctrl+Click* as we're used to with the mouse on our PC. So what do we do? One of the properties of the `SelectionList` object is `SelectType`, which has a number of built-in options:

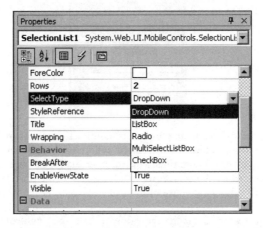

We'll use checkboxes here rather than `MultiSelectListBox` – that works more like a standard HTML list box. If we set this property's dropdown to **CheckBox**, this is the result we get:

The small black arrow on the lower right hand corner of the screen shows that we could scroll down to see more names. We have some programmatic control of paging, too, as we'll see later.

Validating Input

Validation and input work hand in hand with Mobile controls just as they do in regular web applications. The validation server controls create the server and client-side script necessary for the browsing device to confirm the validity of input.

The Mobile Internet Toolkit supplies five validators, and a summary control. They include:

Control Name	Description
RequiredFieldValidator	Checks that a field has a value provided.
CompareValidator	Checks that input matches that of another control. Handy for those "Enter your e-mail address twice for verification" situations.
RangeValidator	Verifies that numeric input falls within a specified range, for example a date.
RegularExpressionValidator	Very useful mobile implementation of the .NET RegularExpressions namespace.
CustomValidator	Allows us to write our own validation routines.
ValidationSummary	Instead of showing each error one at a time, this control collates them for display together. Can help readability.

The basic principles of using the validators are quite straightforward. Let's set one up now. Drag a RequiredFieldValidator from the **Mobile Web Forms** tab of the Toolbox onto the top of Form2. Note that it will be invisible to the user unless the field we set for it is empty when the command button is clicked. Open the Properties window, set the control to be validated using the ControlToValidate property dropdown: in our case, use TextBox1. Also set the Text property to a suitable error message, such as **The field is empty!**, as below:

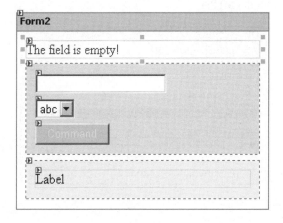

We don't need to change any code to use this control here, but we do need to change the `SelectType` property of the `SelectionList` control back to **DropDown**. Now run the example, and click the command button without typing anything in the textbox. The empty field will be detected, and the error message shown:

This is just the beginning of what the validators can do, though. Take the Regular Expressions validator for example. Regular Expressions are a mature technology dating from the early Unix era, and use a special notation to specify precise patterns of characters within a string. They are a ubiquitous part of the Perl programming language, and are beginning to make a real dent in the Microsoft arena as well. The .NET Framework has an excellent implementation of the Regular Expressions language, found in the `System.Text.RegularExpressions` namespace.

Delete the `RequiredFieldValidator` that is currently on `Form2`, and replace it with a `RegularExpressionsValidator` from the Toolbox. In the Properties window, set the `ControlToValidate` property to **TextBox1** as before. This validator has a property called `ValidationExpression` in place of the `InitialValue` property of `RequiredFieldValidator`. Click the ellipsis button (...) of this property to bring up a dialog listing some pre-set Regular Expressions that come with the MIT:

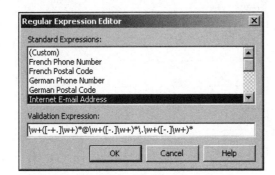

Even if you're reasonably well acquainted with Regular Expressions, figuring out the pattern to correctly match all possible e-mail address formats can be a real headache, and here it is, ripe for the clicking! Select this expression for the `ValidationExpression` property, and then enter a suitable error message in the `Text` property. For more information about Regular Expressions, check out Knowledge Base article Q308252, "*HOW TO: Match a Pattern Using Regular Expressions and Visual C# .NET*" (http://support.microsoft.com/default.aspx?scid=kb;en-us;Q308252).

Styles

Styles allow the mobile programmer to exert limited influence over how controls are displayed. There may be no advanced animation in mobile web applications, or in-depth control of fonts, but some basic styles are included and a simple CSS-like implementation supplied.

There are three built-in style references for mobile controls. If we wish to define our own, we can do so using a style sheet. The three included styles are **error**, **subcommand**, and **title**, and they are all available in the `StyleReference` property dropdown of text type controls. Here are the results of applying each style to our label in the lower panel on `Form2`:

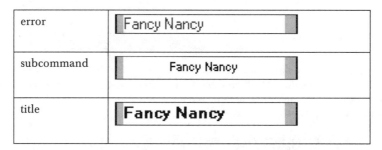

So, if we wish to create other styles than those shown above, we need to use the `StyleSheet` control. This control allows us to define styles for a complete `.aspx` page, and it can only be placed at the page level. To define styles for an entire application, an external style sheet must be used. Drag a `StyleSheet` control from the Toolbox onto a blank area of the page. It will look like this:

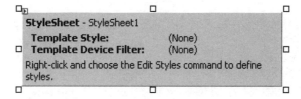

As it says, we can right-click this control and select **Edit Styles** to open a property page for this control which allows us to redefine the standard styles, and create our own:

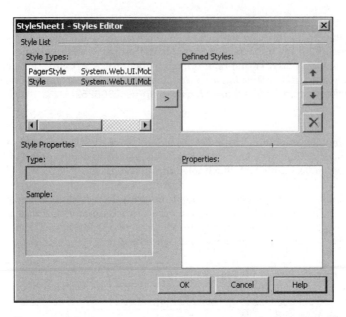

The styles editor allows us to create instances of style types, name them and set their display properties in the upper **Style Types** section. Click on **Style** in the **Style Type** pane, and move it over to the **Defined Styles** area by clicking the '**>**' button. We'll create a new style called `Header` (right-click and choose **Rename**), and set its properties as shown below:

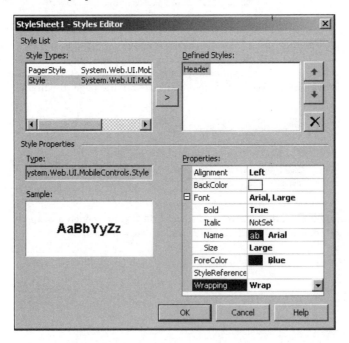

When we go back to our development environment, and check the `StyleReference` of the `Label1` control we were playing with earlier, we find a new reference – Header. This is how it looks:

Fancy Nancy

Images

Currently, mobile devices are far from offering an image-rich platform. Here in the States, the vast majority of mobile phones are monochrome devices, with four levels of grayscale at best, and just 164x300 resolution. For US developers, spending effort creating a rich image control might seem futile now, but it is likely to become a mandatory enhancement for any professional-level application in the near future. Outside the US, however, many devices such as those currently in use in parts of Asia already support higher resolutions and full color. Also, devices like the iPaq and the Palm 505 are color and can access web with a wireless modem.

The MIT `Image` control has a handful of simple capabilities:

❑ Reference an image via its URL, much like the `<img>` tag in HTML

❑ Set a navigation page for the image, possibly linked to a click event

❑ Set the `alt` text and other HTML-like properties

Drag a new form (which should be called `Form4`) onto our ASPX page, and place an `Image` control on it. You'll see the familiar image icon established by the NCSA Mosaic browser so many years ago. The `ImageURL` property lets us set a URL for the image, but first we have to add an image to our project by following these steps:

1. Right-click on the project in Solution Explorer

2. Select Add | Add Existing Item

3. Change Files Of Type drop down to Image Files

4. Navigate to the `Common7/Graphics/Bitmaps/Assorted` folder in the `Visual Studio .NET` folder in `Program Files`

5. Select `Balloon.bmp` – the first in the list

6. The image file will now be listed in Solution Explorer

When we now click on the ellipsis button (...) of the `ImageUrl` property, the **Select Image** dialog appears (readers familiar with Visual InterDev may recognize this dialog). The new `Balloon.bmp` image should appear in the **Contents** pane on the right. Select it, and click **OK**. The image control on `Form4` will change to depict the file we've just associated with it.

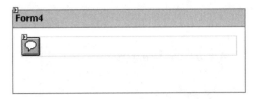

Let's also set the `NavigateUrl` property in the Navigation section of the Property window to #Form1 so that the user is redirected to the start form when they click the image.

Before we can run the sample, we must do a little housekeeping so that the new form can be reached. Add a link to the `List` control on `Form1` for `Form4`, either using the Items Collection Builder or by typing directly into the HTML view as before. Also we need to add a `case` statement to the `switch` construct in the code behind to navigate to the new form.

Setting Device Filters for Images

The more alert among you must by now be wondering what's going on – displaying images on mobile phones can't be this simple: different devices support different image types. In fact, most Wireless Markup Language (WML) 1.1 devices support only a special format of image file: the Wireless Bitmap, or WBMP. Other devices accept only GIF images. The mobile `Image` control handles this through the **Device Filters** mechanism, which provides a list of images in various formats for the server control to select from according to the capabilities of the browsing device. The Applied Device Filters dialog can be opened with the ellipsis button of the `AppliedDeviceFilters` property in the Device Specific group within the Properties window:

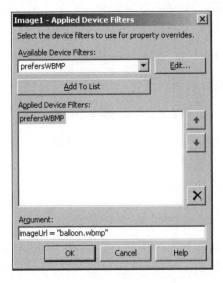

The Calendar Control

The Calendar control is the baby brother of the eponymous control of regular ASP.NET applications. Just like all the mobile controls, it is smart enough to scale down the scope of the display for devices that cannot support its more sophisticated functionality. Go ahead and add a new form (`Form5`) to the ASPX page, and drag a calendar and label onto it:

Before we look at the way the control changes for different browsers, let's play around with some of this control's cool features. Double-click on `Calendar1` to add a `SelectionChanged` event handler to our code-behind file. We'll use this event to change the label's `Text` property based on the date currently selected on the calendar:

```
private void Calendar1_SelectionChanged(object sender, System.EventArgs e)
{
    Label2.Text = Calendar1.SelectedDate.ToString("D");
}
```

As before, we must add a link to the `List` control on `Form1` for this form, along with a new `case` statement in the code-behind file, before we can access the new form. The calendar control isn't much to look at in the MME. Since there isn't really the space or power for a real date picker, the user is run through a sort of wizard that allows them to select the date required:

This is not really the optimal option for most users, but it is the best that the control can produce for this level of browser, and in most cases will suffice. Our page will, after the user digs through the five step wizard, show the date in string format in the `Label` control:

In the Windows CE emulator however, which comes with the embedded tools package downloadable from MSDN, the interface is much richer. We get a formatted calendar, month change buttons, hypertext day labels, the whole nine yards. This is a fantastic example of the flexibility of Mobile Web Server Controls.

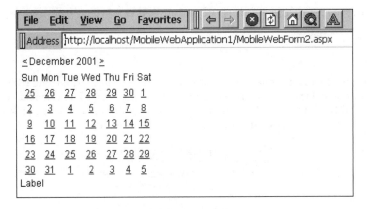

Advertising Controls

The final control we'll examine before going on to our sample application is the advertising rotator control. This control is almost identical to the regular AdRotator of ASP.NET, except for the additional ImageKey property. Just like the mobile Image control, it can be set up for a variety of image formats for various devices. As we go over the component and its features, remember that usage is practically the same as the equivalent control used in regular ASP.NET applications.

The AdRotator stores key information in an XML file describing advertisements to display. As a well-formed XML file, there can only be one top-most <Advertisements> element, which contains any number of <Ad> child elements. Each <Ad> element must contain one, and only one, instance of an <ImageUrl> element and a <NavigateUrl> element. These indicate the preferred image file to use and the URL to redirect to when the ad banner is clicked. There may be as many <OptionalImageUrl> elements as we have <ImageKey>s. Here is the DTD:

```
<?xml version="1.0" ?>
<Advertisements>
```

```
[<Ad>
  <ImageUrl>
    The URL of the preferred image to display
  </ImageUrl>
  <NavigateUrl>
    The URL of the preferred page to display
  </NavigateUrl>
  [<OptionalImageUrl>
    URL of alternate image to display
  </OptionalImageUrl>]*
  [<OptionalNavigateUrl>
    URL of alternate page to display
  </OptionalNavigateUrl>]*
  <AlternateText>
    The text to display as a ToolTip
  </AlternateText>
  <Keyword>
    The keyword used to filter
  </Keyword>
  <Impressions>
    The relative weighting of the advertisement
  </Impressions>
</Ad>]*
</Advertisements>
```

This file is clearly the heart of the rotator. There are a few properties of the control itself, but the most important is the `AdvertisementFile` property, pointing to this file. Each `<OptionalImageUrl>` needs to be matched to the `ImageKey` of the alternate images requested by various devices. You can make custom changes to this system using `<choice>` subtags inside the HTML `AdRotator` call, but we'll come back to this in the *Mobile Capabilities* section of the chapter.

Using a few images from the root `InetPub` directory, let's build a simple XML file called `ads.xml` using the above format and put it in the project.

```
<?xml version="1.0"?>
<Advertisements>
  <Ad>
    <ImageUrl>../web.gif</ImageUrl>
    <NavigateUrl>http://www.wrox.com</NavigateUrl>
    <AlternateText>Wrox Web Stuff!</AlternateText>
    <KeywordFilter>balloon</KeywordFilter>
    <Impressions>80</Impressions>
  </Ad>
  <Ad>
    <ImageUrl>../win2000.gif</ImageUrl>
    <NavigateUrl>http://www.wrox.com</NavigateUrl>
    <AlternateText>Wrox Windows 2000 stuff!</AlternateText>
    <KeywordFilter>beans</KeywordFilter>
    <Impressions>80</Impressions>
  </Ad>
</Advertisements>
```

Then build a new `AdRotator` on a new blank form (`Form6`) and a label. Double-click on the rotator to add the `AdCreated` event handler and add some code to tell us which advert is being used:

```
private void AdRotator1_AdCreated(object sender,
System.Web.UI.WebControls.AdCreatedEventArgs e)
{
   Label13.Text = e.AlternateText;
}
```

When we run the program, the advert is displayed as an image, and we get the `alt` text as well:

Mobile Capabilities

The diversity of mobile devices on the market – and the continuing flood of new devices arriving – makes the old problem of coding for IE and Netscape seem like child's play. Each device has a slightly different configuration, screen size, and input mechanism.

ASP.NET provides a `BrowserCapabilities` object with many useful properties to help make rendering choices in our code based on what a particular browser supports. With the MIT, we get the `MobileCapabilities` objects – a similar set of tools, which can determine the specifics of the device using the application. Moreover, this is controlled entirely locally; it's not just a set of `SERVER_VARIABLES` for the mobile world. We can add new devices ourselves as and when needed, or install patches from the mobile device design community.

To access these useful properties, we must first declare an instance of the class, found in `System.Web.Mobile`. We are then free to access the properties of `Request.Browser` as it relates to mobile tools. In this example, we bind a list control to the collection of available properties:

```
<%@ Page language="c#" Codebehind="MobileWebForm3.aspx.cs"
Inherits="MobileWebApplication1.MobileWebForm3" AutoEventWireup="false" %>
<%@ Register TagPrefix="mobile" Namespace="System.Web.UI.MobileControls"
Assembly="System.Web.Mobile, Version=1.0.3300.0, Culture=neutral,
PublicKeyToken=b03f5f7f11d50a3a" %>
<%@ Import Namespace="System.ComponentModel" %>
<%@ Import Namespace="System.Web.Mobile" %>

<script runat="server" language="c#">

private void Page_Load(object sender, System.EventArgs e)
```

```
{
  MobileCapabilities myCapabilities = (MobileCapabilities)Request.Browser;

  PropertyDescriptorCollection allProperties =
    TypeDescriptor.GetProperties(myCapabilities);
  List1.DataTextField = "Name";
  if (allProperties != null)
  {
    List1.DataSource = allProperties;
    List1.DataBind();
  }

}
</script>

<body Xmlns:mobile="http://schemas.microsoft.com/Mobile/WebForm">
  <mobile:Form id="Form1" runat="server">
    <mobile:List id="List1" runat="server"></mobile:List>
  </mobile:Form>
</body>
```

Here are all of the properties that were available at press time – showing the real depth of control we as programmers can have if we so desire. More information about each property can be found in the member list of the mobile capabilities class. Realistically, the properties are pretty self-descriptive.

- ❏ IsMobileDevice
- ❏ RequiresUniqueHtmlCheckboxNames
- ❏ CDF
- ❏ MajorVersion
- ❏ SupportsDivNoWrap
- ❏ SupportsFontColor
- ❏ Platform
- ❏ Browser
- ❏ RequiresHtmlAdaptiveErrorReporting
- ❏ RendersWmlSelectsAsMenuCards
- ❏ Beta
- ❏ CanRenderOnEventAndPrevElementsTogether
- ❏ RequiresAttributeColonSubstitution
- ❏ CanRenderPostBackCards
- ❏ PreferredRenderingType
- ❏ MobileDeviceManufacturer
- ❏ InputType
- ❏ SupportsJPhoneSymbols

- ❑ RequiresUrlEncodedPostFieldValues
- ❑ MobileDeviceModel
- ❑ SupportsDivAlign
- ❑ ScreenPixelsWidth
- ❑ CanRenderMixedSelects
- ❑ MinorVersion
- ❑ CanCombineFormsInDeck
- ❑ Cookies
- ❑ SupportsIModeSymbols
- ❑ Crawler
- ❑ ClrVersion
- ❑ GatewayMinorVersion
- ❑ PreferredRenderingMime
- ❑ RendersBreaksAfterWmlInput
- ❑ GatewayMajorVersion
- ❑ SupportsInputIStyle
- ❑ RequiresContentTypeMetaTag
- ❑ RendersBreaksAfterHtmlLists
- ❑ RequiresUniqueFilePathSuffix
- ❑ CanInitiateVoiceCall
- ❑ Tables

So, for instance, if we need to test whether the browsing device in question accepts cookies, we could use something like this:

```
if(myCapabilities.Cookies == true)
{
   //Put some code in here
}
```

Device Adapter Code

The MobileCapabilities object is used in a set of server controls that provide adapters for easy manipulation of code between devices. The Device Adapter code includes three useful tools:

- ❑ Device filters
- ❑ The DeviceSpecific control
- ❑ Templates

These three tools are a one-two-three punch in Microsoft's battle against platform-specific web coding. The device filters provide definitions we can use to describe differences between platforms. We've already touched on this control when discussing how to set multiple image types for different browsers, but as we shall see, it also applies to other areas. The `DeviceSpecific` control allows us to instantiate those definitions in a specific form, and finally, the templates help us to actually lay out our pages based on this information.

Device Filters

We can access the device filters by clicking a control in the Designer, then clicking the ellipsis button of the `AppliedDeviceFilters` property. If we click the Edit button on the dialog that pops up, we are taken to the dialog below, which allows us to specify certain parameters that our application needs to know for various platforms:

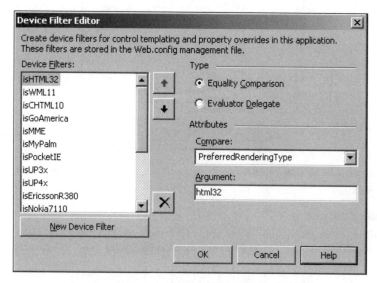

In addition to the list of standard filters provided, we can add a new filter by clicking the New Device Filter button at the bottom of the list. Do this now, and name it prefersJPG. Select the `PrefersImageMIME` property in the Compare box, and enter image/JPEG in the argument box. Click OK, and we can now set values for controls in the Argument box of the previous dialog based on the existence of this filter argument:

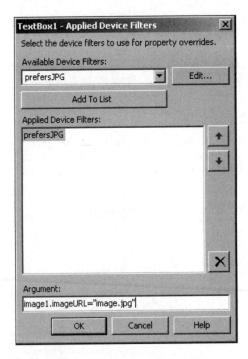

These filters can also all be controlled by code – the `<DeviceFilters>` section can be found in the `web.config` file.

The DeviceSpecific Control

The `DeviceSpecific` control allows us to apply filters to a container control. Drag one of these controls from the Toolbox onto a form or panel, and Visual Studio .NET will display a box like this:

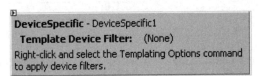

To apply our new `prefersJPG` filter to an image control, for instance, we would drag the `DeviceSpecific` control onto a form that contains an `Image` control. We then right-click on the `DeviceSpecific` control and select **Templating Options** to select a filter:

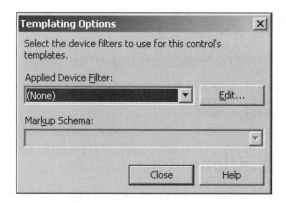

Click on the Edit button, and choose prefersJPG from the list of Applied Device Filters. Click OK and we can select a schema to use if the device supports JPEGs. In addition, we can set the argument specific to this form if the device supports JPEG in the Applied Device Filters dialog box. The default argument we set above appears, and we can change it for specific needs – for instance to change the image used in this form.

Templates

Templates are associated with device filters. Developers can set custom templates for controls and apply then in the templating options dialog box. Making custom templates is a bit beyond the scope of this book, but more information can be found in the documentation for the MIT – our next topic.

Help Documentation

The Mobile Internet Toolkit installs with some of the most comprehensive documentation yet seen in a Microsoft product, and includes:

- ❑ **Integrated help** – The help files are integrated into Visual Studio .NET, and are a real help. There are many options in the Dynamic Help panel, and most of the dialogs, as we see above, have active help buttons.

- ❑ **The QuickStart tutorial** – Installed with the toolkit is a comprehensive set of samples and examples – and they are easy to use. The demos have been very nicely designed, and don't require cumbersome changes to Visual Studio settings to use them. All code is available in both C# and VB.NET.

- ❑ **Release Notes** – For the first time, we've actually got some useful information in a product's Release Notes! Good information about Palm devices, specific phones, and other known issues.

Smart Device Extensions

At the time of writing, the SDE is in a very rough form, and as we've already said, we will not go into much depth. Essentially, where the MIT provides ASP.NET for mobile devices, the SDE provides Windows Forms for mobile devices. It uses the .NET Compact Framework, which is similar to the regular Framework but, as the name implies, smaller.

Visual Studio guides us quite well through the development loopholes one normally finds in the compact device world. If we are developing for PocketPC or Windows CE, for example, we have a richer control set. If we choose a mobile phone platform, fewer controls are available with a poorer support structure. All of this is determined through the project type we select.

From there, we have access to most of the forms controls, the `System.Drawing` namespace, and other user-interface related tools. For debugging, we can utilize a device connected to the network, or one of many emulators included with the SDE.

Design Considerations

Knowing the controls isn't enough when designing a mobile application with Visual Studio. The software model strongly encourages and facilitates good design and structure of an application.

The rules we follow in designing good desktop applications apply equally to mobile applications. In fact, they are probably more crucial because the richness of the platform is even less than that of the World Wide Web, where design is of the utmost importance.

When we talk design, we don't just talk about control placement, font, and graphics. Good design encompasses the overall architecture of the application. There are two main points to keep in mind: the first is separation of duties, and the second is the Software Development Life Cycle.

Separation of Presentation, Logic, and Data

The Windows platform makes this part easy, and it's pretty much the same when we develop for mobile devices. In fact, most of us try to separate the presentation, logic, and data of our applications already – think of a typical web application that might use old style ASP (the presentation layer), and be powered by a DLL file (the logic layer) and SQL Server (the data layer).

This becomes even more important when dealing with mobile devices, however. The point here is that by following this golden rule, we can port the logic from our desktop applications to our mobile applications very easily. If however our ASP code uses inline SQL rather than stored procedures, we are sunk, because we would have to rewrite all of the code into the mobile web forms, or at least copy and paste. Even then, changes have to be made in two places.

If we follow good n-tier design practices, though, we can use the same data-calling methods in both the ASP.NET applications and the mobile web applications. Since we are abstracted from the functionality of actually filling that dataset, or setting that variable, we can make all of our database changes in just one place.

Document, Code, and Test

The software development lifecycle is just as important of a part of the development effort for mobile web applications as it is for anything else. Plan, Develop, Test, Implement – and document as you go. Just because the platform is small doesn't mean the effort is small.

Simplicity is King

We've all grappled with those tiny mobile phone keypads. They are a pain. Keeping the application simpler but functional is always best.

Keep Individual Pages Simple

One of the better design recommendations is to set up pages in a wizard-like fashion, rather than several fields on one form. On a smaller screen, it is better if the action button is visible to the user. For instance, even with two fields, say first name and last name, the page gets a little unwieldy:

Accepting one field at a time, though, on multiple forms, erases this problem:

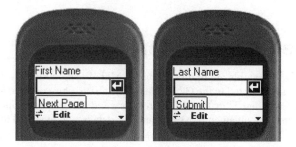

Reduce Keystrokes

Another good idea in general, is to reduce the total number of keystrokes required to finish a form. One well-known WAP provider surprised me with a 14-field signup form on the phone. If the application really does require such a hefty sign-up procedure, let users sign up online and then give them a WAP username and password.

Recognize Usefulness of Mobile Platforms

Despite the poor press that mobile applications had after the initial hype, they really can be powerful tools in the corporate arsenal, and they should not be underestimated. Certain things make the mobile platform useful – first, they easily replicate desktop functionality and logic. Second, they make it easier to access data on the go.

Reuse Business Logic from Desktop Applications

Don't rush in and write new mobile applications from scratch – wherever possible, repurpose existing web or desktop applications as Mobile Web Forms. Use the business logic already compiled. Use the same databases. As long as those existing applications followed good design principles, all you need to rewrite is the user interface for the new medium.

Planes, Trains, and Automobiles

On that same note, don't rewrite the entire intranet. Think of particular information that will be useful to a person on the go within your company. These are some typical tasks that can be very useful if available to employees while out of the office:

❑ Inventory

❑ Basic reporting

❑ Company directory

❑ Directions to company locations

❑ Client lists

The custom Exchange e-mail front end probably won't make a good port to a mobile application, nor will that flash sales presentation. Just keep in mind who uses these applications – people on planes, trains, and automobiles.

The Employee Directory Application

Let's now create a real-world sample application using the MIT. We'll build a directory of salespeople that can be searched by the regions listed in the GlobalMarket database. Our goal is to allow a user to click on a region, and get a list of territories. They then click a territory and get the salespeople that control that territory. Finally, they can click on an employee to get their details, and even call that person.

Setting Up

Start by making a new Mobile Web Application project at http://localhost/GlobalMarketMobile. On the default web page, add a few components to get things going:

❑ Three form controls, to make a total of four.

❑ Three List controls, one on each of the first three forms.

❑ The Employees, Region, and Territories tables from the SQL Servers node in Server Explorer (as you add them onto the page, Visual Studio .NET will make a sqlDataConnection object, and a sqlDataAdapter for each, placing them in the Component Tray). Now rename the sqlDataAdapters as shown in the following table:

Table Name	Adapter Name
Region	sqlRegion
Territories	sqlTerritories
Employees	sqlEmployees

❑ A single `DataSet` for all of those tables – right-click on each, select **Generate Dataset** selecting all of the tables and click **OK**. When complete, we can view the `DataSet` by selecting it in the Component Tray, and choosing **Data | View Dataset Schema** from the menu:

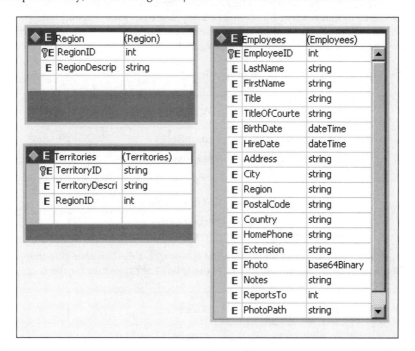

Shut the `DataSet` view, to return to the Designer for `MobileWebForm1.aspx`. Add two `Label` controls above the `List` on `Form1`, and set the following properties:

Control	Property	Value
Label1	StyleReference	title
	Text	GlobalMarket Directory
Label2	Text	Choose a region below

Next, set the following properties for the `List`:

243

Property	Value
DataSource	dataSet11
DataMember	Region
DataTextField	RegionDescription
DataValueField	RegionId
ID	GmRegions

Moving on to Form2, we'll again have two labels above the List, with the same property values set as those on Form1, except that the text for the lower label (Label14) should read **Please select a territory:**. The easiest way is to simply copy and paste the labels from Form1 onto Form2, not forgetting to change the Text property for what will be Label14 as described.

Now select the List and set the following properties:

Property	Value
DataSource	dataSet11
DataMember	Territories
DataTextField	TerritoryDescription
DataValueField	TerritoryID
ID	GmTerritories

On Form3, copy and paste the two labels as we did for Form2, this time changing the Text property for Label16 to **Finally, select an employee:**. Now set the following properties for the List:

Property	Value
DataSource	dataSet11
DataMember	Employees
DataTextField	LastName
DataValueField	EmployeeId
ID	GmEmployees

Form4 is the final form where we'll display details of the selected employee, and so it breaks from the pattern set by the previous two forms. However, we can still copy and paste the top title from a previous form. Then add three further labels beneath, and enter their IDs as employeeName, employeeTitle, and employeePhone respectively. Also set the second label's (Label18's) StyleReference property to **subcommand**.

Lastly, place a `PhoneCall` control from the Toolbox at the bottom of `Form4`. If the user is viewing on a phone that supports this functionality, it will allow a phone call to be made directly from our application. We need to set a default value for the `PhoneNumber` property to make the thing compile – even though we will always set this property through code. Just enter any old number for this – we used 411. Also, set the Text property of this object to Call this person.

That wraps up setting up the controls in the Designer. Our four forms should now look like this:

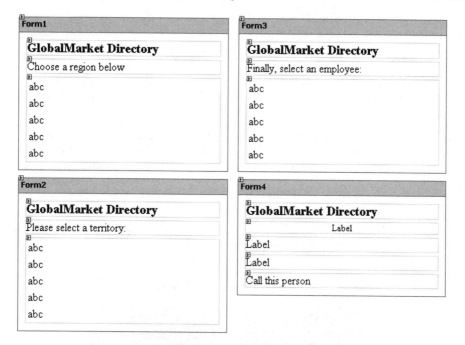

Drilling Down from Region to Territory to Person

Before we build, we need to bind up the data in the dataset. This appears in the `Page_Load()` method.

```
private void Page_Load(object sender, System.EventArgs e)
{
  //fill the dataset from the adapter
  sqlRegions.Fill(dataSet11);

  //Bind the GMRegions control
  GmRegions.DataBind();
}
```

If we build and browse the application now, the first form will appear showing a list of regions. We want to set those list items so that the next form is loaded with specific information about the region clicked.

To do that, we need to do two things. The first is to write an event handler for a list click event. The second is to modify the generated code for the `SelectCommand` that matches the `sqlTerritories` Data Adapter to accept the `TerritoryId` as a parameter. The code below shows `sqlSelectCommand3`; however, in your code it may be numbered 1 or 3. To check this look at the `GmTerritories` properties window.

Double-click the `GmRegions` list in the designer, and add this event handler:

```
private void GmRegions_ItemCommand(object sender,
System.Web.UI.MobileControls.ListCommandEventArgs e)
{
    sqlSelectCommand3.Parameters["@RegionId"].Value = e.ListItem.Value;
    sqlTerritories.Fill(dataSet11);
    GmTerritories.DataBind();
    ActiveForm = Form2;
}
```

Next, we need to change the `sqlSelectCommand3` information, and add a parameter. Expand the **Web Form Designer Generated Code** region, and find the `sqlSelectCommand3` code (it will be preceded by a descriptive comment), and replace the statements there with the following:

```
this.sqlSelectCommand3.CommandText = "SELECT TerritoryID, TerritoryDescription,"
    + "RegionID FROM Territories WHERE RegionID = @RegionId";
this.sqlSelectCommand3.Connection = this.sqlConnection1;
this.sqlSelectCommand3.Parameters.Add(new System.Data.SqlClient.SqlParameter(
    "@RegionId", System.Data.SqlDbType.NVarChar, 20, "RegionId"));
```

This allows us to send the parameter to the `DataSet` without having to write our own data code. When we run the application, we can click on a region to get a related list of territories:

Now we do it all again for `Form2`, adding a click handler to the `GmTerritories` list, and editing the `SelectCommand` for the **Employees** table. The `ItemCommand` handler for the list looks like this:

```
private void GmTerritories_ItemCommand(object sender,
System.Web.UI.MobileControls.ListCommandEventArgs e)
{
```

```
    sqlSelectCommand1.Parameters["@TerritoryId"].Value = e.ListItem.Value;
    sqlEmployees.Fill(dataSet11);
    GmEmployees.DataBind();
    ActiveForm = Form3;
}
```

This time check the GmEmployees properties window to determine the sqlSelectCommand numbering.

The new code for sqlSelectCommand1 looks like this:

```
this.sqlSelectCommand1.CommandText = "SELECT Employees.* FROM Employees "
    + "INNER JOIN EmployeeTerritories ON Employees.EmployeeID ="
    + "EmployeeTerritories.EmployeeID WHERE EmployeeTerritories.TerritoryID ="
    + " @TerritoryId";
this.sqlSelectCommand1.Connection = this.sqlConnection1;
this.sqlSelectCommand1.Parameters.Add(new System.Data.SqlClient.SqlParameter(
    "@TerritoryID", System.Data.SqlDbType.NVarChar, 20, "TerritoryID"));
```

These changes make the territories into links to bring up a list of employees for that territory. The last step is to build a click handler that will fill the employees screen. We'll use a DataReader for that, just to mix it up a little. Normally, we would have a standardized data access system, but since we don't, let's take the opportunity to work with a few different systems. The DataReader is a code solution – nothing needs to be added to the designer. Double-click on the GmEmployees list to create and wire up the event handler:

```
private void GmEmployees_ItemCommand(object sender,
System.Web.UI.MobileControls.ListCommandEventArgs e)
{
    System.Data.SqlClient.SqlDataReader sqlDataReader1;
    System.Data.SqlClient.SqlCommand EmployeeSelect;
    EmployeeSelect = new System.Data.SqlClient.SqlCommand();
    EmployeeSelect.CommandText = "SELECT * FROM employees WHERE EmployeeID ="
        + "@EmployeeID";
    EmployeeSelect.Connection = sqlConnection1;
    EmployeeSelect.Parameters.Add(new System.Data.SqlClient.SqlParameter(
        "@EmployeeID", System.Data.SqlDbType.NVarChar, 20, "EmployeeID"));
    EmployeeSelect.Parameters["@EmployeeID"].Value = e.ListItem.Value;
    sqlConnection1.Open();
    sqlDataReader1 = EmployeeSelect.ExecuteReader();
    if (sqlDataReader1.Read())
    {
        employeeName.Text = sqlDataReader1["FirstName"].ToString() + " "
            + sqlDataReader1["LastName"].ToString();
        employeeTitle.Text = sqlDataReader1["Title"].ToString();
        employeePhone.Text = sqlDataReader1["HomePhone"].ToString();
        PhoneCall1.PhoneNumber = sqlDataReader1["HomePhone"].ToString();
    }
    ActiveForm = Form4;
}
```

This produces a clickable list of employees (well, probably only one – but it is capable of handling more than that!), linked to a details page on Form4:

Summary

Usually feature-driven development tools are as much a hindrance to the developer as a help – we want a functional package, without the bells and whistles. In the messy world of mobile device development, however, it is quite refreshing to have software that is designed to make our lives easy. In that regard, the MIT, and the SDE, both meet their design briefs superbly.

Mobile Devices are clearly a focus of Microsoft, and are becoming a much more popular development platform in the real world as well. When a new access method starts showing up in Microsoft ads, we developers would do well to take notice, because it is surely going to be on the task list soon.

We discussed a number of things in this chapter to help get started with mobile device development using Visual Studio .NET, including:

- The MIT and its components in depth
- The early incarnation of the SDE
- Some design issues relating to mobile devices
- A short example – the directory for the GlobalMarket database

This should be enough to get started with mobile web development, and as devices get stronger and smarter, the capabilities of mobile applications will increase exponentially. That's when programmers like you and I will be able to reap the benefits of the extensibility that Microsoft has built into the .NET model, and Visual Studio and our applications will grow right along with the device technology.

If you crave more meat on this subject, take a look at *ASP.NET Mobile Controls Tutorial Guide* (ISBN 1-861005-22-9, goes in to a lot of detail about using the MIT) and *.NET Compact Framework* (ISBN 1-861007-00-0, an introduction to the Compact Framework and the SDE), both published by Wrox Press.

9

Deployment Features

In the highly competitive Windows application market, every little detail will impact the overall success of a product. A user's first impression of an application is going to be formed when they install it, and so we should never overlook this first step. A professional and cohesive installation process will give our users the confidence in an application that they require.

Back in the days when DOS was king, installing an application was simply a matter of copying all files – usually from a floppy – over to the hard disk. You would then simply run the executable, and that was that. When Windows came along, things changed. Installing Windows applications generally requires not only copying required files, but also registering libraries and creating shortcuts in the Start menu or on the desktop, just to name a couple. Microsoft initially bundled setup creation tools with Visual Basic and Visual C++, and other companies have made a big business out of creating powerful and flexible application installation tools.

Microsoft's Windows Installer first appeared with the release of Office 2000, and it represented a quite new Windows application installation mechanism. Later versions of Windows Installer were released with Windows 2000 and Windows Millennium Edition. Microsoft also integrated the Visual Studio Installer developer's tool into Microsoft Visual Studio version 6 and above. As the Windows Installer evolves, third-party installation toolmakers also update their products to allow the creation of Windows Installer packages.

With the advent of the .NET Framework and Visual Studio .NET, Microsoft's Windows Installer 2.0 has now entered the scene. Visual Studio .NET includes a new project category, **Setup and Deployment Projects**, which contains templates to create different types of projects for the deployment of other applications. In this chapter, we see how to use these new project types to deploy applications, as summarized in the following list:

❑ Deploy Windows applications using the setup project

❑ Distribute the .NET Framework Runtime with application installation packages

❑ Deploy applications manually

❑ Package component assemblies in merge modules

❑ Deploy component assemblies in merge modules using setup projects

❑ Create web setup projects for deploying Internet applications

❑ Create CAB projects for deploying applications and components through the Internet

The next section presents an overview to the Windows Installer and Visual Studio .NET deployment projects. In the following sections, we will create several small, focused setup and deployment applications in order to explore the different types of setup and deployment projects and demonstrate the correct techniques for producing user-friendly installation packages for different types of applications.

Windows Installer and Visual Studio .NET

An installation package performs a set of tasks, such as copying files to specific locations on the target machine, registering components, and creating shortcuts for program executables and other application elements. Windows installation is carried out according to a procedural model: that is, the installer typically performs these tasks in a sequential manner. While installation tools should hide the low-level details from application developers, they all create a predefined sequence of steps for the installation of the target application(s). When creating installation packages, then, we must attempt to devise a clear sequence that will result in the installation of the application elements required for the options selected by the user. We need to think about when and how an element should be installed. Traditionally, if any program files should become corrupt later on, the user will generally have to reinstall the whole application.

From the developer's point of view, the Microsoft Windows Installer is a Windows application deployment service that is data driven. Rather than specifying the exact sequence of steps to follow, we specify what files need to be installed, where they should go, what registry entries need to be created or modified, any other operations need to be executed, and so forth. The Windows Installer then handles the execution of tasks itself: our focus is on the installation data rather than the process.

The Windows Installer also supports self-repair. If some files become corrupt or destroyed, our application has the ability to detect and repair those files automatically. In most cases, the user will need to have the installation package, such as the distribution CD, to hand in order for the self-repair to work, but that's not too surprising really. However, rather than leaving it to the user to detect and diagnose run-time errors, software installed using later versions of Windows Installer is more proactive in detecting and fixing potential problems.

The deployment projects available in Visual Studio .NET provide tools for application developers to quickly create installation packages based on this Windows Installer technology. We can create and test an installation package in the familiar and feature-rich Visual Studio .NET IDE. Visual Studio .NET offers four types of deployment project templates.

- ❏ **Setup Projects** allow us to create installation packages for deploying Windows desktop applications.

- ❏ **Web Setup Projects** create installation packages that can deploy ASP.NET applications on Microsoft Internet Information Servers. However, in conjunction with Setup projects, they can be used to deploy desktop applications over the Internet or an intranet.

- ❏ **Merge Module Projects** are for the pre-packaging of application components. Setup and Web Setup projects can then use merge modules to include the components in the installation packages.

- ❏ The **Cab Project** type allows us to create Internet download packages for ActiveX controls.

Each of these project types requires an application as its deployment target. In this chapter, we'll create a couple of simple applications that we'll use as deployment targets to illustrate how we can create setup and deployment projects for them in Visual Studio .NET. It's a fairly simple matter to swap these for any other application that you may have created already, should you so wish.

We'll start with the Visual Studio .NET Setup project type for desktop applications, and a general discussion on basic features common to all setup and deployment projects. After that, we'll go on to examine the other types of setup and deployment projects.

The Setup Project Type

The Setup project type creates the files required to successfully deploy an application on client machines. In this section, we'll see how to create Setup projects for various types of Windows applications and take a good look at the features common to all setup and deployment projects.

Setup projects can be simple when the applications to be deployed are small, but they can become complex and involved as the target applications increase in size.

A Simple Windows Application

First of all, we'll create a simple application to use as the deployment target application for our projects in this chapter. Open Visual Studio .NET and create a new Visual C# Windows application project called HelloWorld. Delete the automatically created form, and add a new one called GreetingForm by right-clicking on the project name and choosing **Add | Add Windows Form**. Change the form's Text property to **Greetings**. Next, drag a button from the Toolbox, and name it btnSayHello. Set its Text property to **Say Hello**. The form should look like this:

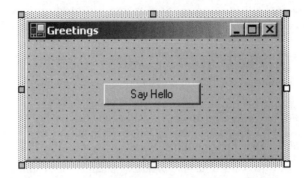

Next, double-click the Say Hello button and add the following code to its click event handler:

```
private void btnSayHello_Click(object sender, System.EventArgs e)
{
    MessageBox.Show("Hello World!", this.Text);
}
```

Now build and run the project by pressing *F5*. When you click the Say Hello button, you should see this message box:

That'll do for our working sample application, so we'll now move on to create our first Setup project.

The Setup Project Type

Descriptions in this section reference the HelloWorld application, if you prefer to use your own project instead, just replace it with your own application.

To create a Setup project for the HelloWorld project, right-click the solution name in Solution Explorer and select Add | New Project. In the Add New Project dialog box, select Setup and Deployment Projects in the Project Types list and select the Setup Project Template. Give it the name HelloWorld_Setup:

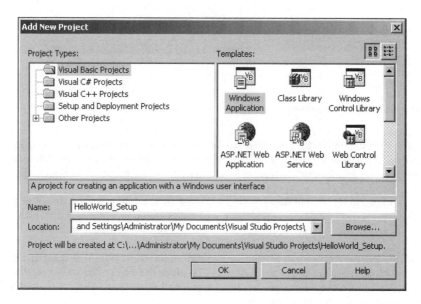

Once you click the OK button, the Visual Studio .NET IDE adds the project to the solution as seen in Solution Explorer. In addition, the toolbar specific to Setup projects appears at the top of Solution Explorer, as shown in the figure below. These buttons invoke the Visual Studio Editors for various setup tasks, and we'll cover each later. You can of course move your mouse over each button to see a tooltip specifying which Editor that button opens.

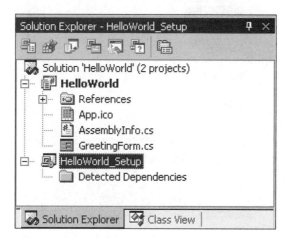

When Visual Studio .NET creates a Setup project, it opens the File System Editor shown overleaf. You can also click the first button on the toolbar to display it:

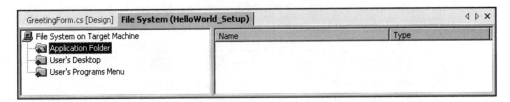

The left pane shows a list of certain folder mappings, each representing a folder on the installation target machine. The **Application Folder** represents the folder where your application will be installed, and you can probably deduce what the other two represent from their names. We can also add other folders by right-clicking the top **File System on Target Machine** node, and selecting **Add Special Folder**.

If we select a folder in the list, all files we want to create in that folder will be shown in the right pane. Since we have just created a new Setup project, all folders are empty. We specify which files are to be installed in a given folder by adding those files to each folder, as we will see shortly.

So as I said, we use the **Application Folder** (or its subdirectories) to store files directly relating to our application, such as the executables and help files. To place the HelloWorld executable in there, right-click the **Application Folder** item in the left hand pane, and select **Add | Project Output** to bring up the **Add Project Output Group** dialog box shown below:

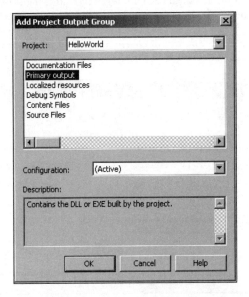

The **Project** dropdown at the top of this dialog lists all application projects in the current solution, and so it only shows the HelloWorld project in this case. Note that deployment projects themselves are naturally not included in the list. In the pane below, which lets us select which file types from the application we're dealing with here, select **Primary output** to indicate the build output of the selected application, namely HelloWorld.exe. The **Primary Output** of the application project corresponds to its **Output File** property as you can see in the Properties Window for the HelloWorld project:

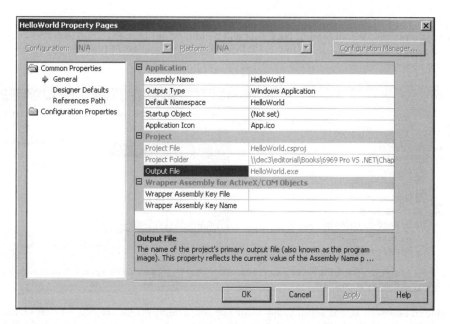

Note that by default, the Setup project uses the `HelloWorld.exe` file produced by the currently active configuration of the `HelloWorld` project. For instance, if the active configuration is Debug, it will use `HelloWorld\bin\Debug\HelloWorld.exe`. If you in fact want to deploy the release version, for instance, you can select that from the Configuration drop-down box.

> **Be careful about which configuration you choose. If for instance you specify a release version of the primary project output, but only the debug version of the application has been built, Visual Studio .NET won't automatically perform a release build for you to create the required output. In fact, it will simply create the setup package without even warning you of the lack of the required project output. When the setup package is then run, however, it will fail with error code 2709, which indicates that the application executable file is missing from the package.**

Click **OK**, and we are ready to go ahead and build the Setup project. If you watch the build messages in the Output window closely, you see the following a warning:

WARNING: This setup does not contain the .NET Framework which must be installed on the target machine by running dotnetfx.exe before this setup will install. You can find dotnetfx.exe on the Visual Studio .NET 'Windows Components Update' media. Dotnetfx.exe can be redistributed with your setup.

This message is telling us that .NET programs require the Microsoft .NET Framework runtime to work, and it often makes sense to include the .NET Framework redistributable file in our Setup project. As the message states, we need to include `Dotnetfx.exe` in the project. If the target machine then doesn't already have the .NET Framework runtime installed, the setup process can install it before installing the application. If however you are certain that all your users will have this file on their machines already, you can keep your setup redistributable's size down by skipping this – the runtime is not particularly small!

In fact, if you expand the Detected Dependencies folder under the HelloWorld_Setup node in Solution Explorer, you see that Visual Studio .NET lists a dependency on `dotnetfxredist_x86_enu.msm`, which is a merge module containing the .NET Framework runtime. We'll find out about merge modules later in the chapter.

The problem, however, is that Setup projects (or any other deployment projects for that matter) created using Visual Studio.NET can't include `dotnetfxredist_x86_enu.msm`, even though the Setup project identifies it as a dependency. Therefore its `Exclude` property is True, meaning that it will not be installed by the Setup project. If you try to change its `Exclude` property to False, you will get another error when you build the Setup project:

dotNETFXRedist_x86_enu.msm must not be used to redistribute the .NET Framework. Please exclude this merge module.

However, we should ignore this message, and keep its `Exclude` property set to False. I will explain how to work around this limitation so that you can install the program on machines that have not had the .NET Framework runtime installed later.

Testing the Setup Project

Right-click the Setup project in Solution Explorer and select Install from the context menu. We are now taken through the series of steps that will perform the installation of the `HelloWorld` application. Although the installation process is smooth enough, it looks a little plain to say the least, so we'll add a little polish in the next section.

Once it has installed, we can test the uninstall functionality, by right-clicking in Solution Explorer and selecting Uninstall. A nice feature of Visual Studio .NET is that you don't have to explicitly uninstall a previous installation before installing a new version. When you select Install from the context menu, Visual Studio .NET automatically detects whether or not a previous installation exists. If one does, it will be automatically removed before the new version is installed.

Alternatively, you can run the `Setup.exe` file in your Setup project's output folder – either the `Debug` or the `Release` subfolder depending on the configuration – to perform the installation procedure. In this case, however, you need to explicitly uninstall a previous version if one exists before starting a new installation.

Ideally, you should test the final Setup project on a variety of operating systems before you roll out your application. Unless you are absolutely certain that the user machines will always have the .NET Framework runtime installed, you should also test on machines with and without that component. At the moment, our setup package for the HelloWorld program will only work on machines that do already have the .NET Framework. *The .NET Framework Runtime Package* section later in this chapter introduces some of the ways we can include the .NET Framework redistributable in setup packages.

Additional Setup Features

The way we've installed the HelloWorld program, if we want to run it, we'd have to find the HelloWorld.exe file, perhaps using Windows Explorer, and then run it directly. This isn't an ideal solution, unless of course it's an application that will not be started by the user manually. Normally, we'd want to at least create a shortcut to HelloWorld.exe in the usual places, such as the Programs menu or the Desktop.

It isn't difficult to set this up. In the File System Editor, right-click the **Primary output from HelloWorld (Active)** node in the right-hand pane, and select **Create Shortcut to Primary output from HelloWorld (Active)**. This will create the shortcut file in the Application Folder. This is still not quite what we want, which is to put it in the user's Programs menu. We need to drag and drop the shortcut into the **User's Programs Menu** folder in the left hand pane. Similarly, we can add a shortcut to the user's desktop by creating another shortcut in the Application Folder and moving it to the **User's Desktop** folder. Alternatively, we can create a shortcut directly within a virtual folder by selecting that folder, and right-clicking in the left hand pane of the File System editor. From that context menu, we choose **Create New Shortcut** to open up the Select Item in Project dialog, where we specify the target of the shortcut – which in this case would be the project's primary output file:

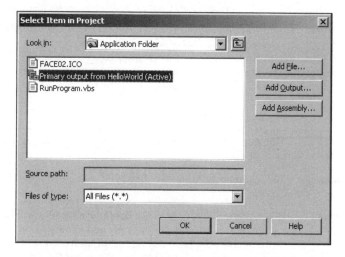

Note that, however you create it, the name of the shortcut file is **Shortcut to Primary output from HelloWorld (Active)** by default, so we want to rename it to something more suitable, such as **Hello World**, by right-clicking the shortcut file and selecting **Rename**.

If we're going to create several shortcuts in the user's Program menu, for instance, one for the main program file and another for the user documentation, it's a good idea to create a subfolder in that virtual folder and place all the shortcuts there. This simply requires us to right-click the User's Programs Menu folder and select Add | Folder. Once the subfolder has been created and named, we can create as many shortcuts as we need inside it.

We can further improve things by replacing the shortcut icon with an application-specific design. Note that even if we've already set up an icon for our main application, the setup project will still use the vanilla Windows executable icon rather than 'inheriting' the application's one. So, to assign the shortcut a smiley face icon:

1. Right-click the Setup project, and select Add | File.

2. Browse to the new icon file. Normally, you'd want to use the same icon as the application you are installing, which would generally be located the application's project folder. The smiley face icon is named Face02.ico, in the Microsoft Visual Studio .NET\Common7\Graphics\icons\Misc folder. It will be added to the virtual Application Folder.

3. Select the Icon property of the shortcut, click the down arrow, and select Browse. In the Icon dialog box, click Browse and then open the Application Folder. Select the Face02.ico file that should be listed there.

We can now build the setup project and install the HelloWorld program to check that the shortcut to HelloWorld.exe appears with a smiley icon in the target machine's Programs menu.

During the install, you'll notice a few things that don't look very professional and are a little confusing. For instance, the installation title is **Welcome to the HelloWorld_Setup Setup Wizard** and the default application folder is [YourCompany]\HelloWorld_Setup (where YourCompany is the company name you entered when Visual Studio .NET was itself installed). We can modify such settings by changing the corresponding properties of the Setup project. Below is the minimum set of properties that we should set for a reasonable-looking setup process:

Element	Purpose and Value
Dialog Title	The value of the ProductName property appears as the title of setup dialogs.
Application Name	The ProductName is also displayed as the name of the application in dialogs.
Default Installation Folder	When the installation is created, application files will be placed in a folder named after the ProductName property value, within a folder that takes its name from the Manufacturer property value. This will be created inside the user's Program Files directory. If you entered your full company name when installing Visual Studio .NET, you may want to change the Manufacturer property to be something shorter. For instance, we might prefer to use Wrox rather than Wrox Press Ltd.

The figure below shows the welcome dialog after the `ProductName` property has been set to Hello World Program:

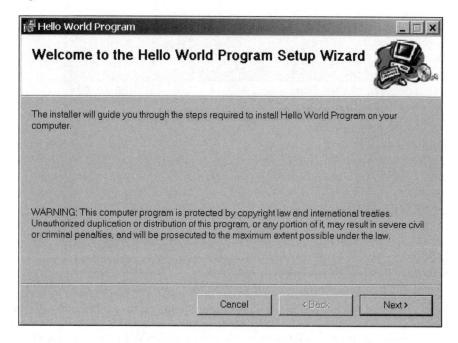

Link Up the Setup and Application Projects

Now you have learned to create setup packages for .NET applications using the Visual Studio .NET setup project. Before we move on to other topics, let's look at one small but handy feature in the Visual Studio .NET.

After following the previous steps, you should now have a single Visual Studio Solution containing both the application and the Setup projects. There's no reason why we can't continue to modify the application project after having created the Setup project for it, and many developers do this. You just need to remember to rebuild the Setup project once you have made your changes and rebuilt the primary application.

However, we can automate the build process so that both are built together, in the correct order. When we create a Setup project for an application project in a solution, Visual Studio .NET automatically creates a dependency for it. That is, it marks the Setup project as dependent on its target application project, because the Setup project contains the primary output of the application project. It also configures the build order to so that the application project is built first, followed by the Setup project. Therefore you can select Build Solution in the Build menu, or click the Build Solution button on the Build toolbar if you have it displayed, to have Visual Studio .NET automatically build both projects in the correct order for you.

You can check out this feature by right-clicking the Solution node in the Solution Explorer and selecting Project Dependencies:

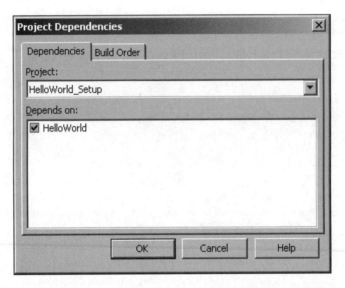

Since the Setup project depends on HelloWorld, Visual Studio .NET will build HelloWorld before building HelloWorld_Setup. We can check the order by clicking the Build Order tab. Note that although Visual Studio .NET can build both projects in the correct order, you don't have to build both all the time. If you only need to build one of them, just right-click that particular project and choose Build. Selecting the Build Solution command from the Build menu or the Build toolbar will build all projects.

Further Customization

In addition to the File System Editor, a Setup project has a number of other editors, which offer a range of further configuration options.

The User Interface Editor

The User Interface Editor allows us to customize the dialogs and other visual elements of the installation process. By default, an installer created by a Setup project presents users with the following five dialog boxes:

1. Welcome screen

2. Select installation folder screen

3. Confirm installation screen

4. Installation progress indicator

5. Setup complete screen

The User Interface Editor provides a way to add our own dialog boxes or even remove some of the default ones, and is accessed by clicking the User Interface Editor button on the Setup toolbar at the top of Solution Explorer. To see the dialog boxes that are available, right-click the Start node and select Add Dialog.

Let's create a checkbox-based dialog to allow users to specify whether the installer should create a registry entry on the user's machine. You will see how to add registry entries in the next section. Suppose that our HelloWorld program could display random greeting phrases, we could use this dialog to offer several related choices for the user to select.

First, right-click the Start node in the User Interface Editor and select Add Dialog. An installation can include at most three checkbox-type dialogs, each containing up to four checkboxes. Select Checkboxes (A) in the Add Dialog dialog box and it will be presented after the Confirm Installation dialog. For some reason, all custom dialog boxes in the Start section must appear before the Installation Folder dialog. If you leave the newly added dialog where it is, you will get this warning:

All custom dialogs must precede the 'Installation Folder' dialog

when you build the Setup project. So right-click Checkboxes (A) and select Move Up to move it one place up, and repeat this so that it ends up above Installation Folder. You may also simply drag-and-drop it to its desired location. Now change the following properties:

Property Name	Description	Value
BannerText	Dialog title	Greetings
BodyText	Dialog text appearing before the checkboxes	Please select the optional greeting phrases.
Checkbox1Label	Label of checkbox 1	Hello .NET
Checkbox1Property	Unique identifier of checkbox 1. If you use more than one dialog, each element must have an installation wide unique ID.	GREETING_DOTNET
Checkbox1Value	Whether or not checkbox 1 should be selected by default	*unchecked*
Checkbox1Visible	Whether or not checkbox 1 is visible	True
Checkbox2Label	Label of checkbox 2	Hello Universe

Table continued on following page

Property Name	Description	Value
Checkbox2Property	Unique identifier of checkbox 2. If you use more than one dialog, each element must have an installation wide unique ID.	GREETING_UNIVERSE
Checkbox2Value	Whether or not checkbox 2 should be selected by default	*unchecked*
Checkbox2Visible	Whether or not checkbox 2 is visible	True
Checkbox3Visible	Whether or not checkbox 3 is visible	False
Checkbox4Visible	Whether or not checkbox 4 is visible	False

If you build and run the installer, you will see the dialog box showing two checkboxes. In the next section, you will see how you can pick up the user choice and create the corresponding registry entries.

Registry Editor

The Registry Editor provides a tool to add application-specific entries to the system registry on the target machine. You can create registry entries in the same way as you would with the system registry editor, regedit.exe, to edit the registry. You can add entries to any of the four top registry groups:

1. HKEY_CLASS_ROOT

2. HKEY_CURRENT_USER

3. HKEY_LOCAL_MACHINE

4. HKEY_USER

You should follow the standard convention when adding entries to the registry. For instance, add user-specific settings to HKEY_CURRENT_USER\Software\YourCompany and system-wide settings to HKEY_LOCAL_MACHINE\Software\YourCompany.

Let's create two registry entries based on what the user selects from the checkbox dialog created in the last section, so that when the installer runs, it will pick up the entries specified here and merge them into the system registry on the user machine.

Expand the **HKEY_CURRENT_USER** node, and right-click the **[Manufacturer]** node appearing under **Software**. In the context menu, select **New** and then **String Value**. Change the new entry properties as shown in the table below:

Property	Description	Value
(Name)	Registry entry name	Greeting #1
Condition	An expression indicating whether or not this registry entry should be created	GREETING_DOTNET
Value	Registry entry value	Hello .NET

Repeat the above process to create a second entry (Greeting #2) but this time with the value **Hello Universe**. Before you go, go back to the **[Manufacturer]** node and change its `DeleteAtUninstall` property to **True**. This will delete the registry entries when **HelloWorld** is uninstalled. Now build the setup project and verify that it will only create registry entries when you check the corresponding checkboxes.

File Types Editor

The File Types editor offers you the ability to associate your applications to certain file types. For instance, if you are writing an XML editor, you could associate all files with the extension `.xml` or `.xsl` to your application. Once you have added a file type and provided it with a descriptive name, such as Greeting Vocabulary File for this case, you can specify its extension and associate it with an executable file in your application.

When the installer runs, it will create the association as specified here on the user's machine. It's always preferable, particularly if the file type is a standard one such as `.xml`, `.txt`, or `.jpg`, to ask the user if they wish to associate those files with your applications before doing so. Unfortunately, Visual Studio .NET Setup projects don't let you set such a condition for file associations, and you will have to use the Windows Installer SDK if you wish to have such a feature. You can read more about the Windows Installer SDK in the MSDN Library or the Platform SDK documentation.

Custom Action Editor

In addition to customizing the installer using the aforementioned editors, we can also specify additional operations the installer should perform. A custom action can run one of the four types of files:

- ❑ Executable file (`.exe`)
- ❑ Library file (`.dll`)
- ❑ VBScript file (`.vbs`)
- ❑ Jscript file (`.js`)

Let's create a custom action that invokes a VBScript file to display a thank-you note at the end of the installation. Custom actions using other file types work in the same way.

Create a new VBScript file, RunProgram.vbs, in the HelloWorld_Setup project folder with just one statement:

```
MsgBox "We hope you enjoy the program", , "Thank you"
```

Next, add it to the project by right-clicking the HelloWorld_Setup project node in Solution Explorer and selecting **Add | File**. Follow the steps below to create a custom action to run this script:

1. Open the Customer Actions Editor

2. Right-click the **Install** node and select **Add Custom Action**

3. In the **Select Item in Project** dialog box, open the Application Folder and select **RunProgram.vbs**.

4. A custom action will appear under **Install**. Rename the action to something suitable, such as **Run Program**.

Build and run the Setup project, and you should see the message box pop up right before the installation finishes. All custom actions under **Install** are executed at the end of the installation process. Files used by custom actions, such as RunProgram.vbs, will be not installed on the target machine by the installer, unless specifically set to do so in the file system editor.

We may also add custom actions for un-installation, and we can also specify a condition for a custom action. Finally, we can pass parameters to the action file by assigning them to the CustomActionData property.

Launch Condition Editor

The Launch Condition Editor allows you to specify the installation prerequisites. If a user's machine doesn't meet those conditions, the installation will stop. You will see how to add and customize launch conditions using the Launch Condition Editor in the next section.

This concludes the introduction to creating Setup projects. In the next section, you will see how to deploy your application using Setup projects.

Deploying Applications

Once we have built an application setup project, we can deploy it on any machine running Windows 98, ME, NT 4 with Service Pack 6, 2000, or XP using the files created by Visual Studio .NET in the HelloWorld_Setup project's output folder, as described below:

File Name	Description
HelloWorld_Setup.msi	The Windows Installer package for the HelloWorld project. We can change its name to something more conventional by modifying the Output file name property in the setup project's **Property Pages** dialog.

File Name	Description
InstMsiW.exe	The ANSI version of the Windows Installer redistributable file. If the target machine runs Windows 98 or Millennium Edition and does not have Windows Installer 2.0 already installed, this file will be executed to install the required Windows Installer files before the application installation package starts.
InstMsi.exe	The UNICODE version of the Windows Installer redistributable file. If the target machine runs Windows NT 4.0 (Service Pack 6), 2000, or XP and does not have Windows Installer 2.0 already installed, this file will be executed to install the required Windows Installer files before the application installation package starts.
Setup.exe	The setup bootstrapper file. This is the file you should run to start the installation. It will install the correct Windows Installer redistributable file if necessary and then run the application MSI file.
Setup.ini	The initialization file used by Setup.exe to perform the required operations. In a simple setup project like this, it contains only a reference to the MSI file containing the application's Windows Installer package, although in more complex installations, it will contain other information too.

Windows Installer

To distribute an application, we usually should include all five of the above files in our installation package. The users can run Setup.exe, which installs the correct Windows Installer redistributable if necessary, and then invokes HelloWorld_Setup.msi to install the HelloWorld program on their machines.

If you are certain that your users will always have the correct version of Windows Installer available, you can get away with only distributing the application installation .msi file (such as HelloWorld_Setup.msi). You can then change your setup project's Bootstrapper property so that it does not create any bootstrapper files. To do so, right-click the project node in the Solution Explorer and select Properties to open the Property Pages dialog shown in the figure overleaf:

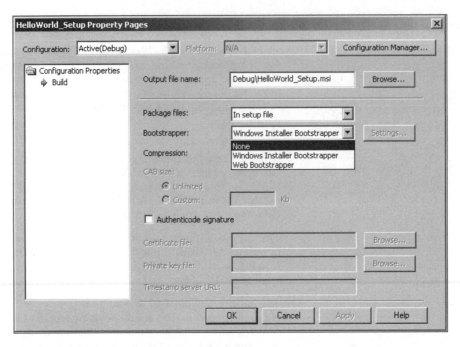

By default, a setup project will create a Windows Installer Bootstrapper as determined by the **Bootstrapper** dropdown. Change it to None to have Visual Studio .NET only build the application installation MSI file and skip all other files. Now you can distribute just this file to the users and they will run it directly to install the application.

The third option, Web Bootstrapper, is normally used to create Setup packages for deployment over the Web, as discussed in the section headed *A Web-Oriented Setup Project* later in the chapter.

The .NET Framework Runtime Package

There is a catch to the .NET installation process though. The setup program will only run if your users already have the .NET Framework installed on their machine.

If they haven't, you will need to supply the redistributable .NET Framework Runtime Package (a single file, `Dotnetfx.exe`) for installation on users' machines. You can obtain it from several sources including:

❑   The Visual Studio .NET CD – in the `\WCU\DotNetFramework` folder.

❑   Microsoft MSDN Download Center – in the package `DotNetRedist.exe`. From the MSDN home page, click on **Downloads**, and select **Software Development Kits | Microsoft .NET Framework Redistributable** in the Table of Contents on the left hand side of the screen. When downloaded, you need to run it to extract `Dotnetfx.exe`.

Dotnetfx.exe contains the Windows Installer 2.0 redistributable. If the target machine does not already have this version of the Installer, Dotnetfx.exe will install it first, and then install the .NET Framework runtime. On some versions of Windows such as Windows 98, Windows Installer 2.0 installation may require a reboot. In such case, Dotnetfx.exe will need to be invoked a second time after the restart.

You may recall that I briefly discussed an issue with the Visual Studio .NET Setup project type that prevents our including Dotnetfx.exe in a project. From a developer's point of view, there are two workarounds: you can ask your users to manually install Dotnetfx.exe, or you can use a Setup bootstrapper file provided by Microsoft. Let's look at both of these two options now.

Install Manually

Having your users install a component for your application manually is far from ideal – you need to provide clear instructions, and risk giving an unprofessional impression. For these reasons, you may find that this option is really only suitable for internal projects where a member of the IT department is available to carry out this installation process.

If this is suitable however, you can include Dotnetfx.exe on the CD if that is how you will distribute your project. Alternatively, you can also point your users to the MSDN Download Center to download it – the file is about 21 Mb in size.

If we run Setup.exe on a machine without the .NET Framework Runtime, we see a message box like this:

We can't expect our users to know that this means they should go find Dotnetfx.exe and run it, and so we need to provide more details, by customizing the above default message set by Visual Studio .NET Setup projects. To do so, right-click the Setup project in Solution Explorer, and select View | Launch Conditions. Alternatively, with the Setup project selected, click the Launch Condition Editor button on the Solution Explorer toolbar:

Either way, the Launch Condition editor and MsiNetAssemblySupport then appear in the Launch Conditions folder. If you click on it, you will see its Message property has the value [VSDNETMSG], which represents the default message shown in the previous figure. Simply replace this with your own message text, and build and run the setup package again. The customized message should then appear on any machine without the runtime installed, such as the one shown below:

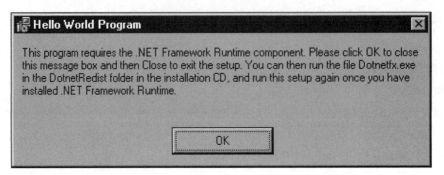

This is kind of message is much more helpful to users and we can be more confident that they will be able to install and run our applications correctly.

Install with Microsoft Bootstrapper

Asking users to manually install .NET Framework Runtime is workable, but most situations call for better than this. Realizing this problem due to the inability to integrate the .NET Framework Runtime and Visual Studio .NET Setup projects, Microsoft has released a freely redistributable Setup.exe bootstrapper. This program will check whether the host machine has .NET Framework Runtime. If it can't find the runtime, it will install Dotnetfx.exe before running your application installation file. You can obtain this file and associated Settings.ini file from the MSDN Download Center:

http://msdn.microsoft.com/downloads/default.asp?url=/downloads/sample.asp?url=/msdn-files/027/001/830/msdncompositedoc.xml

Because the Visual Studio .NET Setup project creates its own Setup.exe bootstrapper by default, we need to remove it from our project in order to use the new bootstrapper. We also have to modify the downloaded Setup.ini file to include your installation files.

1. Change the Bootstrapper property of the HelloWorld_Setup project to None and rebuild. The output directory now should only contain the HelloWorld_Setup.msi file. Note that Dotnetfx.exe contains Windows Installer 2.0 redistributable files and will install it if necessary. Therefore no separate InstMsiA.exe or InstMsiW.exe is required.

2. Copy Dotnetfx.exe to the HelloWorld_Setup output directory.

3. Copy the downloaded Setup.exe and Setup.ini files to the HelloWorld_Setup output directory.

4. Modify the `Settings.ini` file as shown below:

```
[Bootstrap]
Msi=HelloWorld_Setup.msi
ProductName=Hello World Program
DialogText=Do you want to install Hello World?
CaptionText=Hello World Installation
FxInstallerPath=.\
```

If you now run `Setup.exe` on a machine without the .NET Framework Runtime, it will invoke `Dotnetfx.exe` to install the required runtime files silently without user intervention before installing the `HelloWorld` program. On machines that do already have the runtime of course, the setup will detect that and continue to install the HelloWorld program straight away.

Check for Microsoft Data Access Components (MDAC)

HelloWorld is a simple program that doesn't depend on anything but the .NET Framework runtime. Most real-world applications, on the other hand, deal with some kinds of data storage. If your applications need to use MDAC such as OLE DB or ADO, you will need to ensure that the correct version of MDAC is installed on your users' machines. Because the .NET Framework requires MDAC 2.6 or later, you should check the presence of MDAC version 2.6 or later as a prerequisite to installing an application. Note that although MDAC 2.6 is a .NET data access requirement, `Dotnetfx.exe` does not include the MDAC redistributable, and we must handle this ourselves if required.

The latest version of MDAC installed on a machine is indicated in the system registry under the key `HKEY_LOCAL_MACHINE\SOFTWARE\Microsoft\DataAccess\FullInstallVer`. Your Setup project can query this value to decide whether or not the installed version is adequate.

To check for installed version of MDAC, you create an installation launch condition using the Launch Condition editor. In the editor window, right-click the **Search Target Machine** node and select **Add Registry Search**. You can change the search name to something more meaningful such as **Search for MDAC Version** and set its properties as shown in the table below:

Name	Value	Description
Property	MDACVERSION	The launch condition name
RegKey	Software\Microsoft\DataAccess	The registry key path
Root	vsdrrHKLM	A constant that denotes the HKEY_LOCAL_MACHINE registry group
Value	FullInstallVer	The registry value name

The next step is to add a launch condition to check the MDAC version returned from the search. In the Launch Condition Editor, right-click the **Launch Conditions** node and select **Add Launch Condition**. You may rename it something more descriptive, such as **MdacSupport**. Next, change its `Condition` property value to **MDACVERSION >= "2.6"**, where **MDACVERSION** specifies the above search. Of course, if your application uses a higher version, you will use a correct version number string here.

If the launch condition is not satisfied, the installation will display the message specified by the value of the launch condition's `Message` property, and terminate. Therefore you should enter clear instruction in this property.

Now you can rebuild the setup project. If you followed the instruction in the last section, just remember to reset the Bootstrapper property to Windows Installer Bootstrapper before you build. When you run the setup on a machine without the required MDAC version, you should see a dialog box containing the text entered for the `Message` property. The installation will then terminate.

Your user will then have to install the correct MDAC version manually, probably by following your instructions. For instance, they can run `Mdac_Typ.exe` from the distribution CD. You can automate the process, just as we did for distributing the .NET Framework runtime, although there is no ready-made solution such as the one we used in the last section to install the .NET Framework runtime. So you will have to make your own using either the Windows Installer SDK or a third-party installer tool. This is one of the major annoyances of Visual Studio .NET Setup projects – let's hope Microsoft acts to remedy it soon.

Applications with Dependent Assemblies

It is common to create applications that use custom assemblies not included in the .NET Framework. A Visual Studio .NET Setup project for the parent application can automatically detect and include any dependent assemblies. To see how this works, we'll create two projects in Visual Studio .NET.

Create a Server Library

Firstly, create a Visual C# Class Library project and name it `DotNetServer`. Next, change the name of the automatically generated class from `Class1` to `DotNetClass` and create a new function as listed below:

```csharp
using System;

namespace DotNetServer
{
  public class DotNetClass
  {
    public string GetInfo()
    {
      return this.ToString();
    }
  }
}
```

Build this project, and we now have an assembly for other projects to use.

A Client Application

Create a client application by following the steps described below in a new solution:

1. Create a Visual C# Windows Application and name it **DotNetClient**.

2. Change the name of the automatically generated form from `Form1` to `ClientForm`, then change its `Text` property to **.NET Client Form**.

3. Add a reference to the `DotNetServer` assembly: in Solution Explorer, right-click the **References** node in the `DotNetClient` project, and select **Add Reference**. In the **Add Reference** dialog, click the **Browse** button and find and select **DotNetServer.dll**. The DLL file will appear in the **Selected Components** list. Click **OK** to close the dialog.

4. Add a button to `ClientForm.cs` in the Designer. Then change its `Name` property to **btnCall** and its `Text` property to **Call .NET Server**. Double-click that button to set up a click handler, and enter the following code:

```
namespace DotNetClient
{
  public class ClientForm : System.Windows.Forms.Form
  {
    private System.Windows.Forms.Button btnCall;

    //...

    private void btnCall_Click(object sender, System.EventArgs e)
    {
      DotNetServer.DotNetClass obj = new DotNetServer.DotNetClass();
      MessageBox.Show(obj.GetInfo(), this.Text);
    }
  }
}
```

5. Build and run the project to verify that it runs correctly.

Create a Setup Project

Now you have both the client application and its dependent assembly, add a Setup project named `DotNetClient_Setup` to the solution. You can add the primary output of the `DotNetClient` project to the Application Folder of the `DotNetClient_Setup` project. This time you will notice that Visual Studio .NET automatically detects that `DotNetClient` uses `DotNetServer`, and so it adds the `DotNetServer.dll` into the **Application Folder**.

If you prefer, modify the relevant Setup project properties as you did with the `HelloWorld_Setup` project. Once you are happy with the settings, build the project and install it. As you would expect, the installation will also copy `DotNetServer.dll` to the application folder.

This example shows how Visual Studio .NET Setup projects detect dependencies and create a Windows Installer package that ensures our applications are correctly installed with all required dependent assemblies.

A Setup Project for Applications Using COM

Creating brand new applications that use only .NET managed components is fun. However, there are many unmanaged code applications created before .NET was released. If you have been developing applications on Microsoft platforms for more than a couple of months, it's likely that you already have a library of useful and fully-tested COM and COM+ components. Unless your company has a lot of money to burn and plenty of time to kill, it makes sense to reuse these tried-and-trusted components in new .NET applications to maximize return on investment.

The .NET Framework provides COM interop services to enable managed objects to communicate with COM objects. If you have already played with COM interop, you'll know that it's fortunately very easy to use existing COM components in a .NET application. When it comes to deployment time, creating setup projects to deploy applications that use COM components is just as easy. This section will guide you through the process. You may wish to take a look at *Professional Visual Basic Interoperability* (Wrox Press, ISBN 1-861005-65-2) if porting existing COM components is a big concern for you.

If you already have a favorite COM DLL, you can use it for this exercise. Otherwise, you can use a simple COM DLL, ComServer.dll, included in the download for this book. The following text will reference ComServer.dll and use a class, ComClass, in the DLL, so substitute them with your own DLL and class if you wish. We need to register the DLL before we can use it, by opening a Command Prompt window, and changing to the directory where the DLL resides. For ComServer.dll, we then enter the command:

```
Regsvr32 ComServer.dll
```

Now we are ready to create a client application for this DLL, and a setup project for that client application.

The Client COM Application

First, create a Visual C# Windows Application project and name it ComClient. On the automatically generated form, add a button. The table below lists the properties to set for the form and button:

Object	Property Name	Property Value
Form	Name	ClientForm
	Text	COM Client Form
Button	Name	btnCall
	Text	Call COM Server

In order to use ComClass in ComServer.dll, you need to add a reference to the DLL file to the project. In the Solution Explorer, right-click the **References** node in the ComClient project and select **Add Reference** from the context menu. In the **Add Reference** dialog box, click **Browse** and find the ComServer.dll file. Click **OK** to close the dialog box, and you should see the registered **ComServer** listed in the **References** list.

Next, double-click the `btnCall` button in the Designer, and enter the code below:

```
private void btnCall_Click(object sender, System.EventArgs e)
{
    ComServer.ComClass obj = new ComServer.ComClassClass ();
    MessageBox.Show("The COM Server is " + obj.GetVersion(), this.Text);
}
```

Note the .NET interop creates a wrapper class for `ComClass` and names the wrapper class by appending the `Class` suffix to the COM class name. Here we still declare `obj` as an instance of `ComClass`, but we could have declared it as an instance of the wrapper class: both have an identical effect. Now build and run the project. When you click the button, a message box should appear as shown:

The next step for us is to create a Setup project that will deploy this application.

Creating a Setup Project

Add a new Setup project named `ComClient_Setup` to the solution. As usual, add the primary output from `ComClient` to the Setup project. You should see that it automatically adds two dependent classes, the original DLL, `ComServer.dll`, and `Interop.ComServer.dll`, which is a Runtime-Callable Wrapper (RCW) generated in `ComClient` by Visual Studio .NET.

Perform any routine configuration setting changes as in the previous sections, and build the Setup project. It generates the same five files in the output directory, just as before. And that's pretty much it. Try installing it on another machine to verify that it works, and that Visual Studio .NET has indeed made it very easy to use and deploy COM components.

When You Don't Need Setup Projects

We've now seen the basics of creating and using Setup projects to deploy applications. Before moving on to learn more, let's hold back a little. The three setup projects essentially copy the application files to a user's file system. For example, `HelloWorld_Setup` copies `HelloWorld.exe`, while `DotNetClient_Setup` copies `DotNetClient.exe` and `DotNetServer.dll` to the nominated application folders. There may be more files to copy for other projects, but the principle will be the same.

One feature of .NET is that assemblies are self-descriptive. That is, the .NET Framework runtime can retrieve relevant information from each assembly when it's loaded. This means that, unlike COM and COM+ components that need to be registered in the system before they can be used, .NET assemblies do not have to be registered. Therefore there is no automatic registration process involved in the installation process. In other words, for simple applications, we can in fact just copy the required files to the user's machine without needing to go through the trouble of creating setup projects for them. This is what is known as **XCopy Deployment**.

XCopy Deployment

While the term XCopy deployment may sound either futuristic or spooky, especially if you're a fan of The X Files, it really just refers to using the trusty DOS XCopy command of old. The XCopy command is used to copy a file system folder, along with all its files and subfolders, to another location. We can of course achieve the same result using Windows Explorer, and a simple drag-and-drop.

With XCopy deployment, we can distribute all our application files using any media, so long as they are properly organized in the same directory hierarchy to be used on the target machine. We can burn them onto CD, compress them as a .zip or .cab file for download off the Internet, or copy them to an internal file server for installation from the company network. In the last case, internal users can even run the application directly off the file server if they like. Try out these different XCopy deployment methods on the DotNetClient program to see how simple it can be.

Another good use of the XCopy installation approach is for deploying ASP.NET web applications and Web Services. A typical web application consists of middle-tier components, mostly DLLs, and UI elements such as HTML or ASP pages. Since .NET assemblies need not be registered, you can deploy the whole web application by simply copying the files to the web server.

As promising as XCopy deployment sounds, it has its limitations:

- ❑ An obvious drawback of XCopy is that it won't automatically create shortcuts on the desktop, in the Start menu, and so on. Users have to either run the application directly, or manually create shortcuts themselves.

- ❑ If an application uses folders that don't belong to a single top-level folder, your users will need to run XCopy multiple times.

- ❑ If your application uses COM or COM+ components, you still have to register those components. This is a task you definitely don't want your users to do.

- ❑ You can't install components in the Global Assembly Cache (GAC). We cover this process in the section below.

- ❑ For web applications, you need to manually configure the web server to create any necessary virtual directory, set access privileges and so on.

So, we still need the Setup projects. However, there are other deployment tasks that can't be achieved using the simple Setup project type or XCopy, so we'll now take a look at the tools Visual Studio .NET offers for those tasks.

Merge Module Projects

The whole process of creating Setup projects, or using XCopy deployment, to install applications seems fairly simple and well designed. However, if you are a savvy developer, you probably have noticed one missing piece. DotNetServer.dll is installed in the application folder so that it can't easily be used by other applications. What if you have designed DotNetServer.dll to be used by more than one client application, and want to distribute it as a shared component?

What the `DotNetClient_Setup` project does is to make a copy of the current dependent assembly, `DotNetServer.dll`, and install it as a private component of the target application. If you have another application that also uses it, the setup project for that application may make another copy of it and install it as a separate private component of the second application, resulting in two copies of `DotNetServer.dll` on that machine.

If this approach seems inefficient at first, it is intentional, and is designed to address the infamous Windows "DLL Hell" problem, where two applications may install different versions of the same DLL on one machine. The later version will overwrite the early one because there is only one registry entry for any given DLL. If the new version is not binary compatible with the older version, applications that rely on older versions may not work properly or even at all once a new version is installed. Being able to install a private copy for each application removes the hidden dependencies among applications that use the same DLL.

On the other hand, the shared DLL technique still has some advantages over having multiple copies of the same DLL. As long as you keep each version of the DLL binary compatible to a common interface, applications that were built against an older version should continue to work with the latest version. Updating a single copy of the DLL is much easier and less error prone than updating each copy separately. If a new DLL is released with a bug fix, we only need to install it once for all applications benefit from it.

This same logic also applies to .NET assemblies. If we plan to have one assembly shared by many applications, installing it in a common area accessible to all applications is a good idea (but we'll then have to ensure it remains backward compatible of course). To do this, we can package the server assembly separately and link it into the client application setup packages. The first client application will install the server assembly, which will then be accessible to other client applications. The Visual Studio .NET Merge Module Project provides the functionality we require to package up one or more shared server assemblies.

Furthermore, you can also create merge module projects to package server assemblies that are not to be shared. In essence, a Merge Module project provides a way for you to package any server assemblies. You can reuse a Merge Module project in many other deployment projects no matter how they intend to deploy the server assembly – shared or private.

In order to allow client deployment projects to decide how they want to deploy the server assembly, you configure the merge module project to allow client application setup packages to dynamically specify the installation location of the server assemblies. For instance, they can install a server assembly to the application folder, making it private to the application. Similarly, they can install a server assembly to the global assembly cache (GAC) and therefore allow it to be shared by other applications. This section provides a walkthrough to create a Merge Module project and use it in a Setup project.

A Merge Module Project

Add a new Merge Module Project to the solution used in the previous section, and name it `DotNetServer_Package`. As usual, add the primary output from the `DotNetServer` project to `DotNetServer_Package`. Notice that the **Primary output from DotNetServer (Active)** is added to the **Common Files** folder, which represents the `Program Files\Common Files` folder of the target machine. We can now build the project, which creates a file called `DotNetServer_Package.msm` in the `Debug` or `Release` subfolder.

Unlike Windows Installer files that can be run to install target applications, we can't run a merge module to install its target components. We must merge it into other installer files that use its target components. To test how the Merge Module project works, create a new Setup project, and call it `DotNetClient_Setup2`. You will use this project to package the `DotNetClient` project and the `DotNetServer_Package` Merge Module project.

As when creating the `DotNetClient_Setup` project, add the primary output from the `DotNetClient` project to the `DotNetClient_Setup2` project. Since we will now install `DotNetServer.dll` using `DotNetServer_Package`, we need to exclude this DLL file from the project by right-clicking it, and selecting **Exclude**. Alternatively, you can select it and change its **Exclude** property to **False**.

Next, add the `DotNetServer_Package` merge module by right-clicking the `DotNetClient_Setup2` project in Solution Explorer, and selecting **Add | Project Output**. In the **Add Project Output Group** dialog box, select **DotNetServer_Package** from the **Project** drop-down box. This time only **Merge Module** appears in the list:

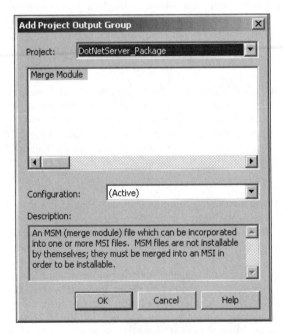

Click **OK** to close the dialog box. We can now build the project and install it with no problem.

Installation Locations for Merge Module Projects

What you probably didn't expect is that if you actually try to run the installed DotNetClient program, it will fail with a message similar to the one shown here:

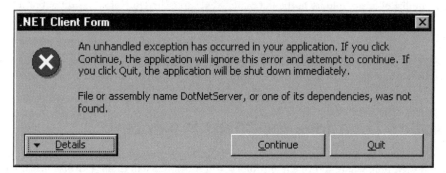

This is essentially complaining that it can't find DotNetServer.dll. What the installation does is to put the application executable, DotNetClient.exe, in the application folder and the library, DotNetServer.dll, in the Program Files\Common Files folder. When the .NET Framework runtime looks for a server assembly – DotNetServer.dll in this case – it will firstly check the folder where the client assembly, that is where DotNetClient.exe resides, and, if it can't find it there, it will next try to find it in the GAC. Either way, it doesn't look at the Common Files folder.

So in other words, placing DotNetServer in the Common Files folder in the DotNetServer_Package merge module is not a good idea at all. The logical place is really the GAC. Of course, DotNetServer must be strongly named if it is going to be installed in GAC.

If you haven't created strongly named assemblies before, follow the steps below to assign DotNetServer a strong name:

1. Open a Command Prompt window, and change the current directory to the DotNetServer project folder.

2. Type in the command sn -k DotNetServer.key and press *Enter*. This creates a key file called DotNetServer.key in the current directory.

3. Go back to Visual Studio .NET IDE and double-click the AssemblyInfo.cs class in the DotNetServer project.

4. Scroll to the bottom of the file and enter the path to the key file for the AssemblyKeyFile attribute, as listed below:

```
[assembly: AssemblyDelaySign(false)]
[assembly: AssemblyKeyFile("..\\..\\DotNetServer.key")]
[assembly: AssemblyKeyName("")]
```

5. Rebuild the `DotNetServer`, project

Now we are ready to install `DotNetServer.dll` in the GAC. Firstly, right-click the **File System on Target Machine** node in the File System editor, and select **Add | Global Assembly Cache**. This adds the GAC to the list of target folders in the left pane. Next, drag the DotNetServer.dll out of the `Common Files` folder, and drop it into the **Global Assembly Cache** Folder. Finally, rebuild the `DotNetServer_Package` project and the `DotNetClient_Setup2` project.

Now we're all set to install `DotNetClient`. Once installed, run it to verify that it works this time. If we inspect the GAC in the `assembly` subdirectory off your Windows installation folder, we'll also find `DotNetServer.dll` there.

Installation Locations for Client Projects

While you can set the installation locations of assemblies in merge module projects, you may not always know at design time where future client projects will want to install them. For instance, a client project may need to include an assembly in a merge module as a private component and therefore want to install it in its own application folder. By forcing the assembly to be installed in the GAC in the merge module, client projects would not be able to install it in the application folder. It would be more flexible if we could allow client installers to decide where to install components based on their own requirements, even long after the merge module was created.

Installing in the Application Folder

The merge module project provides an easy way to make an application's components configurable by client installers. In the File System editor for the `DotNetServer_Package`, there is a **Module Retargetable Folder**. Place a component in this folder to make its installation location configurable by client installers. We can test this on the `DotNetServer_Package` project, by dragging the **Primary output from DotNetServer (Active)** out of the **Global Assembly Cache** Folder and dropping it into the **Module Retargetable Folder**, and then rebuilding the project.

The next step is to configure the client installer, `DotNetClient_Setup2`, to specify the installation location of `DotNetServer.dll`. Select the **Merge Module from DotNetServer_Package (Active)** node in Solution Explorer and find the `Folder` property in the Properties window. Its value will be **Application Folder**, which is the default setting for Setup projects. If we want to install `DotNetServer.dll` as a private component in the application folder, leave this value unchanged and rebuild the project. We can then run `DotNetClient_Setup2` to install the application and verify that `DotNetServer.dll` is installed in the application folder.

Installing in the GAC

In order to install `DotNetServer.dll` in the GAC, we need to add the GAC to your target folder list in the File System editor for the `DotNetClient_Setup2` project, just as we did when we added the GAC to the `DotNetServer_Package` project. Next, click the **Merge Module from DotNetServer_Package (Active)** node in Solution Explorer, and then find the `Folder` property in the Properties pane:

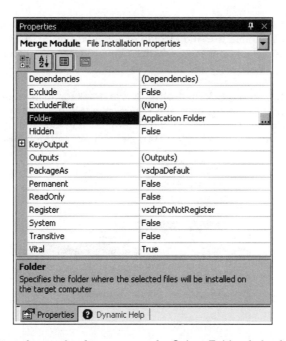

When you click the ellipsis button for this property, the **Select Folder** dialog box appears. Select **Global Assembly Cache Folder** and click **OK** to make the GAC serve as the installation folder for `DotNetServer.dll`.

There is, however, one more twist. If we build the project, we get this error message:

Unable to build project output group 'Merge Module from DotNetServer_Package (Active)' into the Global Assembly Cache; the outputs are not strongly named assemblies.

Visual Studio .NET seems unable to detect that the `DotNetServer_Package` project contains a strongly named assembly. The workaround is to reference the compiled version of both the server assembly and the merge module like so:

1. Remove the **Primary output from DotNetServer (Active)** component from the `DotNetServer_Package` project.

2. In the File System Editor for the `DotNetServer_Package` project, right-click the **Module Retargetable Folder**. Select **Add | Assembly** to open the **Component Selector** dialog box. Then click the **Browse** button and find `DotNetServer.dll`. Once you have selected the DLL, click **OK** to close the dialog box.

3. Rebuild `DotNetServer_Package`.

4. Remove **Merge Module from DotNetServer_Package (Active)** from `DotNetClient_Setup2` project.

5. In Solution Explorer, right-click the `DotNetClient_Setup2` project node. Select **Add |
Merge Module** to open the **Add Module** dialog box. Locate the entry for
`DotNetServer_Package.msm` and click **Open** to close the dialog box, and add the file to
the project.

6. In Solution Explorer, click the **DotNetServer_Package.msm** node under the
`DotNetClient_Setup2` project and expand the **(MergeModuleProperties)** node in the
Properties window. Click the **Module Retargetable Folder** and then the down arrow on the
right. In the drop-down list, select **Browse** as shown in the figure below:

7. In the **Select Folder** dialog box, select **Global Assembly Cache Folder** and click **OK** to
close the dialog box.

8. Rebuild the `DotNetClient_Setup2` project.

As usual, run the setup and verify that `DotNetServer.dll` is installed in the GAC and that
`DotNetClient` works as expected.

That pretty much wraps up our introduction to merge module projects. In the next section, we will look
at the Cab Project, which packages assemblies for distribution over the Internet.

Cab Projects

The primary objective of the Cab project type is to provide a means for downloading ActiveX controls from the Internet or an intranet via a web browser. The .cab file type takes its name from the word cabinet, because it is used to store multiple files and folders, and is pretty much like a .zip file in concept. To see how the Cab project type is used, let's walk through an example.

The ActiveX Control

First, we need an ActiveX control to play with. You may use any ActiveX control that you've already written, or use ClockControl.ocx as provided in the code download for this book. We'll refer to this ClockControl ActiveX control in this section, so substitute this with the name of your own ActiveX control if you'd rather do that. Either way, you need to ensure that the ActiveX control is registered on your development machine.

To register ClockControl, open a Command Prompt box, and change to the directory where you placed the ClockControl.ocx file. Then enter this command:

```
Regsvr32 ClockControl.ocx
```

The ClockControl contains a control called FlashingClock, which displays a digital clock on the hosting web page. It refreshes the time and changes its background color every second, as illustrated below:

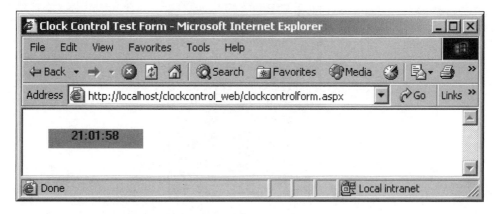

Now we're ready to create a cab file to distribute this control.

Placing the Control within a Cab Project

In Visual Studio .NET, create a new Cab Project and name it ClockControl. Then right-click the project node in Solution Explorer, and select Add | File. In the Add File dialog box, locate ClockControl.ocx and click Open. This should now appear under the ClockControl project.

There is not much to configure for the cab project type, so just go ahead and build it and we are done. In the project output directory, you should see the file ClockControl.cab. We now need to create a web interface to install this control on a user's machine.

A Simple ASP.NET Project

Create a new Visual C# ASP.NET Web Application with Visual Studio .NET and name it
`ClockControl_Web`. Next change the name of the automatically created web form from
`WebForm1.aspx` to `ClockControlForm.aspx` and double-click it to display the form in design mode.
Then follow the steps below to complete the project:

1. In Solution Explorer, right-click the project node and select Add | New Folder. Rename
the new folder Downloads. Next, right-click the Downloads folder node, and select Add |
Add Existing Item. In the dialog entitled Add Existing Item – ClockControl_Web, find
`ClockControl.cab` created by the `ClockControl` cab project in its output directory,
and click Open. The file `ClockControl.cab` will now appear under the Downloads
folder node.

2. Right-click the Toolbox in Visual Studio, and select Customize Toolbox. Check
ClockControl.FlashingClock in the Customize Toolbox dialog box, and click OK. The
`FlashingClock` control should now become available right at the bottom of the Web
Forms tab of the Toolbox, as illustrated below:

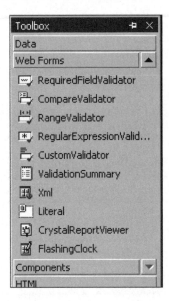

3. Double-click the `FlashingClock` control to add it to the web form.

4. Click the control on the web form, select the `codebase` property in the Properties pane,
and set it to Downloads/ClockControl.cab.

5. Build the project. If you run it on your development machine and the Initialize and script ActiveX controls not marked as safe option for Local Intranet is disabled in Internet Explorer, you may see an error message similar to the one below:

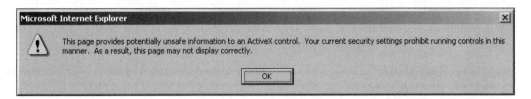

For simplicity, the ClockControl is not by default marked as safe for initialization or scripting, nor is it digitally signed. Check out the following articles on MSDN for more information on these subjects:

❑ Signing and Checking Code with Authenticode (http://msdn.microsoft.com/workshop/security/authcode/signing.asp)

❑ Creating, Viewing, and Managing Certificates (http://msdn.microsoft.com/library/en-us/security/cryptotools_6er7.asp)

❑ Safe Initialization and Scripting for ActiveX Controls (http://msdn.microsoft.com/workshop/components/activex/safety.asp)

❑ Microsoft Knowledge Base Article Q182598 – *HOWTO: Implement IObjectSafety in Visual Basic Controls* (http://support.microsoft.com/support/kb/articles/Q182/5/98.ASP)

For this exercise, just click OK and the clock will display because the FlashingClock control is already registered on your local machine.

6. On another machine that has not had ClockControl registered, you will need to enable the following Internet Explorer security settings:

❑ Download unsigned ActiveX controls

❑ Initalize and script ActiveX controls not marked as safe

7. Open the ClockControlForm.aspx in Internet Explorer. The control will be downloaded to the Downloaded Program Files subfolder in the Windows or WinNT directory. The web page then will display the clock.

So that's the procedure for creating Cab projects to deploy ActiveX controls. Don't forget to reset your IE settings to their previous values if you've had to change them.

Limitations

If you have already developed web pages utilizing ActiveX controls, you know the concept of cab file deployment is not new. The Visual Basic 6 Package and Deployment Wizard provides a convenient way of creating cab files which package ActiveX controls for distribution. You can even mark your controls as safe for initialization and scripting when you create the distribution cab file. Sadly, such an ability is as yet absent from the new Visual Studio .NET Cab project.

Only Microsoft can explain the exact reasons for such a limited Cab project type. A good guess would be that because with the release of the .NET Framework, ActiveX controls are on their way out. We should perhaps view ActiveX as a legacy technology that Microsoft would rather we no longer use.

The Cab Project as a Compression Tool

Another use of the Cab project type is simply as a compression tool. For instance, we can package all our Setup project output files in a cab file so that users can download it over the Internet. They can then extract the setup files and install the application locally.

This isn't difficult to try out if you wish. Open the `DotNetClient_Setup` project in Visual Studio .NET, and create a new Cab project. Next add the project output from the `DotNetClient_Setup` project to the new Cab project. When we now build the Cab project, all setup files created by `DotNetClient_Setup` will be packed up into a single cab file. You can put this cab file on a web server so that users can download it.

There is also another way of making Windows applications available for installation over the Internet, but I'll come back to that later in the chapter. For now, let's turn our attention to the Web Setup Project.

Web Setup Project

The primary purpose of creating a Web Setup project is to deploy a web application to other web servers. Like the Cab project, the concept of deploying web applications from a development machine to a server is not new in .NET. In Microsoft Visual InterDev, we could deploy a web application on the fly. As stated earlier, we can also use XCopy to install web applications. So before we move on to the Web Setup project type, let's look at how to use XCopy to install a web application.

XCopy Deployment for Web Applications

If we wish to use XCopy to copy a web application to a new server, the first thing we need is write access to the drive or parent folder where we wish to place the web application. For instance, if we want to install the web application to `C:\Inetpub\wwwroot\ClockControl_Web`, we must have write access to either the `wwwroot` folder, or at least the `ClockControl_Web` folder, assuming it already exists.

Assuming that the wwwroot folder on the web server is shared as wwwroot$ and that we have the required write permission, we would perform an XCopy installation by following the steps below:

1. Copy the ClockControl_Web folder from your development machine to the C:\Inetput\wwwroot\ClockControl_Web folder on the web server. You can either use drag-and-drop and Windows Explorer, or enter the XCopy command below at a Command Prompt window:

xcopy ClockControl_Web "\\WebServer\wwwroot$\ClockControl_Web" /i /e /y

Note that you'll need to substitute **WebServer** in the above command with the name of the machine where the web application is to be installed.

2. On the web server containing the new installation, open the Internet Information Services MMC snap-in. Under **Default Web Site**, right-click the ClockControl_Web folder and select **Properties**.

3. In the **ClockControl_Web Properties** dialog box that now opens, click the **Create** button towards the bottom to configure the folder as an application accessible as a web site, and click **OK**.

That's the minimum required to deploy a web application using XCopy. If we don't carry out the third and final step above, users will be unable to browse to our web pages. We may wish to set other properties, such as the default start page or the application's protection settings, in which case there will be a few more things to do manually.

Note that the XCopy method copies *all* files, even though a lot of them (such as the project files) are not required at run time. In a production environment, we should really remove such files manually. Needless to say, if your web application uses tried-and-trusted COM+ components, we also have to manually install those. Web Setup projects can automate such tasks, and more.

Deploy a Web Application

In this section, we'll create a Web Setup project to deploy the ClockControl_Web application. Before we start, make sure that the ClockControl_Web project is loaded in Visual Studio .NET.

Add a new Web Setup project to the solution and name it ClockControl_Web_Setup. In Solution Explorer, right-click the ClockControl_Web_Setup project node, and select **Add | Project Output** from the context menu. In the **Add Project Output Group** dialog box, select the ClockControl_Web project and then select **Primary Output** and **Content Files**. Click **OK** to close the dialog box.

The Web Setup project will create a virtual directory on the target web server for the target web application (the ClockControl_Web project). By default, the virtual directory takes the name of the Web Setup project. Normally we'd want it to be named differently, for instance, to have the name of the web application. To do that, click the **Web Application Folder** in the File System editor and change its VirtualDirectory property value to ClockControl_Web. As I said, Web Setup projects also allow us to change other web settings such as the default starting page or the application protection level. For this example, change the ApplicationProtection property value to high using the Properties window.

Now build the `ClockControl_Web_Setup` project. The last step is to copy all files from the project output directory to the web server, and run `Setup.exe` there. Once the setup completes, our web application is all ready to go.

Deploy a Windows Application

In the Setup project section, we saw how to create Setup projects to deploy Windows applications. The Setup project creates a set of files that can be distributed using CDs or a network. In addition to such "traditional" media, we can also distribute such applications over the Internet, expanding our potential userbase to pretty much the entire planet.

A simple way of distributing a Windows application on the Internet is to package it in a single zip or cab archive. Users can then download this file, uncompress it, and run `Setup.exe` to install. However, this method has its drawbacks. In order allow users who don't have the latest installer version on their machines to install our applications, we need to do one of the following:

1. We can choose to include the Windows Installer redistributable files in the application distribution package, which increases the size of the package by about 3.4 megabytes if we include both the ANSI and the UNICODE distributable files. However, users who have already installed the latest Windows Installer on their machine will also have to download those files, even though they don't need them.

2. We could create two setup packages, one with the Windows Installer redistributables and the other without. Users with the right installer version can choose to download the smaller package, while others would need to download the full package. However, this puts the responsibility on our users to know what Windows Installer version they have on their machines.

3. We can choose to exclude the Windows Installer redistributables from our package and make them available for download separately. If the setup process detects that the latest installer version is not present on the host machine, it would need to display a message like that shown in *The .NET Framework Runtime* section earlier to instruct them to download the Windows Installer redistributables. However, this is an inconvenience to users, who may give up, and choose a competitor's product that makes things simpler for them.

There are other options, such as using third-party tools, but they are beyond the scope of this book. However, Visual Studio .NET has a much better way, based on a combination of Setup and Web Setup projects. We create a Setup project for an application, and then create a Web Setup project to deploy the Setup project output files to a web server. Users can then install the target application directly from your web server. We'll have a go at doing this now.

A Web-Oriented Setup Project

First, create a Setup project for the `DotNetClient` application just as we created the `DotNetClient_Setup` project. This time name it `DotNetClient_Setup3`. Before you build it, change its `Bootstrapper` property to **Web Bootstrapper**, which will open the **Web Bootstrapper Settings** dialog box shown below:

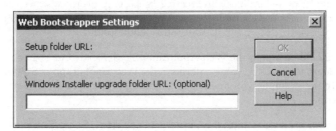

As discussed in the previous *Deploying Applications* section, the bootstrapper `Setup.exe` performs some pre-installation checks and then loads the application MSI file to install the application. For normal installation, the application MSI file is located in the same folder as `Setup.exe` and there is no problem for `Setup.exe` in finding the application MSI. In a web installation scenario, the user downloads and runs `Setup.exe`, which obviously needs to know where it can find the application MSI file. You specify the location of the application MSI file by entering the URL of the folder containing the application MSI file in the **Setup folder URL** box. For this example, enter `http://MyServer/DotNetClient_Setup`, where `MyServer` denotes your deployment web server.

On the other hand, if `Setup.exe` detects that the user's machine does not have the required Windows Installer runtime during the pre-installation check, it will try to find the correct Windows Installer redistributable and update the user's machine, by looking in the URL given in the **Windows Installer upgrade folder URL** box. If this is in the same folder as the application MSI file, just leave this field blank.

Close this dialog box now, and build the Setup project. If you look at the project output folder, you will see these four files:

File Name	Description
`DotNetClient_Setup3.msi`	The application installation Windows Installer package
`InstMsiA.exe`	The ANSI version of Windows Installer redistributable
`InstMsiW.exe`	The Unicode version of Windows Installer redistributable
`Setup.exe`	The web-oriented setup bootstrapper

Comparing this list with the output files created by the regular setup project, `DotNetClient_Setup`, we see that this setup project doesn't produce the bootstrapper initialization file, `Setup.ini`. Instead, it includes the locations of the setup MSI file and the Windows Installer redistributable files within the `Setup.exe` bootstrapper itself. This allows `Setup.exe` to run without having to look up details in `Setup.ini`.

Note that it is possible to simply copy those four files to folder on your web server, à la XCopy. Knowing the limitations of the XCopy method, however, let's create a Web Setup project to fully automate the deployment process.

Deploying Installation Files with Web Setup Project

By now, you should be quite familiar with creating Web Setup projects, so we can skip the walkthrough this time. Just create a new Web Setup project, call it `DotNetClient_WebSetup`, and add the Build Output of `DotNetClient_Setup3` to its Web Application Folder.

One setting you should change is the Web Application Folder's `VirtualDirectory` property, which must match the Setup folder URL value entered in the Web Bootstrapper Settings dialog box shown in the last section. In the example, you must enter `DotNetClient_Setup`. You may also change other settings as you wish.

When you point your browser to http://MyServer/DotNetClient_Setup/Setup.exe, you will see a File Download dialog something like the one shown below:

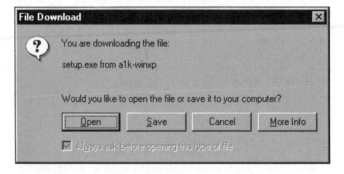

You can either open and run the `Setup.exe` file directly, or save it locally and run it later. The result is the same: in both cases `Setup.exe` will run and automatically try to download and run `DotNetClient_Setup3.msi` to install the application. Because this file is not digitally signed, your browser might not download it, or it may display a warning similar to this:

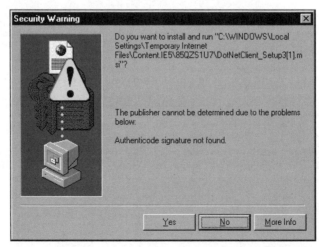

For this exercise, just click Yes and the installation will start. In a production environment, we really do need to digitally sign it so that our users will feel comfortable installing it. An alternative would be to provide users with the option to download all setup files, including `DotNetClient_Setup3.msi`, and install locally. You can package them all up together in a cab, as described earlier, or a zip file, and create a link for the users to download them all.

Summary

Deploying applications has traditionally been less than straightforward and has required a lot of groundwork. Visual Studio .NET provides a collection of setup and deployment project types that make it easy for us to package and deploy applications. This chapter has attempted to introduce those project types, discussing along the way the commonly used techniques when creating different setup and deployment projects.

Setup projects offer application developers the power and flexibility to package Windows applications and customize their installation behaviors. Web Setup projects let us deploy and update web applications across multiple web servers. We can also combine the two project types to distribute Windows applications over the Internet.

Visual Studio .NET also includes the Merge Module project type, which allows application developers to create setup packages for individual system components and assemble them in Setup and Web Setup projects. The Cab project provides an easy way for making components and applications available for download via the Internet.

Knowing that we can create deployment packages easily for an application, and that we can synchronize the setup and deployment projects with the application during its development cycle, lets us focus more on producing high quality software, confident that our applications will be deployed successfully. We can rest assured that our users will enjoy a hassle-free professional-quality installation process, setting them up to fully appreciate the quality of our .NET applications.

10

Crystal Reports

A New Chapter in Reporting

In 1993, certain versions of Visual Studio included a fairly unknown reporting application called Crystal Reports. Now, as with so many other features, Crystal Reports is fully integrated into Visual Studio .NET. The creation of Crystal Report files is part of the Add File dialog; the programming controls are part of the default toolbar.

Crystal Reports is a drag-and-drop-style report generator that has been around for nearly eight years. Crystal Reports is owned by Crystal Decisions (http://www.crystaldecisions.com/), a division of Seagate. Crystal Reports provides very simple creation of very complex reports. The new version of Crystal is a welcome sight to those of us working us with it every day, and especially those with just the occasional need.

For Those who Haven't had the Pleasure

For those who may not have worked with Crystal before, it is essentially a very in-depth, powerful report builder in the style of the Microsoft Access reports tool. It provides access directly into the data in its full version, and even in this version it will completely integrate itself with a dataset, providing a variety of grouping and sorting operations. When it comes down to it, Crystal allows us to present report information much more prettily than if we were to use a Windows Form or HTML.

Crystal Reports are saved as .rpt files, and can be compiled right into projects. They are viewable with ActiveX controls similar to Adobe's PDF reader, which can now be dropped on a web or Windows form. Now, we can also expose Crystal Reports as Web Services.

There are many books written about Crystal Reports, and since this is a Visual Studio book, we will cover Crystal as it relates to Visual Studio. After covering some introductory material, we will discuss:

❑   Creating reports with experts – wizards that allow us to quickly generate common reports

❑   Data Connections

❑   Field Explorer – gives us the ability to drag fields onto a report or generate formulas

❑   Integration – putting reports into our project

❑   Runtime Customization

Included in the Box

By far the best feature of Crystal Reports for .NET is its integration into the IDE. First, working with report files is like working with any other file in Visual Studio. The Report Designer is fully integrated into Visual Studio .NET. Crystal Reports for Visual Studio .NET is a native .NET solution written in C# and Managed Extensions for C++. Now, this is really just a feature of .NET. Third, the viewer is now a server control. We can directly drag it onto a web or Windows form to allow the user to view the report without Crystal Reports having to be installed on their system.

Certain Features Available with Visual Studio .NET

There are several things that are newly available as part of the Visual Studio .NET package. Things we only get with the integrated package, and have not had before.

❑   **Reports as Embedded Resources** – Now, by default, when reports are added to a project, they are set to be embedded in the resources of your project .exe or .dll. This allows better encapsulation of reports in your application without the need to manage .rpt files. Of course, reports can still be loaded from external files as well.

❑   **Report Web Services** – in a major expansion of functionality, reports can be exposed as Web Services. This allows users outside of the scope of our system to use not just our data, but our report format as well.

❑   **Documentation** – The amount of documentation provided has been greatly increased.

❑   **Caching API** – Now we can control the way reports are cached on the server side. This API enables cache timeouts, sharing restrictions, and more, to be configured dynamically.

❑   **Unicode Support** – For the first time, reports fully support unicode data types, so reports can be created in a multilingual manner.

Still Third-Party

It's still a third-party application, as it always has been. Don't be surprised when you are asked to register the product the first time you use it. We just added a new Report File to our project, and were surprised to be confronted with the registration screen.

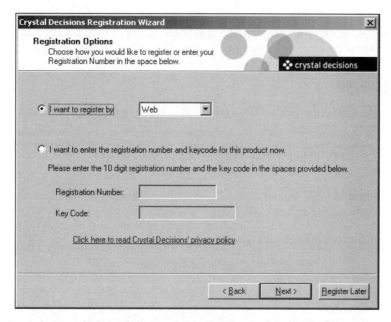

The registration is just to tell Crystal that you are using the product – no payment is required. Also, only 5 concurrent users can view reports on a Web Project, and a purchase of Crystal Enterprise is required beyond that.

Support

Crystal Decisions' support for the product is available from several places. First, its support web site is much improved and can be found at http://support.crystaldecisions.com. There is also the Developer Zone web site at http://www.crystaldecisions.com/products/dev_zone/. The information is very well organized and the site search engine works well.

Creating Reports with Crystal Designer

Let's take some time and go over the various ways to make a report in Crystal Reports for .Net.

Data Connections

The included Crystal Designer works with datasets in the project at hand. In this section, we'll create a simple dataset, and then generate some simple reports that we can use in various ways.

For this little sample:

1. Create a new dataset by right-clicking on the project, and selecting Add I Add New Item I Data Set.

2. Drag the Customers, Products, Orders, and OrderDetails tables from the GlobalMarket database in Server Explorer onto the dataset.

Another simpler way to access the information needed for this chapter is to set up the report to utilize the ODBC connection we set up earlier in the *Introduction* or any other OLE DB connection. Each time we use the connection, the report will ask us for the tables we need as part of the Report Expert.

Report Experts

When we add a new report to a project, we get the Report Expert wizard, allowing us to put together nice, quick reports.

Make a new Windows Form project, right-click on the project file, and select Add | Add New Item ... | Crystal Report.

Selecting this will add a .rpt file to the project. This file will actually be compiled into the project, ending the problems of external, unreferenced files. We can still reference external files, and should if we need to update those files often without a recompile. The next thing we get is the Crystal Reports Gallery dialog that shows the different types of reports available.

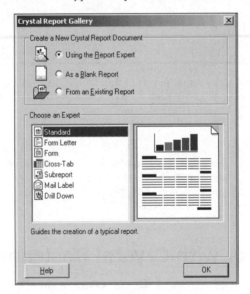

This gives the options to either work from existing or blank files, but we are interested in using an Expert. This is more or less the same as the New Report wizards in the Crystal Reports program proper, starting in Version 4. It is a tab-style wizard, with many of the same steps as the original. Let's walk through a quick example.

1. Select Standard report from the wizard and click OK. The Standard Report Expert will then be displayed.

2. On the Data tab, open the Project Data | ADO.Net DataSets | WindowsApplication1.Dataset1 in the left pane.

3. Double-click on the four tables we added to the dataset or select a table and press Insert Table, to add them to the Tables in report window.

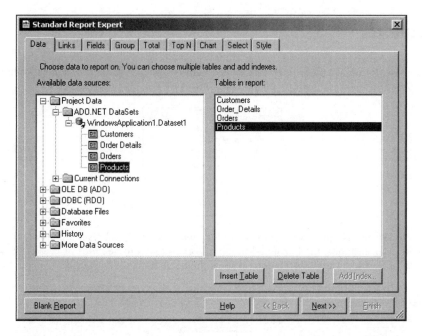

4. Click **Next**. The **Links** tab verifies the data relationships. Note the primary-foreign key relationships that show up in the diagram.

5. Click **Next** to get to the **Fields** tab. Add `Customers.CompanyName`, `Order_Details.UnitPrice`, `Order_Details.Quantity`, `Orders.OrderDate`, and `Products.ProductName`.

6. Click **Next** to get to the **Group** tab and group the data by **CompanyName**.

7. Click **Next** to get to the **Total** tab. Note that Crystal Reports assumes we want to sum the **Quantity** and **UnitPrice** fields.

8. Click **Next** to go to the **Top N** tab. We can summarize customer orders by state, for instance. This doesn't apply to this example, but it's useful!

9. Click **Next** to get the **Chart** tab. Select a pie chart.

10. Click **Next** for the Subset wizard under the **Select** tab. The subset wizard assists us in only seeing data under certain circumstances, like when an order isn't filled, or we want to filter our data. We want to see it all, so we'll skip this.

11. Click **Next** to get to the **Style** tab.

12. Select **Executive, Leading Break**.

13. Click Finish.

Field Explorer

Not much has changed in the field explorer since Version 6. We still have access to the fields in the linked database, formulas and groups. The Field Explorer appears in the tool panels when we open a Crystal report document, or can be opened with *Ctrl + Alt + T*.

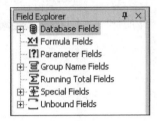

The ability to create custom strings, convenient formulas, and other labels is still available through the field explorer. For instance, the Formula Builder allows us to combine fields or create totals using a broad reach of functional tools and a derivative of the old VBscript 5.0 engine.

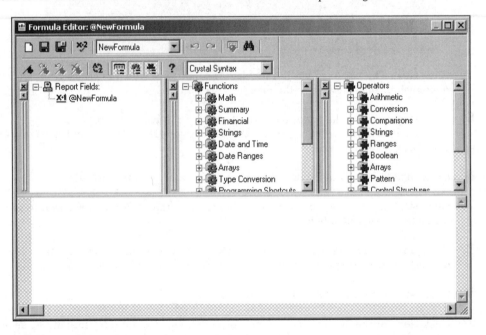

Areas of the Report

The report designer hasn't changed much either. The areas of the report are divided into headers, footers and details, and each can be suppressed or viewed based on the data in the section. Here is the report that is presented by our work in the wizard above:

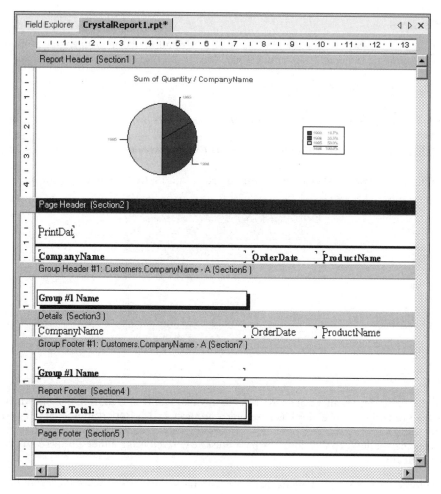

In general, the report headers and footers are the first and last things on the report, and appear only once – even on a multi-page report. The page headers and footers are just as they seem. The group headers and footers wrap around the groups we defined in the wizards – in this example, it's **Customers**. The detail is the data itself.

Integration of Reports

Now that we have a report, what do we do with it? Three main things: we can give access to it as part of a web site, embed it into a Windows Form, or send it out as a Web Service.

Windows Applications

Integrating into a Windows application is interesting, because we actually include the compiled viewer in a Windows Form.

Forms Viewers

In the application we have been playing with, we have a Windows Form just hanging around. If not, or if you're just jumping in here, set up a project like this:

1. Create a new Windows Application.

2. Set up a new dataset as discussed in *Data Connections* previously.

3. Set up a new report as discussed in *Report Experts* previously.

4. Then, drag the CrystalReportViewer control from the toolbox onto the form:

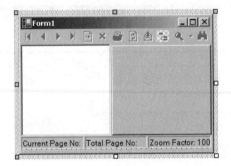

Binding

Once we have the viewer, all we need to do is tell it which report to load from default, which can be done in the Properties panel under Misc., setting a property called ReportSource. Set that value to the report we just made, CrystalReport1.rpt. Interestingly, we can't type in the path, and it must be the full path for the windows application. The path must be entered using either a browse box or programmatically.

Note that there are a number of events that work with the report viewer. Click the Event button in the Properties panel to see them.

These include:

❑ **Drill** – Event fires when a report is drilled down on

❑ **DrillDownSubreport**– Event fires when the user drills down on a subreport

❑ **HandleException**– Event fires when an exception occurs in the Viewer

❑ **Navigate** – Event fires when the user navigates through a report

❑ **ReportRefresh**– Event fires when the data in the report is refreshed

❑ **Search**– Event fires when text is searched for in the report

❑ **ViewZoom**– Event fires when zoom level of the viewer changes

Since the Crystal Reports namespace allows for an unusual amount of control over the substance of reports, the information or formatting of the report can be changed on the events with some ease.

Web Applications

Traditionally, web applications are the most common use of Crystal Reports, because of the useful viewer available for distribution. Not much has changed there. The advent of the .NET Framework has changed the implementation slightly, and that is what we will focus on here.

To get started, make a new web application and copy `CrystalReport1.rpt` and `DataSet1.xsd` into the web project, so that the project looks something like this:

Web Viewers

The ActiveX viewer that we are all used to is still present in the .NET world, but it is now a server control, allowing much easier delivery to the client. Before, we had to write a lot of JavaScript to ensure delivery of the control – now we can just drag it onto the page.

In order to set the report in design time, we must set the **DataBindings** property to the filename of the report, using its **full path**. The browser used by Windows Forms isn't available, and the full path of the file is used. And even then, we have to issue a databind command. Not as easy as we would like, but we can't ask for everything.

Open the `WebForm1.aspx` file and drag the **CrystalReportsViewer** control onto the page.

This server control will provide the viewer most appropriate for the browser requesting the report. IE will get the ActiveX version, and Netscape will get the Java Applet version. To set up a default report at design time, we'll use the **DataBindings** property.

Binding

Setting a default report at runtime requires a custom binding to be set up in the **DataBindings** dialog. Click the control, then the **DataBindings** property box. Push the ellipsis (...) button and the **DataBindings** dialog will appear.

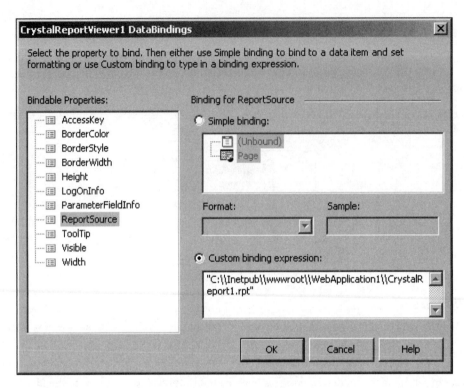

Select **ReportSource** from the **Bindable Properties** list. Click the radio button next to the **Custom Binding Expression** and put the full physical path in the box, surrounding the path with double quotes, if there are spaces, and using double backslashes. The report will appear in the design viewer, with sample data collected at design time.

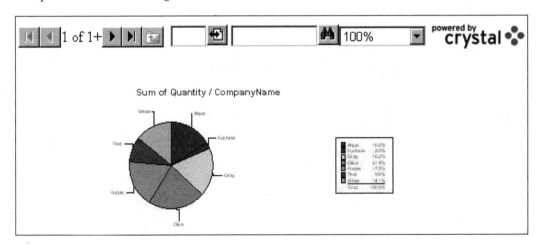

To run the page as part of a web application, add the `DataBind` code to some event handler, like `Page_Load`.

```
private void Page_Load(object sender, System.EventArgs e)
{
  // Put user code to initialize the page here
  CrystalReportViewer1.DataBind();
}
```

Web Services

Web Services are the next big thing, and providing a Crystal XML Web Service interface is a good move on Crystal Decisions' part. Essentially, this allows client applications to view a Crystal Report via a viewer – without the normal difficulty of the file transfer and data validation. Since SOAP uses the HTTP protocol, we don't have the normal security and network constraints.

For example, usually we would save a report as part of a client application (client-server, compiled VB application, for instance) and create a connection to a remote or local database to get the data. Now, that isn't necessary. The report can be remote and a client-server application can still access it by calling the associated Web Service, at which point the report schema and data are downloaded. In .NET, the client application has to have the viewer control installed, but it's still a step in the right direction.

Even in the web examples, the use of a pay-per-view report could make a large difference to some developers. Centrally controlling the source of the report is also a benefit. If working in a distributed environment, this is a major benefit.

Let's first look at how to create a report as a service, then use it as part of a web application and Windows Form.

Creating a Report Web Service

This is a remarkably simple process.

1. Create a new ASP .NET Web Service project.

2. As we did previously, copy the report and dataset from the Windows application at the beginning of the chapter.

3. Right-click on CrystalReport1.rpt and select Publish as a Web Service.

4. The `CrystalReport1Service.asmx` file that is created is the new service.

5. Now build the project.

6. Right-click on the CrystalReports1Service.asmx file and select View In Browser.

7. A very useful set of methods is exposed by the new service.

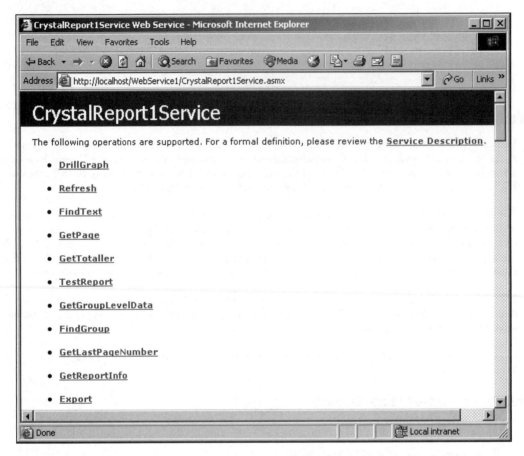

Not only is there a good selection of methods here, but also they are all code editable, since with the Framework, everything is managed. If we don't like the way any of the service works, we just change it. At present not everything is really fully hackable, but it's a good start.

We aren't going to get into the advanced functionality here, because there will be other books that cover things in greater depth. There is one feature we should look at, and this is cache keys. We can easily change the cache key designed by default as part of the service. Crystal has provided a public method for our editing pleasure, and has exposed the code in the `CrystalReport1.cs` or `CrystalReport.vb` file built along with the report file.

```
public virtual String GetCustomizedCacheKey(RequestContext request) {
    String key = null;
    // // The following is the code used to generate the default
    // // cache key for caching report jobs in the ASP.NET Cache.
    // // Feel free to modify this code to suit your needs.
    // // Returning key == null causes the default cache key to
    // // be generated.
    //
    // key = RequestContext.BuildCompleteCacheKey(
```

```
//      request,
//      null,       // sReportFilename
//      this.GetType(),
//      this.ShareDBLogonInfo );
  return key;
}
```

This could allow us to base the data connection on user ID or NTFS permissions, for example.

Consume a Report Web Service

Consuming a report service is, as one would imagine, a combination of consuming a normal service, and viewing a normal report. It is also a fairly simple process.

1. Open the Windows application project we used above, or a new Windows application project.

2. Right-click on the project name and select **Add Web Reference**.

3. Just as if we were adding any other web reference, the UDDI selection dialog appears.

4. Select the **Web References On Local Web Server** link

5. The information from the local server appears.

6. Click on the **WebService1** link, from the application we just created:

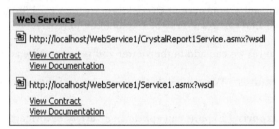

7. Click the **Add Reference** button.

Now we have generated a proxy for the Crystal Report methods we viewed above.

We bind the report via code – there is no interface available, even from the **DataBindings** dialog we worked with above. This is because we are binding to an instance of the report object, of the `CrystalReports` namespace.

It is still fairly simple to add the binding. Since we have added the web reference, we can just change the `ReportSource` of the `CrystalReportViewer1` object, after the `InitilizeComponent` call.

```
public Form1()
{
  //
```

```
    // Required for Windows Form Designer support
    //

    InitializeComponent();

    crystalReportViewer1.ReportSource = new localhost.CrystalReport1Service();

    //
    // TODO: Add any constructor code after InitializeComponent call
    //
}
```

Concluding Integration

There are two take-home lessons here, no matter how we are going to expose the report. First, we need a viewer. There are separate viewer controls for web forms and Windows Forms, but they work in very similar namespaces. Second, we must bind the report to some data source. There are a number of ways to accomplish this. We focused on binding that uses Visual Studio's interface, but there are a number of ways to do it with code as well, as we saw in the *Consume a Report Web Service* section previously.

Run-time Customization

Run-time customization is, generally speaking, writing event handlers at design time that tweak the users' interaction with the Crystal Reports view or report engine. It is a fairly advanced feature of Crystal Reports, and not all of it is part of the Visual Studio development environment. We include it here because it is a significant new feature of Crystal Reports for Visual Studio .Net. It is, however, dependent on the Crystal Enterprise server, which is an extra purchase.

Some of the kinds of features we can add to the viewer and report engine are:

❑ **New viewer features** – We can toggle the appearance of the various toolbars and auxiliary viewers

❑ **Customizing exports** – Exports can appear in a variety of formats

❑ **Data presentation** – Grouping, parameter changes, and sorts are all available

❑ **Errors** – A number of specific errors are thrown by the viewer and engine

We'll cover all of these below.

Customize the Viewer

Display

The presentation of the display can be changed as necessary by changing the parameters of the report viewer. You can change them at design time with the Appearance panel, or at run time with event handlers that change the values. By default, all of the appearance values are set to True.

Appearance	
BackColor	Control
BackgroundImage	(none)
Cursor	Default
DisplayBackgroundEdge	True
DisplayGroupTree	True
DisplayToolbar	True
Font	Microsoft Sans Serif, 8.25pt
ForeColor	ControlText
ShowCloseButton	True
ShowExportButton	True
ShowGotoPageButton	True
ShowGroupTreeButton	True
ShowPageNavigateButtons	True
ShowPrintButton	True
ShowRefreshButton	True
ShowTextSearchButton	True
ShowZoomButton	True

One possible application of this is to allow the user to change the parameters with a checkbox. For instance, we could provide a checkbox that allows the user to remove the toolbar from the report viewer to gain more screen space. If we were to drag a checkbox onto the form containing the viewer, we could add code to the `CheckedChanged` event to remove the toolbar.

```
private void checkBox1_CheckedChanged(object sender, System.EventArgs e)
{
  if (checkBox1.Checked)
  {
    crystalReportViewer1.DisplayToolbar = true;
  }
  else
  {
    crystalReportViewer1.DisplayToolbar = false;
  }
}
```

Mark the checkbox as checked by default in the property panel for the checkbox control, change the text property to "Toolbar" and run the project.

Clicking on the checkbox will then remove the toolbar from the viewing area, dynamically. We could also do things like decide that certain people can't export or print.

Grouping

We have the option to change the grouping options we set up at design time with the `DataDefinition.Groups` collection. This allows us to essentially alter the grouping level with a combo box, similar to above with a checkbox, at run time. The objects used in grouping are part of the `CrystalDecisions.CrystalReports.Engine` namespace; make sure you add the `using` statement to the header of your code. For more information, see the documentation.

Export options

The Export Expert

The export features of Crystal are pretty impressive. By default, the Expert will export to several formats:

- ❑   Excel
- ❑   Word
- ❑   HTML
- ❑   Crystal Report
- ❑   Rich Text
- ❑   Adobe Portable Document Format

Also, we have several options for where to put the file:

- ❑   Disk file
- ❑   Exchange folder
- ❑   Web folder
- ❑   MAPI Mail

Of course, the export function is replaceable by code, and we can create a new handler for the Export event that does exactly what we want. This has a number of options in Windows applications, including creating client document that we can work with in later parts of our program.

Coding Specific Export Handlers

We can create an Export button that will generate an Excel spreadsheet in a file location of our choosing. To create a custom export button:

1. Create a new Windows Form with a report viewer and a bound Crystal Report

2. In the property panel of the viewer, set the **DisplayToolbar** property to `False`

3. Add a button to the `form1` control and change the text to `"Export"`

4. Add the `CrystalDecisions.Shared` namespace and other needed namespaces to the declarations

```
using System;
using System.Drawing;
using System.Collections;
using System.ComponentModel;
using System.Windows.Forms;
using System.Data;
using CrystalDecisions.Shared;
using CrystalDecisions.CrystalReports.Engine;
using CrystalDecisions.ReportSource;
```

5. Add event handler code to the Click event of the button, to set the export options. It will need to set the `DestinationType`, `FormatType`, and `DiskFileName` properties at least, because there are no default options for these properties.

```
private void Export_Click(object sender, System.EventArgs e)
{
  //Set our objects up
  ExportOptions ExportOptions1 = new ExportOptions();
  ExcelFormatOptions ExcelFormatOptions1 = new ExcelFormatOptions ();
  DiskFileDestinationOptions DiskFileDestinationOptions1 = new
DiskFileDestinationOptions();

  //Define the Export Options
  ExportOptions1 = ReportDocument.ExportOptions;

  //Set the excel options
  ExcelFormatOptions1.ExcelUseConstantColumnWidth = true;

  //Set the export options
  ExportOptions1.ExportFormatType = ExportFormatType.Excel;
  ExportOptions1.FormatOptions = ExcelFormatOptions1;
  ExportOptions1.ExportDestinationType = ExportDestinationType.DiskFile;

  //Set the Destination
  DiskFileDestinationOptions1.DiskFileName = @"c:\ExcelOutput.xls";

  //Finalize by setting a file as the target
  ExportOptions1.DestinationOptions = DiskFileDestinationOptions1;
}
```

6. Run the project, and clicking the Export button should create an Excel version of the report on the local C: drive.

Data Options

The Crystal Data Presentation Customization is more or less the ultimate in run-time customization for Crystal Reports. The ability to create a subset report, group and sort it, then do the other functions gives users the ad hoc reporting they are clamoring for.

Along with other run-time customization, this feature doesn't require changes to the reports. We are modifying – in this case – the data stream to the report with the code provided in the `CrystalReports` namespace. Formerly, this kind of customization would require major changes to the stored procedures or the report itself. In this case, practically nothing about the report has to change.

Selection Formulas

We can generate simple filters with user interface elements and pass them through the `ReportViewer` or the `Report` object.

1. Create a form with the viewer object bound to our report that lists all of the customers.

2. Add a textbox and a button to the form:

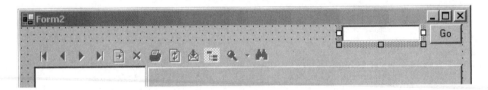

3. Add the needed references to the declaration section of the `.cs` file.

```
using CrystalDecisions.Shared;
using CrystalDecisions.CrystalReports.Engine;
using CrystalDecisions.ReportSource;
```

4. Add a little code to the `Click` method of the button to pass the value of the textbox to the `ReportViewer`.

```
private void button1_Click(object sender, System.EventArgs e)
{
  string selectionFormula;

  //Build the string - the postal code is text!
  selectionFormula = "{Customers.PostalCode} = \"" + textBox1.Text + "\"";

  //Set the SelectionFormula property
  crystalReportViewer1.SelectionFormula = selectionFormula;

  //Refresh the report
  crystalReportViewer1.RefreshReport();
}
```

5. Run the program, and enter a zip code like 87110:

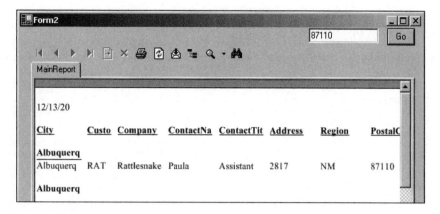

Groups and Sorts

Groups and sorts work essentially the same way as Selection, except they utilize the `DataDefinition` object as do the display customization tools. Similar to above, we have the option to add field names to the `SortFields.Item` collection, or send a field name to the `ConditionField` property for grouping.

Error Handling at Run Time

Crystal Reports provides a couple of slick features for error handling. First, it has its own set of classes for errors. These classes are inherited from the `System.ApplicationException` class, and have all of its features as well as some of their own:

- ❑ `EngineException` – the base exception class
- ❑ `DataSourceException`
- ❑ `ExportException`
- ❑ `FormattingException`
- ❑ `FormulaException`
- ❑ `InternalException`
- ❑ `InvalidArgumentException`
- ❑ `LoadSaveReportException`
- ❑ `LogOnException`
- ❑ `OutOfLicenseException`
- ❑ `ParameterFieldCurrentValueException`
- ❑ `ParameterFieldException`
- ❑ `PrintException`
- ❑ `SubreportException`

All of these are rather self-explanatory, and give a good idea of where the errors occurred. To further ease the error trapping process, the classes have an added property called ErrorId – really a rather common addition – that gives the specific problem. So, on trapping an error, we have the area the problem occurred and the exact nature of the problem. A simple and elegant solution. The values for the ErrorId include:

- DataSourceError
- ExportingFailed
- IndexOutOfBound
- InternalError
- InvalidArgument
- InvalidExportOptions
- InvalidFormula
- InvalidParameterField
- InvalidParameterValue
- InvalidPrintOptions
- LoadingReportFailed
- LogOnFailed
- MissingParameterFieldCurrentValue
- OpenSubreportFailed
- OutOfLicense
- PageFormattingFailed
- PrintingFailed
- SavingReport

To use these, we have to write code that catches errors in the two main objects of the Crystal namespace – the viewer itself, and the current document.

In the Viewer

The viewer provides a HandleException event, since it is a server control. We can add code to that event to deal with the value of the ErrorId in the exception object, and pass errors up to the user in that fashion. Alternatively, we can depend on Crystal to pass the error, but the messages are somewhat cryptic.

For instance, the default login error prompts the user for the name of the database and stuff in its default format. After prompting the user for information they don't know, it says:

We choose this error because it is fairly easy to replicate – just take the network cable out of the back of your PC. Anyway, we would rather have an error message that makes the system administrators happy. So we need to add a `HandleException` event. Add the method `crystalReportViewer1_HandleException` to the Events panel of the viewer.

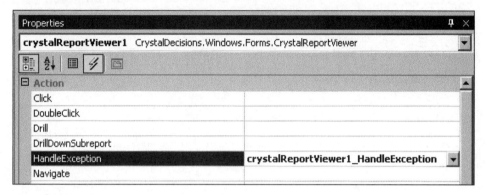

Then add a little code to catch the `LogOnFailed` error.

```csharp
private void crystalReportViewer1_HandleException(object source,
                          CrystalDecisions.Windows.Forms.ExceptionEventArgs e)
{
  if (e.Exception is EngineException)
  {
    EngineException EngineException1 = (EngineException)e.Exception;

    if (EngineException1.ErrorID == EngineExceptionErrorID.LogOnFailed)
    {
      e.Handled = true;
      MessageBox.Show
        ("The database is down for maintenance.\n
          Please try again in 5 minutes.");
    }
  }
}
```

When we try the report again (with the network cable unplugged) we get a much more useful error message:

In the ReportDocument Object

The other possible mechanism for error handling is the report itself. While the `ReportDocument` object does use the same class for errors as the viewer, it isn't a server control so it doesn't have a `HandleError` event.

In order to handle errors in the `ReportDocument`, we'll need to do it the old fashioned way, with a `try ... catch` block. This would be the equivalent of the above error.

```csharp
private void button1_Click(object sender, System.EventArgs e)
{
  try
  {

    EngineException EngineException1 = (EngineException)e.Exception;

    //Bind your report here

  }
  catch (LogOnException EngineException1)
  {
    MessageBox.Show("The database is down for maintenance./n
    Please try again later.");
  }
}
```

Essentially, if we are using the viewer, we should use the viewer object. If we are working with the report object before it gets to the viewer, then we need to use the report error trapping. It's all a matter of if the project is using some kind of structured error handling, and if it is OK that the viewer gets the error.

Summary

This chapter isn't designed to be the ultimate Crystal Reports reference, but it gives the basics, and gets us started. We went over the most important – and the most Visual Studio-oriented – features of the Crystal Reports, including:

- ❑ Creating reports with experts
- ❑ Data connections
- ❑ Field Explorer
- ❑ Integration
- ❑ Run-time customization

11

Debugging

If you develop web and Windows forms applications you have probably said something like this to yourself before: "Why does it have to be so difficult to debug a web application? It's so easy to step through a desktop application; why can't debugging a web application be as simple?" We are delighted to say that now it can be. Visual Studio .NET has made debugging every type of application almost exactly the same, with the IDE providing the same tool for each task. Because of this, we will not look at every common practice in each of them. For this reason we suggest reading this chapter from start to finish. It's not long and can make the difference the next time a deadline is bearing down.

It should be pointed out that this chapter isn't going to look at debugging non-managed C++ applications, ATL Servers, or the interaction between managed and non-managed code while debugging. If you're doing that, chances are you've already used a C++ debugger before (perhaps even Visual Studio 6) and can manage by yourself. With Visual Studio .NET comes the promise of managed code and that's what we're sticking to here. In this chapter then, we'll look at debugging ASP, ASP.NET, Component Classes, Windows Forms, Console Applications, and XML Web Services.

The Basics

Debugging is a very exacting science with the end result being that your applications run almost perfectly and there's not a lot you don't know about exactly how they work. Working systematically through the list of errors and unforeseen behaviors, you and your debugger will encounter many and varied syntax, logical, and system errors before reaching the end.

❑ **Syntax errors** are the easiest spot – a misspelling of a variable name, missing semi-colon, unclosed block of code, and so on. They are literally your mistakes in trying to follow the syntax of the language you're using to write your programs. They're easy to spot because your application won't compile, and if using Visual Studio .NET will be listed for you in the Task List window after compilation has been aborted. If IntelliSense is working, they'll also appear in the Task List window as they are made.

❑ **Logical errors** on the other hand can remain elusive for a good while, showing themselves as flaws in the programming logic – adding when subtraction should occur, division by zero, incorrect output, using an object that doesn't exist, and so on. They might also disguise themselves as something else, for example, a lack of system resources because garbage collection has been waived when it shouldn't be. It is to the trapping of these bugs that the Visual Studio .NET debugger and this chapter are dedicated.

❑ If you're lucky, you'll never see a **system error** – these are caused by a bug in ASP.NET, the Common Language Runtime, or Windows itself. Also lumped into this category are such occurrences as web server failure, hardware failure, or exhausting the server's memory. It's not usually possible to fix these errors without waiting for a service pack to appear from Microsoft. Again, hopefully, you'll never encounter one, but with an estimated 50,000 bugs still in Win2000 and WinXP just released, you probably will.

So how do we go about debugging our application once we've written it and found there are some problems? It's a three step process: **diagnosing an error**, **isolating the cause**, and **creating a solution**.

In Visual Studio .NET, treating syntax errors is almost trivial. Each error is listed and described after an aborted compilation attempt in the Task List window. Double-clicking on an error will take you to the line of code (give or take) where it can be found and its description should tell you exactly what's wrong and thus how to fix it.

Logical errors meanwhile take a little more work. There are the kinds that make themselves known by hanging or crashing your application, then there are those that don't stop an application from working but do make it do something unexpected. It's up to you and your application's testers to note the inconsistency and report it with enough information that you have a place to start tracking it down, it's to this task that the Visual Studio .NET debugger is attuned.

We've a few options to isolate the cause of a logical error:

❑ We can try adding code into our application to follow the path of execution up to the point when an application fails or starts behaving erratically. This method is known as tracing.

❑ We can step through the code a few lines at a time and see whether or not executing those few lines produces the inconsistent behavior we're looking for. The behavior could manifest itself in the value of a variable, call stack, system heap, or memory allocation table, for example, so a lot of the skill here is in knowing what you're looking for in the first place. Visual Studio .NET provides several ways to specify how far to go through the code before it suspends itself and many tool windows to monitor the various possible places the error could show itself in.

Visual Studio .NET also allows you to configure how much debugging information an application contains when it is compiled and built. Of the defaults, debug and release, the latter configuration is set up to optimize the code for release and contains no debug information whatsoever. The former, as you can guess, does, but you can add more by creating your own build configuration as we'll see in the next section.

The tools may be the same for the different types of application we want to debug but we have various strategies for the different application types we can build in Visual Studio .NET.

Some of these are:

❑ A program running outside of Visual Studio .NET in its own process can be 'just-in-time debugged'.

❑ Associated applications operating in different processes can be debugged concurrently by switching between them using the debug location toolbar.

❑ Web applications based on a remote server can be debugged just as if they were located on a local server.

❑ VC++ 6 users should note that unmanaged C++ and mixed-mode (a combination of managed and unmanaged) code can be debugged in Visual Studio .NET just like managed code. Like VC++ 6, you can dump debug information to a file for debugging later on, but unlike VC++ 6 you can now edit your code and then continue to step through it – a feature new to Visual Studio .NET.

In this chapter, we'll first look at the various features of Visual Studio .NET that make debugging easier than using the command line; we will then work through several examples to illustrate how to put them to use. Again, we'll not cover the debugging of unmanaged and mixed mode code.

Helping Visual Studio .NET Help You

The auto-generated code for an application is always perfect until we add some of our own, so it is up to us to help ourselves correct it as we go. Try to make your code clear so that someone else can read it and understand what's going on. Writing neat code, having frequent comments, using `try...catch` blocks, handling exceptions, and following a scheme for naming variables always help, as do a number of your own tricks. We are sure you've picked up many useful things along the way. We're sure you wouldn't want to have to debug six thousand lines of confused code written by someone else.

In this section, we'll look at the areas of Visual Studio .NET that help us diagnose and isolate the cause of a bug.

Debug and Trace

You're probably familiar with the trick of writing messages to the page containing the debug information so you can see what's going on behind the scenes. It's a crude method but effective and .NET has several useful features up its sleeves for those of you who want to write and manipulate code to help debug your applications.

The `System.Diagnostics` namespace in .NET contains two functionally identical classes, `Debug` and `Trace`, which allow you to send debugging information to the **Output** tool window as the application in question executes. The `Debug` and `Trace` classes correspond to the **Conditional Compilation Constants** defined in the build configuration properties box we will see later. If the constant is not defined there or in the code itself, then the calls to the respective class will not be included in the build of the project.

Both classes contain:

❑ `Write` and `WriteLine` functions, which will send the text given it as a parameter to the output window.

❑ `WriteIf` and `WriteLineIf` functions, which do as `Write` and `WriteLine` but only if a given condition is true.

❑   `Indent` and `Unindent` functions to format the output messages so that they are more easily readable.

❑   An `Assert` function with which you can check that a condition is true at a certain point in the application's execution. If it is false, an exception will be raised and the application stopped.

So why have both `Debug` and `Trace`? `Debug` is only meant for development time while `Trace` is meant for development and production. We can recall times when an error in production seems to happen for no rhyme or reason. This would be a case to use `Trace` to write information to logs to analyze what happens. Note that `System.Web` also contains a `Trace` class used specifically for tracing and profiling ASP.NET applications.

Exceptions

Exceptions are a great way for an application to deal internally with errors as they occur but they're not so great when they automatically handle the problems you're trying to fix, especially when automatic handling results in the program being terminated. What we need is a way to specify what happens when a particular type of exception is thrown. Then we can be sure that we have the information we need to find out what's happened to cause it without removing your well designed code or adding in large numbers of `try...catch` blocks.

Fortunately, Visual Studio .NET provides just such a way found under **Debug | Exceptions**. Here you'll find a dialog box that allows you to search through the various exceptions that can be thrown and the action taken when they are thrown.

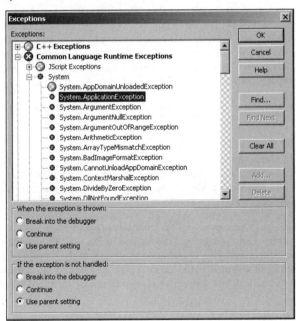

You can choose to have the application continue executing or stop and open the debugger at that point. Each exception inherits its exception class's parent setting by default unless you need to specifically override it. Note that this dialog won't initially know about your own custom exceptions to begin with, but they can be added manually as required. Just select the top-level node in the dialog you want to include your class under, click on the **Add...** button and type in the name of your new exception.

Build Configurations

Visual Studio .NET has the ability to create and store different build configurations for your application – a very handy feature. When you are debugging you want a different application behavior from when preparing your application to be shipped. In debugging mode, the application needs to be verbose and easily navigable so we can track down the bugs in the code. In production, we want our applications to be as small as possible and as fast as possible for the end user. Code is optimized, with debug symbols and code not included in the executable.

When you create a project, Visual Studio .NET automatically sets up two build configurations for it:

❑ **Debug** – Debug symbols will be generated and no code optimization will be performed

❑ **Release** – No debug symbols are generated and code optimization is used

As the names imply, these are generic configurations for creating builds for debugging and for release candidate software. If need be, you can create your own configuration for the project you're working on or simply alter some of the settings in those that already exist.

To alter the configuration options:

1. Right-click the project in the Solution Explorer and choose Properties.

2. In the left pane of the Property Pages displayed, select Configuration Properties.

The Property Pages will look like the following.

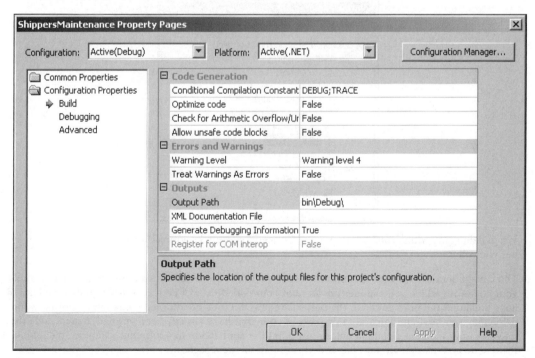

At the top of the Property Pages dialog are two drop-down boxes. The value in the **Configuration** box determines the configuration options that are currently displayed. **Platform**, is the platform the application targets. The **Configuration** in the previous screenshot shows **Active(Debug)**. This shows the configuration currently in use. The dropdown will contain the configurations created for the current project. An **All Configurations** option is also provided to allow for easy alteration of all configurations at once. For our use we will use **Debug**.

In the left pane underneath **Configuration Properties** are three property pages: **Build**, **Debugging**, and **Advanced**. Any alterations to the properties within these apply to the configuration currently selected. For debugging we will focus on **Build** and **Debugging**. Both of these pages are broken down into three sections:

❑   The **Build** page has **Code Generation**, **Errors and Warnings**, and **Outputs** sub-sections

❑   The **Debugging** page has **Debuggers**, **Start Action**, and **Start Options** sub-sections

Of particular interest in the **Build** page are the **Conditional Compilation Constants** and **Generate Debugging Information** properties, which directly influence how much debugging information is contained in the build of our project. Setting the latter option to `True` creates a set of debugging symbols into the build that map the intermediate language (IL) for the application to the source code.

By default, these debugging symbols are stored in a Program Database under the `bin` directory in a file called `projname.pdb` where `projname` is of course replaced with the name of your project. Looking in Solution Explorer, you'll find this directory by clicking the **Show All Files** button. The `bin` folder appears semi-transparent, as do the icons for the files within it, because they are not part of the project. They are part of the project in that Visual Studio .NET knows that they are associated with the project but they are not listed in the project file.

When debugging with Visual Studio you won't need to access Program Database (PDB) files directly, but you will use them.

The **Conditional Compilation Constants** property allows you to define custom preprocessor symbols in your code with which you can identify areas of your code (just as `#region` does) to the compiler and have them ignored or included in the build as required. Using conditional compilation constants for debugging can be useful for excluding parts of code that have already been verified, bypass code that may not work while in development, or just point the application to a different database. We'll look at the two defined by default – `DEBUG` and `TRACE` – in the next section.

The options on the Debugging page are somewhat more self-explanatory:

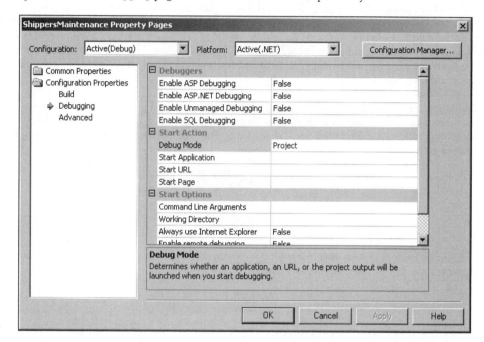

The **Debuggers** section allows you to enable specific debugging modes for ASP, ASP.NET, unmanaged, and SQL code, while the **Start Action** section lets you determine what is launched when debugging begins. Finally, the **Start Options** section lets you set a few options for command-line applications, and most importantly, lets you enable remote debugging if you need it.

In general, you shouldn't need to fuss around with configurations too much. You might want to set up two builds for enterprise and professional-level versions of the same application but that's more of a deployment issue as seen in Chapter 9. However, you will need to be able to select the appropriate configuration depending on why you are building your project, and it is useful to know what the effects of the different configurations are.

Navigating Code

With your project given the correct build configuration, it's time build the executable and see how much you got wrong. By now you've probably figured out how to run code using *F5*. This is fine for those of us who write perfect code. In fact, these people can start their code with *Ctrl+F5* to disable debugging. For the rest of us, the ability to execute in a very controlled manner is very important and there are a couple of concepts we need to be aware of as we do this in Visual Studio .NET.

The first is break mode – the state in which the execution of an application has been paused. You can put an application in break mode programmatically with the `Stop()` function, or by defining a point in the code at which to pause. It won't matter whether the code running at the time is your own or some Windows routine your application makes use of – it will stop. The only difference to you is that the debugger will display a message saying that 'no source code is available' if the application is in the middle of a system routine when it is paused.

The second is the concept of 'stepping through your code'. If you recall in Chapter 3 we discovered how a Windows form worked by stepping through the auto-generated code a line at a time to see the order in which code was executed and what happened. What we were actually saying to Visual Studio was 'execute the next line of code and then go into break mode'. Actually, we have a bit more flexibility in this and are not limited to stepping through the code a line at a time. We can choose to execute a function without jumping into its code, and create **breakpoints** in the code marking places where the application should pause.

Visual Studio .NET's debug toolbar is our pilot through the debugging process and is displayed by default when execution is started without disabling debugging. If you start execution with *Ctrl+F5* the Debug toolbar will not be displayed because Visual Studio will not be attached to the running code. There are ten items here and they're all important.

Start (*F5*) – Start is used for starting or running an application. Execution will continue until a breakpoint is reached or the program terminates.

Break All (*Ctrl+Alt+Break*) – Pauses the execution of the currently running code by placing it into break mode. Although it is possible to pause code like this for debugging, we do not suggest it. Setting breakpoints or using Run to Cursor is much cleaner. We usually find this useful when we put the processor into an endless loop, but suggest using the keyboard shortcut gives a slightly cleaner break in this case.

Stop Debugging (*Shift+F5*) – Ends debugging immediately. In many situations this will also halt execution of the program being debugged.

Restart (*Ctrl+Shift+F5*) – Stops the execution of the current debugging session and restarts it. We find that we use this when we have changed code in the source window while the program is executing. The same effect as using restart can be achieved by clicking Stop Debugging followed by Start.

Show Next Statement (*Alt+Num **) – If the next line to be executed is not shown, it will be will brought within view. We find this to be useful when we go digging through dozens of windows to find something and can't find our way back to continue the execution.

Step Into *(F11)* – Executes a single line of code (.NET or assembly) then enters break mode. If the line of code is a user-defined function call, it will enter the function call.

Step Over *(F10)* – Executes a single line of code then enters break mode. If the line of code is a function call it will be treated as a single line to execute. The entire function will execute (unless it contains a breakpoint) then the program will enter break mode immediately afterwards. We find this to be helpful when we are debugging code that has a lot of function calls not all of which are suspected to be the cause of the problem we are working on.

Step Out *(Shift+F11)* – Executes all lines of code remaining in the current function, it then enters break mode when at the first line of the calling function. If a breakpoint is encountered, execution will be paused as normal.

Hex – Set Visual Studio to display integers in Hex. This can be seen in the IDE windows such as Command and Immediate.

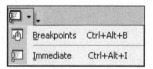

The last button, as shown expanded above, while not debugging, brings up a list of debug tool windows to pull into view. It's in these windows (covered in the next section) that the internals of our application will be displayed freeze-framed at the point where it entered break mode. When debugging, the list will be larger. The list is duplicated in the **Debug | Windows** menu.

An option not included in the toolbar that helps with debugging is the Run To Cursor option. Run To Cursor will cause the program to execute until it gets to the current line the cursor was on. When the specified point is reached, the program will enter break mode. If the line is never reached the execution will not stop. To use Run To Cursor, right-click the line to pause at and select **Run To Cursor** from the context menu. It is like setting a breakpoint, pressing Start, and then removing the breakpoint when/if the line is reached. Run To Cursor will not break more than once or place any visual marker.

Visual Studio .NET also gives you the ability to edit a program's code while it is running thanks to the versatility of the CLR. All you do is edit the code while the application is in break mode and then 'un-break' it. This feature is known as 'Edit and Continue' and is enabled by default.

Breakpoints

As we know, breakpoints are user-defined pauses in the execution of code. Visual Studio will enter Break Mode when a breakpoint is reached either on all instances or based on a certain set of criteria that are set with a given breakpoint. Visual Studio has four types of breakpoints:

- ❑ **Function** – Pauses execution when a specific location in a function is reached. This is the most common type of breakpoint.

- ❑ **File** – Pauses execution when a location in a file is reached.

- ❑ **Address** – Pauses execution when a specified memory address is reached.

- ❑ **Data** – Pauses execution when the value of a variable changes. This breakpoint type is only available in C++, native code.

Visual Studio will not allow you to enter invalid breakpoints such as Data breakpoints in C#.

There are a few ways to create breakpoints. The easiest is to click the gray margin to the left of the line of code you wish to pause at. Breakpoints cannot be set on any line without code to execute.

```
private void BindRegions()
{
    dalRegions RegionsComponent = new dalRegions();
    DataGrid1.DataSource = RegionsComponent.GetAllRegions();
    Page.DataBind();
}
```

A red dot, referred to as a glyph by the documentation, is placed in the margin area for the line of code. A breakpoint can also be added by placing the cursor at the line of code and clicking *F9*. You can remove the breakpoints in the same fashion. To have more control when adding a breakpoint launch the New Breakpoint dialog by choosing **New Breakpoint** from the **Debug** menu or pressing *Ctrl+B*.

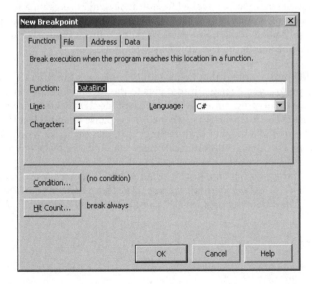

As you can see, tabs are provided for creating breakpoints of the four types. The DataBind value was placed into the Function textbox because when we launched the dialog our cursor was placed on this word in our code. Visual Studio will try to interpret the values of a breakpoint you might be adding to save you some trouble. Next, switch to the File tab. Notice how the File, Line, and Character values are filled in from the current position of the cursor.

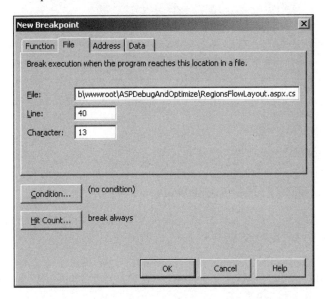

Below the tabs are two buttons. The first is Condition. Clicking Condition will display another dialog allowing you to specify an expression to be evaluated when the breakpoint is reached.

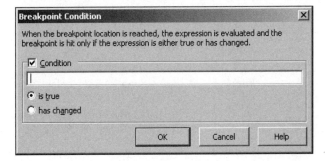

This can be very useful for narrowing problems to specific cases. When you enter a condition it will be displayed next to the Condition button on the New Breakpoint dialog.

The other button, Hit Count, allows the definition of when a breakpoint should halt based on the number of times the breakpoint has be reached. This button displays the Breakpoint Hit Count dialog.

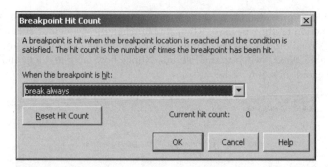

The dropdown allows us to define when the hit count will pause execution. The options are:

❑   Break always (default)

❑   Break when the hit count is equal to

❑   Break when the hit count is a multiple of

❑   Break when the hit count is greater than or equal to

When any choice other than the break always option is selected, a textbox will be displayed allowing us to enter a hit count to evaluate for the rule.

Our breakpoint will not require a condition or hit count. These options are often useful when dealing with looping constructs. After clicking OK on the New Breakpoint dialog the breakpoint is added.

As we mentioned earlier when you add a breakpoint to a line, a red dot, know as a glyph, is placed in the gray part of the left margin. If you have played with breakpoints already, you may have noticed that not all of them are solid red. The following are a list of glyphs you may encounter and the breakpoint state they represent.

Icon	Type of icon	Description
●	Enabled	Since Enabled is the default type you will see it most often.
○	Disabled	Visual Studio allows you to disable breakpoints without removing them.
❓	Warning	You can get a warning glyph when setting breakpoints for code without setting up debugging. If you haven't enabled ASP debugging then any breakpoints within ASP will show up as Warning when the project is run.
◉	Mapped	Mapped breakpoints occur when a breakpoint is placed in client-side script while in the ASP source.
❶	Error	As it should be, getting a breakpoint into an error state is difficult. The breakpoint can be in an error state if you give an invalid condition for the breakpoint. For example, a > 0, but a isn't accessible in that code block.

Because breakpoints are so extensive Visual Studio has provided them their own window. The Breakpoints window lists all of the breakpoints set within the solution.

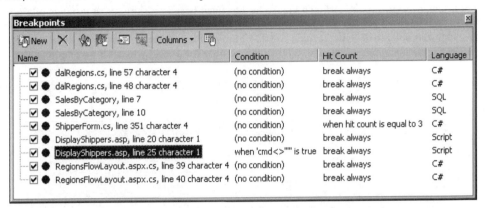

Name	Condition	Hit Count	Language
☑ ● dalRegions.cs, line 57 character 4	(no condition)	break always	C#
☑ ● dalRegions.cs, line 48 character 4	(no condition)	break always	C#
☑ ● SalesByCategory, line 7	(no condition)	break always	SQL
☑ ● SalesByCategory, line 10	(no condition)	break always	SQL
☑ ● ShipperForm.cs, line 351 character 4	(no condition)	when hit count is equal to 3	C#
☑ ● DisplayShippers.asp, line 20 character 1	(no condition)	break always	Script
☑ ● DisplayShippers.asp, line 25 character 1	when 'cmd<>"" is true	break always	Script
☑ ● RegionsFlowLayout.aspx.cs, line 39 character 4	(no condition)	break always	C#
☑ ● RegionsFlowLayout.aspx.cs, line 40 character 4	(no condition)	break always	C#

To the left of each breakpoint is a checkbox indicating if the breakpoint is enabled. The small toolbar at the top provides quick access to some options for altering breakpoints and the display of the list within the window.

Working across Processes

If you've a set of projects that should be working together as a solution but in fact aren't, it's also possible to debug across projects (executables) working in separate processes in Visual Studio .NET. For example, we can start a Web Service from the IDE without debugging (Debug | Start without Debugging). The Web Service then starts in IE, and we can attach the debugger to the process "aspnet_wp.exe".

Under .NET, each application runs in its own process, so Visual Studio .NET regards debugging multiple applications simultaneously as swapping between processes as and when we need. We've seen that each solution defines one project as the startup project when it is asked to run. You can also define multiple startup projects by right-clicking on the solution icon in Solution Explorer and hitting Set Startup Projects... This will bring up a new dialog from which you can choose which projects to start and which not.

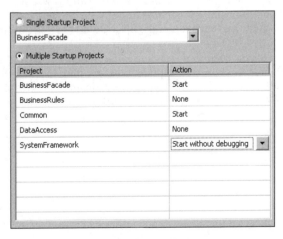

The three choices you have from this dialog are None, Start, and Start without debugging.

Up until now, everything we've shown you so far has been based on running an instance of a project within Visual Studio .NET for debugging purposes. However, it is also possible to debug a process that has been started outside of Visual Studio .NET. This could be anything or anywhere – an application on a remote machine, a windows service, a DLL, and so on – but the way to set it up remains the same.

1. In Visual Studio .NET go to Debug | Processes.... A new dialog appears displaying the processes currently running on your local machine.

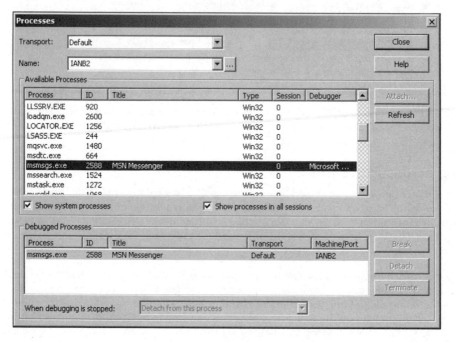

2. If you're looking to debug a remote process, you can browse for the machine using the Name box. Choose your target machine and if your process can't be contacted using DCOM, then switch the Transport entry from Default to TCP/IP (Native Only).

3. Select the process you want to debug and click Attach... This will bring up another dialog to tell the debugger what kind of application is running in this process. Note that unmanaged code is referred to here as native code and that ASP.NET processes should be referred to as Common Language Runtime and Script.

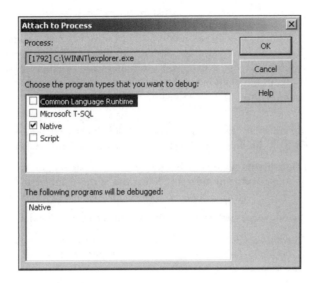

4. Press OK when you're done and the process will appear in the Debugged Processes list at the bottom of the dialog box.

5. With the debugged process selected in the lower listbox you can also tell it what to do when debugging has finished, by choosing an action from the drop-down listbox 'When debugging is stopped'.

6. To stop debugging the process, select it and choose Detach. The process will continue to run, but Visual Studio .NET will no longer take an interest in it. Alternatively, you can pres Terminate, which will stop the process executing altogether. Do be sure you won't crash any other running processes if you choose this option.

So now we've got all the projects and processes running together, we need to see how they interact. The Debug Location toolbar lets us change the current debug view between the various processes running as well as letting us see what's going inside the various threads and stacks that our processes are running on or with. This will appear automatically if you start to debug multiple processes inside Visual Studio .NET or by choosing View | Toolbars | Debug Location.

Inspecting Code with the Debug Windows

The cause of logical errors can be hard to find. The knowledge that something isn't going to plan doesn't help when it comes down to diagnosing and isolating a bug. We've seen how to walk through the code, a line at a time if necessary, and it's in the debug windows that you can monitor what exactly each line of code is doing to the variables and system resources it touches.

There are twelve debug windows including the Breakpoints window we've already seen:

❑ The Locals, Watch, and Autos windows each display the values of variables in use at the point the application entered break mode, with these values being editable. The Locals window will display all local variables. Autos will display the variables from the current and previous lines of code. If you're using C# the Autos window will display variables for the current statement and three ahead of it and three before it. Lastly, the Watch Window displays only what we add to it, but we can put a watch on expressions (for example, db.connection) and registers here.

❑ The This window displays the class members of the object attached to the method currently running. Again, you can alter the object's property values from this window as well.

❑ The Running Documents window is handy when you're debugging script or ASP pages as it proffers a list of the documents currently being run at the point Visual Studio .NET entered break mode.

❑ The Modules window is a list display of the modules currently loaded.

❑ The Call Stack window allows you to dig through the calls currently being made by the application on the stack. The list is in reverse order with the first call shown at the bottom of the stack and the most recent at the top.

❑ The Threads and Memory windows shouldn't need to be used when debugging managed code, because .NET looks after the handling of threads and memory itself. However, if you do want to make a note of the threads being used or the values in certain memory locations while debugging, you can use these windows.

❑ The Disassembly and Registers windows let you view an application at its lowest level – assembler. The disassembler in particular may appear when your project calls into a process for which debugging symbols aren't available.

We won't make use of all of them in the examples to follow but those that we do use are indicative of the others.

Getting Down to It

We could spend a whole book talking about the various strategies to which you can put the tools in Visual Studio .NET. By the nature of this book then, we're going to work through some small examples that we've prepared and included in the download for this book.

Console Application Debugging

Our first trial by bugs is a console application – one that is run inside a console window from a command prompt. Although not many console applications are complex, they can require debugging. Our sample application is not very adventurous. It consists of a single C# file, debugging.cs, which in turn holds only one function, Main(), retrieving all of the objects in a SQL Server database by executing the sp_help command and writing out the response.

```
static void Main(string[] args)
{
  Console.WriteLine("Welcome to Visual Studio .NET brought to be by Wrox");
  Console.WriteLine("Here is the list of objects in the Global Market DB");
```

```
OleDbConnection cnnConnection = new OleDbConnection
("Provider=SQLOLEDB.1;Integrated Security=SSPI;" +
  "Persist Security Info=False;Initial Catalog=GlobalMarket;" +
  "Data Source=[DBName];Use Procedure for Prepare=1;" +
  "Auto Translate=True;Packet Size=4096;Workstation ID=[MachineName];" +
  "Use Encryption for Data=False;" +
  "Tag with column collation when possible=False");
cnnConnection.Open();

Debug.WriteLine("Connection Opened");
OleDbCommand cmdSPHelp = new OleDbCommand("sp_help", cnnConnection);

OleDbDataReader drDataReader;
drDataReader = cmdSPHelp.ExecuteReader(CommandBehavior.CloseConnection);

while(drDataReader.Read())
{
  Trace.WriteLine(drDataReader.GetString(0));
  Console.WriteLine(drDataReader.GetString(0));
}

Debug.WriteLine("Loop Complete");
drDataReader.Close();
cnnConnection.Close();

Console.WriteLine("");
Console.WriteLine("Press Enter to close.");
Console.Read();
}
```

Trace and Debug

Let's start by working with `Trace` and `Debug` to see how they will write information to the Output window. As you may have noticed, there are two `Debug.WriteLine` and one `Trace.WriteLine` commands in our code. As mentioned previously, these commands will only display to the Output Window when the `TRACE` and `DEBUG` constants are assigned in the Conditional Compilation Arguments. Since we are working under the Debug configuration they are added by default. Start the program; *F5*. A console window will display, write out the object names, and then wait for the user to press *Enter* to close. Before pressing *Enter*, switch back to Visual Studio and open the Output Window. It will look something like the following:

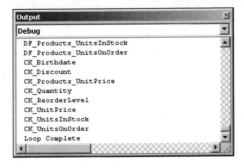

As mentioned in the Trace and Debug discussion earlier, Debug is meant for use in development while Trace is meant for development and production. If we remove TRACE from the Conditional Compilation Constants the output will look like this:

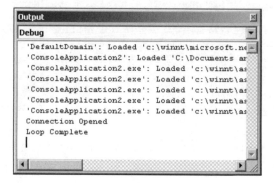

Note that the first seven lines in the output in this screenshot are generated by Visual Studio .NET to let you know how it is dealing with your application.

Locals, Watch, and Autos

As we learned earlier, the Locals, Watch, and Autos windows let you inspect and alter the current values of variables and expressions in use by your application when it enters break mode. In particular, the Watch window displays only what we add to it. In the case of the above code we may want to add a watch to the cnnConnection.State.

To add a watch to cnnConnection.State:

1. Enter break mode if you're not already there.

2. Select the first blank line in a Watch window.

3. Type cnnConnection.State and press *Enter*.

The new watch will look like this:

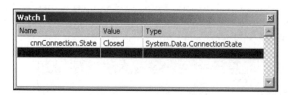

Watches can also be added using the context menu:

1. Enter break mode.

2. Right-click the code to add a watch for that point.

3. Choose Add Watch from the context menu.

The following is a screenshot of a watch added for drDataReader. The first level properties have been expanded for display.

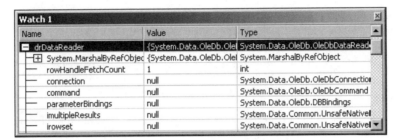

Here is a shot of the Locals window at the same point. Because Locals displays all variables within the current scope, drDataReader is in the list.

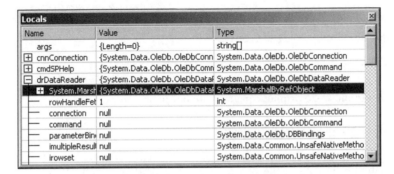

The true purpose of windows like this is to track values we have found ourselves, using it to find properties we were looking for. The documentation for the .NET Framework is good, but sometimes we just can't find the property we are looking for. So, we find ourselves expanding the tree view in either the Locals or Watch window and digging for it. Not the usual way to find a property, but very useful at times.

ASP and ASP.NET

How many of you reading this have ever tried to debug an ASP application on a remote server using Visual InterDev 6.0? For those of you without InterDev, there was the script debugger – again not that effective – and even just the simple echoing of values to the screen with Response.write. It worked, but it wasn't very efficient.

Fortunately, Visual Studio .NET takes debugging to the next level by making debugging server-side code like debugging a desktop application. Set your breakpoints, run the application, evaluate the program as it goes. It works equally well with both ASP and ASP.NET pages inside the same project, as our example will demonstrate. The pages you'll find in the download for this Chapter simply try to reference the GlobalMarket database we've used before and retrieve some information out of it.

Server-side debugging is not without a little bit of set-up work first, however. To use ASP and ASP.NET debugging we need to enable them in property pages for our `ASPDebugAndOptimize` project.

1. Create a virtual directory in IIS called `ASPDebugAndOptimize` that points at the directory containing the `ASPDebugAndOptimize` project files.

2. Open the project up in Visual Studio .NET.

3. Right-click the project in the Solution Explorer and choose **Properties**.

4. In the left pane of the property pages displayed, select **Configuration Properties | Debugging**.

5. Set **Enable ASP Debugging** and **Enable ASP.NET Debugging** to `True`.

6. Set **Start URL** to the location of the web such as **http://localhost/ASPDebugAndOptimize/**.

7. Set the **Start Page** to `DisplayShippers.asp`.

We also need to have Visual Studio create debugging symbols.

8. Change to the **Build** property page in the left pane.

9. Set **Generate Debugging Information** to `True`.

The `web.config` file for our ASP debugging project must have the attribute `debug="true"` (default) for the compilation section. Since the `web.config` file is XML, remember to watch case sensitivity. For this example the compilation section looks like this.

```
<compilation
  defaultLanguage="c#"
  debug="true"/>
```

If the web page you are working with does not specify the debug attribute but a parent web page does, the value from the parent web page will be inherited.

By setting up the `web.config` file for debugging we have configured the web application to emit debugging symbols. ASP.NET gives us further control over the creation of debug symbols. Each page, **DOCUMENT** in the **Properties** window, has a debug property that decides if the page will be compiled with debug symbols. Since this value can inherit from the `web.config`, it's not necessary to set this value to `True` when working with a project in Visual Studio .NET.

If we forget to set `debug="true"` in the `web.config` file, but do enable the properties in the property pages mentioned above, when we run our application Visual Studio .NET will display the following message:

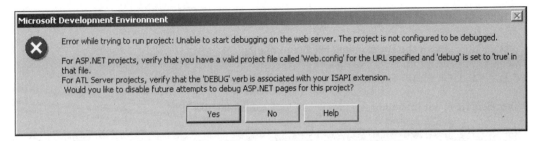

Notice how the message tells you how to fix it for this type of project.

With the environment set up, now we can see it in action. First we will look at DisplayShippers.asp, a list of the Shippers from the GlobalMarket database. Open the DisplayShippers.asp file in Visual Studio to view the code. Click in the gray area in the left margin to add breakpoints to the following lines of code:

- ❏   cmd.CommandType = 1
- ❏   <td><%=rs.Fields("ShipperID").Value%></td>

This should produce the following within the IDE:

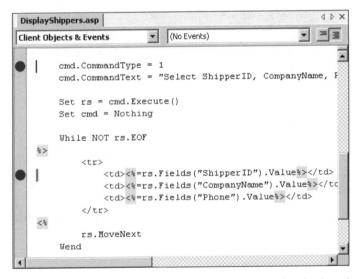

Edit the properties of the second breakpoint and set the Hit Count to break when the hit count is greater than or equal to 3.

1. Right-click the breakpoint in the Breakpoints window and choose Properties.

2. In the Breakpoints Properties window click the Hit Count button.

3. In the Breakpoint Hit Count dialog set the dropdown to "when hit count is greater than or equal to."

4. Set the next number in the textbox at the right to 3.

5. Click OK on the Breakpoints Hit Count dialog.

6. Click OK on the Breakpoints Properties dialog.

When complete, our breakpoints window will look something like this:

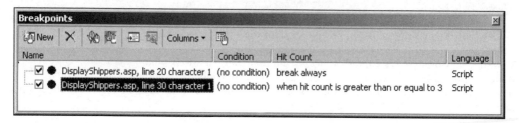

Start the project, by pressing *F5*, and wait for the browser to launch and Visual Studio to stop at the first breakpoint. We have noticed that you may be prompted to enter a user name and password with rights to debug ASP pages on the web server. This will occur before the browser is launched. When prompted, the dialog will look like this:

We have also noticed that we are prompted by this dialog even when the ID we have logged into Windows with has sufficient rights to start ASP debugging.

When Visual Studio .NET encounters the first breakpoint it enters break mode, which looks like the following.

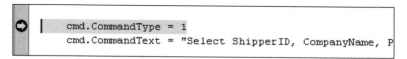

The yellow arrowhead overlaying the breakpoint symbol is referred to as the execution point marker. This marker indicates the next line of code to be executed. The line of code to be executed will have a yellow background. This yellow marker can be dragged forward or backward within the current scope to change the next line of execution. This can be very useful when you find a piece of code you wish to avoid or want to rerun a section.

Press Step Into, or use *F11*. This executes the current code line by line.

Press Start, *F5*, to run the program to the next breakpoint.

```
       While NOT rs.EOF
%>
           <tr>
               <td><%=rs.Fields("ShipperID").Value%></td>
               <td><%=rs.Fields("CompanyName").Value%></td>
               <td><%=rs.Fields("Phone").Value%></td>
           </tr>
<%
           rs.MoveNext
       Wend
```

The second breakpoint is configured to stop only when it has been reached three or more times. Since our program stopped, the breakpoint must have reached a hit count of three. The breakpoints window shows us this in the **Hit Count** column in parenthesis. We can also see that the **Hit Count** is at one for the first breakpoint.

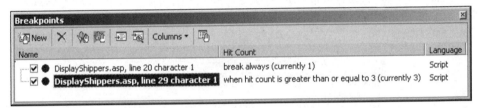

Press **Start** again and the page will finish, assuming you have only three records returned by the query.

Refresh the web page to send another request for it. Notice the **Hit Count** values in the **Breakpoints** window. The values are not reset between requests. Visual Studio will now stop each time the second breakpoint is reached because the Hit Count for it has already been reached.

To stop debugging click Stop Debugger, *Shift+F5*, or close the browser launched by debugging.

In the next example we will set breakpoints in our ASP.NET page, `RegionsList.aspx` and the component class, `dalRegions.cs`, it calls. The steps taken previously to enable debugging are almost all we need for the environment.

1. Right-click the `RegionsList.aspx` page in the Solution Explorer.

2. From the context menu select **Set As Start Page**.

3. Set breakpoints in `RegionsList.aspx` and `dalRegions.cs`.

4. Open the code for `RegionsList.aspx`.

5. Set a breakpoint at the following line of code in the `BindRegions` method:

```
DataGrid1.DataSource = RegionsComponent.GetAllRegions();
```

6. Open the code for `dalRegions.cs`.

7. Set a breakpoint at the following line of code in the GetAllRegions method.

```
drDataReader = cmdCommand.ExecuteReader(CommandBehavior.CloseConnection);
```

Start the program, *F5*, and wait for Visual Studio to stop at the first breakpoint.

```
    private void BindRegions()
    {
        dalRegions RegionsComponent = new dalRegions();
        DataGrid1.DataSource = RegionsComponent.GetAllRegions();
        DataGrid1.DataBind();
    }
```

This line makes the call to the component. Press Step Into, *F11*, to step into the call to the method. The program will enter break mode at the first executable line within the method.

```
    public OleDbDataReader GetAllRegions()
    {
        string strSQLTemp = "GetAllRegions";
        OleDbConnection cnnConnection = new OleDbConnection("Provider=SQLOLEDB.1;I
        OleDbCommand cmdCommand = new OleDbCommand(strSQLTemp, cnnConnection);
        cnnConnection.Open();
        cmdCommand.CommandType = CommandType.StoredProcedure;

        OleDbDataReader drDataReader;
        drDataReader = cmdCommand.ExecuteReader(CommandBehavior.CloseConnection);

        return drDataReader;
    }
```

The integration of stepping between the layers is seamless. Press Step Out, *Shift+F11*, to run from the current position to the next execution in the calling procedure. In this case it will be the same line we entered from because of the assignment of the `DataReader` to the `DataSource` property of the `DataGrid`. Finish execution of the page by pressing Start once more.

Here are a few things that you should know about ASP and ASP.NET debugging. When you set breakpoints they apply to all requests for the page, not just the requests made by the launched browser or even just your PC. If a request is being debugged and another page is requested that also has debugging enabled, the second request will be forced to wait for the first to complete. To recreate this, follow these steps using the previous example.

1. Enable ASP and ASP.NET debugging.

2. Start the project and wait for it to stop at a breakpoint in `RegionsList.aspx`.

3. Using another browser request the `DisplayShippers.asp` page.

4. Notice that before the second request can be processed the first must complete.

5. Stop debugging.

6. Disable ASP debugging.

7. Start the project and wait for it to stop at a breakpoint in `RegionsList.aspx`.

8. With the second browser request the `DisplayShippers.asp` again.

9. Notice how this time the request for `DisplayShippers.asp` is not held up by the first page being debugged. If debugging is set to true for a page and the page is requested two times, the same would be the case. It would wait for debugging to finish in the first page and then display the next page.

We don't need to set the Start Page to the page we plan to debug, but it makes it easier. If you are working on a site that requires you to login, you may find it easier to either set the start page to the login or use another window and start debugging only when needed.

Debugging is hard on the server. It can take a lot of resources to perform debugging so use it wisely and don't attempt to measure performance when the project has been built for debugging.

Debugging in ASP and ASP.NET is like any other managed code. The use of the debugging tool windows such as Watch and Output is enabled as is the use of Trace and Debug, although watch out for using trace. The `System.Web` class library also has a trace class with a server-side-specific set of methods, which is more useful than the one in `System.Diagnostics`.

Microsoft has been moving towards a model of developing on your local computer and then committing the changes back to the main project. You will see more about this when we talk about pending check-ins in the *Visual SourceSafe* chapter (Chapter 13). This model makes debugging ASP and ASP.NET more practical because you will not be interfering with other developers. It also doesn't require a large number of people to have rights to debug on the server, just on their local computer.

Component Class Debugging

Components – for example, `dalRegions.cs` in the previous example – can be debugged like any other managed code using the Visual Studio .NET debugger and its utilities as for anything else. But what if you want to invoke the component class in a different way – perhaps via a DLL in an enterprise application rather than an ASP.NET page? If you develop in a tier-segmented environment you may only be involved with writing a component and testing it. The following example shows how to set up the configuration for this scenario. Here, we will reuse the object `dalRegions`, in its own project called `ComponentClassDebugging`.

❑ Close any solution in Visual Studio .NET and open the project `ComponentClassDebugging`.

To test it, we'll need to create a client project to make use of it. Here we will use a Windows Forms client.

❑ Add a new C# Windows Application folder to the solution. Call it ComponentClassDebuggingClient.

The project will be added and the Solution Explorer will look like this:

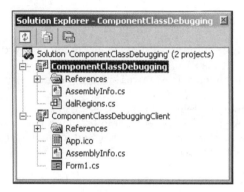

The next step is to create a button linked to a small amount of code to call the GetAllRegions method of dalRegions. Right-click the ComponentClassDebuggingClient project and choose Project Dependencies. Check the box next to ComponentClassDebugging in the listbox. It will look like the following when complete.

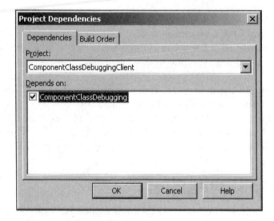

To add the reference to the ComponentClassDebuggingClient project:

1. Right-click the ComponentClassDebuggingClient project and choose Add Reference. The Add Reference dialog will be displayed.

2. Select the Projects tab.

3. Choose ComponentClassDebugging from the list and click Select. ComponentClassDebugging will now show in the Selected Components list at the bottom.

4. Click OK to add the reference.

5. Drag a button from the Toolbox onto the form Form1.cs.

6. Add the following lines of code to import the `ComponentClassDebugging` and `OleDb` classes to the form code:

```
using ComponentClassDebugging;
using System.Data.OleDb;
```

7. Add the following code to the click event of the button:

```
private void button1_Click(object sender, System.EventArgs e)
{
    dalRegions RegionsComponent = new dalRegions();
    OleDbDataReader drResult = RegionsComponent.GetAllRegions();
    MessageBox.Show("Call Completed");
}
```

8. Right-click the ComponentClassDebuggingClient project in the Solution Explorer and select Set As Startup Project.

Before running the project check that the Debug configuration is selected in the Solution Configurations in the toolbar.

We are now ready to debug and run the project. Set some breakpoints as we did in our previous example, start the project, *F5*, and wait for the display of the message box or an error.

The example we walked through is not the only way to test a Class Component. The properties under the Start Action section of the Debugging property page can be configured to use a URL or another application.

Windows Forms Debugging

To debug a Windows Forms application is a matter of controlling the execution of the program, much as we did in Chapter 3, *Building Windows Forms*. All the power of debugging is available in Windows Forms. Breakpoints, Trace, and Debug are all available. We can very easily do step execution and use our debugging tool windows.

Rather than take you through another example of actual debugging, we'll use the `ShippersMaintenance` project created in Chapter 3 to let us look at a some more of the debugger windows that we mentioned earlier but haven't yet covered. We'll start by opening the project, setting a breakpoint, and entering break mode to view the windows.

1. Open the `frmShippers` code in the `ShipperForm.cs` file.

2. Set a breakpoint at the following line:

```
this.sbrShippersBottom.Panels[0].Text = "DataSet Record Count = " +
dsShippers1.Tables["Shippers"].Rows.Count;
```

3. Start the project, *F5*, and wait for it to enter break mode.

The Call Stack Window

First, let's look at the Call Stack window by choosing Debug | Windows | Call Stack or pressing *Ctrl+Alt+C*. Recall that it allows you to dig through the calls currently being made by the application on the stack. The list is in reverse order with the first call shown at the bottom of the stack and the most recent at the top. In this case, the call stack is not very deep.

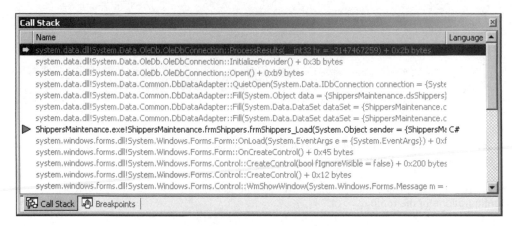

So then, the line at the top is the current program location. If you've a Locals, Autos, or Watch window open, double-click on another line with black font in the Call Stack and see the contents of the variable windows change. At any one time, these windows show you the values of the variables in the current stack frame. Double-clicking any other line in the call stack window will trigger the others to show you what's available in the appropriate stack frame.

Note that those entries grayed out are calls made by the system's .NET DLLs rather than your own.

You might also find the Call Stack window helpful digging through someone else's code, or when you're trying to figure out the recursion in your application. These are times when we may set a breakpoint and not worry about how it gets there until there is a problem. Being able to see the path can be very helpful.

Threads

Threads are not often manually controlled or monitored because programs are usually single-threaded. However, for those times when the necessity presents itself the Threads window can be used. To display the Threads window select Debug | Windows | Threads or *Ctrl+Alt+H*. Displaying it from the previous example will look like this:

Memory

Another infrequently used window, for managed code development at least, is Memory. The Memory windows are used to display the information at a specified address. They can also be useful in C++ to display the contents of a string too long to show up in the variables/watch windows. Those strings' displays are limited by window width and tooltip limits; if you double-click on them, you typically see the address rather than the characters – bringing up a **Memory** window on the address/variable shows the lot. For most development purposes we will not use it, but it's still available while debugging. To launch the window select **Debug | Windows | Memory | Memory 1** or *Ctrl+Alt+M* followed by *1*. At the stopped point in our application the window will appear like this.

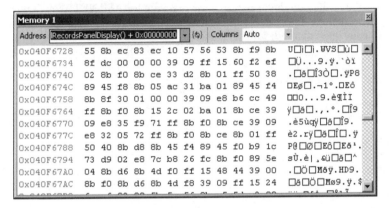

Modules

The Modules window is a list display of the modules currently loaded. It can sometimes be useful just to know what has been loaded and the path it was found at. What we find most helpful about the Modules window is the **Information** column. The information column states if symbols have been loaded for a specific module. In our case, symbols have been loaded for `ShippersMaintenance`. To display the Modules window select **Debug | Windows | Modules** or *Ctrl+Alt+U*.

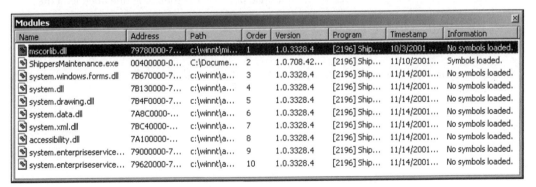

ASP.NET Web Services

As you know, the 'next big thing' heralded by the arrival of .NET is the enabling of distributed applications with Web Services. As you've seen, creating a Web Service is very easy with Visual Studio .NET and we're happy to report that debugging ASP.NET Web Services is just as simple. All the windows and code techniques we've shown above can applied here as well.

To demonstrate, have a look in your code download for the WebServiceDebugging project and open it up. In the file SimpleDebuggingService.asmx, you'll find the two methods we want to get to grips with. The first, GetDataSet(), returns a blank DataSet to the client. The other is a modified version of the HelloWorld() method that is part of a the template for ASP.NET Web Services, except that it's commented out by default. This version is uncommented and takes a string to describe the type of world. The code for these methods looks like this.

```
[WebMethod]
public string HelloWorld(string TypeOfWorld)
{
  Debug.WriteLine("Hello " + TypeOfWorld + " World");
  return "Hello " + TypeOfWorld + " World";
}

[WebMethod]
public DataSet GetDataSet()
{
  DataSet dsRegions = new DataSet();
  return dsRegions;
}
```

Since ASP.NET creates a test page for Web Services that we create, we can save a lot of time.

To use Visual Studio .NET to debug our Web Service we need to enable ASP.NET debugging in the project's Debugging property page. Also ensure that the **Debug Mode** is **Project** and **Start Page** is SimpleDebuggingService.asmx. Next set a breakpoint on the following line of code in the GetDataSet example:

```
DataSet dsRegions = new DataSet();
```

Start the project *F5*, and wait for the test page to be rendered. When the test page is displayed is will look like this:

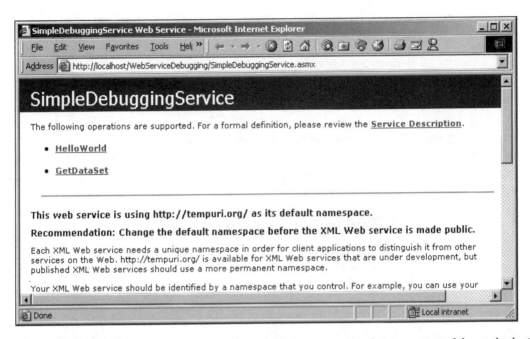

Click the HelloWorld link. The page will reload displaying inputs for the parameters of the method with an Invoke button.

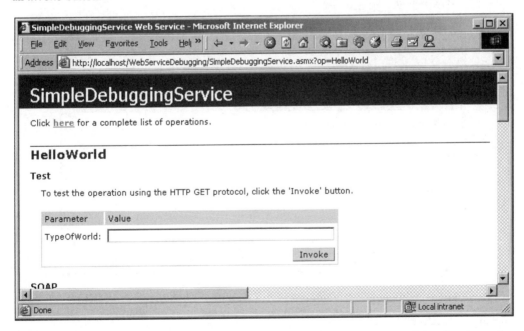

Enter Brave New in the value textbox for the TypeOfWorld parameter and click Invoke. A new browser is launched calling the method and displaying the result.

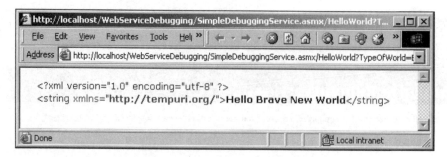

Change to the instance of Visual Studio debugging the Web Service. The Output window should have a line with Hello Brave New World in it:

Restart the program, *Ctrl+Shift+F5*. This time select GetDataSet from the list of methods. The invoke page will be displayed. Since there are no parameters to the method only an Invoke button is present. Click the Invoke button.

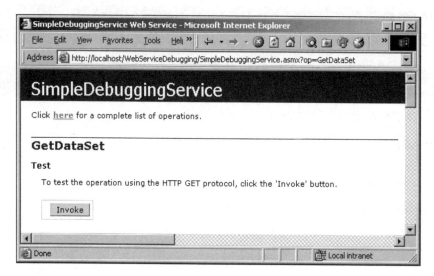

A new browser is launched to invoke the method. The current window will switch to Visual Studio .NET stopped at the breakpoint. Press *F5* again to finish the call. The calling browser will be displayed showing the results of the call.

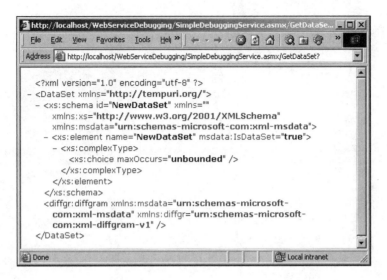

Summary

As we have said throughout this chapter, debugging is the same across nearly all projects. Understanding the use of breakpoints and controlling program execution with Step Into, Step Out, Step Over, and Start are excellent ways to easily watch the execution of your program. Utilizing Trace and Debug within Visual Studio .NET and beyond can provide additional help for finding the hard-to-follow problems. The IDE windows used for debugging can provide us with a plethora of information.

So what is the final word on debugging? Don't let it intimidate you. Visual Studio .NET makes it very easy even if we choose to use only a few of the features that it is supplied with.

12

Working with Data

Working with data may be the most common thing that developers do on a daily basis. Almost all applications use data of some sort. Databases are the mainstay for data storage, with flat files still lingering in dark corporate corners, and verbose XML cropping up in more places every day. Although it would be wonderful if we could get to a point of using only one storage format, we have to accept that this really a pipe-dream. Like everything else, each data storage method has its drawbacks, forcing us to work with whichever best suits our current requirements.

If you are familiar with Visual Studio 6 you know that there is no intrinsic GUI support for XML. There are add-ins available, but Microsoft didn't include a visual XML editor. This isn't too surprising as XML has only become popular recently, while Visual Studio 6 was released a number of years ago. To fill this void many companies have released external tools for XML.

As is par for the course with Microsoft, it has now brought out XML tools of it's own. It has included tools with Visual Studio .NET to work with databases, XML, and XML Schemas. And if we desire, we can open flat files using the simple code editor. All these tools are fully integrated within Visual Studio.

This chapter will be slightly different from most of the previous ones, because instead of working towards a final goal of working sample code, we'll cover how to perform various data-access tasks that we will use in our everyday applications.

Server Explorer Basics for Databases

Server Explorer is the essential Server RAD tool for Visual Studio .NET, and is covered in some detail in Chapter 5. Here, though, we will focus on the data tools.

Let's start by looking at how to work with databases in Server Explorer. To open Server Explorer, select View | Server Explorer from the menu bar or hit *Ctrl+Alt+S*. Server Explorer is available regardless of whether or not a project is currently open. Below, we can see the local PC, which has been given the name TECRA8100, underneath the Servers node:

The name of this node, Servers, indicates that the machine is capable of acting as a data server (not necessarily a networked one, but it will have that capability). For this reason, you will need to be running a Win NT derivative OS, namely Windows 2000 Professional or above.

If you wish to use another computer as the server:

1. Right-click the Servers node and select Add Server.

2. The Add Server dialog will be displayed:

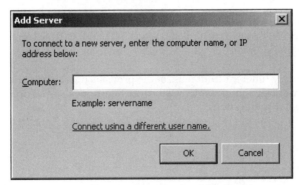

3. Enter the computer information. As the text indicates, you can enter either the IP address or the computer name.

4. To connect as a user other than the currently logged-in Windows user, click Connect using a different user name to display the Connect As dialog. If not, then skip to Step 6.

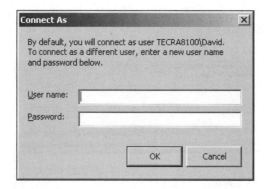

5. When the Connect As dialog is displayed, the help text tells us the user we are logged in as. Enter the user name and password then click OK.

6. Click OK on the Add Server dialog.

7. The dialog will disappear and, unless a problem occurs, the server will be added to the list in Server Explorer.

Note that if you enter the server name incorrectly, Visual Studio .NET won't make you wait long before telling you it couldn't connect!

With the SQL Servers node expanded, we see all installed instances of SQL Server, including any powered by the cut-down MSDE package. Expand these sub-nodes to see the SQL Server databases they contain:

You'll notice that the databases have the 'unavailable' icon next to them. This is the default state, because for the sake of efficiency Visual Studio will not automatically connect to a database unless required. The same is true for the SQL Server node itself.

If you have a tool that does in fact automatically open multiple connections in this way, be careful that your DB admin doesn't track you down, because it could get ugly...

If the SQL Server you are attempting to display is 'stopped' (not running) and you try to select it within the tree view, a prompt is displayed (sometimes after a long wait) for the authentication details to connect with:

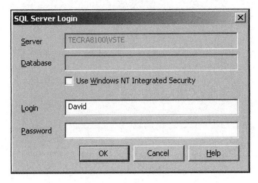

Entering this information won't actually do anything because Visual Studio will not start the SQL Server from the databases node even if you have the rights – although it will in the **Services** node. What will happen is that Visual Studio will change your cursor to an hourglass and make you wait twiddling your thumbs before showing this message:

We need to start the SQL Server manually, and we can then expand the node within Server Explorer to see and manage the objects within the database:

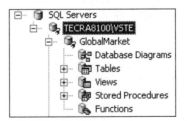

Understandably, the objects that Visual Studio allows us to work with are the sort of things a developer would need, rather than a DBA. We'll see more about creating and editing the objects later. You will need a separate database management tool to perform user and role management, or to start and stop the database server.

Data Connections

Data Connections in Visual Studio are connections to databases residing locally or remotely. You have already been through this process in other chapters. Creating data connections is not a difficult or new process. The first thing we'll do is look at how to create a connection to MSDE running on the local PC. Note that the location of the database is not important to the examples for making a connection.

Creating a Data Connection to an MS SQL Server Database

1. Right-click the Data Connections node in Server Explorer and select Add Connection. The Data Link Properties dialog will be displayed showing the Connection tab. Here, we can add properties to connect to a MS SQL Server.

Data Link Properties is a standard database dialog for creating connection strings so you may already be very familiar with it.

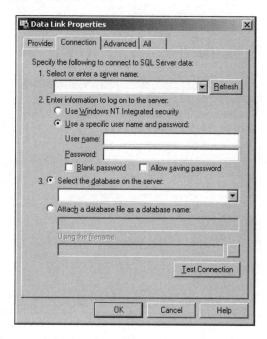

2. Enter the server name and authentication information in parts 1 and 2 of the tab.

3. To connect to the GlobalMarket database on the server, we can either select it from the dropdown, or type it in directly. If the SQL Server instance has a large number of databases running, if your connection is slow, or the server is a little underpowered, then it can be frustratingly slow to click the dropdown.

If you do use the dropdown you can skip the next step (testing the connection) because if you managed to get the database name from the list, it means that the connection must be OK.

4. Click the Test Connection button. If all is well, a message box will appear to tell you that the test completed successfully.

5. Click OK. The dialog will disappear and the new connection will be displayed in Server Explorer.

Now we'll see how to connect to an Access database.

Creating a Data Connection to an MS Access Database

1. Right-click the Data Connections node in Server Explorer and select Add Connection. The Data Link Properties dialog will be displayed showing the Connection tab.

This time, change to the Provider tab, select the Jet provider you wish to use to connect to the Access DB, and click the Next >> button.

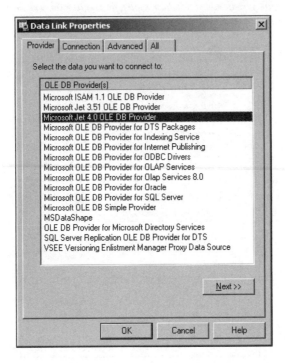

2. The Connection tab is now displayed. Type in, or browse to, the Access database location:

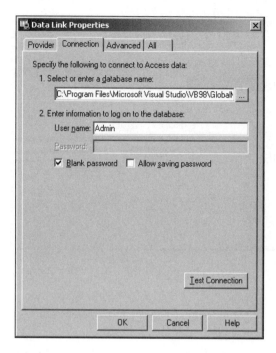

3. Enter the login information in section 2, and click the **Test Connection** button. If all is well, a message box will tell you the test completed successfully.

4. Click **OK**. The dialog will disappear and the new connection will be displayed in Server Explorer as before.

Once you've added both connections, your **Data Connections** node in Server Explorer will look like this:

Default Connections

The default connection uses a database connection icon with a red arrow inside green box when viewed in Solution Explorer. To change the default connection right-click the connection in Solution Explorer and select **Set as Project Default**. The default connection will originally be set to the connection selected when the project was created. Unfortunately the default connection cannot be changed while designers are open.

Copying a Connection String

Even if you don't plan to work with database objects through Server Explorer, you might still find that creating a connection this way can be very useful. If you are not very knowledgeable about connection strings, creating them by hand can be a little daunting. When a connection has been created in Server Explorer, though, the connection string is always readily available. We simply need to select the connection in Server Explorer, and open the **Properties** window to see the information that relates to it:

All properties are read-only, but we can copy the value of `ConnectString` to use within our code whenever we need to set up a connection.

Having a connection can be useful when adding connection objects to a form, which you might want to do some time.

5. Add an `OleDbConnection` object to a windows form. It will be displayed in the component tray.

6. Select it and open the **Properties** window.

7. Select the **Connection String** property and expand the dropdown.

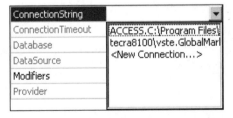

The connections within Server Explorer that can be used for this connection type are displayed. If we had added a **SqlConnection** instead, then only SQL Server connections would be displayed in the list. Notice also the **<New Connection...>** option in the list. This will launch the **Data Link** dialog and start the process of adding a new data connection.

> The type of database you are connected to will determine the objects Visual Studio shows. For instance, an Access database doesn't support Functions, while MS SQL Server 2000 does. Naturally, Visual Studio will not display items that a database doesn't support, but it will show any items that the edition of Visual Studio you are using can view but not alter.

Some options are available regarding what things are displayed in Server Explorer and how. Select Tools | Options from the menu bar, expand the Database Tools folder, and select the Server Explorer page:

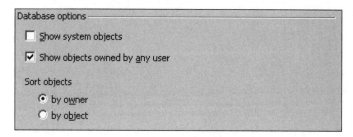

I find defaults of not showing system objects and showing objects owned by any user the most effective. However, I find it more intuitive to change the Sort objects option to by object.

Working with Database Objects

Many objects can be manipulated via Server Explorer using either a Data Connection or the Servers node as we will see later, but this isn't always enough. Having scripts and queries grouped in one place would make them easier to manage. **Database Projects** are the way.

From the menu bar select File | New | Project. The New Project dialog will be displayed:

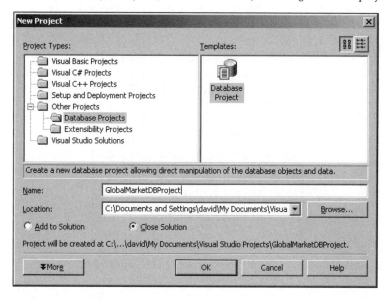

1. As above, expand Other Projects under Project Types, and select Database Projects.

2. Next, in the Templates list at the right, select Database Project.

3. Name the project GlobalMarketDBProject, and click OK.

4. Since we already have two database connections established in Server Explorer, the Add Database Reference dialog is displayed next:

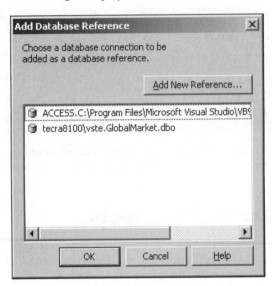

5. Select the MSDE connection, tecra8100\vste.GlobalMarket.dbo in my system, and click OK.

The dialog will disappear and the project is created. If we had not already created connections within Server Explorer then we'd have seen the Data Link Properties dialog displayed instead of the Add Database Reference.

By default, two folders will be created within the new project: Change Scripts and Queries, although the Enterprise edition also has a Create Scripts folder. A Database References node is also created under which the connection we selected is created:

The folders are created for convenience. They can be renamed or deleted if desired. The reference to the database is a shortcut back to Server Explorer, which will be opened if it's not already.

Creating Database Queries and the Query Designer

The Query Designer is also referred to as the View Designer in the documentation and many dialogs. Since a view is essentially just a query it makes more sense to refer to it here as the Query Designer. It is also called the Query Builder in some cases, such as when working with a single piece of SQL.

The Query Designer can be launched in many ways. For example, opening a table from Server Explorer automatically runs a `SELECT * FROM TableNameQuery`. Initially only the Results pane is displayed, but the others can be displayed by using the toolbar buttons or shortcut keys, as we'll see later on. Some other ways that the Query Designer can be useful are shown later in the chapter.

Let's start by creating a new Database Query object to retrieve the orders for a customer showing the most recent first. To begin with, we need to add a Database Query object to our project.

1. To add a new item, right-click the project in Solution Explorer and select Add New Item. The Add New Item dialog box will open:

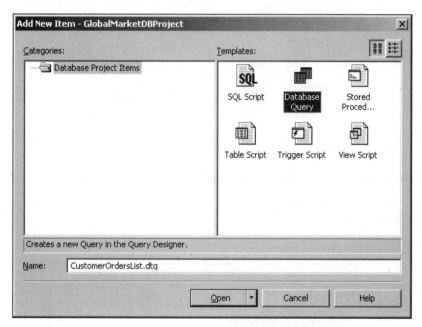

Like all other types of projects, predefined templates for projects and items within them are provided to make the job easier. The templates for a database project are of two types: Query and Script. A Database Query is a single query stored in a file. Adding a Database Query will launch the Query Editor. The SQL Script template starts a blank file in the code editor – a little like a free SQL session. The script can be executed as a whole or SQL statements can be edited/executed separately in the Query Designer. The rest of the scripts (Stored Procedure, Table, Trigger, and View) are all templates to create new instances of these items. All of the templates except Database Query will create a standard `.sql` file (a normal text file with a `.sql` extension) that we can easily work with in other programs.

2. Select Database Query, name it, and click OK. In this case I named it `CustomersOrdersList.dtq`. The dialog will disappear and the new query file will be shown in the Solution Explorer. The Query Editor will then be opened and the Add Table dialog displayed, provided we have a default connection selected:

In this case the **Add Table** dialog also allows for additions of views or functions, which is dependent on the format of the underlying database.

3. Select the **Customers** table and click **Add**, or just double-click the table.

4. Click **Close**. The **Customers** dialog will disappear and the **Customers** table will be added to the designer.

In the top pane of the designer, **Diagram**, the **Customers** table will be displayed. If the pane is not already displayed click the **Show Diagram Pane** button on the menu bar or press *Ctrl+1*.

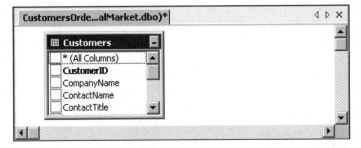

The **Diagram** pane shows a visual layout of the query including joins, sort orders, and filters.

5. Add the **Orders** table to the query by dragging it from the **Tables** section of the database connection within Server Explorer onto the diagram. This could have been accomplished by right-clicking and selecting **Add Table** to redisplay the **Add Table** dialog to select it from, but it can be simpler to drag it out from Server Explorer. The join will now be displayed between the two tables:

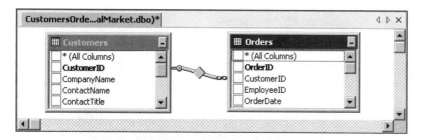

6. The boxes next to each column are to select them for inclusion in the query. Check Customers.CustomerID, Customers.CompanyName, and Orders.OrderID.

Below the **Diagram** pane will be the **Grid** pane. If it's not already displayed, click the **Show Grid Pane** button on the menu bar or press *Ctrl+2*.

Column	Alias	Table	Output	Sort Type	Sort Order	Criteria	Or...	Or...	
CustomerID		Customers	✓						
CompanyName		Customers	✓						
OrderID		Orders	✓						

The **Grid** pane is used to select what columns or expressions to display in the result set, define criteria for the query, and set sorting options. Here we can see the **Orders** columns we have already added.

7. Add the Orders.OrderDate field to the query by clicking the dropdown within the first open row of the **Grid** pane:

Below the **Grid** pane will be the SQL pane. If it's not already displayed, just click the **Show SQL Pane** button on the menu bar or press *Ctrl+3*.

```
SELECT    Customers.CustomerID, Customers.CompanyName, Orders.OrderID
FROM      Customers INNER JOIN
            Orders ON Customers.CustomerID = Orders.CustomerID
```

8. In the SQL pane, add the following WHERE clause to the SQL code:

```
WHERE (Customers.CustomerID = 'MAISD')
ORDER BY Orders.OrderDate DESC
```

9. Click the Verify SQL Syntax button on the menu bar. A message box will be displayed indicating if errors were found with the SQL. In this case it indicates all is well:

Notice now how the Diagram and Grid panes have been updated to show the WHERE clause and sort order.

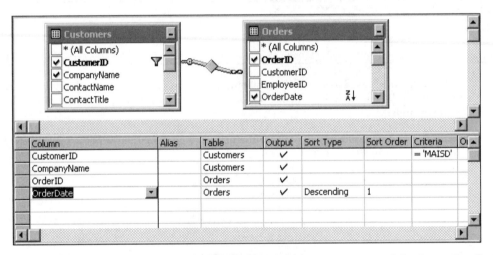

In the Diagram pane the Filter icon is added next to CustomerID and the Ascending Sort icon next to OrderDate. The Grid pane shows the sort in the Sort Type and Sort Order columns and the filter in the Criteria column.

10. Execute the query by clicking Run Query on the toolbar bar or pressing *Ctrl+R*. This will populate the Results pane at the bottom of the page:

CustomerID	CompanyName	OrderID	OrderDate	
▶ MAISD	Maison Dewey	11004	4/7/1998	
MAISD	Maison Dewey	10978	3/26/1998	
MAISD	Maison Dewey	10896	2/19/1998	
MAISD	Maison Dewey	10892	2/17/1998	

We can now navigate the results by using the scroll bar on the right or the Row feature for jumping to a specific row in the resultset. Right-click and select Row from the context menu. The Go to Row dialog will be displayed:

The "of *" next to the box indicates that not all rows have been retrieved from the data source. If we had scrolled to the bottom first it would display "of 7" instead.

Let's assume that this query will be used to show the list of the three most recent orders. For this a TOP clause will need to be added.

Adding a TOP Clause

1. To add a TOP clause using the designer, open the property pages by right-clicking in any open area of the Query Designer and selecting **Property Pages**. If necessary, select the **Query** tab.

2. Check the **TOP** checkbox.

3. In the textbox below it, enter 3.

> *Below the textbox is a SQL Comments box for documenting the query. Comments can also be added to a query in the SQL pane by using the syntax:* /* My comments */ *– but it must be at the beginning or end of the query. If we do this, they will be stripped out and placed in the SQL comments box.*

4. Click OK to close the dialog. TOP 3 will be added to the query in the SQL pane.

5. Rerun the query. As expected, only three rows are returned:

	CustomerID	CompanyName	OrderID	OrderDate
▶	MAISD	Maison Dewey	11004	4/7/1998
	MAISD	Maison Dewey	10978	3/26/1998
	MAISD	Maison Dewey	10896	2/19/1998
*				

The records can actually be edited within the results pane. The blank row at the end of the list with the asterisk (*) at the beginning is used for adding records. This won't always work for a number of reasons, such as not having all required fields present in the resultset to enter.

Since we plan to eventually use this query for getting a specific customer's orders it makes sense to have a parameter for the CustomerID instead of hard-coding MAISD. This is not a difficult change to implement.

6. Reopen the property pages, and change to the **Parameters** tab.

7. A nice feature of the Query Designer is that it allows us to specify how parameters are identified. Appropriate prefix and suffix characters can be chosen for this purpose. At some point down the line, we'll probably want to change this to a stored procedure, so to specify parameters we will use the @ – the required format for SQL Server. Other databases use different formats. Enter @ in the **Prefix characters text box**.

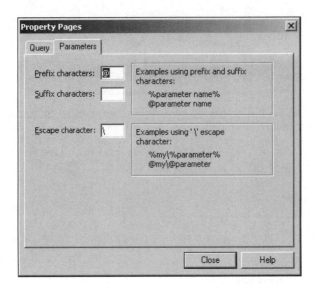

8. Click the Close button.

9. In the SQL pane, add @CustomerID in the Criteria column of the CustomerID field, and rerun the query.

10. When the Define Query Parameters dialog is displayed, enter GODOS for the @CustomerID parameter:

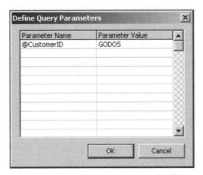

11. Click OK. The query will run and the results pane be populated.

Lastly, we can save the query by pressing *Ctrl+S* or File | Save CustomersOrdersList.dtq from the menu.

Tables were used in this example, but views and functions can be used too. When tables are added to the query their relationships are shown in the Diagram pane, but the designer doesn't limit us to them. A join can be altered by right-clicking it in the Diagram pane. New joins can be created by dragging a column from one table to a column in another.

The Options dialog allows us to set which panes are displayed by default, as well as a few other things. Select Tools | Options from the menu bar. Expand the Database Tools folder and select Query/View Designer.

Result Set Timeout

The designer maintains a connection to the server for the resultset fetches. Because of this, Visual Studio will display messages such as the following, asking if you wish to continue using the results if they have not been used for a while:

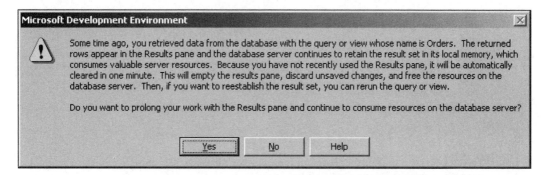

It's generally not a good idea to keep a resultset alive for a long time. If you fail to respond to this question after a while the results pane will be cleared automatically and this message displayed:

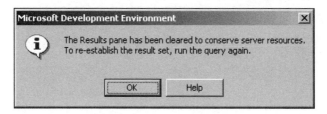

Here a new SELECT query was created. Other types of queries can be designed also. To change the query type click the Change Type button on the toolbar and select the new type:

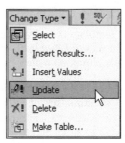

Change type is also available from the context menu within the designer.

Creating a View Using the View Script Template

Let's now look at an example of a script object by creating a new view.

1. Open the Add New Item dialog by right-clicking the project in Solution Explorer and selecting Add New Item. The Add New Item dialog will be displayed.

2. Select the **View Script** template and name the new script. The view will retrieve the territories of employees with the descriptions for them, let's use the name v_EmployeeTerritory.

3. Click **OK**. The dialog disappears, a script is added, and shown in the code editor.

4. The template has four major sections. The first section searches for the existence of a view with the same name. If one is found, it's deleted:

```
IF EXISTS (SELECT * FROM sysobjects WHERE type = 'V' AND name = 'View_Name')
    BEGIN
        PRINT 'Dropping View View_Name'
          DROP  View View_Name
    END
GO
```

The second section is just a comment template for the view. The third section is where the SELECT statement for the view will be placed:

```
PRINT 'Creating View View_Name'
GO
CREATE View View_Name
as

    /*INSERT_SELECT_STATEMENT*/

GO
```

And the last section is used to grant rights to the view:

```
GRANT SELECT ON View_Name TO PUBLIC

GO
```

None of the SQL added by the template is what you might call rocket science. But it does save some time when creating an object, and I find it can be very nice for those mornings when I can't seem to remember my SQL syntax no matter how many cups of coffee I have.

5. Replace the View_Name placeholder used in the template with the name you want for the new view. Here I have chosen to name the view the same as my SQL script.

6. In the third section, delete the /*INSERT_SELECT_STATEMENT*/ comment.

7. Right-click there and select **Insert SQL** from the context menu. The Query Builder will be displayed if we have a default connection.

If the query designer is not already set to a SELECT query, right-click in the designer and choose **Change Type | Select** from the context menu.

8. Add the `EmployeeTerritories`, `Territories`, and `Region` tables. The **Add Table** dialog can be displayed by right-clicking in the designer and selecting **Add Table**. Tables can also be added by dragging them from Server Explorer to the **Diagram** pane of the Query Builder.

9. Select the following columns for output:

- ❑ `EmployeeTerritories.EmployeeID`
- ❑ `EmployeeTerritories.TerritoryID`
- ❑ `Territories.TerritoryDescription`
- ❑ `Region.RegionDescription`

10. Run the query (*Ctrl+R*) to ensure that the results are as expected.

11. Close the **Query Builder** window.

The window will prompt you to save changes. Notice how it's asking to save changes to the original view file name. What it is really asking is if the changes in the Query Builder should be committed back to the initial location in the original window.

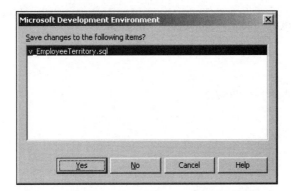

12. Click Yes. The dialog will disappear and the original window for the view will be displayed, with the new SQL selected:

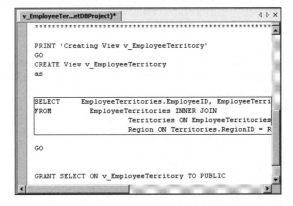

A blue outline is drawn around the SELECT statement. This box indicates that Visual Studio recognizes this as a Data Manipulation Language (DML) command – that is, a SELECT, INSERT, UPDATE, or DELETE statement. We can now edit the DML command using the Query Builder if we right-click within the DML outline and select Design SQL Block.

If we had forgotten to run the query before closing the editor we can do so now by right-clicking the entire selected block and choosing Run Selection. The results will be displayed in the Output Window.

13. If you want, add some descriptive information to the comments section.

14. Save the script. The script must be saved before it can be run. If we forget to save it, Visual Studio displays a message prompting us to do so.

15. Run the script. There are a number of ways to do this, as we'll see in the next section. For now, simply execute it by right-clicking within the designer and selecting Run from the context menu. This will run the script on the default connection.

16. Select the connection to execute the create view script on and click OK. The Output Window will be displayed and the results shown:

Executing script C:\Documents and Settings\david\My Documents\Visual Studio Projects\GlobalMarketDBProject\v_EmployeeTerritory.sql

No rows affected.
No more results.
(0 row(s) returned)
Creating View v_EmployeeTerritory
No rows affected.
No more results.
(0 row(s) returned)
No rows affected.
No more results.
(0 row(s) returned)
No rows affected.
No more results.
(0 row(s) returned)
Finished executing script C:\Documents and Settings\david\My Documents\Visual Studio Projects\GlobalMarketDBProject\v_EmployeeTerritory.sql

Running Scripts

There are a couple of ways to run a script other than right-clicking and selecting Run. One is to drag the file inside Solution Explorer onto the connection to execute it with. Visual Studio warns that doing this will execute the script on the connection.

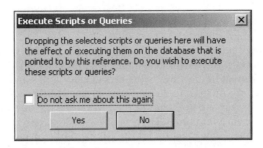

I find this method a bit risky because I worry I will get lazy and drop it on the wrong connection. This is more worrying should we check Do not ask me about this again.

The last run option is the Run On option. Right-click the query file in Solution Explorer and select Run On. The Run On dialog will be displayed:

This is the same dialog that we'd get if we didn't have a default connection. It shows all configured connections. The first two are the database references added to our project. Just as in Solution Explorer, the default connection will have a red arrow boxed in green in the icon. The third is a connection that I have established with Server Explorer, but not added to the references for this project. You can tell that it's not referenced because there's no link arrow.

The last item, <temporary reference>, will display the Data Link properties dialog to create a connection only for executing the script this time. When this option is used the connection created will not be added to Server Explorer or the Database References for the project. This can be useful for rolling scripts out to production environments because it's not a good idea to keep a constant connection to this environment. If we wanted to create a connection that would persist we could click the Add Reference button to open the Data Link Properties.

Database Diagrams

Database diagrams are more than just nice things to hang on the cubicle wall. They provide developers with a way to view the objects in the database and their relationships in a "quick glance" format. We also often find that they are great in meetings with users to assist in fleshing out data requirements and guide design changes. They can be used to display a lot of detail about tables and fields, or just an overview of the entire database in a bare-bones format. Regardless of how you decide to use them, I think you will find the editor for them provided by Visual Studio to be very handy. We will have a go at working with them by creating a new diagram for the GlobalMarket database.

Creating a New Database Diagram in the GlobalMarket Database

1. Locate the Database Diagrams node for the GlobalMarket database in Server Explorer.

2. Right-click it, and choose New Diagram.

3. From the Add Table dialog, select the tables you wish to include. In this case, select Orders, Shippers, and Customers.

4. Click Add to add the selected tables, and Close to close the dialog. The tables will be arranged on the form:

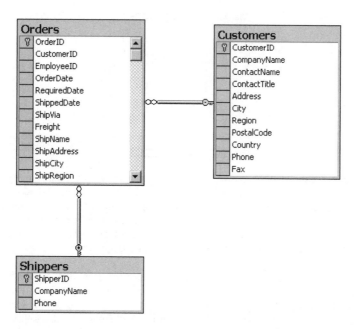

Save the diagram by selecting File | Save DatabaseDiagram1 from the menu bar, or using *Ctrl+S*.

5. When the Save New Database Diagram dialog is displayed, enter a name such as OrdersToShippersAndCustomers.

6. Click OK. The diagram is saved and listed in Server Explorer within the database:

Beneath the database diagram, the tables it contains also appear. The tables can even be expanded to show their columns.

Adjusting the Display

With a new diagram in hand, let's turn our attention to adjusting the display and working with the diagram within our editor. We will begin by adjusting the display area of the diagram within the IDE. Click and hold the small icon located in the bottom right corner of the designer where the horizontal and vertical scroll bars meet. A small window will be displayed on top of the icon.

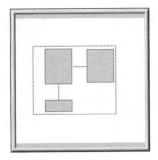

A shadowed overview of the diagram is displayed along with a dotted box that represents the visible area in the designer. We can use the mouse to move and size the box, and observe the effects of our actions in the IDE window in real time. As expected from a diagram designer, the zoom can be adjusted. A dropdown is provided on the toolbar with standard zoom sizes, but custom sizes can be entered also. The zoom and shape of the designer will determine the shape of the layout box. Not surprisingly, this is pretty processor-intensive so when using a slow machine you may prefer to use the scroll bars.

When creating the diagram we saw that tables can be added using the Add Table dialog. To redisplay this dialog click the Add Table button on the toolbar or select Add Table from the context menu. Tables can also be added by dragging them from Server Explorer onto the diagram. A feature I find particularly handy for databases I am not familiar with is Add Related Tables. Just as it sounds, this will add all tables related to the selected table to the designer. To use it, click on the Add Related Tables button on the toolbar, or select Add Related Tables from the context menu. For the Customers table, this would add the CustomerCustomerDemo table. If the table(s) selected have no relationships, or the tables they relate to are already included on the diagram, this option is disabled.

To remove a table, we have two options. If we simply want the table removed from the diagram, we can click the Remove Table from Diagram button on the toolbar or select Remove Table from Diagram from the context menu. If we really, really don't want the table, we can remove it from the database entirely, by selecting the table and clicking the Delete Table from Database button on the toolbar or Delete Table from Database from the context menu. The remove options are side by side on the toolbar and one after the other on the context menu, so it's very easy to select Delete Table from Database accidentally. Don't worry too much if you do, as you will be prompted to confirm the delete. Even if you accidentally confirm the delete the change isn't committed to the database itself until the diagram is saved, at which point you will be warned of changes like this.

Arranging objects is also simple. To arrange all tables click the Arrange Tables button on the toolbar. To arrange only the selected tables, click the Arrange Selected Tables button on the toolbar or choose Arrange Selected Tables from the context menu. The icons may look the same, especially in a book or on a laptop, because the only difference is that one table in the icon is a slightly different color to show it's selected. This is one case where the tool tip is the best way to tell.

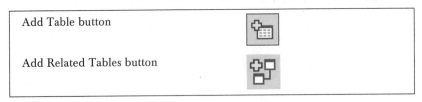

| Add Table button | |
| Add Related Tables button | |

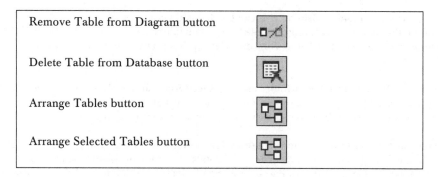

Remove Table from Diagram button	
Delete Table from Database button	
Arrange Tables button	
Arrange Selected Tables button	

Table Layout

The table layout has enough possibilities to satisfy almost anyone. To adjust the layout of the table, use the Table View dropdown on the toolbar or Table View from the context menu. The following shows each view for the Shippers table.

Standard

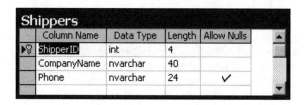

Column Name

Keys

Name

If these don't meet your needs, a Modify Custom option is also provided. This option displays a dialog for the selection and ordering of a custom layout. The custom layout is applied using the Custom option from Table View.

The default view of a table is custom. This can be changed via the Options dialog. Select Tools | Options from the menubar. Expand the Database Tools folder and its child Database Designer. Select the General page. The Default Table View dropdown can be set to any of the views types shown above, including Custom.

Also under the Database Designer folder are pages for Oracle and SQL Server. These tabs allow for setting default variable lengths and the default type for new columns. If your design practices strongly favor char or varchar over nchar and nvarchar this is a simple option to set to save time.

In the previous Standard view of the Shippers table, notice how the table has extra space at the right. This can be easily adjusted using the cursor, but can also be auto-configured using the Autosize Selected Tables button from the toolbar or Autosize Selected Tables from the context menu. Doing this to the Shippers table in Standard view produces the following:

Shippers

Column Name	Data Type	Length	Allow Nulls
ShipperID	int	4	
CompanyName	nvarchar	40	
Phone	nvarchar	24	✓

As would be expected, these actions are applied to all selected tables and the standard shortcuts (such as *Ctrl+A* for Select All) can be used. One thing I find quite frustrating is that actions taken on database diagrams are not recorded for undo, so when we change something, hitting *Ctrl+Z* is not going to set it back. It's not committed to the database until we close the diagram and save though – but choosing not to save can mean losing prior changes of course.

One last quite helpful feature is the ability to add text blocks to a diagram. To do this, select an area on the diagram and either click the New Text Annotation button on the toolbar, or select New Text Annotation from the context menu. Here's an example of a note placed above the Orders table:

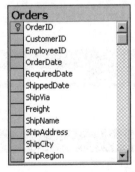

Orders is related to Order Details also which is not shown here.

Orders

OrderID
CustomerID
EmployeeID
OrderDate
RequiredDate
ShippedDate
ShipVia
Freight
ShipName
ShipAddress
ShipCity
ShipRegion

Printing

With our diagram laid out, we now need to prepare it to print it respectably. To see how the diagram will print, click the View Page Breaks button on the menu bar. I've spread out the tables here to take up two pages for illustrative purposes only:

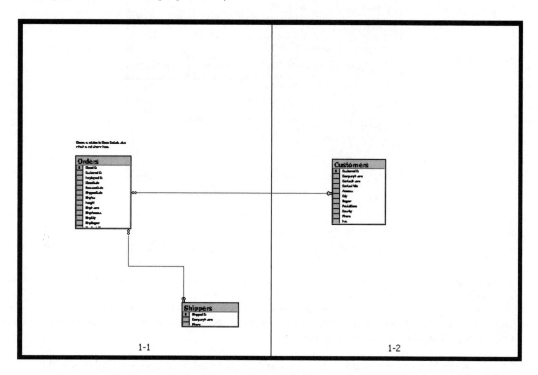

The bottom of each page shows which position the page is located at in a grid format. Here, the only pages are 1-1 and 1-2. Since the diagram designer will not always update the page layout automatically, we need to use the Recalculate Page Breaks button on the toolbar.

Property Pages

So far, we have done a lot for layout but little with table changes. Changes to the tables are accomplished via the Property Pages for a table:

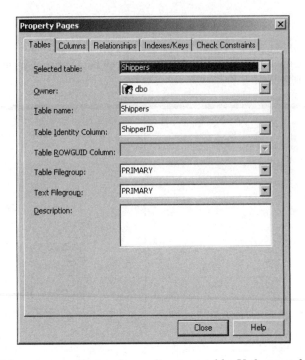

The tabs provide all the necessary choices for configuring a table. Unfortunately, this is a bulky dialog that can't be docked. The good part is that it's not modal so, if required, we can leave it open while doing other things, and it will adjust its display to the currently selected table. If having it open covers your entire diagram, the Selected Table option on the Tables tab, shown above, can be used to change tables rather than clicking on the diagram.

The use of the Property Pages is not the only way to adjust a table. Properties displayed within any of the views can be adjusted directly.

SQL Change Scripts from Database Diagram Changes

The last and what I feel the most significant feature of the database diagram designer is the creation of **change scripts**. Let's assume that we had a request for the following changes:

- ❑   Add an OrderDesc field of type nvarchar(100) Nullable to the Orders table
- ❑   Add a Fax field of type nvarchar(24) Nullable to the Shippers table
- ❑   Delete the Customers table from the database

To implement these changes using a database diagram:

1.   Create a new database diagram, but don't save it.

2.   Add the Orders, Shippers, and Customers tables to the diagram.

3.   Add the fields we mentioned above.

4. Remove the `Customers` table by clicking **Delete Table from Database**. At this stage, the table hasn't been completely deleted, we've only told the designer that we intend to delete it. Remember that if you don't really want to delete the table, don't commit the changes at the end of this exercise.

5. Click the **Generate Change Script** button on the toolbar to display the **Save Change Script** dialog. Depending on the extent of the changes this can take some time to complete.

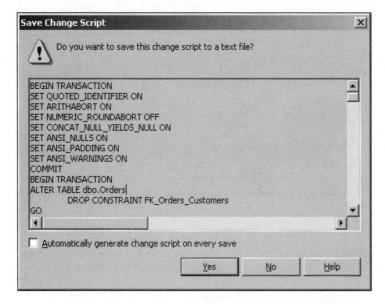

6. Click **Yes** to display the standard Windows **Save As** dialog. Enter a name and select a location to save the script to and click **Save**. At this point, we still haven't changed the actual underlying database.

7. The generated script, too lengthy to show here but included in the download, even handles the mindless task of writing the SQL required to maintain the current data in the tables and recreate the permissions.

Since these changes will likely have to be applied to multiple environments, this can be a great help. This is not a new feature created by Microsoft, but it is new as an integrated component of the Visual Studio environment negating the need for an extra tool.

If we take it an extra step and save the changes, a prompt will be displayed warning us of the table changes that will be committed. This is the point at which your database will be permanently modified, so if you want to keep things as they were, back out now:

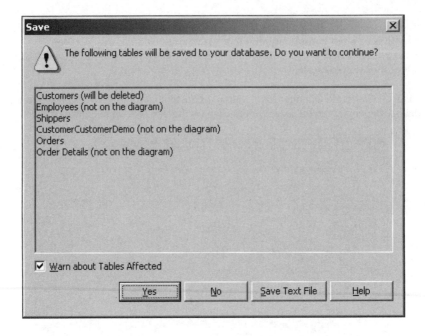

Tables

Working with tables is simple and intuitive, using the same designer for both adding and editing. The list of columns is on top, and the properties are to found underneath:

Selecting a column will display the values in the **Columns** tab at the bottom. Addition of columns is performed by simply typing in new fields at the bottom of the list or using the **Insert Column** option from the context menu. **Delete Column** is also available from the context menu.

From a developer's perspective, this has several helpful features. I can recall many times when I have made a request to my DBA for a simple addition or an alteration to a field. They would tell me to send them a script to make the change. They'd then review it and send it back because I had made a trivial mistake. Since I can't claim to be a total T-SQL wizard I'd get it slightly wrong a couple of times, eating up precious hours. Using VS.NET, we can now knock up the correct SQL in no time.

Creating a Quick Table Change Script

For illustration, let's suppose that we want to change the `Phone` field of the `Shippers` table to a `char` instead of a `varchar`. We'd follow these steps:

1. Right-click the `Shippers` table in Server Explorer and choose **Design Table**.

2. Change the `Phone` field data type to `char`.

3. Click the **Generate Change Script** button on the toolbar.

4. A validation warning will likely be displayed telling us that data may be lost because we are changing the data type. Click **Yes** to continue:

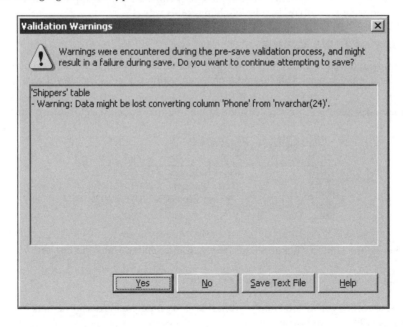

5. When the **Save Change Script** dialog is displayed, select and copy the script, ready to be pasted into an e-mail or a file and shipped off to the DBA:

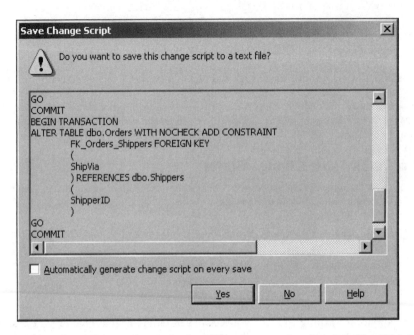

This example takes about 15 seconds to complete, but can save a lot of typing. The DBA is also likely not to get as annoyed if you request a lot of changes this way.

Inline Editing of Table Values

Another simple and useful feature when working with tables is being able to edit the table values. Tables can be opened and the values can be changed within the grid. Let's try it out.

1. Right-click the Shippers table within Solution Explorer and select Retrieve Data from Table:

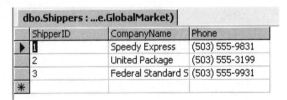

2. Change the United Package company name to United Package Limited.

3. Change cells to commit the changes to the database.

If this example strikes you as too simple, well, it is. This simple feature can save us from having to write a SQL statement like the following:

```
USE GlobalMarket
GO
UPDATE Shippers SET CompanyName TO 'United Package Limited' WHERE ShipperID = 2
```

This isn't particularly difficult SQL, but it is bound to take more time to write this for every change you may wish to make than to use the VS tool.

Views

Because views are essentially queries, we've seen how to edit them in our earlier look at the Query Designer. To create a new view, right-click the Views node for the database in Server Explorer, and select New View. Visual Studio will open the designer for the new view. To edit or delete a view, right-click it in Server Explorer and select the appropriate option.

Stored Procedures and Functions

Working with Stored Procedures and Functions in Visual Studio is done in a very similar way, so we will cover them both together.

A Function for Use Within a Stored Procedure

1. In Server Explorer, right-click the Functions node of the GlobalMarket database and select New Scalar-valued Functions.

2. Change the function text to the following. This function is designed to calculate a price after 5.75% sales tax:

```
CREATE FUNCTION dbo.CalculatePriceWithTax
    (
@Price as money
    )
RETURNS money
AS
    BEGIN
        SET @Price = @Price +
            CAST(CONVERT(decimal(10,2),(@Price * 0.0575)) as money)
    RETURN @Price
    END
```

3. Save the function. The function will immediately appear in the Functions list within Server Explorer.

4. To test it, right-click the function name, and select Run Scalar-valued Function.

5. The Run scalar-valued function dialog will be displayed showing the parameter list. Enter a value for the @Price parameter:

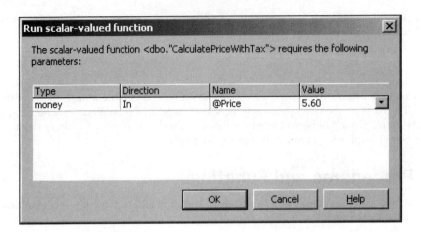

6. Click **OK** to run the function. The Output window will be displayed showing the results. Be aware that if the Output window is set to auto-hide, then it tends to display and hide very quickly:

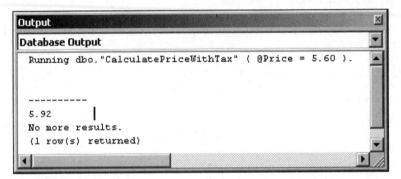

7. Check the value returned to ensure that the function calculated correctly. Assuming all is well, it's time to use it from within a stored procedure.

8. Find the CustomersOrdersDetails stored procedure in Server Explorer, right-click it and select **Edit Stored Procedure**. This stored procedure is part of the original Northwind database we copied as GlobalMarket. Add a new output column using the function created. Once complete the stored procedure will look like this:

```
ALTER PROCEDURE CustOrdersDetail @OrderID int
AS
SELECT ProductName,
  UnitPrice=ROUND(Od.UnitPrice, 2),
  Quantity,
  Discount=CONVERT(int, Discount * 100),
  ExtendedPrice=ROUND(CONVERT(money, Quantity * (1 -Discount) * Od.UnitPrice), 2),
   dbo.CalculatePriceWithTax(OD.UnitPrice) as PriceWithTax
FROM Products P, [Order Details] Od
WHERE Od.ProductID = P.ProductID and Od.OrderID = @OrderID
```

9. Save the stored procedure.

10. The designer for the Stored Procedure will display the DML blue box around the SELECT statement, as we saw earlier in the chapter:

```
dbo.CustOrder....GlobalMarket)                                                    ◁ ▷ ✕
    ALTER PROCEDURE CustOrdersDetail @OrderID int
    AS
    SELECT ProductName,
        UnitPrice=ROUND(Od.UnitPrice, 2),
        Quantity,
        Discount=CONVERT(int, Discount * 100),
        ExtendedPrice=ROUND(CONVERT(money, Quantity * (1 - Discount) * Od.UnitPrice), 2),
        dbo.CalculatePriceWithTax(OD.UnitPrice) as PriceWithTax
    FROM Products P, [Order Details] Od
    WHERE Od.ProductID = P.ProductID and Od.OrderID = @OrderID
```

11. If we right-click anywhere within the blue box and select **Design SQL Block**, the **Query Designer** will be displayed in a new window for this statement. Saving changes to the query within the Query Designer will commit them back to the original window. Everywhere DML can be found, a separate blue box will be displayed.

The DML box would have been displayed when we were creating the CalculatePriceWithTax *function if we had used* SELECT *to assign the* @Price *value instead of* SET.

12. Save the stored procedure. Now right-click CustOrdersDetail within Server Explorer, and select **Run Stored Procedure**.

13. The Run stored procedure dialog will be displayed, showing the parameter list. Enter a value for the @OrderID parameter:

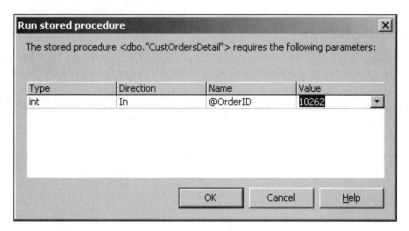

14. Click OK to run the stored procedure. The Output window will show the results:

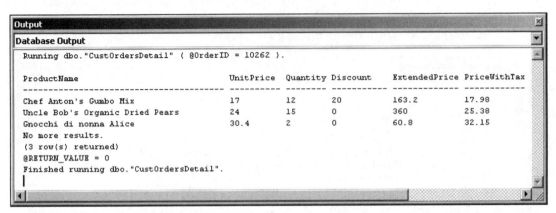

```
Output                                                                          ×

Database Output                                                                  ▼

Running dbo."CustOrdersDetail" ( @OrderID = 10262 ).

ProductName                          UnitPrice  Quantity Discount   ExtendedPrice PriceWithTax
------------------------------------ ---------- -------- ---------- ------------- ------------
Chef Anton's Gumbo Mix               17         12       20         163.2         17.98
Uncle Bob's Organic Dried Pears      24         15       0          360           25.38
Gnocchi di nonna Alice               30.4       2        0          60.8          32.15
No more results.
(3 row(s) returned)
@RETURN_VALUE = 0
Finished running dbo."CustOrdersDetail".
```

The display in the Output window shows all of the columns returned, along with the values of the parameters and the return value. If our stored procedure had returned more than 500 rows they would not have been displayed, due to a setting in the Options dialog. Change this by selecting Tools | Options from the menu bar, expanding the Database Tools folder and selecting the Server Explorer page. In the Connection options section, you'll find a property called Limit SQL results sent to Output window:

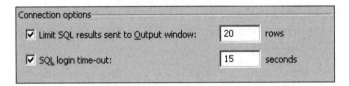

```
Connection options
  ☑ Limit SQL results sent to Output window:    [20      ]  rows
  ☑ SQL login time-out:                         [15      ]  seconds
```

This option limits the total results, not just the rows for each resultset returned. If three resultsets were sent back from a stored procedure, then the third wouldn't even be shown. I find it more useful to uncheck this option.

Creating Databases

The ability to create an MS SQL Server database is also available. This is more of a DBA function and doesn't expose all of the properties you really need to set up a database well, but it can suffice for some purposes.

1. Right-click the Data Connection node in Server Explorer, and select Create New SQL Server Database to bring up the Create Database dialog:

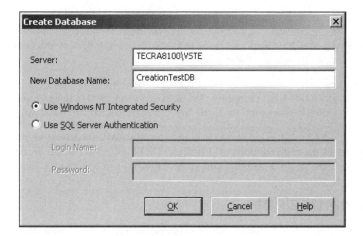

2. Enter the **Server, New Database Name,** and authentication information if necessary. Be sure to use an ID with sufficient rights to create a database.

3. Click OK. The dialog will disappear and a new Database Connection with the specified name will be added to the list in Server Explorer:

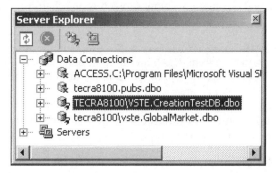

The documentation states that a new Oracle database cannot be created in this way, but there is still the possibility of Oracle, a third party, or an individual writing an add-in for this purpose. For more information about add-ins, see Chapter 7.

XML

Three years ago only a select few people were using XML – the Extensible Markup Language. Articles and books were few and far between. This has changed in a major way, although we don't yet live in a world where we serialize ourselves to XML to be beamed to our destinations in a twinkling of an eye, as the initial hype might have suggested. Nevertheless, a chapter about working with data would be incomplete without some discussion of this data format. In the same way, Visual Studio .NET would be incomplete without tools for working with XML.

Visual Studio .NET has tools for working with XML and XML Schemas – it has no support for DTDs. Since DTDs are the limited and less favored predecessor to schemas, this is to be expected. XSD (XML Schema Definition) is the W3C-approved way to mark up schema documents, and Microsoft does now appear to be sticking to standards where it can.

We'll spend our time in this section looking at the XML Schema Editor and the XML Editor. There is a lot more to XML and ADO.NET than those two tools, but they will make a good starting point. They also happen to be the only two visual tools for XML, which is what we're looking at in this chapter.

Our scenario is this. We need to be able to accept orders in XML format from our partners. In order to do that, we must pass them through the appropriate XSD file to make sense of the XML messages. To that end, we'll generate an XSD schema, add some fields, and validate some XML against it.

XML Schema Designer

XML Schema Definitions (XSDs) are written, not surprisingly, in the XML Schema definition Language (XSDL), which is itself an XML dialect. Hence, Visual Studio .NET allows us to code using this language in the XML Editor, but in addition, it provides a specialized visual tool for the their creation and editing.

The Order Template Example

1. To get started with the XML Schema designer, open a new Empty Project by going to File | New | Project and clicking on Empty Project. Name the project OrderMessages and click OK.

Create a new XML Schema document in the project by right-clicking on the project and selecting Add | Add New Item. Click on the XML Schema icon and name the schema OrderSchema.xsd. Click the Open button to create the file, and the XML Schema Editor will appear.

2. Add a connection to the GlobalMarket Database to the project by right-clicking on the Data Connections icon in Server Explorer and selecting Add Connection just as before.

3. From the Tables sub-tree, drag the Orders table onto the designer.

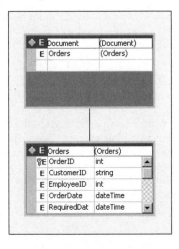

We now see the above graphical view of our nascent schema. It tells us that the root object is an `<Orders>` element, and that there are instances of individual orders beneath. If we click the tab at the bottom of the designer marked **XML**, we see the actual code that sets this up:

```
<?xml version="1.0" encoding="utf-8" ?>
<xs:schema id="OrderSchema" targetNamespace="http://tempuri.org/OrderSchema.xsd"
elementFormDefault="qualified" xmlns="http://tempuri.org/OrderSchema.xsd"
xmlns:mstns="http://tempuri.org/OrderSchema.xsd"
xmlns:xs="http://www.w3.org/2001/XMLSchema" xmlns:msdata="urn:schemas-microsoft-
com:xml-msdata">
  <xs:element name="Document">
    <xs:complexType>
      <xs:choice maxOccurs="unbounded">
        <xs:element name="Orders">
          <xs:complexType>
            <xs:sequence>
              <xs:element name="OrderID" msdata:ReadOnly="true"
               msdata:AutoIncrement="true" type="xs:int" />
              <xs:element name="CustomerID" type="xs:string" minOccurs="0" />
              <xs:element name="EmployeeID" type="xs:int" minOccurs="0" />
              <xs:element name="OrderDate" type="xs:dateTime" minOccurs="0" />
              <xs:element name="RequiredDate" type="xs:dateTime" minOccurs="0"/>
              <xs:element name="ShippedDate" type="xs:dateTime" minOccurs="0" />
              <xs:element name="ShipVia" type="xs:int" minOccurs="0" />
              <xs:element name="Freight" type="xs:decimal" minOccurs="0" />
              <xs:element name="ShipName" type="xs:string" minOccurs="0" />
              <xs:element name="ShipAddress" type="xs:string" minOccurs="0" />
              <xs:element name="ShipCity" type="xs:string" minOccurs="0" />
              <xs:element name="ShipRegion" type="xs:string" minOccurs="0" />
              <xs:element name="ShipPostalCode" type="xs:string" minOccurs="0"/>
              <xs:element name="ShipCountry" type="xs:string" minOccurs="0" />
            </xs:sequence>
          </xs:complexType>
        </xs:element>
      </xs:choice>
    </xs:complexType>
    <xs:unique name="DocumentKey1" msdata:PrimaryKey="true">
      <xs:selector xpath=".//mstns:Orders" />
      <xs:field xpath="mstns:OrderID" />
    </xs:unique>
  </xs:element>
</xs:schema>
```

If we are going to validate the orders sent from customers, we need the detail lines. To add these to the schema, drag the `OrderDetails` table onto the `Orders` table, below the single-cell `Document` table to produce this:

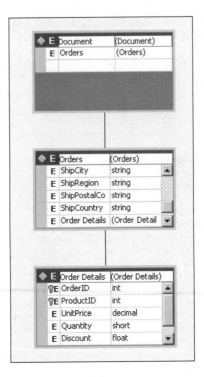

If we now look at the XML, we can see that the OrderDetails are represented as an element under the Orders objects, which are under the Document object.

```xml
<?xml version="1.0" encoding="utf-8" ?>
<xs:schema id="OrderSchema" targetNamespace="http://tempuri.org/OrderSchema.xsd"
elementFormDefault="qualified" xmlns="http://tempuri.org/OrderSchema.xsd"
xmlns:mstns="http://tempuri.org/OrderSchema.xsd"
xmlns:xs="http://www.w3.org/2001/XMLSchema" xmlns:msdata="urn:schemas-microsoft-
com:xml-msdata">
  <xs:element name="Document">
    <xs:complexType>
      <xs:choice maxOccurs="unbounded">
        <xs:element name="Orders">
          <xs:complexType>
            <xs:sequence>
              <xs:element name="OrderID" msdata:ReadOnly="true"
                msdata:AutoIncrement="true" type="xs:int" />
              <xs:element name="CustomerID" type="xs:string" minOccurs="0" />
              <xs:element name="EmployeeID" type="xs:int" minOccurs="0" />
              <xs:element name="OrderDate" type="xs:dateTime" minOccurs="0" />
              <xs:element name="RequiredDate" type="xs:dateTime" minOccurs="0" />
              <xs:element name="ShippedDate" type="xs:dateTime" minOccurs="0" />
              <xs:element name="ShipVia" type="xs:int" minOccurs="0" />
              <xs:element name="Freight" type="xs:decimal" minOccurs="0" />
              <xs:element name="ShipName" type="xs:string" minOccurs="0" />
              <xs:element name="ShipAddress" type="xs:string" minOccurs="0" />
```

```
            <xs:element name="ShipCity" type="xs:string" minOccurs="0" />
            <xs:element name="ShipRegion" type="xs:string" minOccurs="0" />
            <xs:element name="ShipPostalCode" type="xs:string" minOccurs="0" />
            <xs:element name="ShipCountry" type="xs:string" minOccurs="0" />
            <xs:element name="Order_x0020_Details">
              <xs:complexType>
                <xs:sequence>
                  <xs:element name="OrderID" type="xs:int" />
                  <xs:element name="ProductID" type="xs:int" />
                  <xs:element name="UnitPrice" type="xs:decimal" />
                  <xs:element name="Quantity" type="xs:short" />
                  <xs:element name="Discount" type="xs:float" />
                </xs:sequence>
              </xs:complexType>
            </xs:element>
          </xs:sequence>
        </xs:complexType>
      </xs:choice>
    </xs:complexType>
    <xs:unique name="DocumentKey1" msdata:PrimaryKey="true">
      <xs:selector xpath=".//mstns:Orders" />
      <xs:field xpath="mstns:OrderID" />
    </xs:unique>
    <xs:unique name="DocumentKey2" msdata:PrimaryKey="true">
      <xs:selector xpath=".//mstns:Order_x0020_Details" />
      <xs:field xpath="mstns:OrderID" />
      <xs:field xpath="mstns:ProductID" />
    </xs:unique>
  </xs:element>
</xs:schema>
```

This document affords us with three important pieces of the big data puzzle:

❑   First, it can be used to create a Dataset (**Schema | Generate Dataset**)

❑   Second, partners can use it to ensure that their order messages are well-formed.

❑   Finally, we can use it to validate the XML messages of others, even programmatically.

Editing the Schema

First, though, let's add a Validation Code. This is an imaginary number we are using for our example, but we can imagine that it's a number that business partners must affix at the order level in order for our message handler to accept the XML documents.

This column is not in the database yet, so we'll have to add it. We have two options: we can add it graphically or with code alterations – both are equally valid.

Graphically, scroll to the empty row at the bottom of the **Orders** box in the Schema diagram (the middle one), and create a new field, just as we would do in the data tools – by typing directly into the blank row. Name the field `ValidationCode` and give it a file type of `Integer`:

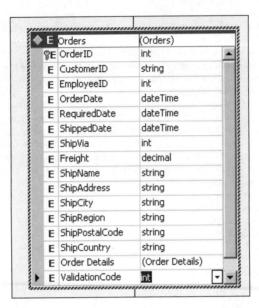

Alternatively, we could add the field into the XML code file. Place the cursor straight after the element in the code called `Order_x0020_Details` (your name may differ slightly), press *Enter*, and type a left angle bracket:

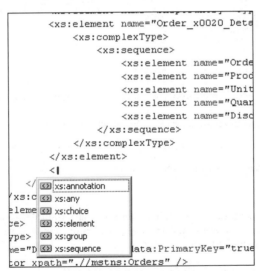

The IntelliSense picks up on the current schema namespace (the `xs` namespace, for Schemas themselves) and offers several choices. Here we are adding an element, and the new code will in the end look like this:

```
<xs:element name="ValidationCode" type="xs:int" />
```

Finally, save the XSD so we can use it during the next section.

The XML Editor

The XML editor is for directly editing the actual data in an XML file, just as the Table editors give us access to the data in a relational database management system such as SQL Server 2000.

Validating an Order

To check out our XSD, we'll take a crack at writing some XML by hand with the XML Designer and Editor. Then we'll run some validation against the XSD and see where we get.

To get started, add a new XML document in the same way as we added an XSD, through the context menus of Solution Explorer. Call it `OrderTest`.

In order for us to use this XML file effectively, we need to add a reference to the XSD document we just used. The Properties panel has a place for that. Just open the XML document we just created and check the **Properties** panel:

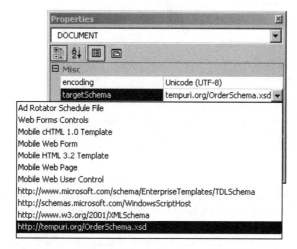

There is our `OrderSchema.xsd`, at the bottom of the list. It is referenced through `TempURI.org` because we didn't set a permanent URI for the root – we should change this in the text of the HTML before release. For now, just use it as it stands.

IntelliSense in XML

After adding the reference, we have a `Document` root of our XML document.

```
<?xml version="1.0" encoding="utf-8" ?>
<Document xmlns="http://tempuri.org/OrderSchema.xsd">

</Document>
```

This gives us everything we need to have IntelliSense assist us with the creation of a hand-coded XML document. Place the cursor between the opening and closing `Document` tags, and type a left bracket to get a list of objects that are under the document root. Since `Orders` is our only object at that level, it should be the only available option.

Go ahead and press *Tab* and a right bracket to accept. The closing `Orders` tag should appear. Next, type another left bracket between the two `Orders` tags. Lo and behold, the list of available tags at this level appears:

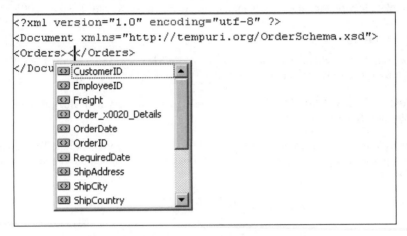

Select `OrderID`, and type in the closing bracket, followed by the number 1. We now have a simple – but invalid – XML document:

```
<?xml version="1.0" encoding="utf-8" ?>
<Document xmlns="http://tempuri.org/OrderSchema.xsd">
    <Orders><OrderID>1</OrderID></Orders>
</Document>
```

Validating XML

In order to validate this document, click on the **XML | Validate XML Data** menu in Visual Studio. A task is generated in the Tasks window, which describes all the fields we are missing according to our schema:

```
C:\Documents\Visual Studio Projects\OrderMessages\OrderTest.xml(3): Element
'http://tempuri.org/OrderSchema.xsd:Orders' has incomplete content. Expected
'http://tempuri.org/OrderSchema.xsd:CustomerID
http://tempuri.org/OrderSchema.xsd:EmployeeID
http://tempuri.org/OrderSchema.xsd:OrderDate
http://tempuri.org/OrderSchema.xsd:RequiredDate
http://tempuri.org/OrderSchema.xsd:ShippedDate
http://tempuri.org/OrderSchema.xsd:ShipVia
http://tempuri.org/OrderSchema.xsd:Freight
http://tempuri.org/OrderSchema.xsd:ShipName
http://tempuri.org/OrderSchema.xsd:ShipAddress
http://tempuri.org/OrderSchema.xsd:ShipCity
http://tempuri.org/OrderSchema.xsd:ShipRegion
http://tempuri.org/OrderSchema.xsd:ShipPostalCode
http://tempuri.org/OrderSchema.xsd:ShipCountry
http://tempuri.org/OrderSchema.xsd:Order_x0020_Details'. An error occurred at (3,
31).
```

Data View

If we don't feel like typing all of this by hand, the Data View window will help us out. Click on the Data tab at the bottom of the XML Editor, and we get a database-style entry screen pre-tabbed with access to the Order Details related table:

If we fill in valid data for all the requested fields, a valid XML file will be created to represent that data. Of course, we could also load an external XML file and validate that just as easily, using the ADO.NET tools to validate programmatically. Some suitable books for that purpose are mentioned at the end of the summary.

Summary

As we've seen, there are a tremendous number of features in Visual Studio .NET for dealing with data.

We started with Server Explorer, which is undeniably a very powerful tool in the enterprise developer's VS.NET arsenal. Specifically here, we looked at how it lets us work with servers and create data connections.

Next, we moved on to the large topic of database objects, and covered a lot of things there, including:

❑ Database Projects

❑ Query Designer

❑ View Script Template

❑ Database Diagram creation

❑ Making change scripts from diagrams

❑ Table view

❑ Inline editing of tables

❑ Views

❑ Stored Procedures

❑ Functions

From there, we took a quick view of the XML designer, taking in the Schema Designer and XML Viewer. These are powerful tools in VS.NET because of the close relationships between ADO.NET Datasets and XML.

This is not a book about data design – too bad, because there is a lot more to say. The relationship between the XML Designer and the ADO.NET Dataset alone is worth a few chapters.

For more information on ADO, Wrox has a book on ADO.NET called, *ADO.NET Programmer's Reference* (ISBN 1-861005-58-X) that I recommend for every programmer's bookshelf. Also, check out *Professional XML for .NET Developers* (ISBN 1-861005-31-8).

Anyone who is working with data on a regular basis would do well to look quite carefully at XML. It's slow to process compared to traditional methods, but it is so incredibly flexible that it really will change everything for cross-platform programmers and web developers. This chapter aims to set everyone on the right path in using the data tools of Visual Studio .NET, but there is much more out there to learn.

13

Visual SourceSafe

Source control is an often-underused part of software development. Especially for Microsoft developers, the choices have been few and far between. Visual SourceSafe (VSS) – the most fully integrated solution – has had a rough time of it, getting so-so ratings from the experts for years. Many users, frustrated with the unintuitive structure of source control programs in general, just dropped it in favor of good backups long ago.

At this point, you're either nodding your head knowingly, or thinking "What is source control, and why would I want to use it?" Let us put it this way. Have you ever worked in a team of developers, and been working on the same source code at the same time as another person? Ever both tried to save your work and ended up in that game of chicken – last one out wins – and one set of changes are completely lost? A source control system in its most basic form can help you avoid situations like this by allowing you to 'check out' source code files as if from a library. When you have a file checked out, your colleague won't be able to make changes until you check it back in. That's probably a little oversimplified, but there you have the very basics.

A good source control system can help you organize your work, which is especially useful when a large team of developers are at work on the same project, or if you have a large, complex project (where you can have various lines/branches of development, separate teams for testing, and so on). It provides a lot that a normal development environment can't provide on its own, and that would be hard to keep track of manually. We'll go into this briefly in our source control primer.

We said earlier that VSS hasn't always been welcomed with open arms, so what's been the problem? If you're working in teams, once you get into the habit, source control is worth having; that said, there were still a host of features missing from VSS 6.0b, the version *before* the one we have in Visual Studio .NET.

❑ **Project level tracking** – the 'projects' in VSS 6.0b are nothing more than folders

❑ **Web integration** – SourceSafe was not designed to handle the specific problems of web design, and had a habit of messing things up if you tried

❑ **Slow** – VSS has traditionally been a little sluggish over RAS, IP, or Terminal Server

❑ **Checkin procedure** – other source control systems like ClearCase have had advanced integrated source control options for years that have been missing from VSS

This is just to provide a bit of contrast and background for the rest of this short chapter, where we will focus on the source control system's latest version, 6.0c; its integration and automation with Visual Studio .NET, and new features. First, though, we'll start with a primer on source-control use.

Source Control for Developers

Source control refers to controlling the process of modifying software by mediating changes.

❑ It lets us control who can make changes and when

❑ It helps to prevent conflict that could occur when many people edit the same source

❑ It lets us save multiple versions of source code and choose the one we would like to use

❑ It gives us a centralized point for backup

❑ It lets us review the history of changes made to a file

❑ It lets us save configurations, or **baselines**, which are lists of collections of files and revisions that are part of a common release

❑ It gives us the ability to review the history of changes to a file

Many organizations use some form of source control system, and some do not. Visual SourceSafe is excellent for smaller development groups. As we'll see later, version 6.0c is also excellent for individual developers.

Adding Source Code

SourceSafe thinks in projects, which are folders that do not necessarily represent the folders in the directory structure. This gives us the ability to get files from different solutions and aggregate them for a build, or organizational reasons.

The SourceSafe client is under Programs | Microsoft Visual SourceSafe in the Windows Start button menu. It will ask for a login, and the default for the local database is admin with no password. Here's what the main screen looks like:

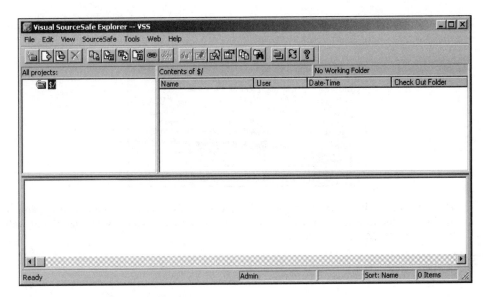

Adding a SourceSafe Project

Let's now build a simple project:

1. Click the Create Project icon. The following dialog will then appear:

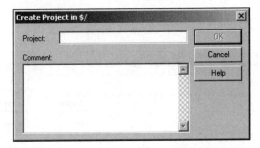

We can enter a folder name here and it will add a folder to the project tree.

2. Click the Add Files button (the file icon with a gold plus (+) sign) to add a source file. A standard file dialog will then appear:

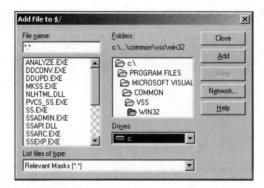

This lets us add files to be source controlled. These files will be marked read-only, and can only be written to when they are 'checked out'. Let's use the default web page in our web root, `C:\InetPub\WWWRoot\iisstart.asp`.

3. SourceSafe will ask for a comment. Type Adding for a test. and click OK. The file disappears from the list of available files.

4. Click Close.

Check Out and Check In

We now have a source-controlled project. The file has been marked read-only, and we have to check it out to use it. Let's look at the checkout procedure.

1. Right-click on the `iisstart.asp` file and select Check Out.

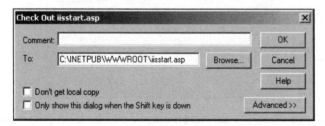

2. Enter a comment like Checking out, and click OK.

3. The file now appears checked out. The User, Time, and Date fields are filled in:

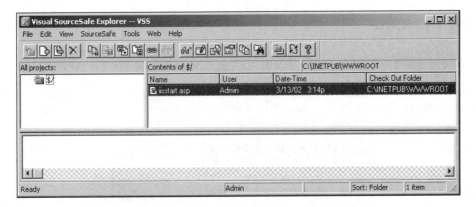

Now the file is read/write accessible, but SourceSafe will track changes to the file for us once we check it in again.

To check the file back in right-click the file in the Explorer and select Check In... A dialog will then appear showing the comment that was listed for the file when initially checked out.

Good Source Control Habits

The key to using SourceSafe is to build good habits.

❑ Use the **Set Working Folder** command to build a local repository of locally checked out files.

❑ Check in files when they are not being used. This allows others to edit them, and ensures that change is actually controlled.

❑ Despite the usability of the source-control client we saw above, get in the habit of using the integrated features. We'll look at these next.

Integration of VSS with Visual Studio .NET

By far the biggest story in the 6.0c version is the integration with Visual Studio .NET. Though earlier versions were fairly well integrated with VC++ 6 and InterDev, things have changed even from that point. There are five main new integration features:

❑ The tree view in **Add Project**

❑ **Checkout For Edit**

❑ The new **Options** dialog

❑ **Pending Checkins**

❑ Silent checkout

SourceSafe 6.0c is a separate disk, and a separate installation. There are two pieces – the server, with the database, and the client that both integrates with Visual Studio and has its own standalone program as well. We will focus on the client side for the purposes of this chapter.

Adding Projects

This is very easy to do. After VSS has been installed, right-clicking on a project in Visual Studio's Solution Explorer and selecting **Add Solution to Source Control...** will add it to the database.

What has changed, however, is the flexibility we have when adding a project. For instance, a tree view control has replaced the less intuitive interface used in integration with products like VC++ 6. It now gives us the option to add a directory for the solution.

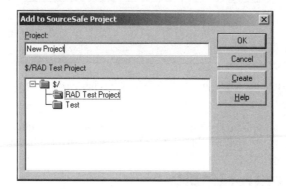

In this example, we clicked the **Create** button to add the **RAD Test Project** (from Chapter 5 (RAD for the Server), and are about to add another project called **New Project**. What's nice about this is that if we are using a large database, we could navigate to find it, rather than pasting the path into a textbox.

Check Out for Edit

If we open a checked in file, then attempt to edit it, we are prompted with the **Check Out For Edit** dialog – a nice addition to the process.

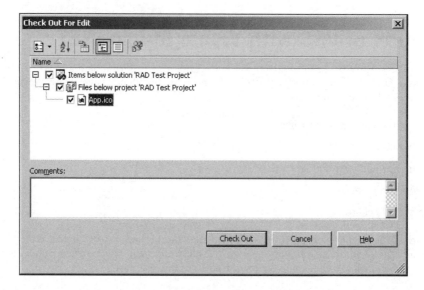

There are a few neat features here in the icon bar:

Symbol	Description
	Options – pull-down dynamic options specific to what you are doing
	Flat view
	Tree view – display file in tree format as seen above
	Compare versions – similar to the VSS report of the same name

If we choose to check out the file, we can edit as normal, and check in as normal. The checkout tree view above is also used for check in.

Options for Source Control

As part of the more careful integration, VSS now gives Visual Studio .NET developers more of a chance to customize the way they do business with source control. Among other things, there are 'profiles' for the corporate or independent user, as well as a user-modifiable custom setting. These profiles each have preset option configurations for different ways of using the tool. To get to the options, just select Tools | Options | Source Control in the menu bar.

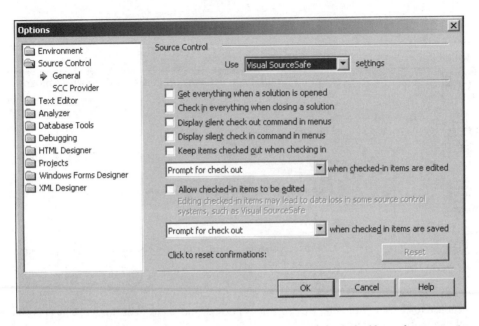

For more in-depth information on these options, you should read the help files – they are quite extensive for this option box.

Pending Checkins

The pending checkins screen provides us with a way to easily view the entire project's status in SourceSafe from one dialog box. Bring it up by right-clicking on your project in the Solution Explorer and selecting Pending Checkins.

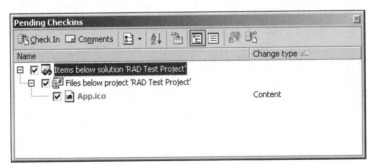

This toolbox gives us the ability to:

❑ Add text comments about the checkin status

❑ Compare files checked out with our copy

❑ Undo checkouts

❑ Most importantly, do a selective, global checkin

Previously, this required an actual instance of VSS to be running. This is just another example of the integration that Microsoft has done to collate the tools a developer needs to get the job done.

Silent Checkout

As part of the **Independent Developer** option profile, Microsoft makes certain assumptions about our development environment. First, files are kept checked out after they are checked in. This is reasonable, since we probably don't want to actually release the file for anyone else to edit, only to mark a version in the change control.

Another feature that is included in this set of options is silent checkout/checkin. This rather elegant name is nothing more than the automatic bypassing of the checkin box when you want to check in a file.

Note that this means that you can't leave any checkin comments.

When we select the **Independent Developer** option in the **Options** box, the context menu changes to show **Check In Now** for a checked out file, thus allowing us to bypass the intermediate step of the checkins box.

If we haven't made any changes, then the file is not actually checked in.

Not much more other than that, I'm afraid – but a useful feature nonetheless. One of the reasons independent programmers don't use source control more often is because it is more suited to enterprise developers. Several of the features of Visual Studio are aimed toward fixing that, though it's unfortunate in that regard that SourceSafe is only included with the Enterprise versions of the software.

Automation of VSS

The second minor breakthrough of Visual SourceSafe 6.0c is bringing the `SourceControl` object to the realm of the people. Though it has previously been accessible from C++ (however badly documented the APIs were), it is now part of the `DTE` namespace in the Script for the .NET Framework. This means that we can now include source control features in our automation macros.

As part of the `DTE.SourceControl` property, which returns a `SourceControl` object, we have six methods easily grouped into three pairs.

- ❑ `CheckOutItem` – Checks out the specified item
- ❑ `CheckOutItems` – Checks out the specified items
- ❑ `ExcludeItem` – Excludes the specified item from source control
- ❑ `ExcludeItems` – Excludes the specified items from source control
- ❑ `IsItemCheckedOut` – Retrieves a Boolean value that indicates whether the specified item is checked out
- ❑ `IsItemUnderSCC` – Retrieves a Boolean value that indicates whether the specified item is under source control

Checkout

`CheckOutItem` and `CheckOutItems` are exactly what they seem. The principal use for these would be to add source-control capabilities to existing macros. Chapter 7 includes a lot more on the Automation model. For instance, if we have a macro that adds text to selected files, we may want to check them all out first. This could be accomplished with a macro similar to the following:

```
Imports EnvDTE
Imports System.Diagnostics

Public Module Module1

  Sub CheckOutSelectedFiles()

    Dim OurFile As SelectedItem

    For Each OurFile In DTE.SelectedItems
      DTE.SourceControl.CheckOutItem(OurFile.Name.ToString())
    Next

  End Sub

End Module
```

Exclude

The `ExcludeItem` and `ExcludeItems` method perform as expected as well. If we needed to remove all images from the source control package, we could run a macro to do so:

```
Imports EnvDTE
Imports System.Diagnostics

Public Module Module1

  Sub RemoveImagesFromSS()
    Dim OurProject As Project
    Dim OurProjectItems As ProjectItem

    OurProject = DTE.ActiveSolutionProjects(0)
    For Each OurProjectItems In OurProject.Collection
      If InStr(OurProjectItems.Name.ToString, ".gif") <> 0 Then
        DTE.SourceControl.ExcludeItem(OurProject.FullName.ToString(),_
                                  OurProjectItems.Name.ToString)
      End If
    Next

  End Sub

End Module
```

IsItem

There are two different `IsItem` methods. They complement the above series of methods.

The first is `IsItemCheckedOut`. This determines if source control is required to check out an item. We could use it, pretty much as expected, to determine if a checkout operation would be required at all.

```
Imports System.Diagnostics

Public Module Module1

  Sub CheckOutSelectedFiles()

    Dim OurFile As SelectedItem

    For Each OurFile In DTE.SelectedItems
      If Not DTE.SourceControl.IsItemCheckedOut(OurFile.Name.ToString()) Then
        MsgBox(DTE.SourceControl.CheckOutItem(OurFile.Name.ToString()).ToString())
      End If
    Next

  End Sub

End Module
```

The second, `IsItemUnderSCC`, could be used in a similar manner in conjunction with the `Exclude` methods.

Summary

In this short chapter, our goal was to put across the fact that Visual Studio .NET has in Visual SourceSafe 6.0c a more integrated and usable way to manage source control. SourceSafe is one of the defining differences between the Enterprise edition of the product and the other variants. Not enough developers use source control, and we think that should change.

To that end, we introduced the new integration features of VSS 6.0c. These included:

❑   The tree view in **Add Project**

❑   **Checkout For Edit**

❑   The new **Options** dialog

❑   **Pending Checkins**

❑   Silent checkout

These features will certainly make working from home easier than ever, and reduce headaches for VSS administrators. Also, on the enterprise side, we discussed the DTE object for source control and those three useful categories of methods.

❑   Checkouts

❑   Exclusion

❑   IsItem

In today's RAD environment, when even losing a day's work to someone overwriting your changes can mean a lot, source control is something that everyone should be doing. Hopefully the changes to Visual SourceSafe for Visual Studio .NET will open a few eyes.

14

Application Center Test

When people talk about application testing, they mostly talk about testing the software to discover bugs and prove the correctness of the application's behavior. We often refer this kind of testing as functional testing. On the other hand, there's the fact that sometimes you run up against performance problems that need to be rectified in order to make your applications viable. Consequently, we also need to test applications in order to discover performance problems and prove that the application performs as expected or required. The software industry has developed many test strategies, techniques, and tools to combat the potential bugs and performance bottlenecks in software. In this chapter, we will take a close look at one performance testing tool, namely Application Center Test, which comes with Visual Studio .NET Enterprise Editions.

Different types of applications demand different types of performance testing techniques and tools. As one of the most commonly used development environments, Visual Studio contains a wide range of debugging and testing tools such as integrated debuggers, profiler, and remote debugging tools. As we are developing more and more Internet and intranet applications, we find that Visual Studio has sadly been lacking a web application performance testing tool and so we often need to use other tools.

With the release of Visual Studio .NET, things have changed. Visual Studio .NET Enterprise Editions include Application Center Test, or ACT, which provides powerful features to make web application performance testing easy to create and operate.

In this chapter, you will learn:

- ❑ What ACT can (and can't) do
- ❑ How to create and configure ACT projects and tests
- ❑ How to run tests
- ❑ How to analyze test results
- ❑ How to customize test scripts

In the following sections, we'll have an overview of performance testing issues and ACT. Later in the chapter, we'll then go into more detail to explain the tasks involved in testing web applications using ACT.

Performance Testing

Web applications typically support a large number of concurrent users. It is critical that development teams understand the capacity of both the web servers and the applications themselves in order to deliver successful applications that perform well under all conditions, especially during peak periods. Performance testing of a web application provides us with concrete and quantified data to measure how well the application performs when under heavy load, and to identify any potential problems that may affect the application's performance.

A successful web application should have the following three performance characteristics:

❑ **Low response time**. The response time is often measured as the delay between the time when a request is sent by a client and the time the client receives the full response to the request. Technically, the application response time is the sum of the response times of all components including the web server, database server, network connections, and so on. In general, response time increases as the number of client requests increases. When the system's resource is under a low load, the response time increases slowly because the system has the capacity to serve more clients. When the system is under heavy load, response time increases sharply as the system lacks the resources to serve additional clients.

❑ **High throughput**. The web application throughput is the number of client requests the system processes in a unit of time, normally a second. It measures the actual figure, not the maximum capacity. When the system load is light, throughput increases proportionally to the number of client requests. As the number of client requests continues to rise, it reaches its peak eventually at a certain point and starts to degrade.

❑ **High scalability**. Scalability is measured by how well the application performs when the number of requests increases, and how much the application's performance increases when the system is upgraded. It is common for business to outgrow their supporting applications. For instance, say a business anticipates that it will have 10,000 customers per day, but soon finds that it now attracts 100,000 customers per day. A good application should be able to scale up by simply upgrading its system hardware without significant redesign and recoding. For instance, it should be able to increase the throughput proportionally with faster or more processors and more memory.

In most applications, system requirements normally include the first two measurements. For instance, an online bookshop application's requirement specification may be to provide up to 1,000 concurrent users the ability to search the catalog with an average response time of 30 seconds. Development teams must then design and build the applications to satisfy such requirements. While the high scalability measurement is not always clearly stated, it's still a real requirement in most applications.

During the development cycle, the development team must conduct numerous performance tests with different objectives. At the early design stage, performance testing provides data for the team to decide on hardware and software requirements. At the implementation phase, developers execute performance testing to ensure that the application will provide the required performance with the given hardware and software. If the application fails to achieve the performance target, developers must investigate the problem, normally by identifying and resolving the bottlenecks of the application. In the testing phase, testers and customers also execute performance testing to prove that the system performs as required.

With proper performance testing, we can measure the application performance, discover existing and potential problems, and improve the application performance. A good performance testing tool provides us with statistics about not only the performance of applications, but also any potential problems. ACT is one such performance testing tool.

Overview

ACT is the second incarnation of a web application performance testing tool created by Microsoft. In 1999, Microsoft released the Web Application Stress tool (WAS), a tool that can simulate multiple requests to web application pages. ACT builds on WAS and includes most of the useful features available in WAS.

> *If you don't have ACT included in your version of VS.NET, you can download WAS from www.microsoft.com/technet/itsolutions/intranet/downloads/webstres.asp. Note that Microsoft has not made any new improvements to WAS since early 2000, and it is not clear whether it will continue to make WAS available now that ACT has been released.*

ACT comes in two editions. The ACT Enterprise Edition is included with Application Center 2000, a deployment and management tool for web applications. The Developer Edition is shipped with Visual Studio .NET, and is also called ACT for Visual Studio .NET. The latter edition has a subset of the features available in the former. In this chapter, we will be looking at the Developer Edition and the term ACT will always denote this edition unless explicitly stated. If you'd like to learn more about the ACT Enterprise Edition, please read the Application Center 2000 documentation. At the time of writing, there is very little documentation about the Enterprise Edition available on the Microsoft web site.

ACT is a simulation tool that can be used to stress test any web applications compliant to the HTTP 1.0 and 1.1 protocols. As the primary purpose of stress testing is to discover and analyze application performance and scalability issues, ACT provides a valuable tool for web application developers to test their applications against their performance requirements. In addition to normal testing features like the ability to generate test scripts, automate testing, and collect and report test results, ACT provides other features that are more specific to web applications.

As I mentioned earlier, web applications typically support a large number of concurrent users. ACT allows us to create multiple simultaneous connections to simulate such situations. It records, collates, and presents test results, which can be analyzed to work out the performance of many web application elements and pinpoint any potential problems. By their nature, web applications are open to misuse, hackings, and so on. As businesses are increasingly aware of security issues, especially those associated with web applications, more and more web applications are protected with security mechanisms such as the Secure Sockets Layer (SSL) in combination with user authentication. ACT supports testing incorporating both of these, but with some limitations. Before we get into detail about how to use it, it is important to understand what ACT can do and what it can't do.

What ACT Can Do

ACT provides a set of functionalities sufficient for most common web application stress testing requirements. Below is a list showing ACT's features.

- ❑ ACT is a web application performance testing tool. It is designed (and should be used) to test how well applications perform.

- ❑ ACT can create a number of simultaneous browser connections for each test run, and it is therefore capable of collecting realistic results data that reflects the server performance under heavy traffic.

- ❑ ACT supports both 40-bit and 128-bit SSL encryption. You can test URLs with HTTPS.

- ❑ ACT supports all four Microsoft Internet Information Server (IIS) authentication methods – anonymous access, basic authentication, integrated Windows authentication, and digest authentication for Windows domain servers.

- ❑ ACT supports the simulation of a large number of unique user connections. You can create test users and user groups.

- ❑ ACT stores test results for later analysis and comparison.

- ❑ ACT provides simple graphic representations of test data.

- ❑ ACT supports browser session recording. You can generate test scripts by recording activities performed in a browser session and rerun the test at a later time.

- ❑ ACT can collate test data for pages on the same or different web servers. If your test script sends requests to pages on different web servers, ACT can log performance statistics for each of them and calculate various average results.

- ❑ ACT supports test automation and scheduling by providing two well-designed object models – `Application` and `Test`. You can use any programming language or script capable of instantiating COM objects and invoking COM methods to automate ACT or to execute tests.

What ACT Can't Do

It's important to know right up front what ACT can't do, at least so you can start to try to find alternative ways around certain things. The list below shows the features I feel would be great but that aren't in the current version (1) of ACT:

- ❑ ACT is not a functional testing tool. That is, it doesn't provide you with the ability to verify the correctness of the target applications. In situations where you need to perform functional testing, you should use functional testing tools such as Rational TeamTest.

- ❑ While ACT can run on both client and server machines, it doesn't provide the ability to coordinate multiple test-client machines to execute tests. While it's possible to use high performance test-client machines to create and execute tests, in most cases test clients are less powerful than target web servers. Therefore, you often need to run tests simultaneously using multiple test clients in order to stretch the web server. The lack of test client coordination is rather surprising given that the older WAS does offer this capability, although it's not always easy to set the clients up and it may take some time to configure all test clients properly. You can work around this limitation by distributing tests to multiple client machines and running them simultaneously. However, you will have to either manually coordinate them or write your own program to do so.

- ❏ Although ACT supports SSL, it can't send client certificates nor verify server certificates.

- ❏ ACT can't simulate different network bandwidths between the test client and web server. Users of web applications normally use different connection media; some use corporate network, some use broadband Internet connections, others use dialup through analog modems. Users on low-speed connections normally generate much fewer requests than those on high-speed connections. When you test a web application under development, you typically run tests across the high-speed corporate network. The test result may not always be a true reflection of real-world scenarios. This is also a surprising omission considering it was implemented in WAS.

- ❏ ACT does not support the form-based authentication used by most Internet applications.

What the above list implies is that, if you already use WAS or other tools for web application performance testing, you should not abandon them yet, because they still provide a few features you can't get from ACT. I know that until ACT catches up, I'll keep WAS handy alongside ACT for my own work. In addition to WAS, there are other tools that offer more sophisticated functional and performance testing features, including those missing from ACT. Such tools include LoadRunner by Mercury Interactive (http://www-svca.mercuryinteractive.com/), Rational TeamTest by Rational (http://www.rational.com/), Web Performance Trainer by Web Performance Inc (http://www.webperformanceinc.com/), and e-Load by Empirix (http://www.empirix.com/).

First Look at ACT

ACT is available as a part of both Visual Studio .NET Enterprise Architect and Visual Studio .NET Enterprise Developer editions. If you selected to install ACT during the installation of Visual Studio .NET, you can find the shortcut to the ACT program in the Visual Studio .NET Enterprise Features folder. When it runs for the first time, it loads a sample project entitled ACTSamples. If this project does not appear, you can find it in the ACT program folder and open it. By default, it's installed in Program Files\Microsoft ACT\Samples\ACTSamples.

ACT provides a well-organized integrated development environment (IDE) that allows you to easily create and execute tests as well as analyzing the test results. The figure overleaf illustrates an example of viewing test results in the ACT IDE.

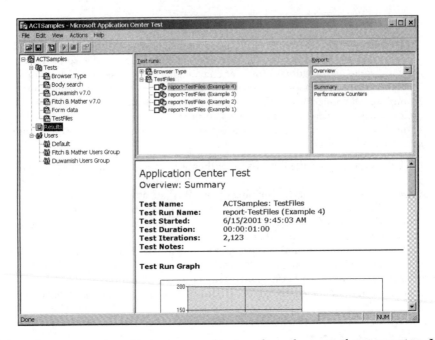

The left pane shows a tree view of tests, users, and test results in the currently open project. I will use the term Project Explorer, if only to be consistent with the Visual Studio .NET terminology, to refer to this pane. The ACTSamples project contains several pre-configured sample tests that can be used to demonstrate the capabilities and features of ACT.

Of the six included sample tests, you can run the following four to test against a set of test pages shipped with ACT.

- ❏ **Browser Type** – sends different HTTP headers with each request, mimicking access by a range of different browsers

- ❏ **Body Search** – checks to see if a specified string is in the body of the response

- ❏ **Form Data** – pulls querystring data from a text file and passes it in a POST

- ❏ **TestFiles** – a dynamic test that uses the sample test files provided

You can see full descriptions of each test in the header comments of the test script. The target test pages are in the Program Files\Microsoft ACT\Samples\TestFiles folder. In order to access and test them, you need to set up the TestFiles folder in IIS in one of two ways:

- ❏ Copy the TestFiles folder to the root directory of your web server

- ❏ Create a virtual root in your web server to point to the TestFiles folder

Once you have done this, you can access the test files through http://localhost/TestFiles/. Note that the sample tests all reference the web server using localhost. Therefore if your web server is on a different machine from the one you run ACT on, you will need to manually modify the test scripts. We'll look at writing test scripts in more detail in later sections. If you need to change the target web server now, simply follow the two steps below:

1. Open each test by clicking it in the Project Explorer. The right pane should then show the test script for the selected test.

2. Change the value of g_sServer from localhost to your web server address.

Now you can run a test by first selecting a test and then either clicking the Start Test button on the toolbar, or the Start Test command in the Actions menu. The test status dialog will appear as shown in the figure below.

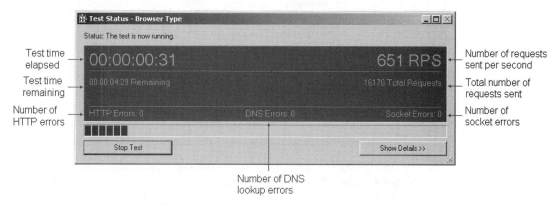

The Show Details button expands the dialog to show the above results in a chart.

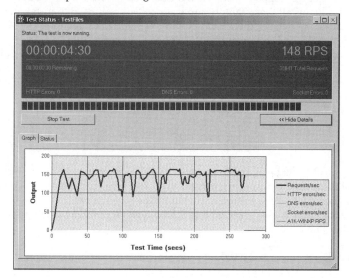

During the test, you can also click the Stop Test button to stop the test. Once a test has been stopped, you can only restart it from the beginning. That is, you can't pause and resume a test. After the test finishes, you can view your test results by clicking the Results node in the Project Explorer.

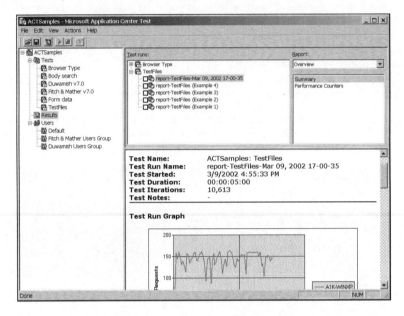

In the right pane, you can see a list of tests and the reports from each run. Later sections explain the test results in more detail. For now just try running a few to get a feel for the process.

The other two tests, Duwamish v7.0 and Fitch & Mather v7.0, target the Duwamish Online and F&M Stocks sample applications shipped with Visual Studio .NET. Because the Visual Studio .NET installer does not automatically install those sample applications, you will need to install them yourself if you want to try these tests. By default, the Visual Studio .NET installation copies the Windows Installer package for both sample applications to the `Microsoft Visual Studio .NET\Enterprise Samples` folder. Please read the `Readme.htm` files for each application for installation instructions.

As with other Microsoft applications, the ACT IDE offers a toolbar for you to quickly perform some common tasks.

The first two buttons let you open another project and save the current project, respectively. The third button is for you to create a new test in the current project. The next two allow you to run and stop a test. If no test is running, the stop button is grayed out as shown above. The last button allows you to see the properties of the currently selected test. These actions are all available from the menu, which also provides a few more functions.

Once you are familiar with the ACT IDE, it's time to create a simple test to get started.

Walkthrough – Creating a New Test

An ACT test is a script that uses the ACT Test object hierarchy to specify the test process. There are two ways to create a new test in ACT:

❑ Create a new test by recording a browser session. You can then modify the generated script if required.

❑ Create a new test by manually entering test scripts using either VBScript or JScript.

Once you are familiar with the Test object model, you can create tests by writing scripts yourself. However, it's often more productive to record a browser session and let ACT generate a script for you. You can then modify the generated script to suit your needs. So, let's start from the beginning by creating a new project and a new test.

Recording a Browser Session

Recording a browser session in ACT is fairly straightforward. The steps below show the whole process.

1. In ACT, select File and then New Project from the menu to create a new project.

2. Click the New Test button on the toolbar to create a new test.

3. In the New Test Wizard, select the Record a new test option. While ACT supports both VBScript and JScript for writing test scripts, recording only creates test scripts in VBScript.

4. In the Browser Record dialog, click the Start recording button. ACT will start a new instance of Internet Explorer.

5. In the Internet Explorer, type in the URL http://localhost/TestFiles/ad_test.asp and press *Enter*. This opens the page in the Internet Explorer. In the background, ACT records the requests sent to the web server. When you run the test later on, ACT will be able to recreate those requests.

Switch back to ACT, click the Stop recording button and then the Next button. Name the test AdTest and click the Next and then the Finish buttons to close the wizard. ACT will automatically generate a test script that will set up page requests when you run the test later on. The test is now ready. The next step is to run it to ensure that it works properly. By default, the test will run for five minutes.

On your web server, open the Windows Task Manager and click the Performance tab to watch the CPU usage. If you run the test from another machine, do the same there as well. You should see that the CPU usage on both machines is much higher than normal. CPU usage is an important indicator of the web site performance and the test effectiveness. We will explain this in more detail in a minute. Let's now turn our attention to configuring and running tests.

Creating a Test Manually

Whether you are an experienced programmer or just starting, you probably have a love for code writing in your blood. Once you have run through the `Test` object model reference in the ACT help files, you may feel the temptation to actually write code yourself. After all, wizards are meant to be for non-programmers, and automatically-generated code is unlikely to be as good as your own code.... You might want to modify a pre-recorded test to get the feel for it first.

If you want, you can create an empty test by selecting Create an empty test in the New Test Wizard (no, you can't avoid the wizard here). You can then select the script language and assign it a name. ACT will still generate one line of code, `Test.SendRequest("http://localhost")`, for you, but I really can't see why it shouldn't be deleted anyway. The rest, of course, is up to you. But don't despair – we'll look at testing in more detail so you will get a better idea of the sort of thing you will need to write.

Project Properties

Before we go any further, let's take a look at the settings you can configure for each test project. Right-click the project in the Project Explorer and select Properties. The project properties dialog presents all configurable project-wide settings.

General Properties

The General tab in the project properties dialog allows you to set whether or not any objects on the web server should be excluded from tests in the project. You can also set proxy server properties if the test clients connect to the web server through a proxy server. The figure below illustrates the configurable general properties:

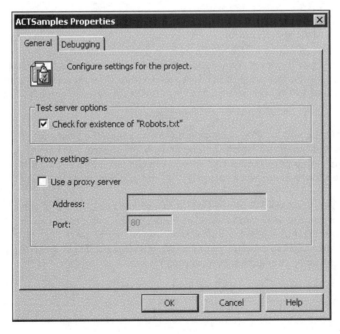

Since search engines became popular to help Internet users find information on the web, system administrators use the web robot exclusion list to instruct the search robots to bypass certain sites or pages that they do not want to be searchable. They usually create a `robots.txt` file on the root directory of a web site to specify a list of pages, or the whole site, that should not be indexed. ACT can check this file to decide whether certain objects on the target web server should be excluded from the tests as well. ACT enables this checking by default, but you can turn it off by clearing the Check for existence of "Robots.txt" checkbox. As ACT ignores all META tags in target HTML pages, it doesn't pick up any exclusion instructions specified in the ROBOTS META tags. Therefore you must use a `Robots.txt` file to specify what pages should be excluded. You can find more information about the `Robots.txt` file at http://www.robotstxt.org/wc/robots.html. A good resource for the robots exclusion protocol can be found at http://www.robotstxt.org/wc/exclusion.html#robotstxt.

Many corporate networks use proxy servers to cache frequently accessed web contents to reduce the traffic between the network and the Internet. If you test a web site outside of the company network, you may have to follow the company policy to go through a designated proxy server. In such cases, you can enable the Use a proxy server option and specify the proxy server address and port.

However, you should be aware of the implications of using proxy servers for stress testing. The first is that you may be getting test responses from the proxy server rather than the actual web server, and this will obviously invalidate the test results. Second, the proxy server itself may become the bottleneck during the stress testing so you don't get the true indication of the target web application performance.

Debugging Properties

You can also configure the test tracing properties for a project. The figure below illustrates the possible settings:

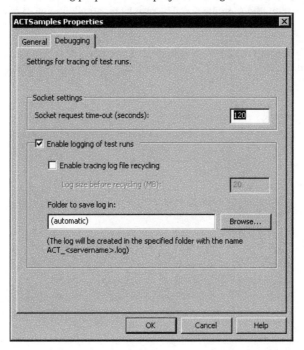

If a connection has been idle for a long time, you may want to close it so that inactive connections don't eat up valuable system resources. You can specify the Socket request time-out value to instruct ACT to drop a connection if the specified number of seconds has elapsed since the last request or response.

While ACT already collects useful test data during a test, you may also want to log extra information about the test status or error conditions in your script. You can instruct ACT to write textual data to a log file by enabling test logging in this dialog and calling the Trace method of the global ACT Test object when required. By default, ACT writes the log data to the ACTTrace.log file located in the Program Files\Microsoft ACT directory. However, you will generally want to store project-specific data in a separate log file by specifying a folder where the log should be placed. ACT will then write the log data to ACT_<ServerName>.log in that folder, where <ServerName> is the name of the target web server.

If your script writes a large amount of data to the log file, the size of the file may increase rapidly. To prevent it from growing too large, you can restrict its maximum size by enabling log file recycling and specifying a threshold size. Once the log file reaches this size, it will be cleared before new data is added to it.

Now you have your project set up exactly as you want, give it a run. This time, let's take a closer look at the results.

Reading and Analyzing Test Results

For each test, ACT presents three different reports. The **overview** report shows the summary of test statistics and major errors encountered during the test. The **graphs** report allows you to generate graphical representations of the test data. The **requests** report lists various test results related to each request.

The overview report consists of two parts – summary and performance counters. The summary shows statistics related to the test itself. The performance counters show the readings of selected performance counters during the test.

Overview Summary

The overview summary shows various test results such as the number of requests sent and the average response time. The figure below illustrates the IDE in the results view.

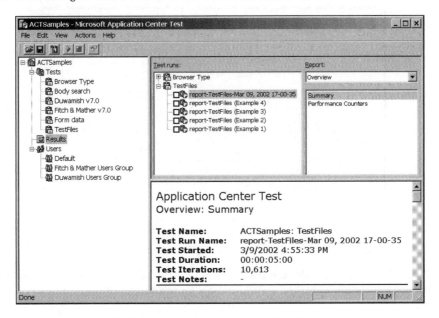

It contains seven sections. Let's look at each section in more detail.

Header

The lower right pane in the above figure shows the header of the overview summary. The results are fairly self-explanatory. The only item that may not be quite so obvious is Test Iterations. This value shows the number of passes the test has run through. This is different from the total number of requests because a test can generate multiple requests in each pass. The test we created with the wizard is quite simple, as each pass generates exactly two requests – one to the ad_test.asp page and another to an image file, logo.gif, used in that page.

Test Run Graph

This graph is almost identical to the one shown in the details view of the Test Status dialog. The only difference is that by default it only shows the number of requests sent during the test, as illustrated below.

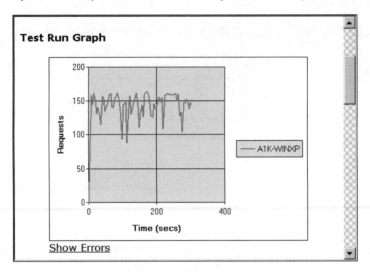

To see the number of socket, DNS, and HTTP errors, you can click the Show Errors link below the graph. We saw those statistics earlier, on the Test Status screen while a test was running.

Properties

This section shows the test type and other configurable properties for the current run.

Properties	
Test type:	Dynamic
Simultaneous browser connections:	1
Warm up time (secs):	0
Test duration:	00:00:05:00
Test iterations:	10,613
Detailed test results generated:	Yes

ACT only supports dynamic tests. A dynamic test is a bit of either VBScript or JScript that sends requests to a web server. When a dynamic test runs, it can change many aspects of the test such as the target URLs, the order in which the requests are sent, and so forth.

You can configure other properties by right-clicking the test in the project explorer and selecting **Properties** from the context menu to open the test properties dialog as shown in the figure below.

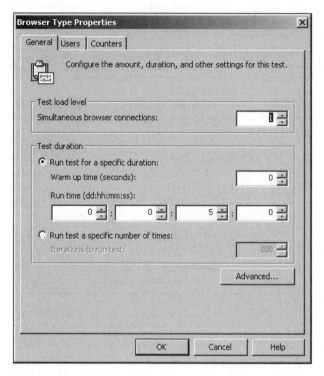

The simultaneous browser connections figure shows the number of concurrent connections to the web server. This test only uses one connection. While HTTP itself is a connectionless protocol, HTTP 1.1 offers the keep-alive feature. A web browser and a web server supporting this feature will establish one connection between them, send multiple requests through the connection, and close it once all requests are sent.

As web servers typically serve many simultaneous connections, a test with multiple connections more accurately represents the real world situation. ACT is capable of opening up to 2,000 simultaneous connections, although you would usually use a lot less because such a large number of connections would overload the client machine running the test. If the client machine is powerful enough, you can configure it with the maximum number of concurrent connections your web application is design to support. In most cases, however, the client machine may not be able to support that maximum number of connections. In such cases, you start with 1 connection and increase it gradually in each subsequent test until the CPU usage at the client machine reaches about 90% during the test. In general, when the CPU usage is above 90%, the client machine can't generate requests fast enough and therefore becomes the performance bottleneck itself. The test results then don't accurately reflect the server performance. You can either watch the CPU usage using the Windows Task Manager, or record it by adding a CPU performance counter to the test. We will cover the latter method in the *Performance Counters* section.

The warm-up time specifies the number of seconds after the test starts and before ACT starts to collect the test results. If you have worked with database before, you will probably know notice that it takes a lot longer to open the first database connection than to open the consequent connections because of the connection pooling feature used to cache database connections. As a result, when you access a web page that needs to open database connections for the first time, the response time may not be representative if included in the test result. Another factor that may cause false long response times is when a page needs to instantiate COM+ components, again due to the COM+ object pooling feature. There are other factors such as connection to other systems via Web Services or SOAP requests.

The test duration specifies the length of time the test should run. Instead of specifying the test duration, you can also specify test iterations to run a test for a particular number of passes. Setting those figures allows you to test the system in continuous operation.

There is another setting, Generate detailed test results, which is accessible by clicking the Advanced button.

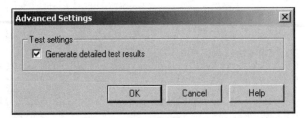

When you enable this setting, ACT will generate statistics for each request, shown in the detailed request statistics report. If this option is disabled, ACT will only generate the average over all requests during the test. While enabling this option will create a more detailed report, it also takes more time to record the data and therefore reduces the test client's ability to generate more requests.

The other two tabs, users and counters, allow you to assign users and add performance counters, respectively, to tests. We will cover adding users in the *Authentication and Users section*, and performance counters in the *Performance Counters* section.

Summary

This section contains the test result summary. It shows the total number of requests and the total number of connections in fairly obvious fashion, as illustrated below.

Summary

Total number of requests:	43,159
Total number of connections:	10,613
Average requests per second:	143.86
Average time to first byte (msecs):	4.08
Average time to last byte (msecs):	4.85
Average time to last byte per iteration (msecs):	19.73
Number of unique requests made in test:	8
Number of unique response codes:	1

Since each test run produces two requests in our example, one to the page and another to the GIF image file, you would probably expect that the total number of connections should be exactly a half of the total number of requests. The report, however, shows that they are the same.

Note that if you stopped the test before it was finished, the total number of connections may be one less than the number of total requests. This is because the test may not have the chance to close and record the connection after it sends a request using the connection.

The reason for this seemingly unexpected result is that the New Test Wizard generates a script where it creates a new connection for each request. It also only posts requests in HTTP 1.0 format. In order to test the server performance with the HTTP 1.1 keep-alive feature, you will have to change the script manually. You will see how this can be done later in the chapter.

The average requests per second figure is also quite obvious; it's just the total number of requests sent divided by the test duration in seconds. The next two figures, though, are more interesting.

The time to first byte (TTFB) shows the time difference, in milliseconds, between sending out a request to the server and receiving the first byte of the response from the server. The time to last byte (TTLB), on the other hand, shows the time between sending out a request and receiving the last byte of the response. The average TTFB and TTLB therefore show the average measurements obtained during the test run.

Both TTFB and TTLB figures measure the **latency,** or response time, of the web server to serve out a page. When the server is heavily in use, the latency increases rapidly. A long TTFB usually indicates that the web server is under stress, that is, the request may be held in the request queue on the server for a long time before it gets processed. The difference between TTFB and TTLB shows how long the application takes to process a request, and therefore is a good indication of how the application performs under heavy load.

The average time to last byte per iteration shows the difference between the time when the first request in a pass is sent and the time when the last byte of the last response is received. Since this test sends out two requests per pass, this figure is roughly double the average TTLB.

The number of unique requests made in this test is two – the `ad_test.asp` page and the `logo.gif` image file. The number of unique response codes reports the response code received from the web server. Note that it only reports HTTP errors. If you stop the web server or pull out the network cable on your development machine, ACT can't record any more response codes because it isn't receiving any HTTP response from the server at all. The Response Codes section shows all HTTP response codes with some more detail.

Error Counts

This section shows the number of HTTP, DNS, and socket errors.

```
Errors Counts

   HTTP:                                        0
   DNS:                                         0
   Socket:                                      0
```

We've already seen these, so I won't go into any more detail about them now.

Additional Network Statistics

As the title suggests, this section reports the network status that isn't reported in previous sections.

Additional Network Statistics	
Average bandwidth (bytes/sec):	553,025.77
Number of bytes sent (bytes):	3,828,297
Number of bytes received (bytes):	29,353,249
Average rate of sent bytes (bytes/sec):	63,804.95
Average rate of received bytes (bytes/sec):	489,220.82
Number of connection errors:	0
Number of send errors:	0
Number of receive errors:	0
Number of timeout errors:	0

The average rate of sent bytes and average rate of received bytes show the number of bytes sent and received, respectively, per second during the test. The average bandwidth shows the sum of the above two. Note that this figure is generally lower than the actual network bandwidth because it only measures the bandwidth actually used by the test. The number of bytes sent and the number of bytes received show the total number of bytes sent and received during the test.

To accurately measure the server performance, suspend as many programs and services that may use the network on the client machine as possible to maximize the network bandwidth available to testing. If the average bandwidth used by the test approaches the actual network bandwidth, the test result may not be accurate as the bottleneck may now be the network connection between the client and server machines. You can add network performance counters to obtain the total network usage during testing in order to compare them with the bandwidth consumed by the test.

The number of connection errors shows the number of times when the test client fails to connect to the web server. Such errors may indicate that the web server is offline, but they can also be caused by the inability of the web server to establish connections under heavy load, a bad router, and so on. The number of send errors and the number of receive errors show the number of times when the test client fails to send out the request or receive responses, respectively. The number of timeout errors indicates the number of times the test client times out between sending out a request and waiting for the response to come back. The default timeout is 120 seconds, which you can change manually in the test script. As most web applications require a faster response time than 2 minutes, you should change it in most cases. A good timeout value should represent the threshold of acceptable server response time. For instance, if a web application requirement specifies that the users should get a response within 30 seconds, setting the timeout value to 30 will help you identify how often this requirement has not been met during testing.

Response Codes

This section lists all response codes the test client received from the server. The Count figure shows the total number of times a particular response code is received, while the Percent figure shows the percentage of a response code count against the total count of all response codes.

Requests

If you have enabled the Generate detailed test results option for the test, you can investigate detailed results for each unique request made in the test. To see the test result for a request, select Requests in the report list and then click the request target.

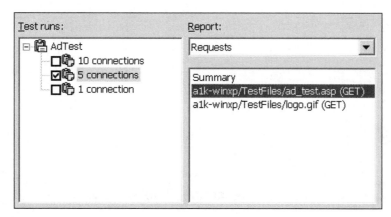

The request details report header is the same as that of the overview report. The report contains four sections. Three of them will be very similar to the corresponding sections in the overview:

❏ The Request Information section shows the server name and the request target path on the server. It also displays the request method, which is either GET or POST.

❏ The Additional Network Statistics section shows the network statistics related to the request. Each result has the same meaning as its counterpart in the Summary and Additional Network Statistics section of the Overview report, except it only reports the test data collected for the particular request.

❏ The Response Codes section is also similar to the corresponding section in the Overview report. Again it also shows the response code received from the response to the request.

The Request Performance section, however, is where you can get more detailed information about the request. The request number shown here is the number of this particular request sent during the test. The request content length is also clear enough. While you already know what TTFB and TTLB mean, the detailed statistics for each of them and the request content length need some more explanation as they show some statistically significant results.

Statistics Review

To understand the importance of your data, it helps to know a little bit of statistics theory. While we won't be able to cover nearly enough here, it would still be a good idea to understand a few terms. A graph will also help.

The graph below shows a distribution of results known as a **normal distribution** of response times. As you can see, in a normal distribution most results are around the same kind of time in the middle of the graph, but we still have a few requests being delivered really quickly, and a few that have taken a bit longer.

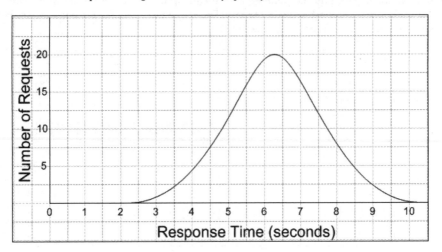

Let's make sure we understand a few terms.

❑ **Minimum** – The lowest individual value in our distribution. Here the minimum is about 3 seconds, with one request achieving the minimum response time.

❑ **Maximum** – The highest individual value in our distribution. Here the maximum is about 9.5 seconds, also with one request achieving the maximum response time.

❑ **Median** – The 'middle' value in our distribution. If we have, say, 99 requests, the median is about 6.5 seconds, which is the response time for the 50th fastest (same as the 50th slowest) request.

❑ **Mean** – what most people just call the 'average'. It is the sum of (response time x number of requests with same time) divided by the total requests. In a perfectly 'normal' distribution, the value of the median and the mean are identical. Most real distributions are actually slightly skewed, so this isn't true.

❑ **Percentiles** – The 25th percentile (for example) is the value below which 25% of the results fall. In our response example, 25% of the requests took less than roughly 5 seconds to answer, so the value of the 25th percentile is 5. Similarly, the 75th percentile is roughly 7.5 seconds. Therefore 50% of the requests receive a response between 5 and 7.5 seconds.

And again, in a perfect world, the 50th percentile would have the same value as both the mean and the median. Although the world is not perfect, in most cases those three values are very close.

❏   **Standard Deviation** – This is a tricky one. This is a measure of how tightly or loosely spread the deviation is. A smaller number indicates a sharper curve, and means that most of our results are quite close to the mean. A curve with the same mean and a much bigger standard deviation would mean that our average speed is the same, but that we're getting a spread of really fast and really slow responses. A standard deviation of zero would mean that every response took exactly the same time.

There's more to statistics than this, and if you get into testing in a real way you'll need to study it a little so you know what your numbers are telling you.

Request Performance

Now that we understand a little statistics, it's a matter of applying the knowledge when reading the request performance data in the request details report. Let's look at a sample set of TTFB statistics as shown in the figure below.

Time to first byte - TTFB (msecs)	
Minimum:	0.00
Maximum:	110.00
Average:	18.17
Standard Deviation:	9.37
25th Percentile:	10.00
50th Percentile:	19.99
75th Percentile:	20.04

The minimum TTFB is 0.00 milliseconds, which is rather strange as it's very unlikely that you would actually receive the response in less than 1/100 of a millisecond. A reasonable guess as to the cause of this is that the response comes so quickly that ACT can't properly record the time difference. Regardless of the cause, this is an exception that we won't concern ourselves with much about. The maximum indicates that the longest wait for a response during the test is 110 milliseconds. What's labeled here as 'average' is really the mean of the test results. The standard deviation of 9.37 indicates a rather sharp distribution. Looking at the value alone won't tell you much about how sharp the distribution is, though, so you should also look at the percentiles. Between the 25th and 75th percentiles, half of our data are found. This means that half of our requests lie in a 10ms range, and a further 25% of our requests are faster than 10ms.

The other 25% lie somewhere between 20.04ms and 110, which is quite a spread and is shown in a broad shallow tail on the slow side of our curve. The diagram below shows a possible curve representing distribution of the response time in this test run.

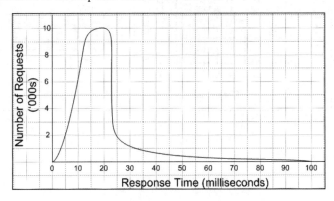

An interesting observation is that the 50th and the 75th percentiles are very close to each other, indicating that the TTFB for the vast majority of requests are very close around the 50th percentile of 19.99 milliseconds. In fact, considering the mean is 18.17 which is also very close to the 50th percentile, you can quite safely say that most requests receive response between 16 and 20 milliseconds. While all this might not be obvious from the quick pass through statistics we've taken, hopefully it illustrates that with a bit of practice you can get quite a lot from a set of 7 figures like the ones we have above.

Graphs

Graphs are a useful tool to identify the web site performance across different conditions. In order to create a good comparison, you need to run the test several times. Each time, you should generally change only one test property. For instance, you can run the test three times, each with a different number of simultaneous browser connections. You can then create a graph comparing the requests per second for each run to see how well your web server handles heavy traffic.

To see how it works, run the test 3 times with 1, 5, and 10 connections. Then select all three tests and report on RPS and TTLB against connections, as illustrated below.

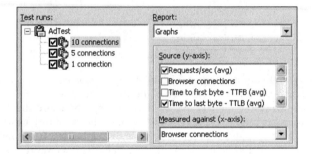

The graph may look like the one shown below:

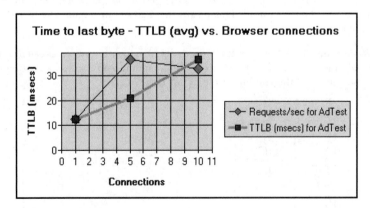

This graph shows that the best performance seems to be achieved when you open 5 simultaneous browser connections to the server. Obviously, you may want to try a few more runs, possibly with the number of connection set to 4, 6, and 8. The graph will show more accurately when the performance peaks and when it starts to suffer. On the other hand, the TTLB increases with the number of connections, as we might expect. In this way, you can better configure your setup to work at its peak performance across all the factors that affect it.

There are too many useful combinations to be covered fully here. In a production project, you should try to play with various test settings to stress your web server and to see how many concurrent users it can satisfactorily support. For instance, if a performance requirement is to support 100 concurrent users with the average response time of 30 seconds, you can try to run 100 simultaneous connections and check the average TTLB. If the average is more than 30 seconds, you reduce the number of simultaneous connections until the TTLB falls to less than 30 seconds. You now know that the current configuration of your application can only support, say, 80 concurrent users.

Such test results provide quantified support to decide whether and when you should consider upgrading or adding new hardware. Note that hardware upgrade is just one of the options to increase your web server performance. You will often find other software bottlenecks by collecting other information by adding some performance counters to your reports.

Performance Counters

To add performance counters to your test, select the Counters tab in the test properties dialog. By default, ACT does not include any performance counters in tests. You can click the Add button to bring up the Browse Performance Counters dialog.

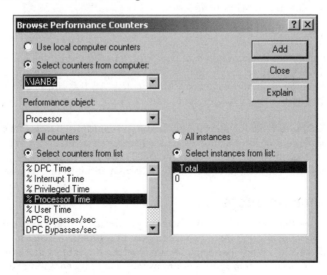

You can add performance counters from both the web server and the test client machines. The reason for collecting server performance data should be obvious, because that's what tests are generally designed to do – test the server performance. However, a less obvious consideration is that you want to ensure that your test really does test the server by removing extraneous bottlenecks that are not related to the performance of the target web server.

The Client Machine

One such bottleneck is the test-client machine. If the client machine is overloaded, it will not be able to generate as many requests during the test. In such cases, the collected test result will not truly represent the performance of the server. For instance, if the test client only manages to send 50 requests per second, the test result will show 50 RPS even though the server may have no problem handling 200 RPS.

A good indication of the client machine's ability to generate as many requests as possible is its CPU usage, which is the Processor Time of the `Process` object. If the CPU usage by ACT is very close to 100%, the client machine may be overloaded and therefore unable to generate requests fast enough. Other useful performance counters for the client machine are:

- ❏ **Memory – Available Bytes**. This shows the available physical memory. If the CPU usage is not very high but you run out of physical memory, the machine will still not be able to generate many requests.

- ❏ **Network Interface – Bytes Total**. This shows the network volume during the test. If it is close to the network bandwidth, you are reaching the limit.

There are several methods to increase the client machine's performance:

- ❏ Suspend unnecessary processes by stopping some non-essential services and other programs on the test client

- ❏ Reduce the number of simultaneous browser connections used in the test

- ❏ Upgrade hardware, for example adding more memory and replace your network card if its capacity is below the network bandwidth

- ❏ Use multiple client machines

Because test client machines are generally less powerful than the server, the best you can get by applying the first three techniques is normally still not enough to really stress test the server. Therefore the realistic solution is to use multiple clients. Unfortunately ACT as shipped with Visual Studio .NET does not have the ability to coordinate testing among multiple machines.

With ACT for Visual Studio .NET, you can install ACT on multiple clients. Once you have created and tested a test on your development machine, you can distribute the test script to all client machines. You can then start the test on all client machines manually. To automate the process, you can write scripts to start a test using the ACT application object model and then add it to the Windows Task Scheduler.

Useful Performance Counters

There are many factors that can affect the application performance. Each application has its own technical characteristics, requiring you to collect a range of test data in order to identify the potential bottlenecks and other issues. While performance analysis is a big subject that warrants the coverage of its own book, the web server system resources are usually the bottlenecks in many applications. Here are some of the most significant performance counters.

The CPU usage (**Processor: %Processor Time: _Total**) tells you when, and by how much, the processor or processors on the web server become the bottleneck. If the processors run constantly above 90%, you should consider replacing them with faster processors. Another indicator is the amount of available physical memory (**Memory: Available Bytes**). If it is constantly low, the system will have to perform a lot of memory paging, which is very slow. In such a case, you should also add the **Memory: Pages/sec** counter, which reports the paging rates. If the paging rates are high, you will want to increase the system memory size.

The IIS itself can also be a bottleneck. If a lot of incoming requests are being queued (**Active Server Pages: Requests Queued**), the server may be overloaded. While this sometimes relates to CPU usage, you should keep an eye on this as well because it may be caused by other factors such as COM+ component overload. If a COM+ component is getting more requests than it can handle, it may block the web server and prevent requests from being processed as fast as the server can normally handle. Of course you can always distribute your COM+ components on a server on their own in the corner if they're going to misbehave.

As most web applications use a database to persist data, you should watch the database server statistics. ACT can only collect this kind of test data through performance counters. If you use SQL Server, you can get most database-related statistics this way. However, using the SQL Server Profiler may provide you with more detailed information. Furthermore, as not all database servers make their performance data available through the Windows Performance Monitor, you have to use their own tools separately to monitor their performance.

Authentication and Users

If the target web server requires authentication, the test client will need to be able to log on. ACT supports all three authentication methods used by the IIS: basic, integrated, and digest. It also supports anonymous access, in which case no login is required. You can provide a list of users for ACT to use for tests, as explained in the next section. Once you have selected users for a test, ACT can automatically detect the web server authentication methods and manage the HTTP authentication with the web server.

On the other hand, ACT does not support form-based logon methods. If the target web server uses such methods, you will need to manually edit the script to specify the username and password.

User and User Groups

ACT allows you to create users and user groups, which are available for all test projects. In ACT, each user can belong to one group only. Although you can create identical user name-password pairs in different groups, a user in a group does not relate in any way to another user with the same user name and password in another group. Furthermore, you can create multiple users with identical user names and passwords in the same group.

By default, ACT provides a default user group containing 200 users with arbitrary names and passwords. You will usually want to create your own user groups containing users on the target web servers. To create a user group, right-click the Users node in the Project Explorer and select Add from the context menu. You can then rename the group by right-clicking it and select Rename from the context menu. To add users to a user group, simply select the group in the Project Explorer and type in the user name and password in the right pane. If the target web server requires domain information, you need to enter user names in the DomainName\UserName format as illustrated overleaf.

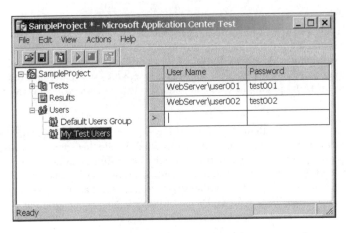

For each test, you can select users in one or more groups. To select a group for a test, select the Users tab in the test properties dialog. The first option, Automatically generate users, allows ACT to automatically generate users during the test. However, it is not clear what rules ACT uses to generate user name and passwords, and it is generally not possible for ACT to create application-specific users. To use your own group or groups of users, select the Specify users option and check all groups you wish to use in the test. When you run a test, ACT cycles through all users in the selected groups and uses them to log on.

If you configure a test with more than one simultaneous browser connection, ACT requires that you use at least one user for each connection. For instance, if you use one user group for a test using five simultaneous browser connections, you need to ensure that there are at least five users in that group. If you use two groups, the total number of users must be five or more. If you don't use enough users, ACT will report an error. The number of users must be at least as large as the number of connections.

Cookies

Many web applications use cookies to store certain application data locally. Once a test creates a cookie for a user, other tests can share this cookie whenever the user is used and the web server requires a cookie. ACT lets you edit or delete cookies between test runs. To edit or delete a cookie for a user, select the user in a group and the **Edit Cookies** command from the **Actions** menu item. You can then edit or delete cookies in the **Edit User Cookies** dialog.

That's it for analyzing data; now let's see how we can get deeper into the realms of customizing our own test scripts.

Customizing Test Scripts

While the ACT browser recording feature does well to construct test scripts that simulate browser requests, there are times when you will want to further customize a test. In general, I'm quite happy with the wizard-generated scripts and have not found many things that I definitely need to change yet. But among the things I have found, one really stands out.

As I mentioned in a previous section, ACT supports HTTP 1.1. However, the wizard generates scripts to create requests only with HTTP 1.0 headers by default. As a consequence, the keep-alive feature available in HTTP 1.1 is not used in the generated scripts. As IIS supports the keep-alive feature and many browsers are capable of generating HTTP 1.1 requests, the recorded scripts may produce test results that do not quite match the real-world performance of the web server.

This presents us with a good reason for customizing the test scripts. If you know VBScript, the required changes to the generated scripts are quite simple. Let's first look at the structure of the wizard-generated script and then see how you can change it to use HTTP 1.1's keep-alive feature.

Test Script Structure

A typical recorded test script contains a `Main` procedure, several `SendRequest` procedures and a single global statement that simply invokes the `Main` procedure.

```
Sub SendRequest1()
   ' code to send the first request
End Sub

Sub SendRequest2()
   ' code to send the second request
End Sub

'...
.
```

```
Sub SendRequestN()
  ' code to send the Nth request
End Sub

Sub Main()
  Call SendRequest1
  Call SendRequest2
  '...
  Call SendRequestN
End Sub

Main
```

The Main procedure is effectively the entry point of the script. You can certainly customize the script in any way you want, or make it adhere to your existing coding conventions. Once you have gained a good understanding of the ACT Test Object Model, you can write powerful test scripts. Both the ACT documentation and the MSDN Library provide good references to the object model.

Modifying Test Scripts

The script for **AdcTest** created in the *Walkthrough – Creating a New Test* section creates two requests, one for the ad_test.asp page and the other for the logo.gif file, in each pass. It creates a connection for each request, and closes the connection after the request has been sent. To simulate a keep-alive browser session, you should change it to create a connection and use it to send both requests. Here is how you do it.

In the SampleProject created in the walkthrough, add a new empty test using VBScript and name it something like AdKeepAlive.vbs. Next, delete the one statement generated by the wizard, then copy and paste the script from AdTest.vbs to AdKeepAlive.vbs. Now you have a script to work with.

First, define a script-level object, oConnection and add two procedures to the script, as below:

```
Option Explicit
Dim fEnableDelays
fEnableDelays = False

Dim oConnection

Function OpenConnection()
  Set oConnection = Test.CreateConnection("MyWebServer", 80, false)
  If Not oConnection is Nothing Then
    OpenConnection = True
  Else
    Test.Trace "Error: Unable to create connection to MyWebServer"
    OpenConnection = False
  End If
End Function

Function CloseConnection()
  If Not oConnection Is Nothing Then
    oConnection.Close
  End If
End Function
```

Remember to replace `MyWebServer` with the name of your web server. Now you have a script-level connection object, and separate procedures to open and close it, you should remove the local connection objects and their corresponding open and close calls in both `SendRequest1` and `SendRequest2` procedures. The code snippet below shows the changes made to `SendRequest1`. Changes to `SendRequest2` are identical. Note that we're commenting out some lines and replacing them with others:

```
Sub SendRequest1()
'   Dim oConnection, oRequest, oResponse, oHeaders, strStatusCode
    Dim oRequest, oResponse, oHeaders, strStatusCode
    If fEnableDelays = True then Test.Sleep (0)
'   Set oConnection = Test.CreateConnection("MyWebServer", 80, false)
'   If (oConnection is Nothing) Then
'     Test.Trace "Error: Unable to create connection to MyWebServer"
'   Else
    Set oRequest = Test.CreateRequest
    oRequest.Path = "/testfiles/ad_test.asp"
    oRequest.Verb = "GET"
'     oRequest.HTTPVersion = "HTTP/1.0"
    oRequest.HTTPVersion = "HTTP/1.1"
    set oHeaders = oRequest.Headers
    oHeaders.RemoveAll
    oHeaders.Add "Accept", _
        "image/gif, image/x-xbitmap, image/jpeg, image/pjpeg, */*"
    oHeaders.Add "Accept-Language", "en-us"
    oHeaders.Add "User-Agent", _
      "Mozilla/4.0 (compatible; MSIE 6.0; Windows NT 5.1; Q312461; .NET CLR
1.0.3705)"
'     oHeaders.Add "Host", "MyWebServer"
    oHeaders.Add "Host", "(automatic)"
    oHeaders.Add "Cookie", "(automatic)"
    Set oResponse = oConnection.Send(oRequest)
    If (oResponse is Nothing) Then
      Test.Trace "Error: Failed to receive response for URL to " + _
        "/testfiles/ad_test.asp"
    Else
      strStatusCode = oResponse.ResultCode
    End If
'     oConnection.Close
'   End If
End Sub
```

Note that while it's still normally valid to check whether the connection is alive in `SendRequest1`, it's neither necessary nor desired. As you usually want the client to be able to generate as many requests as possible, you should minimize the amount of work the client needs to perform. Apart from removing the connection-related statements, the only other change is to specify the HTTP 1.1 protocol for the request so that the connection will be kept alive between the two requests. The last change you need to make is obviously to explicitly open and close the connection in the `Main()` procedure, as illustrated below.

```
Sub Main()
  If OpenConnection Then
    Call SendRequest1()
    Call SendRequest2()
    Call CloseConnection()
  End If
End Sub
```

That's it. If you run the test now, you should see that ACT creates one connection for every two requests by examining the Summary section in the Overview report. The figure below shows a sample test result.

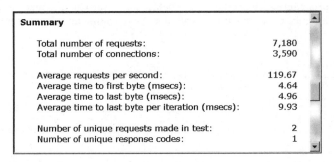

ACT in Visual Studio .NET

In addition to the standalone ACT program, Visual Studio .NET also offers an integrated ACT UI that allows for creating ACT projects directly in Visual Studio .NET IDE. You can add a new ACT project to an existing solution such as one containing a web application, or create it in a new solution. ACT projects created in ACT and in Visual Studio .NET use the same underlying technology for creating and executing tests, and to collect results. The integrated ACT UI also provides you with the ability to run tests and view test results in the Visual Studio .NET IDE.

Creating a Test

Visual Studio .NET provides a special type of project for creating ACT projects and tests. To create a new ACT test, follow the steps below.

1. In Visual Studio .NET, create a new project. In the Add New Project dialog, select Application Center Test Projects under Other Projects. There is only one project template, ACT Project. Just select it and give it a name like VsNetActProject.

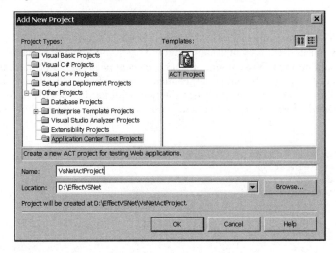

2. Add a new item to the newly created project. As in the standalone ACT program, you can create a browser recording test or an empty test in either VBScript or JScript. For this, exercise, select the **Browser Recorded Test** and name it **AdTest.vbs**.

3. In the **Browser Record** dialog, click the **Start recording** button. Visual Studio .NET will start a new instance of Internet Explorer.

4. In the Internet Explorer, type in the URL **http://localhost/TestFiles/ad_test.asp** and press *Enter*. This opens the page in the Internet Explorer.

5. Switch back to Visual Studio .NET, click the **Stop recording** button and then the **OK** button.

The project file and the script generated by Visual Studio .NET are identical to those in the standalone ACT program. In fact, you can open a Visual Studio .NET ACT project in the standalone ACT program, and vice versa.

Configuring Test Properties

In the Visual Studio IDE, you can also configure project and test properties. However, compared to the set of properties you can configure in the standalone ACT program, the configurable ACT properties in the Visual Studio .NET IDE are rather limited. The table below lists the configurable properties in Visual Studio .NET. The standalone ACT program lets you configure all of these options.

Property	Visual Studio.NET
Proxy server address/port	Configurable
Checking `robots.txt`	Always enabled
Socket settings	Always enabled
Test logging	Always enabled
Simultaneous browser connections	Configurable
Test run time	Configurable
Test iterations	Configurable
Warm-up time	Configurable
Generate detailed test results	Always enabled
Creating and using users and user groups	Not configurable
Performance counters	Not configurable

Reading Test Results

You can also view and compare ACT test results in Visual Studio .NET. Again, the set of result data is also limited. Once a test finishes, the result from the current test run is displayed in the output window.

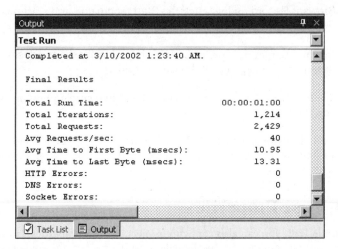

You can also see a list of results from all previous runs by right-clicking the test node in the Solution Explorer and selecting View Results.

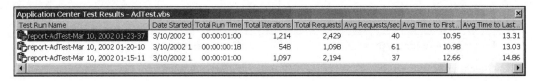

Summary

In this chapter, we've learned how to create ACT projects and tests. When a test runs, ACT collects various performance data. You can interpret the standard set of test data presented to you by ACT. You can also use ACT to collect other performance data that is more relevant to your applications by adding performance counters to tests.

A complex web application has many potential hot spots contributing to good or poor performance. Different applications have different performance characteristics, and therefore require different sets of test data to help in identifying the problems and their causes. You have seen that there are also issues that may affect the accuracy of tests. One of the common traps is that test clients may be overloaded and inadvertently become the bottleneck. It is critical to configure the test settings to avoid such traps.

In the past, we have seen applications that perform well under light load but do not scale well enough. By using ACT, you can discover such dangers early by stress testing your applications. Doing so helps you to identify the cause and resolve the problem before it gets too late. With ACT and other tools, you can develop applications that meet not only functional requirements, but also performance and scalability requirements.

15

Fact-Based Data Modeling with the ORM

According to a recent Gartner Group study, seventy five percent of developers say they feel they need to carry out some kind of data modeling before designing an application, and ninety percent of users would like to see some kind of understandable data model. There is no question that data modeling is an important part of application design – especially for distributed applications. However, in many ways, today's methods of creating models are somewhat inadequate – a problem that Microsoft has attempted to address, and Dr. Terry Halpin has provided one solution: Object Role Modeling.

Object Role Modeling (ORM) is a method for designing and querying database models at the conceptual level, where the application is described in terms easily understood by non-technical users. In practice, ORM data models often capture more business rules, and are easier to validate and evolve than data models found in other approaches. In short, ORM makes the language of data modeling much more oriented around business rules.

Modeling comes before design. ORM does not replace the Entity Relation (ER) model, and it not used to design a database, in the traditional sense. It is a rational model for modeling data storage, just as UML is a rational model for modeling objects. ORM can be used to conceptualize a user's specific ideas to form a generic data model. For instance, a user can sketch a report, and we can generate a generic data model from that information.

There is a lot to cover in this chapter, and we'll have to move away from the GlobalMarket scenario that we've considered in other chapters, because the data model for that is already created. Although we can and will reverse engineer the database, we will also look at some needs for the GlobalMarket enterprise. Here is the routemap for this chapter's foray into ORM:

❑ The concepts of Object Role Modeling

❑ The use of Visio in the modeling process

❑ Making databases with ORM

❑ Finally some example code for illustration

So let's get started by looking at the process, and then move on to work through some examples in Visio. Finally, we'll move some code to Visual Studio.

The Concepts of ORM

ORM provides a visual representation of the relationships between data, and the business rules relating to that data. More than a diagram format, however, it includes a structured fact language among other things, in addition to a procedure for creating diagrams. It is designed to streamline that usually unstructured process of sitting with the end users of an intended application, sketching out what structure the data should take. There are three points to focus on for the data model:

❑ Simple

❑ Accurate

❑ Understandable

Following the usual format of this book, let's now walk through a series of unstructured examples to illustrate key principles. We will do this again using Visio afterwards.

The Parts of the ORM

There are two formats to the ORM, and a process to make them both happen. The first format is language-based. It allows us to describe data relationships and business rules in an understandable way. The second format is a diagram, used to visualize the system. The process we'll discuss later.

Just the Facts

As an example, suppose we are looking at a phone book. We could describe the data in a very binary fashion, such as:

The citizen has name "Bill"

The citizen resides at "123 main street"

"123 Main Street" is found in "Ohio"

The citizen has phone number "555-1212"

"555-1212" exists in Area Code "614"

This data description can be generalized into facts, which are really the base foundation of the ORM for a generic phonebook:

Citizen has name

Citizen resides at address

Address is found in state

Citizen uses phone number

Phone number has area code

Types of Facts

Note that all of these elementary facts have two nouns:

Citizen has name

This is the most common type of fact, a binary element. If the sentence had one noun it would be a property, or a unary element.

Citizen is male

Also, there are ternary and quaternary elements. For example, this would be a ternary, because it contains the three elements 'citizen', 'groceries' and 'Kroger':

Citizen gets groceries from Kroger

The number of nouns in a fact is called its **arity**. This will eventually relate to the constraints we put in the database, but the important thing is that it is a good general way to describe data.

This is modeling – we're not even at a design stage yet. It's important in fact to avoid trying to map everything to a preconceived idea of how the database will look if this modeling process is to be at its most efficient. We'll be amazed at how well things will go when we ask Visio to make a database for us.

Constraints

Another of the many parts of the ORM is the use of constraints. As we'll see, they are mostly defined in the diagram, but they are an important part of the language too.

As part of the elementary facts, we can define uniqueness constraints (which are also to be found in ER diagrams). For instance, we know that one phone number has one area code, but one area code has many phone numbers. We could, if we wished, define this as part of the elementary fact like so:

One phone number is contained by one area code

One area code contains many phone numbers

This isn't usually seen in the language of the roles, but it is usually expressed in the diagrams. We'll look more at that when we use Visio to enter the facts.

The Diagrams

If we replace the nouns, or to use the correct ORM term, predicates, with ovals, and the verbs, or relationships, with boxes, we can construct a visual representation of the facts we have determined:

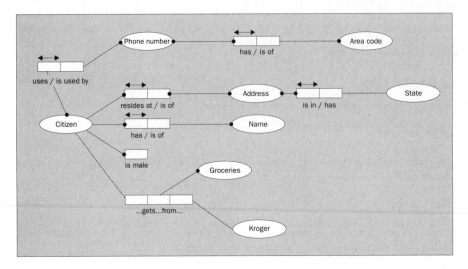

It gets much more complex than this, but essentially, this is the basic look of the design. Compared to an ER diagram (which doesn't effectively show relationships), this is very low in detail. Here's the equivalent ER diagram:

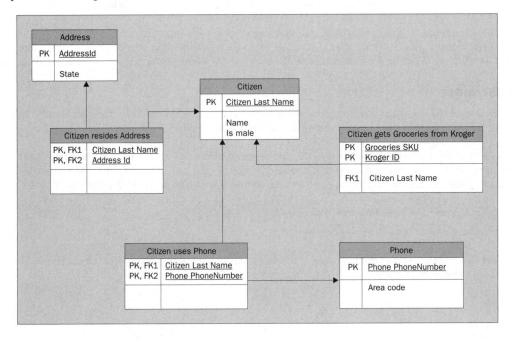

The ER diagram is much less clear due to the unusual codes it uses, and the lack of visible language. This one has the added problem of not really making sense, but it'll do for the sake of this example – it is actually the ER diagram that Visio came up with based on our ORM above. But even with that, anyone would find it hard to read, whereas we could take the ORM and infer the rules directly from it – it's a much clearer and more intuitive system, which is definitely a good thing when dealing with our end users.

The Conceptual Schema Design Procedure

The Conceptual Schema Design Procedure, or CSDP, is the name given to the procedure for creating ORM diagrams. The basic idea is that we start with a user-oriented concept, such as a sample report or form. That is an "information example". We then follow these steps:

1. Transform familiar information examples into elementary facts, and apply quality checks

2. Draw the fact types and apply a population check

3. Check for entity types that should be combined and note any arithmetic derivations

4. Add uniqueness constraints and check arity of fact types

5. Add mandatory role constraints and check for logical derivations

6. Add value, set comparison, and sub-typing constraints

7. Add other constraints and perform final checks

By far, the most important of these is the first, where we change a report into basic business rules. From there on we add essential complexity to the model, which allows us to create an actual database design from the model. Let's go through this process using Visio to get a true feel for things.

Microsoft's Plan

One of the most glaring problems from the architect's point of view has been the lack of available documentation methods for RAD methodologies. Generally, to communicate our design ideas to the users, we've had to show them a prototype, and this prototype will often end up evolving into the final program, and what a mess that could create!

The ORM provides us with a way to talk to our users about data, a text and visual path to show users what we are going to build before we build it. The next step was to provide some functionality to support that.

Enter Visio, and the ORM Source Diagram. We now can enter the rules into a system, have it draw the diagram, use the diagram to enter constraints and object types, then build that into an ER diagram. From the ER, we can add maintenance fields, and finally build a database. This is great for real-world programs, which are most of the time written from the database up.

Using the ORM with Visio

For our example, we have to go back in time, back to before we had a nice data model for GlobalMarket, when we were just two developers with a client. That client was doing their accounting and control with paper-based methods, and wanted to move over to a computerized system.

In that first meeting, we had to pose questions such as "What do you want?", "What do you need it to do?", "How should it work?", "Do you have any existing models we can work from?" and so on. If you're anything like me, this will be boiled down to one question: "Can you draw it?" If they are a power user, they'll probably draw a screen. Most secretaries, accountants, and business owners draw something else, though. They draw reports.

Fortunately, reports are exactly what ORM is designed to work from. So going to the accountants and getting a few reports drawn on a legal pad can be a great start. This is exactly what we got from the accountants at GlobalMarket, including one inventory report, which we will work from here, following the Conceptual Schema Design Procedure.

The Report

Naturally, the bean counters in charge of GlobalMarket need to track inventory. Anyway, they recall a report used at a previous company, and they would like a similar thing here. It looks like this:

Inventory Report

Item#	Item	Price	Quantity	Color	ReorderPt	Category	OrdDate
Q34	Quilt	35.95	23	Red	5	Home	1/2/2000
P34	Pillow	14.95	43	Green	5	Home	3/2/2000
B12	Basket	20.00	12	Brown	1	Garden	2/4/2000

We could, at this point, thank them and leave with the report. We could build an application just from experience that provides this data and be done with it. But Microsoft and those involved with the ORM specification have a different idea. They see a language that is separate from the code of programming, where we can show the users **what we mean**, rather than just showing them the finished product. This language is the ORM.

Step 1 – Create Elementary Facts

Looking at the report, we now know something about the data structure that created it. We know that there are probably lists of categories and colors to choose from. We know that the key of the report is the item, and that items are probably keyed with item numbers. We can sort of get the idea just by looking at this how a database will look, but how can we explain it to our users? How can we make sure that our ideas are right? Object Role Modeling provides us with the tools.

To begin, we will have to create our facts. These are stated, like above, as simple statements about the report as we see it. Afterward, we can ask a few further questions, do a little data entry, and take it from there. Let's take a look at these facts:

Item has item number

Item has price

Item has quantity

Item is of color

Item has reorder point

Item belongs to category

Item has last order date

We then take these rules and discuss them with the users, and we discover that the reorder point is set by category rather than by item – everything in one department has the same order point. It's misunderstandings like these that are hard to pick up were we to show the users an ER diagram. Anyway, we can now revise our set of facts accordingly:

Item has item number

Item has price

Item has quantity

Item is of color

Item belongs to category

Category has reorder point

Item has last order data

Entering the Rules into Visio

This part can be a little tedious – especially if you have a large database – but the output is very clear and makes our efforts worthwhile.

Start by opening Visio Enterprise Architect (part of Visual Studio Enterprise Architect edition). You may need to install this from the CDs if you haven't already. When it opens, select the **Database** option from the category list on the left of the opening screen, which offers the following diagram templates:

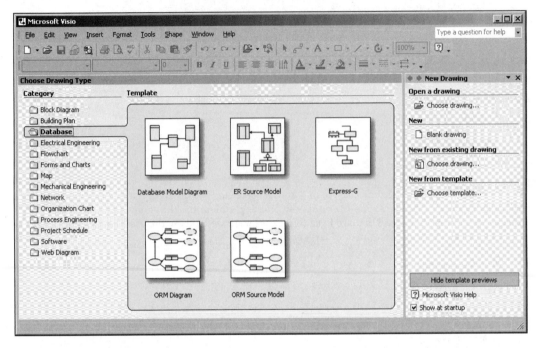

Create a new ORM Source Model drawing project. The ORM Source Model is the ORM interface to the Database Model Diagram. We can also create Database Model Diagram projects, which take our model and compile it into a format that SQL Server can use. The ORM Source Model doesn't offer much in the way of drawing tools – those are found in the ORM Diagram project if we just want to draw.

We use the Source Model to enter the rules above into a diagram using some rather neat templates, which we can then transform an ER model, and from there generate a database. Here's the initial screen:

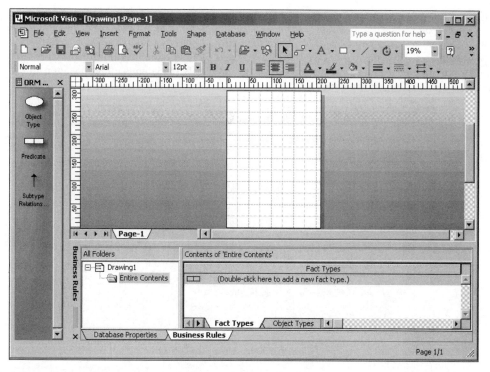

On left are the few diagramming tools that we do have, for the occasional add, edit, and delete. The list of Fact Types that appears in the Contents panel at the bottom is the most important part of this screen. Double-click where it says to bring up the Fact Editor to add a new fact:

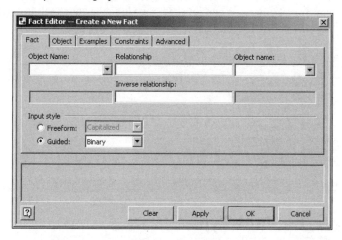

Here, we have the principal option to choose the guided type of rule we are going to enter. We have a choice of binary, ternary, or quaternary. Each of these offers different combinations of names and relationships. However, we can also select the FreeForm input style, and enter our rule all at once, capitalizing our elements. The Fact Editor can then determine the arity according to how many capitalized elements we have entered.

We're going to enter to enter a binary rule. Type "Item" in the Object Name box, the verb "has" in the Relationship box, and "ItemNumber" in the second Object name box. Once we have entered the nouns (which are automatically capitalized), we have the option of entering the opposite verb in the Inverse relationship box. This verb is what we would use to describe the relationship if the order of the two nouns were to be reversed, and serves merely to further clarify the language to the reader. Enter "describes" in this box as shown:

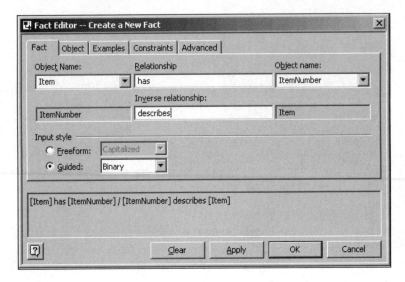

Notice that a verbal equivalent for the fact is shown in the text box at the bottom of the dialog.

Carry on to enter all the facts we established earlier. They will all follow a pretty similar pattern to this example, because they are all binary. When finished, the Contents panel will list all the facts, along with an icon to their left which indicates their arity by the number of boxes it contains:

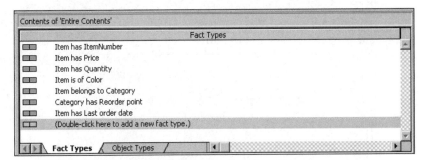

Step 2 – Draw the Fact Types

Save the facts as `Inventory Report Model.vsd`, so that changes are not lost. After saving, we can create our model diagram by simply dragging the rules onto the diagram. We can drag any rule on to get a rule pair like this:

This isn't totally correct yet, because we haven't set the entity types, or the constraints, but it's a start. If we drag all of the facts onto the report screen, we'll get quite a useful diagram. Also, we can right-click on Item, and select Show Relationships. This is a great way to get a subsystem's data model on one page:

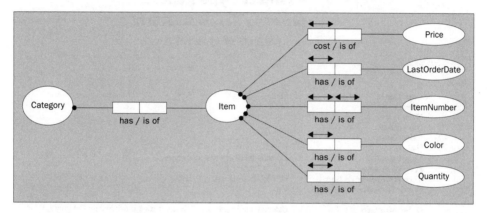

Of course, this doesn't include the Category properties we set up, so show its relationships too to get the full diagram:

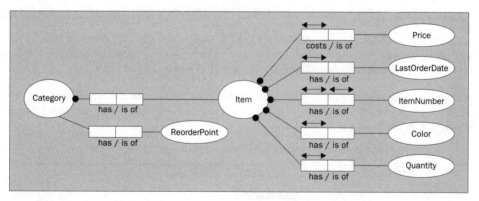

Now we have the beginnings of the diagram. According to CSDP, we should check the population, and assure ourselves that we have all of the objects in the report. Visio has a few reporting options that will help us with that.

In the Database menu, there is a Report option for running a number of useful reports, including:

- ❑ **Constraint type** – Shows details of the constraints, which we haven't yet entered for this example

- ❑ **Fact type** – Shows detail on every object/relationship pair

- ❑ **Object type** – This will help us with the inventory, showing info about the ellipses in the diagram

❏ **Supertype report** – If we have a hierarchical diagram, this shows the hierarchy

The report wizard is a good tool for when you need something other than the rules or the diagram, and will get better as we enter more information into the model during the CSDP. A remarkable amount of information about the objects is reported, aside from just the inventory, which is what we need for this step. Here is how the reports starts out:

Object Type Report
Inventory Report Model.vsd
Objects of type Entity

1   *Category*
   General attributes

ID:	40
Object kind:	Entity
Notes:	
Name space:	
Independent:	No
Value/Range:	
Numeric:	No
Mapping option:	Does not result in a composite type
Portable data type:	SBCS Char(10)
Microsoft Access data type:	CHAR(10)
Personal pronoun:	No
Fact count:	2
Referencing facts:	Category has Reorder point / Reorder point is required for Category
	Item belongs to Category / Category contains Item

   Entity-specific attributes
   Reference scheme: Category has no clear identification scheme.

Notice that there are a lot of gaps. The Object Kind *is* filled in though – for all of the objects we have added, it is automatically set to Entity by the system, which essentially means an Object or Class in an object-oriented methodology. An entity is anything that can have a child object.

To change the entity type, we need to use the Object Types tab next to the Fact Types tab we used above. It allows us to set the **kind**, and also the physical type if we desire. The kind is used to determine if the object is an entity or a property.

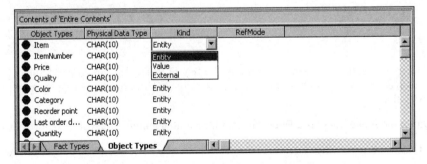

There are three default kinds, and the developer can define kinds as well. External is for an object that is defined in another model, and that won't apply here, and we'll just use the Entity and Value kinds in these examples.

❑ **Entity** – consists of real-world things rather than character strings or numbers. Objects, essentially, the Items and Categories in the model we're currently creating.

❑ **Value** – consists of numbers or character strings. A value object type is generally used to describe an entity object type. In this model, `Color`, `ItemNumber`, `LastOrderDate`, `Price`, `Quantity`, and `ReorderPoint`.

As we change the types and kinds, the model changes to reflect dotted lines in place of the solid around the ellipses of the value objects.

Step 3 – Entity Combination and Constraints

If we had a number of reports, we should check to make sure an Item isn't called a Product on a sales report, and so on. Such duplicate objects need to be "combined". If we have something in this model that is used in another model, we can use the **External** kind in the object types panel to set this at build time. As I've already mentioned, we won't need the **External** kind, or any entity combination, in this model, because we only have one report.

Another important point here is that entities do need names. In other words, we need to include the EntityName rule in the list of facts, because when we otherwise refer to the Entity, we are really referring to the concept of that Entity. The Entity must have a name, along with an ID, to refer to any particular instance of that object. This means that we have to add two new facts to the list we've already drawn up:

Item has ItemName

Category has CategoryName

Constraints are where we get to describe features that make this model more like a database. Constraints define parameters of the relationships between the entities. Visio makes setting these easy, using a question and answer style of information entry. To add constraints for a particular fact, bring up the Fact Editor for that fact (by double-clicking it in the Contents window), and select the Constraints tab:

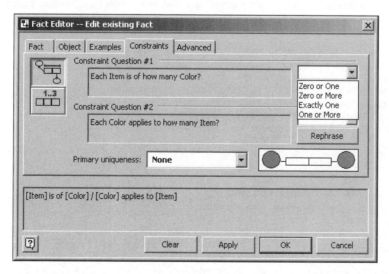

We have the option to select a database-like relationship type for each relationship question using the dropdowns. Then the system provides some text for us, to assist the user further in understanding what is going on, and the diagram is also updated correspondingly.

Another constraint we can set is the primary uniqueness of a given role in the model. In this particular example, neither is unique, but we should set the uniqueness for some, such as the combination of `Item` and `ItemNumber`.

After editing the constraints, we have a pretty much finished visual model, although there are a few more steps to finalize it. The relationships are described by a series of symbols over the relationship boxes, and also by whether or not the lines are terminated by a dot:

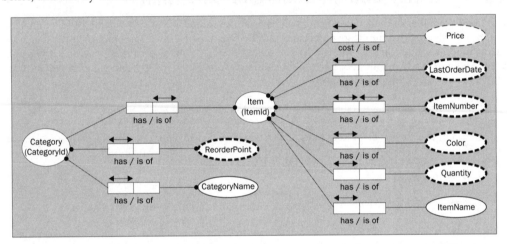

We can clearly see that categories and items are root objects, and the other entities are value types. The relationships are less obvious, but a description in plain text is available, and is essential for communication with users. Bring it up by selecting **Database | View | Verbalizer**. This tool defines our business rules in a state more or less ready for the design documentation:

```
Category has Item / Item is of Category
     Each Item is of some Category.
     Each Item is of at most one Category.
Category has ReorderPoint / ReorderPoint is of Category
     Each Category has some ReorderPoint.
     Each ReorderPoint is of some Category.
     Each Category has at most one ReorderPoint.
Item has Color / Color is of Item
     Each Item has some Color.
     Each Item has at most one Color.
Item has ItemNumber / ItemNumber is of Item
     Each Item has some ItemNumber.
     Each ItemNumber is of some Item.
     Each Item has at most one ItemNumber.
     Each ItemNumber is of at most one Item.
Item has LastOrderDate / LastOrderDate is of Item
     Each Item has some LastOrderDate.
     Each Item has at most one LastOrderDate.
```

```
Item costs Price / Price is of Item
    Each Item costs some Price.
    Each Item costs at most one Price.
Item has Quantity / Quantity is of Item
    Each Item has some Quantity.
    Each Item has at most one Quantity.
```

Steps 4 to 7 – Update Other Object Information

Most of the other steps of the process are for more advanced models than we require here. In more in-depth projects though, the appearance of these kinds of models is a possibility. Check out further details written by Dr. Halpin on www.orm.net, especially his overview white paper.

There are some other model-building features that Visio provides that you may find useful. Some of these are for advanced applications, so may not be of immediate utility, but are interesting nonetheless.

For instance, we can check for errors in the model, per the ORM rules, by selecting the **Database | Model error check** option from the menu. Using the sample model, this produces warnings because we've made the `ItemNumber` and `ReorderPoint` required, even though they are values. This is particularly curious, considering a key field is in the ORM and Visio documentation as an example of a value type:

```
Inventory Report Model.vsd : Starting Conceptual Validation...

Inventory Report Model.vsd : warning C1007: 'ItemNumber'  :
        Value object type playing mandatory role not recommended.
Inventory Report Model.vsd : warning C1007: 'ReorderPoint'  :
        Value object type playing mandatory role not recommended.
Inventory Report Model.vsd : Conceptual Validation complete -
        0 error(s) 2 warning(s)
```

We'll ignore this warning, and leave the kinds as they are. Despite this anomaly, the error check can still be a very useful tool. Another great feature is the Example Data feature. For a given entity/relationship, we can enter the data directly into the report, and Visio will suggest information.

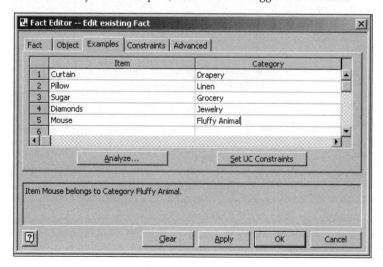

Based on this information, Visio will analyze our constraints and make a few recommendations when we click the Analyze button:

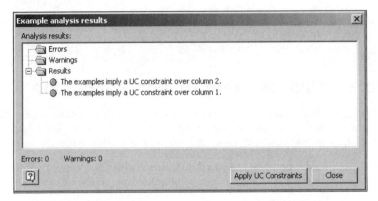

The results suggest that we should add a uniqueness constraint over both columns, which isn't quite right. The more example data we enter, the more valid these suggestions become. I have found that appropriate suggestions are made once six or so entries have been added for most relationships.

Also, we need to tell Visio what to use to define the entity objects. In the Microsoft methodology, key fields for database tables – or objects in OO parlance – are unrelated to the data itself, and are just used to reference the rows. We usually use autonumbering fields or GUIDs to create these keys. Visio just wants to know what to call them.

In order to do this, double-click on the Item is of Color fact to reopen the Fact Editor. This time select the Object tab, and set the Reference / identifier value to ItemId for the Item object, leaving Identification selected in the Ref type box:

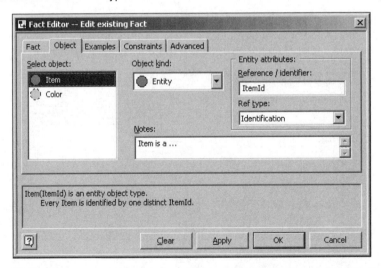

There are other reference types we can select, in order to avoid the unique identifier issue with entities. Microsoft really doesn't advise our doing that, and it's right. The UID design notion is a good one in today's highly relational world.

Generating the Databases

Now the ORM is complete. Aside from having the user look at it, what can we do with it? Visio provides a facility to transform it into an ER diagram, and move that into a database. In order to do this, we need to create a new Database Model Diagram drawing project. Close the current drawing project first, and we'll then import that diagram into the new project using the **Database | Project | Add Existing Document** menu item like so:

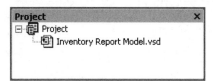

At this point, we can use the **Database | Project | Build** command to generate an ER diagram. Before the build occurs, we need to save the diagram. Use the name `GlobalMarket ER.vsd`.

Similar to the code project build process in Visual Studio, we see errors and warnings encountered during the build. As during the check of the build in the ORM process, we receive warnings about the value objects having unique constraints.

After the build, we get `Items` and `Categories` tables in the Tables and Views window:

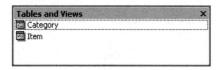

We can drag these into the design view, and we have the start of an ER diagram:

As we see, this is a fairly accurate ER diagram. The `CategoryId` was added as an assumed part of the `Items` table, because of the entity-to-entity relationship. The `ItemId` and `CategoryId` we added as reference values show up as the primary keys of the two tables. In short, we are in pretty good shape.

We can even add tables on this view, and update the ORM. For instance, if we decide we want a color table, we could do the following:

8. Double-click on the Item entity in the diagram to open the Database Properties window, and select Columns in the left hand list of Categories.

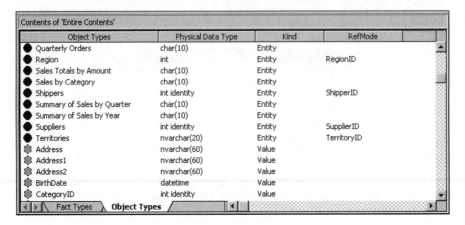

9. Delete the Colors column by selecting the row and clicking Remove.

10. Drag a new Entity from the Shapes panel onto the design view:

11. Click on this new entity, and select Definition in the Database Properties window

12. Change the Physical Name and Conceptual Name to Color

13. Click on the Columns tab

14. Add ColorId as a Primary Key, and ColorName as a required Char(10)

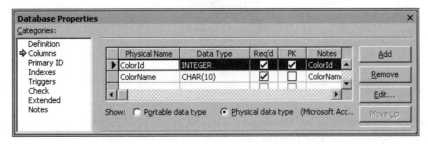

15. Drag a Relationship connector from the Shapes window onto the designer:

16. Drag the arrow side of the relationship to the Color table, and the straight side to the Item table.

17. Double-click on the relationship, and click the **miscellaneous** tab in Database Properties

18. Select **Exactly One** under cardinality

This gives us a new ER diagram. This design is useful should we want to control the specific list of colors available for use, rather than just have a text field.

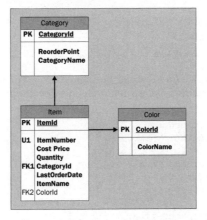

Now we can update our ORM. Click on **Database | Projects | Update Source Models** and we get some migration details. If we double-click on the **Inventory Report Model** in the **Project** panel, we get the new ORM. Color is now an Entity, and needs to be dragged onto the designer, and have its relationships shown by right-clicking and selecting **Show Relationships**:

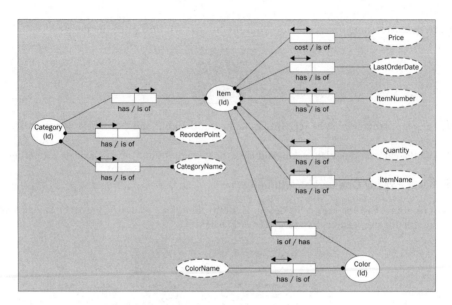

If we now open the Verbalizer, we find that our business rules have been updated to match the diagram. These can be dropped right into the business requirements document, after a little polishing.

```
Color has ColorName / ColorName is of Color
     Each Color has some ColorName.
     Each Color has at most one ColorName.
Item is of Color / Color has Item
     Each Item is of at most one Color.
ColorName is a value object type.
     Physical Microsoft Access datatype: CHAR(10).
Color(id) is an entity object type.
     Every Color is identified by one distinct id.
     Physical Microsoft Access datatype: INTEGER.
Item has LastOrderDate / LastOrderDate is of Item
     Each Item has some LastOrderDate.
     Each Item has at most one LastOrderDate.
Item costs Price / Price is of Item
     Each Item costs some Price.
     Each Item costs at most one Price.
Category has ReorderPoint / ReorderPoint is of Category
     Each Category has some ReorderPoint.
     Each ReorderPoint is of some Category.
     Each Category has at most one ReorderPoint.
Category has Item / Item is of Category
     Each Item is of some Category.
     Each Item is of at most one Category.
Category has CategoryName / CategoryName is of Category
     Each Category has some CategoryName.
     Each CategoryName is of some Category.
     Each Category has at most one CategoryName.
Item has Quantity / Quantity is of Item
     Each Item has some Quantity.
```

```
        Each Item has at most one Quantity.
Item has ItemName / ItemName is of Item
        Each Item has some ItemName.
        Each ItemName is of some Item.
        Each Item has at most one ItemName.
Item has ItemNumber / ItemNumber is of Item
        Each Item has some ItemNumber.
        Each ItemNumber is of some Item.
        Each Item has at most one ItemNumber.
        Each ItemNumber is of at most one Item.
CategoryName is a value object type.
        Physical Microsoft Access datatype: CHAR(50).
ItemName is a value object type.
        Physical Microsoft Access datatype: CHAR(50).
Category(id) is an entity object type.
        Every Category is identified by one distinct id.
        Physical Microsoft Access datatype: INTEGER.
ReorderPoint is a value object type.
        Physical Microsoft Access datatype: INTEGER.
Price is a value object type.
        Physical Microsoft Access datatype: CURRENCY.
Quantity is a value object type.
        Physical Microsoft Access datatype: INTEGER.
LastOrderDate is a value object type.
        Physical Microsoft Access datatype: DATETIME.
ItemNumber is a value object type.
        Physical Microsoft Access datatype: CHAR(10).
Item(id) is an entity object type.
        Every Item is identified by one distinct id.
        Physical Microsoft Access datatype: INTEGER.
```

This is how modeling becomes design in Microsoft land. We can even go to the database from here if we wish. With the `GlobalMarket ER.vsd` project open, select the **Database | Generate** menu item.

19. Select Generate a text file of the DDL script

20. Select a database driver. For SQL Server, use **Generic ODBC**

21. Review the tables

22. Press Finish

23. View your DDL script, which can be run in SQL Enterprise Manager.

```
--      This SQL DDL script was generated by Microsoft Visual Studio
--      (Release Date: LOCAL BUILD).

--      Driver Used : Microsoft Visual Studio - ODBC Generic Driver Driver.
--      Document    : U:\WRITING\PRO VS7\RULES BASED
--      DATA DESIGN\GLOBALMARKET ER.VSD.
--      Time Created: December 21, 2001 11:20 AM.
--      Operation   : From Visio Generate Wizard.
```

```
--      Connected data source : No connection.
--      Connected server      : No connection.
--      Connected database    : Not applicable.

-- Create GlobalMarket database.
create database GlobalMarket

-- Create new table Color.
-- Color : Table of Color
--      ColorId : Colorid identifies Color
--      ColorName : ColorName is of Color
create table Color (
    ColorId INTEGER not null,
    ColorName CHAR(10) not null, constraint Color_PK primary key (ColorId) )

-- Create new table Item.
-- Item : Table of Item
--      "Item id" : Itemid identifies Item
--      ItemNumber : ItemNumber is of Item
--      "Costs Price" : Price is of Item
--      Quantity : Quantity is of Item
--      "Category id" : Category has Item
--      LastOrderDate : LastOrderDate is of Item
--      ItemName : ItemName is of Item
--      ColorId : Color has Item
create table Item (
    "Item id" INTEGER not null,
    ItemNumber CHAR(10) not null,
    "Costs Price" DECIMAL(10,2) not null,
    Quantity INTEGER not null,
    "Category id" INTEGER not null,
    LastOrderDate DATETIME not null,
    ItemName CHAR(50) not null,
    ColorId INTEGER null, constraint Item_PK primary key ("Item id") )

-- Create new table Category.
-- Category : Table of Category
--      "Category id" : Categoryid identifies Category
--      ReorderPoint : ReorderPoint is of Category
--      CategoryName : CategoryName is of Category
create table Category (
    "Category id" INTEGER not null,
    ReorderPoint INTEGER not null,
    CategoryName CHAR(50) not null,
        constraint Category_PK primary key ("Category id") )

-- Add the remaining keys, constraints and indexes for the table Item.
create unique index Item_AK1 on Item (
    ItemNumber)


alter table Item add constraint Item_AK1_UC1 unique (
    ItemNumber)
```

```
-- Add foreign key constraints to table Item.
alter table Item
    add constraint Category_Item_FK1 foreign key (
        "Category id")
    references Category (
        "Category id")

alter table Item
    add constraint Color_Item_FK1 foreign key (
        ColorId)
    references Color (
        ColorId)

-- This is the end of the Microsoft Visual Studio generated SQL DDL script.
```

Reverse Engineering

We can do all of this in the other direction, and create the ORM which corresponds to an existing database. There are typically one or two problems with most generated models, although it's still a very nice feature. With an ODBC connection to the existing GlobalMarket database, we can document, redesign, or show the users what is going on through ER diagrams and ORM.

1. Start a new Database Model Diagram by going to File | New | Database | Database Model Diagram, or by clicking the down arrow on the New button on the Toolbar.

2. In the Database menu, there is a Reverse Engineer option, which fires up a related wizard. Go ahead and do that now.

3. Select the SQL Server driver, and the GlobalMarket data source we created in the introduction.

4. We want to generate all keys, so make sure all object types are selected in the next dialog.

5. Go ahead and add all user tables in the next wizard window – for me, that meant all except the system designed dtproperties table.

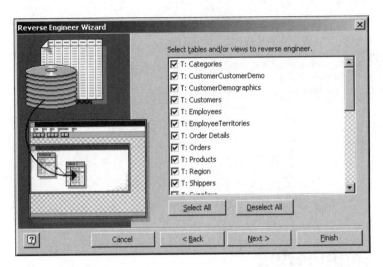

Next add the shapes to the underlying model. This will give us a good look at the existing GlobalMarket data model. As we might imagine, there is a fair amount of information here, and this is what we would print out and hang on our wall while developing the software. But would it be any use to the user?

Usually, no, because of its complexity and technical nature. We'll mostly end up drawing a logical model in Visio anyway for showing to the users, and to use in the user documentation, in the requirements document, and so on.

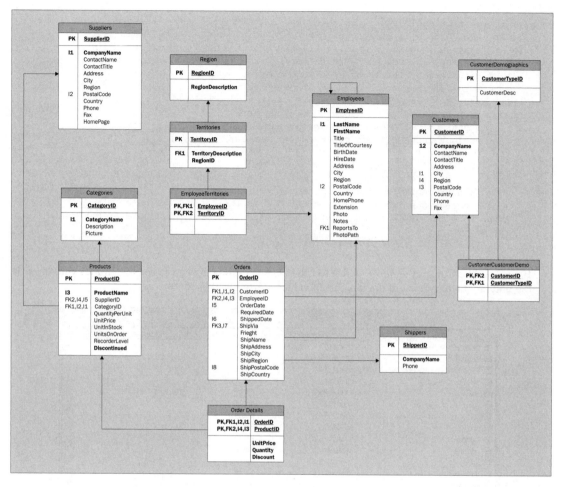

Though this is a very nice ER diagram – considering it took us 2 minutes to make – it just isn't useful to a user. We need a logical model to show our users, that is one that defines objects and rules. Enter ORM.

Creating an ORM from the ER Diagram

Go to the File menu and create a new ORM Source Model. In the new file, click **Database | Reverse engineer**. The same wizard appears as before – repeat the same steps, adding all user tables, and all keys. After the export, we'll find 79 fact types in the Contents panel. More importantly, there is an Entity for each table and a Value for all fields that are not keys in the tables. Right away, we can use the Verbalizer to produce the business rules for the entire GlobalMarket database. Below are the first few lines of what it creates in this case:

```
Orders is of Customers / Customers hasFK_Orders_Customers Orders
        Each Orders is of at most one Customers.
        A non-unique index will be created over the Customers role.
```

```
Orders is of Employees / Employees hasFK_Orders_Employees Orders
    Each Orders is of at most one Employees.
    A non-unique index will be created over the Employees role.
Territories is of Region / Region hasFK_Territories_Region Territories
    Each Territories is of some Region.
    Each Territories is of at most one Region.
Products is of Suppliers / Suppliers hasFK_Products_Suppliers Products
    Each Products is of at most one Suppliers.
    A non-unique index will be created over the Suppliers role.
A non-unique index will be created over the curly-bracketed role of Suppliers in
the fact type:
    Products is of {Suppliers}.
Products is of Categories / Categories hasFK_Products_Categories Products
    Each Products is of at most one Categories.
    A non-unique index will be created over the Categories role.
A non-unique index will be created over the curly-bracketed role of Categories in
the fact type:
    Products is of {Categories}.
```

If we open the Contents window, and select the **Object Types** tab, we can see the entities and, towards the bottom, the beginning of the long list of values, starting with **Address**:

Contents of 'Entire Contents'

Object Types	Physical Data Type	Kind	RefMode
● Quarterly Orders	char(10)	Entity	
● Region	int	Entity	RegionID
● Sales Totals by Amount	char(10)	Entity	
● Sales by Category	char(10)	Entity	
● Shippers	int identity	Entity	ShipperID
● Summary of Sales by Quarter	char(10)	Entity	
● Summary of Sales by Year	char(10)	Entity	
● Suppliers	int identity	Entity	SupplierID
● Territories	nvarchar(20)	Entity	TerritoryID
▓ Address	nvarchar(60)	Value	
▓ Address1	nvarchar(60)	Value	
▓ Address2	nvarchar(60)	Value	
▓ BirthDate	datetime	Value	
▓ CategoryID	int identity	Value	

Fact Types \ **Object Types**

If we add all of the objects to the diagram, we'll end up with an intractable mess. To make something that is of real benefit to our users, we can drag all the Entity objects onto the screen to create more of a logical data model, ORM style. The ORM is designed to show a whole system with some generality, and yet still be capable of showing a sufficient amount of detail for items within a system.

Problem is, there isn't a way to show the relationships between just the objects unless we go and find the specific facts, and drag them to the screen also. The facts that relate to object alone are related by an 'is of' relationship.

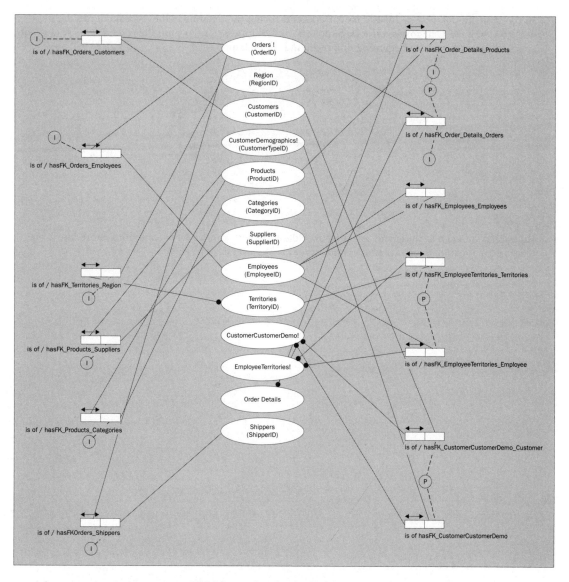

A better option is to create an ORM for each subsystem out of the objects at our disposal. With the original 'back in time' system we worked with above, we ended up with just three tables. That inventory subsystem didn't describe everything, but it would be useful for those accounting users. We can do a similar thing for this reverse engineered database.

In the same model, choose Insert | New Page and accept the defaults in the Add dialog. In the new window, drag the Categories, Orders, Suppliers, and Shippers entities onto the screen. This somewhat sparse diagram forms the beginning of a receiving subsystem:

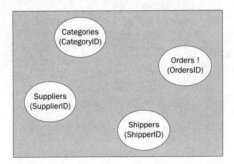

Right-click on each of these and select Show Relationships, and we have something more like a real diagram, that can help us explain the data model to the users:

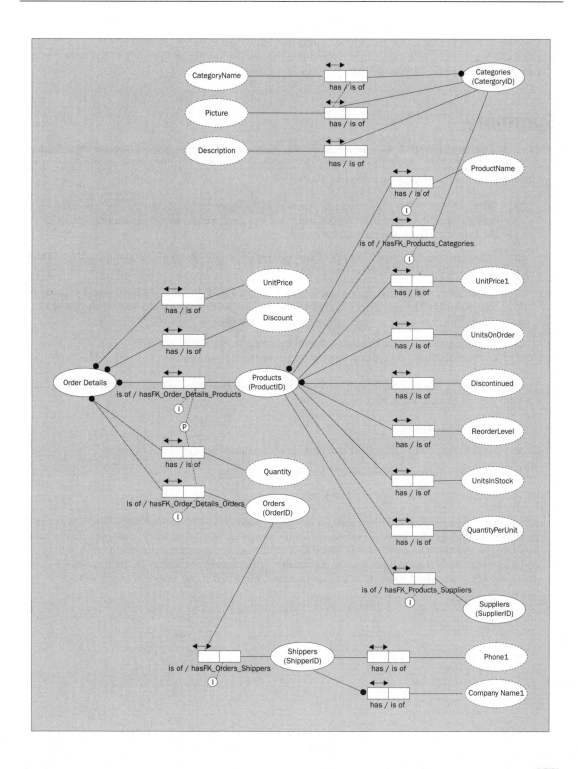

I think you'll agree that this is much more understandable than even the object-entity-only model we created beforehand. The circles labelled I and P represent the indices and primary uniqueness constraints that the ORM engine extracted from the database for us.

Summary

There is a lot more to ORM, even more than Visio can do easily, although there is plenty that Visio can do that we didn't have room for here. If you are interested in using ORM to model data for your users, check out some of the following reference material:

- ❑ www.orm.net – This site, managed by Microsoft's Terry Halpin, is the king of reference material for the Object Role model and is a great start point. There are a number of articles in the Overview page that are must-reads.

- ❑ *Information Modeling and Relational Databases*, published by Morgan Kaufmann (ISBN 1-55860-672-6) – Dr. Halpin's book on the ORM.

- ❑ *Handbook on Architectures of Information Systems*, edited by P Bernus, K Mertins. and G Schmidt, from Springer Verlag (ISBN 3-54064-453-9) – Great book on general architecture, if not cheap. Also has a few good chapters on database modeling.

- ❑ *Object Role Modeling: an Overview* (http://msdn.microsoft.com/library//en-us/dnvs700/html/vsea_ormoverview.asp) – another Halpin article, but with a Microsoft slant.

The information in this chapter should be more than enough to get you started, though. We have covered a lot of ground, including:

- ❑ When to use ORM
- ❑ How to start from ORM facts and end up with a database
- ❑ How to start from a database and end up with ORM facts
- ❑ Using some of the ORM tools in Visio

If I can make a quick personal comment, I'd say that I wasn't really impressed with the ORM at first. From now on though, I will use it exclusively as my means for communicating with users. In the past, I have tended to either gloss over the database side of things, or draw a logical model that they don't understand too well. Now, even if I write the database first, I can generate an ORM diagram for them with ease. It has surprised me with its usefulness, and I hope that it can help you out as well.

16

Software Design with UML

The Unified Modeling Language (UML) is a means for specifying, visualizing, constructing, and documenting objects in a software system. Unlike ORM (Object Role Model), which is a semantic device for describing data and the surrounding rules, UML is a whole-project methodology that encompasses the design of any system.

In 1997, Microsoft began to embrace UML as a standard documentation language for software artifacts, such as objects and tables. But, as the primary business development language of Microsoft groupies – Visual Basic – was not truly object-oriented, not much was done with it.

In 1999 Microsoft bought Visio, the design tool we've already seen in Chapter 15, and circumspectly removed the UML template from it. While nobody is sure why that was done, it's good to see that the template has resurfaced in Visio 2002 Enterprise Architect (EA).

But wait – there's more. Like the ORM diagram, the UML template is tightly interwoven with other Microsoft software, in this case Visual Studio .NET. Properly formulated diagrams can be distilled to code templates, and code can be used to generate certain diagrams. Generally speaking, it is a powerful tool for those who have a need to use UML, such as systems architects.

This chapter is designed to teach the use of Visio 2002 EA with Visual Studio .NET. It is not a chapter about UML. While we will go over some basics, if you don't know UML before reading the chapter, you'll need to read up on it because we can't cover it in enough detail here.

UML isn't something that one can use in a purely visual way. It is a language that is used for a specific purpose, in somewhat the same way as a programming language like C# has a specific purpose. It has its own set of semantics, just like C# has. Moreover, just like C#, you won't get all that far unless you know your way around it.

About UML

You can find some UML references at the end of this chapter if you would like to find out more about UML's core concepts. For our overview, we'll begin with a little bit about the interplay between UML and Microsoft methodologies, then look at each of the eight principal types of UML diagrams one at a time. These are:

- Use Case
- Activity
- Deployment
- Statechart
- Component
- Sequence
- Collaboration
- Static Structure

Within each section, we'll take a look at how one draws the diagrams, the features that make Visio good for this process, and also how we can integrate the diagrams and use them with Visual Studio .NET.

What is UML?

UML is a modeling language, usually presented visually, which can show both the structure and behavior of a system. Its diagrammatic "syntax" is rigorous and expressive, allowing checking and generation by automated tools. The design goals of UML are to:

- Constitute a visual modeling language that users find expressive, simple, and extensible.
- Offer mechanisms for *extension* of core concepts rather than *modification* of those concepts.
- Unify best practices of engineering and software design.
- Be scalable.
- Encourage growth in the use of object-oriented tools and languages.
- Be widely accepted and applicable.
- Be programming language-independent.
- Be development methodology-independent.
- Support both higher- and lower-level constructs in systems
- Handle often-troublesome architectural complexity problems with ease

The Origins of UML

In 1995, Jacobson, Booch, and Rumbaugh gave a talk at OOPSLA (a conference on object-oriented techniques) about the Unified Method – a way to describe objects in a system. Before this time, a number of OO modeling languages had been springing up all over the place, including a language from each of the people mentioned above. In short, the Unified Method caught on. These fine methodologists decided later in 1996 that they could not agree on one method, so they agreed on a language to describe the output of any method of design, and renamed it the Unified Modeling Language.

Late in 1996, Rational Corporation – where the three men worked – brought in a number of other companies, including Microsoft, to form a specification for submission to the Object Management Group. They did so in January of 1997, and UML was born.

Around that time, Microsoft began using a form of UML in its internal specifications. Since that isn't an open model, we know little about it, but it was used to form the Next Generation Windows Services, which as we know later became .NET. This alone should prove that it is a useful tool for projects of any kind, but especially .NET development.

UML is now a widely accepted standard, currently at version 1.3, with 2.0 expected to be released in 2003. Visio 2002 EA is based on UML 1.2.

Visio and UML

Microsoft's tool for the manipulation of UML documents is Visio 2002 EA, just as it is for the ORM diagrams. Visio gives us a good idea of the constructs of the language, but in order to actually use the 'words' we create, our own understanding of UML is necessary. That is why a familiarity with UML is suggested before starting this chapter.

Open up Visio 2002 EA, select the **Software** category on the left, and **UML Model Diagram** from the main **Template** pane. UML is the only such tool that is fully integrated with Visual Studio .NET:

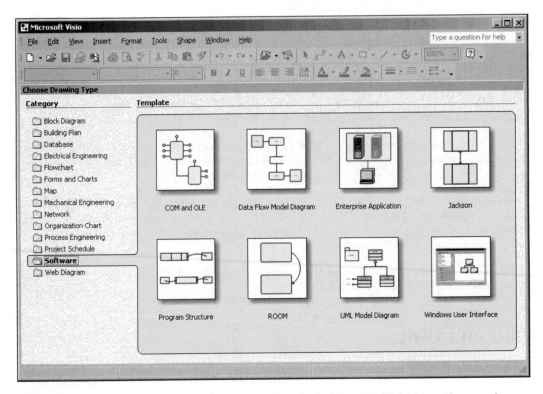

Visio's use of UML is based on a project structure, similar to Visual Studio's approach to a software application. UML model diagrams are collected and interlinked in a single document. After creating a new project, we can see the Model Explorer, which gives a bird's eye view of our project (it's the Visio equivalent of Solution Explorer):

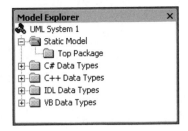

Note that all the diagrams created in this chapter can be found within the single `GlobalMarket` `UML.vsd` Visio file in the download package that accompanies this book.

Designing with Visio

A Visio UML project represents a single software system modeled in one or more different ways, potentially from a variety of viewpoints, and possibly using an assortment of UML diagram types. UML, by design, does not have a particular development process associated with it: you can use it in conjunction with whatever process you are most comfortable with. However, Microsoft has imposed an SDLC (Software/System Development Life Cycle)-style four square process to create new models:

- ❑ The Use Case Model

- ❑ The Domain Model

- ❑ The Design Model

- ❑ The Implementation Model

Use cases are narrative descriptions of processes that we can create as part of a development cycle. They describe the interactions between external agents (known as **actors**) and our system, help us understand the system requirements, and define the terminology used in the domain area. During the use case phase, we will create use case diagrams.

Like the use case model phase, the **domain model phase** is focused on building an understanding of the domain in which we are modeling a system. This is an analysis phase in which we are thinking about objects and relationships in the real world, rather than about programming. During the domain model phase, we create conceptual static structure diagrams, package diagrams, and sequence diagrams.

During the use case and domain model phases, we focus on understanding the requirements and concepts related to our system. In the **design phase**, we apply this understanding and come up with a programming solution.

To develop this solution, we need to use collaboration diagrams to determine how objects will communicate, and class static structure diagrams to define the classes that we will implement in the software. To understand the lifecycle of an object, we will also create a statechart or activity diagram in relation to a particular class or use case.

The **implementation model phase** focuses on the physical and component structure of the development environment. During the implementation phase, we will create component diagrams and deployment diagrams.

To get started, right-click on the Top Package folder and select New | Use Case Diagram.

Use Cases

A use case is a procedure that describes a scenario. Let's look at this with a supporting example.

Say for instance that we want to allow visitors to the GlobalMarket web site to be able to buy items from our catalog. We aren't going to worry about inventory, because everything is going to be shipped direct from the vendor. Here's a short description of what's involved:

A visitor comes to the site and browses through items. After the visitor selects an item, it is added to the shopping cart. When the visitor is ready to pay, the system puts up a list of items purchased and a total cost, and the customer provides their address and payment information. On completion of the sale, the vendor is notified of the sale. Credit for the sale is then given to the sales representative for that customer, determined by their region.

This is essentially a description of one version of what can happen, or a particular **case**. There are other cases, for example, where the customer chooses not to buy anything. Since it is based on the **use** of the system we are designing, we have the term 'use case'.

Usually to make this more useful, we write business rules – similar to those the ORM verbalizer created for us in the previous chapter:

- ❏ Visitor browses site
- ❏ Visitor selects item
- ❏ System adds item to the shopping cart
- ❏ Visitor requests to pay
- ❏ Visitor provides information
- ❏ System provides list of items with total
- ❏ System notifies supplier of the sale
- ❏ System credits site operator for the sale

Notice that a vendor entering the order into their system doesn't come under our use case, because it is outside of the scope of our system. This is an important concept when designing use cases.

Creating the Use Case Diagram

In order to diagram the above, we need a few tools, namely actors, use cases, and relationships.

Actor

An **Actor** is the noun in the above use cases, where the noun is not the system or any part of the system. For instance, in the statement "Visitor Browses Site", the Visitor is an actor, but the site is the system itself, so is not an actor.

Use Case

A **Use Case** object in UML represents the verb in the above use cases that describes actions of the system. For instance, in the use case "Visitor Selects Item", Selects Item would be the UML use case.

Communication

A **Communication** denotes when an actor participates in a use case. The communication must cross the system boundary and more than one actor may communicate with one use case.

The **system boundary** surrounds all of the use cases in the system, but not the actors. Actors are outside the boundary. Communication crosses the boundary.

We can now crack on and start building this diagram. Click on the bottom UML Use Case tab of the Shapes box and drag the system boundary onto the blank chart. Rename it Online Commerce System, by double-clicking on the green boundary itself, and entering the new name in the top title box. We'll now set up other objects of the system:

1. Drag the first actor, our Visitor, onto the page outside the boundary.

2. Right-click on the actor and select Properties (or double-click on the actor). Enter Visitor in the top Name box, and type a brief description in the Documentation box. This will be used by the system later on.

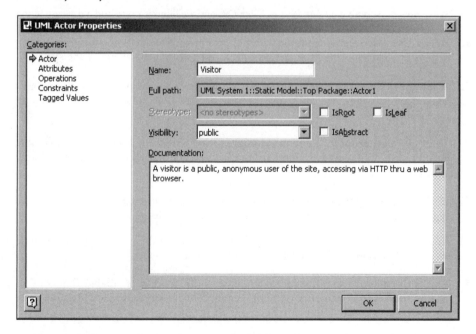

Along with the main Actor category in the left-hand list, the others are, briefly:

❑ Attributes – properties of the actor, like the address, or user name

❑ Operations – things the actor can do in general, like log in

❑ Constraints – business rules, things that modify the behavior of the actor

❏   **Tagged Values** – a screen that brings together a summary of the actor

Together, categories allow us to define the role the Actor plays as an object in our model.

3.   Select **Attributes**, and create the following entries in the blank table on that dialog:

Attribute	Type	Visibility	Multiplicity	Init. Value
Address	VB::String	private	1	
UserName	VB::String	private	1	

4.   Now create a few **Operations**:

Operation	Return Type	Visibility	Polymorphic	Scope
Login	<None>	public	☐	instance
Logout	<None>	public	☐	instance
Checkout	<None>	public	☐	instance
SelectItem	<None>	public	☐	instance

We're now done setting up our Visitor. Click **OK**, and we'll move on to add a use case to the model:

5.   Drag a **Use Case** shape from the Toy box, we mean Shapes box, and place it within the system boundary, as this is something performed within the scope of the system.

6.   Right-click on the use case to access its properties. Like the actor above, we start at a general screen where we can name the case **Selects Item**, and add some documentation information if we wish.

There is a new property category, though, called **Extension Points**. These describe locations within a use case where another action can branch off. We'll come back to them later on.

7.   Choose the **Attributes** category, and add just one attribute, named **PageName**, and with type **VB:String**. Leave the other columns at their defaults as before.

Click **OK**. We've almost completed the first interaction in the model, but we just need to add an association shape to link the actor and the use case together:

8.   Drag a **Communication Association** shape onto the chart (it is labeled **Communi...** in the Shapes box), and attach either one of its endpoints to any of the anchor points of the Visitor (marked with a blue cross).

9.   Drag the other endpoint to an anchor point of the **Selects Item** use case.

10. Right-click on the association, and select **Properties** to access the properties dialog.

I like to name the shape using the verb from the actor's perspective, in this case **Browse**, because the Visitor would say they 'browsed' in order to select the item.

11. That's all we need to set for the association's properties, so click OK.

12. We're not quite finished with the association yet, so right-click again and select **Shape Display Options**, an option which is available for all UML shapes. In this case, we use it to set the endpoints that we don't want to display, and associations that we do, to make it easier to see what's what on our diagram. Check the **Name** box in the **General** section, uncheck all the **End options** checkboxes, and check the last two options so we don't have to change these options for other shapes of this type:

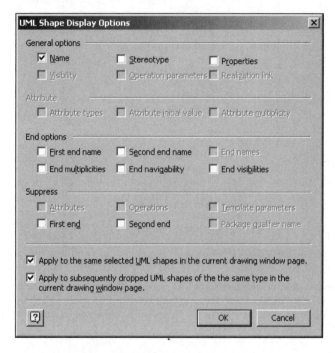

And that's our first UML relationship! To finish off the diagram, add two new actors outsite the system boundary, and name them **Supplier**, and **Site Operator**. We can leave the **Site Operator** as is, but open the properties dialog for the **Supplier**, and add two attributes:

Attribute	Type	Visibility	Multiplicity	Init. Value
Name	VB::String	public	1	
Address	VB::String	public	1	

Now add five new Use Case shapes within the system boundary. All we need to do for these is name them like so:

- ❏ Add Item to Cart
- ❏ Proceed to Checkout
- ❏ Enter Personal Details
- ❏ Provides Total List

❑   Notification of sale

The objects in the diagram are now accessible through the Model Explorer:

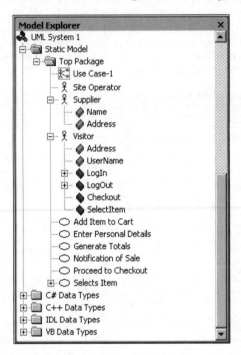

Finally, we just need to connect the Use Case shapes up with the Agents using communication association shapes. We'll also link up a couple of the Use Case shapes to each other. These communication links internal to the system are denoted by the Uses or the Extends shape. Link everything up now as in the diagram below:

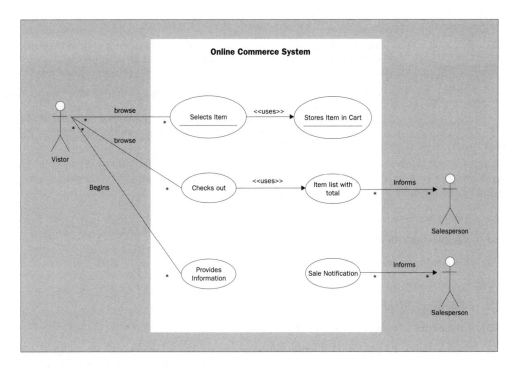

Static Structure Diagrams

Microsoft calls them static structure diagrams. The rest of the world calls them class diagrams. No matter what they're called, they are one of the most important and oldest of the object-oriented design tools. They allow us to conceptually or literally design the actual objects that will do the work in our system, using use case diagrams as a guide.

Conceptual Structures

In the world of conceptual design, we draw the objects that represent the concepts in the domain we are modeling. Essentially, like the use case diagram, this is a model of real world structures and doesn't have much to do with the way the program will work.

These conceptual objects will relate to the system – as above, where the Visitor could LogOn or LogOff. There is often little or no actual attention paid to the underlying language, or the needs of the system.

Conceptual structures are often devoid of detail, and with good reason. Since there is little basis in language, we can't provide more detail. Methods, data types, and parameters tend to be, in many cases, system- and language-dependent.

For this reason, conceptual diagrams tend to be little more than **objects** and **associations**. We can go ahead and make the top classes if we like, by double-clicking on the object and creating them, but it's all too easy to end up putting the cart before the horse.

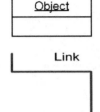

The **Object** is a generic instance of an element in your system. Any noun within the scope of our use case diagram could be an object.

Links simply show how objects interact. Along with the binary association shown on the left, Visio has a host of others, for generalizations, compositions, dependencies, binding, and other object-oriented concepts. All of them can be used in the conceptual diagram, but usually only the binary association is used.

To get a list of the objects, we can look for the nouns that fit inside the scope of the system in our original bulleted list for the use case diagram.

- ❑ Visitor browses **site**
- ❑ Visitor selects **item**
- ❑ System adds item to the **shopping cart**
- ❑ Visitor requests to **pay**
- ❑ Visitor provides **information**
- ❑ System provides list of **items** with total
- ❑ System notifies supplier of the **sale**
- ❑ System credits site operator for the **sale**

With some massaging, this can become our object list for the conceptual model. That is perhaps the hardest part – dragging objects and associations around is child's play after all. We'll end up with a model something like this:

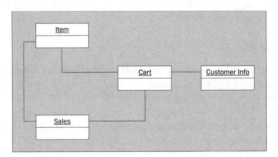

Remember – this is essentially just a sketch of how the class diagram will look a little later. We aren't actually making classes here, so the objects we are drawing aren't showing up in the top-level diagram. That's why most of us usually just go ahead and skip the conceptual model, and go directly into the Class Structure Diagram.

Class Structures

Class structures are usually what are modeled at this stage. Most of us have designed a program or two in the past, and the thought of building a complete theoretical model, then a complete physical model, and only then actually building the software, makes us break out in hives.

Fortunately, the static structure diagramming tools in Visio don't much care if we are building a conceptual or class diagram. For this reason, it might be best to just start with a generic class diagram, and make it more specific as the design improves.

Enough methodology, let's look at the shapes we'll use in the class diagram.

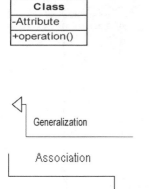

The **Class** is the basic unit in all of these diagrams, when we get right down to it. Classes are entities in the schema that have properties, but no assigned values. Not until they are instances of classes, or objects, do they have values. Thus, since this is a static diagram, in which nothing has happened, we get a look at the empty classes of the model. Classes have Attributes and Operations – which we know as properties and methods.

A **Generalization** shows the use of inheritance. For instance, the dog class and cat class are generalized from the pet class.

An **Association** is a generalized relationship between two classes – for example, when two classes share data.

Adding a Class Diagram to the UML Model

We'll now add a class diagram to our already existing UML model that we've been working on up to now, describing the GlobalMarket web site. Follow these steps:

1. Right-click on the Top Package item in the Model Explorer and select New | Static Structure Diagram.

2. Right-click on the new diagram in the Model Explorer and select Rename (or select with one click, and click again as in Windows Explorer). Give it the name Class Diagram.

3. Drag a Class shape from the UML Static Structure tab of the Shapes box onto the blank chart.

4. Double-click on the shape to open the Class Properties dialog. This is a very important property editor, and is where we'll enter most of the information required to produce good code from our diagrams. Change the name to Product:

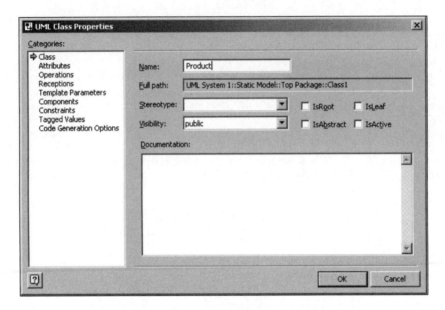

5. Add Name, Price, and Quantity as public attributes of the class:

Attribute	Type	Visibility	Multiplicity	Init. Value
Name	C#::string	public	1	
Price	C#::double	public	1	
Quantity	C#::int	public	1	

6. Next, add Order and Show operations:

Operation	Return Type	Visibility	Polymorphic	Scope
Order	C#::bool	public	☐	instance
Show	C#::object	public	☐	instance
			☐	

7. Note that we can actually enter source code, Object Constraint Language (OCL), or pseudocode for any of these operations by clicking the Methods button to the right of the Operations pane:

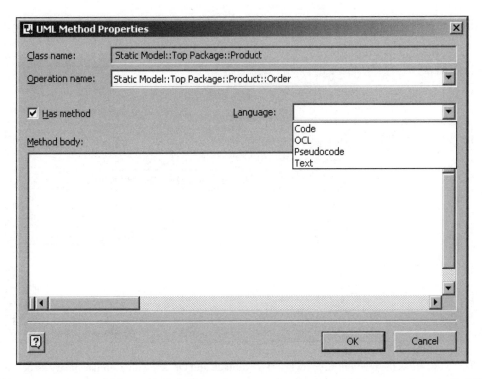

We're not going to do this here, so click **OK**, and return to the diagram. Add two new classes, called **Client** and **Order** respectively. For the **Order** item, create an **AddItem** method (an operation in UML-speak), and **Date**, **Item**, and **Customer** properties (= attributes) set as shown below. Note that the multiplicity of the **Product** property is set to *, indicating that an order can have any number of products:

Attribute	Type	Visibility	Multiplicity	Init. Value
Date	C#::long	public	1	
Customer	Top Package::Client	public	1	
Product	Top Package::Product	public	*	

Now, we want to set up some associations between the classes.

8. Drag a binary association onto the drawing, and use it to connect the **Client** and **Order** classes.

9. Double-click on the new association. Name it **Client makes order** and set the ends as shown in the following screenshot. This shows the relationships between the objects.

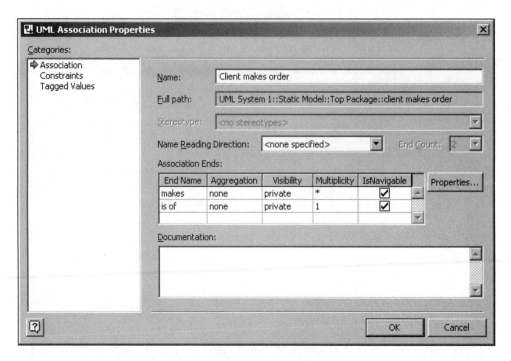

10. Next, show the relationship between the Products and Orders with a similar binary association:

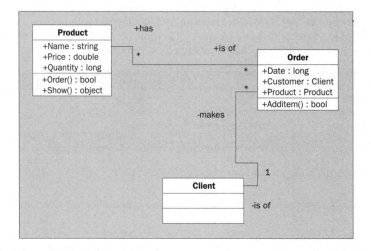

This is a fairly simple example of what these diagrams are capable of, really designed just to provide an introduction to the subject. We'll draw on the work in this class diagram as we go on to explore some other UML diagram types. Due to space requirements, we've also had to make certain assumptions about your understanding of the basic principles of object-oriented design.

Using Packages

Packages are essentially folders in Visio's UML Model Explorer window. We use them to group associated classes instead of dumping them all in one diagram. If we right-click on the Top Package in the tree view, and select New | Package we get the package properties dialog, where we can change the package name if we like. Then a package appears on the tree view, looking like a folder.

This package can be used to subdivide the system. If we were creating **all** of GlobalMarket's software in this diagram, and not just an online shopping mart, we would use packages to define the shipping, receiving, reporting, and sales subsystems, for instance.

We may then decide to create a high-level **package diagram** to illustrate the interaction of the packages. The folder icon from the tree view of the Model Explorer can in fact be dragged straight onto the static structure diagram to show the packages, or onto a class diagram to show interaction with an outside system. Packages are connected with another type of association, the **Dependency**.

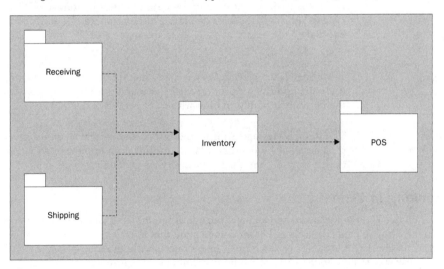

Sequence Diagrams

A **sequence diagram** shows the actors and use cases in the model performing their activities in time. That's really all there is to them! Time is represented in the vertical direction, and the actors are represented along the top in a horizontal direction. The use cases appear in sequence going down the page, interacting as needed between actors.

Sequence diagrams are a fantastic tool for developing even a small application. Using Visio and UML model diagramming tools is just a nice plus, in the grand scheme of things. During our years of multi-tier application development, the sequence diagram has often been the only diagram that we have needed to draw.

So – how do we draw one? Let's start with the shapes, and what they mean.

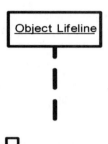

The **Object Lifeline** is the shape that represents the existence of an object throughout the existence of a sequence. It can be ended with a destruction marker (a yellow diamond) or can continue through the end of the sequence. It will often take on the shape of its classifier. For instance, if it is representing an actor, it will have the shape of an actor. Finally, as with other shapes in other diagrams, it turns red when it has semantic errors.

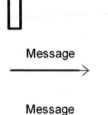

The **Activation** is the period that the object is active. It is glued to the lifeline of the object, and defines the use time of the object while it is alive. This is a rather theoretical concept in these days of object pooling and JIT activation. Usually, unless there are extenuating circumstances, the activation covers the entire time the object is available to the sequence.

Message
$\longrightarrow$

A **Message** is the verb in the use case diagram. In a normal design philosophy, it is a method call, or property reference under some circumstances. It defines the movement of information within the sequence diagram.

Message
$\longleftarrow\ -\ -\ -\ \bullet$

The **Return Message** is for methods that return a value, either as a return parameter, or by reference. We know this is an implementation strategy in a design chapter, but it is the best way we've found to look at it.

Error Checking in Visio

Right-click on the Top Package and add a new sequence diagram. Drag an Object Lifeline onto the page from the Shapes panel. It has a red outline, indicating that it has semantic errors. As we build diagrams, Visio checks for semantic errors in real time. Objects without required information will turn red, in a similar way to how code in Visual Studio containing syntax errors is given a squiggly red underline. We can view the errors in the simple diagram by right-clicking on the object and selecting Display Semantic Errors. We'll see this:

UMLE00153: [Constraint] : UML ModelElement has no name.

UMLE00081: Object Lifeline[ClassifierRole] : [ClassifierRole - WFR2] -
The features of the classifier role must be a subset of those of the base classifier.

UMLE00150: Begins[Association] : UML AssociationEnd may only be
connected to a classifier.

Building the Sequence

The process to build a sequence diagram in Visio 2002 is as follows:

1. For each object (either an actor or use case that could be defined as an object rather than an activity), drag an object lifeline onto the drawing.

2. Double-click the object lifeline to bring up the **UML Classifier Role Properties** dialog.

3. Select a **Top Package** classifier in the **Classifier** dropdown. The actors and use cases generated as part of the use case diagram make up the list.

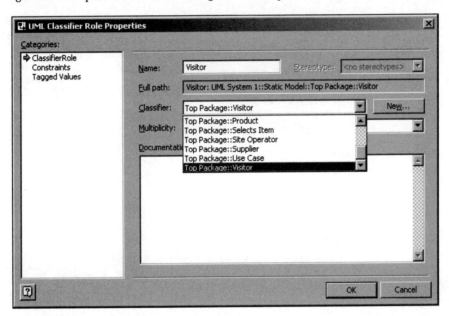

Alternatively, use the **New** button to create a new object in the top-level package. This will be available to all diagrams.

4. Press **OK**. The shape on the lifeline will take on the shape of its classifier:

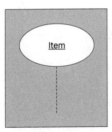

5. In order to show the actual active state of the object through its lifetime, drag an **Activation** shape onto the drawing panel.

6. Glue the **Activation** shape to one of the anchor points along the length of the lifeline.

7. Finally, to show an interaction between two objects, drag a **Message** shape to the drawing pane.

8. The shape should try to link itself to two nearest lifelines. It is possible to drag an anchor point over a lifeline or several lifelines in order to connect disjunctive lifelines.

9. Double-click on the message shape, and the Message Properties dialog opens:

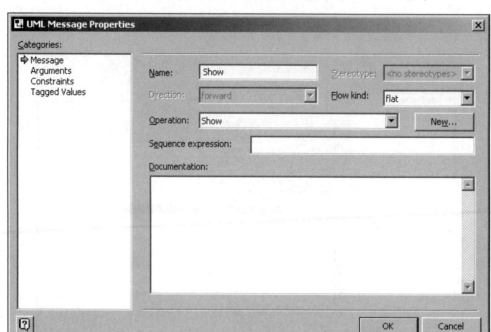

The messages are based on operations, and as long as we have included a class with operations in the message call, this dialog lets us select the operations from the drop down, or add a whole new operation.

For fun, put a few more messages on the diagram. Don't worry about them making sense at this point.

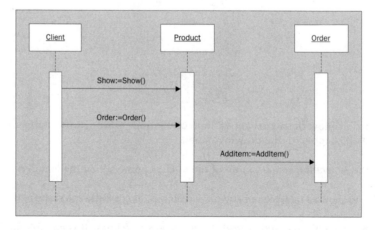

We can also represent the return parameters for the methods with a return message.

Collaboration Diagrams

A **collaboration diagram** is essentially a sequence diagram for one use case. As we get further into UML notation, we begin essentially decomposing the system. This is the first of the real decompositions, taking a use case like Browse Item and showing the order in which the objects communicate, and how they communicate.

Unlike a sequence diagram, there is no way to notate time on a collaboration diagram, so the methods specified are ordered with numbers to indicate the call sequence. The sequence number is stored as a property of the association, so it's more than just a drawing – the application actually knows how things are supposed to flow.

Also unlike the other diagrams we have covered so far, the Collaboration diagram is not about the static classes. It is about objects, or instances of the classes. We can only relate an association role with a classifier role, for instance, if the two classes we are trying to relate are already associated in the class diagram.

Essentially, what we are doing is making instances of the classes found in the static structure diagram, and connecting then with instances of the associations between those classes in the static structure diagram.

There are two essential icons in a collaboration diagram, Classifiers and Associations.

A **Classifier Role** is the instance of a class in the static structure diagram. It is used in the Collaboration diagram to show the order in which methods are called to fulfill the use case in question.

The **Association Role** connector takes on most of the properties of its association in the static structure diagram. They can be used for self-calling operations, or between operations. Just remember that it only works if there is already an association in the static structure!

Let's start with a diagram of the use case Selects Item.

1. Right-click on the Top Package and choose a New | Collaboration. Note that if we were using packages, this would be in the package for the related subsystem.

2. Rename the diagram Selects Item Collaboration.

3. Drag a Classifier Role onto the diagram.

4. Double-click on the Classifier Role to access the properties. Name the role class. Usually, the role is named with the same name as the class in all lower-case letters, unless it is a special use instance.

5. Change the classifier to `TopPackage::Client`.

6. Change the multiplicity to 1. Only one client at a time is selecting items.

7. Drag another Classifier Role onto the page, and set the name to `product`, the classifier to `Product`, and the multiplicity to 1.

8. Drag an Association Role onto the page.

9. Anchor the ends to the handles on the client and product classifier roles.

10. Go back to the class diagram, and add an association for this collaboration:

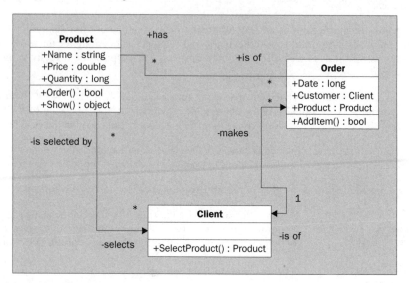

Name the new association between `Product` and `Client` Client selects Product.

11. Also, add a method to the client to enact the association, called `SelectProduct`. It returns an object of type `Product`.

12. Return to the collaboration diagram, and double-click on the association to get the UML Association Role Properties dialog.

Leave the name blank – we are more interested in the association and method name than the name for the role.

13. Select Client selects Product in the Base association dropdown, and change the end roles to selects and is selected by in the Association End Roles grid:

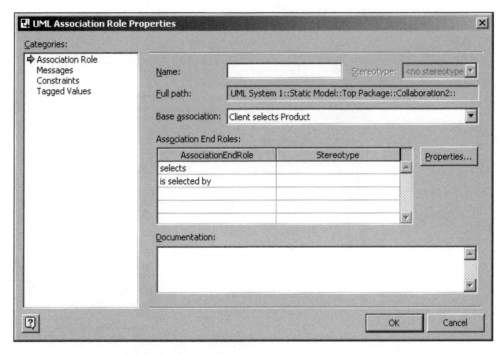

14. Now choose the Messages category from the left hand list, and edit the default message by clicking the Properties button next to the Messages grid.

15. Get the SelectProduct operation from the Operation dropdown. Set the sequence to 1, since it is our first and only method. Set the name to SelectsProduct – model elements such as this (that is, methods) must have names. Depending on how you drew the line, you may need to select the direction as backward in order to get the Client class methods:

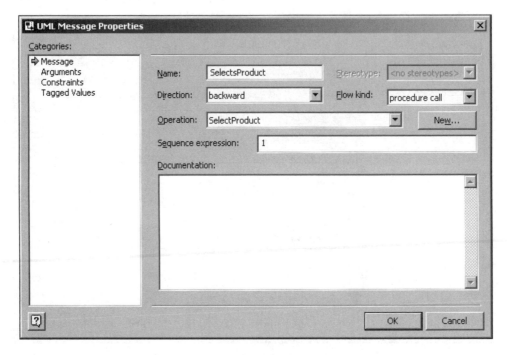

16. Click OK twice, and we have a diagram!

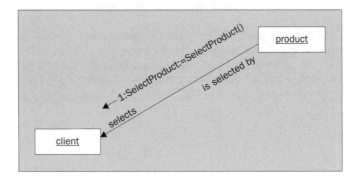

Granted, it's a very simple diagram, and it essentially shows what happens when a user clicks on a link in a web page. Nevertheless, in a sophisticated program it is very useful to know when everything occurs. We just don't have the space to go into as much detail here, but hopefully this will provide a good idea of how to get started.

Statecharts

In addition to the collaboration diagram, Visio can also create **Activity** diagrams. Most of the world – outside of a small area of Redmond in the US – calls these statecharts, and they are very useful for analyzing the crossover from design to implementation at the activity level.

The statechart diagram allows us to interpolate the state of an object in time, during the execution of the project. They really require a book of their own to cover all the details, and they don't interact with Visual Studio, so we've left them out of this chapter. Check the Visio documentation under Activity, or the references in the *Summary*, for more information.

Implementation-Level Diagrams

The last two diagrams in Visio's tool chest deal with implementation rather than design, but we include them for completeness. The **component** and **deployment** diagrams are closely related. The component diagram shows physical dependency between actual DLLs, source files, and data structures. The deployment is more of a state chart, showing instances of the classes, as they exist on pieces of hardware during the execution of a program.

Component Diagrams

As with the package diagram we created above, the component diagram would actually be very simple for this system. In reality, we would likely compile our three classes into one DLL file, and that would be the entire component diagram. For the sake of demonstration, we'll pretend to compile our three classes into two DLLs, one for the client, and one for the product and order.

1. Create a new component diagram by right-clicking on the top package and selecting New | Component diagram. Rename the diagram Component.

2. Drag a new component onto the screen, and double-click to expose the properties window.

3. Call the component Users, and set the stereotype to library if it isn't already.

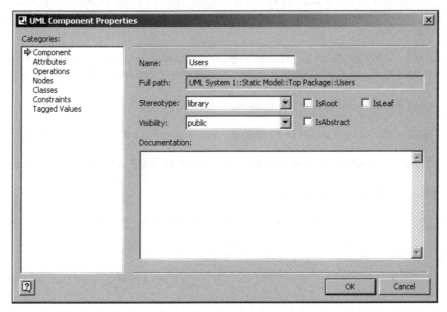

Click on the Classes tab, and set the Client class to be placed within this component by simply clicking the Client checkbox, and then click OK.

4. Drag another component onto the diagram. Set the name to store, the stereotype to library, and include the Products and Orders classes.

5. Drag a dependency onto the drawing. The dependency shows that a change to an object may affect other objects. Connect the handles to the two components.

That's all there is to it. We have an idea of how the compiled application will look now, from a file perspective.

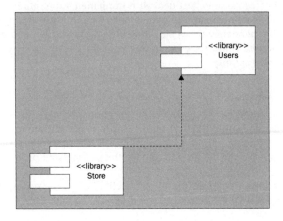

Deployment Diagrams

A deployment diagram shows us where we will be able to find these objects while they are running. Of course, both of these objects will be on the same machine, but we could easily show the existence of a Users Web Service across a network line if necessary here, or a call to a separate server for certain specific information.

In this case, we have a single node instance, with the two library instances within it. Starting with a simple example in the class areas usually means a *really* simple example in the implementation.

1. Drag the node instance to the drawing window.

2. Double-click to get the node properties. This is considered a top-level object.

3. Name it something generic, like Application Server. We'll get specific in a second.

4. Click on the components tab.

Press the Select All button to show that all the system components run on the application server.

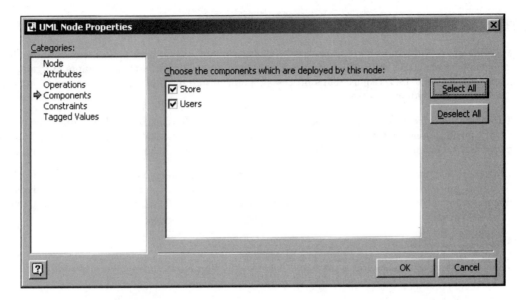

5. Press OK. We are now confronted with the properties for the node instance. This is the actual physical machine. The name of my demo application server is **Gryphon**.

6. Press OK. Widen the node on the drawing, and drag a new component instance onto it.

7. Double-click the new component to get the property window. Set the name to something unique, like oUsers, and specify that it is from component Users in the component dropdown.

8. Repeat this for the Store component instance.

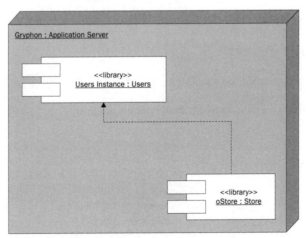

That about closes it up for diagram types. Now we have a complete picture of how the application looks – on (electronic) paper anyway. We know how the users will use it, what classes are involved, when they are called, and how the system is installed and compiled. All that is left is to actually use all of this stuff.

Integrating with Visual Studio

Many organizations require serious amounts of documentation so that their process can be shown to be 'repeatable'. Organizations like the Software Engineering Institute (SEI) and International Organization for Standardization (ISO) require that a process be in place, and that the company can prove that it uses that process to build its software.

Then there are companies that have no documentation, but should have. No one should work without documentation. Even when on a one-person project, we need to communicate with users, and be reviewed by peers. It's tough to do that with just the code, because if there is a mistake we have to start all over.

UML fits both of these scenarios. If we are working in a large organization, our time spent accurately portraying the system in UML translates itself into actual code we can use in the project. If we are the type that sketches the code first to get a prototype, we can translate that into UML for a start to documentation.

Building Code

The neater of these two features is the **Generate** wizard. This tool creates the templates for classes and namespaces for us in the language of our choice.

1. Open the GlobalMarket UML project we've been working in.

2. Go to UML | Code | Generate menu.

3. Set the language to C#, if it isn't already set.

4. Name the project **GlobalMarket**.

5. Set the location, or leave the default.

6. Check the **Add classes to Visual Studio project** checkbox.

7. Select **Empty Web Project**.

8. Name the new solution **GlobalMarket**, and check **Create directory**.

9. Select all of the classes in the **Static Model** on the left.

10. Press OK.

Lo and behold, a little picture of our product:

has actually become a product!

```
// Static Model

public class Product
{

  public string Name;

  public double Price;

  public long Quantity;

  public bool Order()
  {

  }

  public object Show()
  {

  }

}// END CLASS DEFINITION Product
```

Are we ready to compile and run? No. But did we completely waste our time doing the documentation – at least from a code perspective? No! This is actually useful stuff! Both the public properties and the public methods that we created are template-generated for our use.

Working with Options

There are a few options too in code generation. Go to the class diagram (static structure) and double-click on the **Product** class, and select the **Code Generation Options** category.

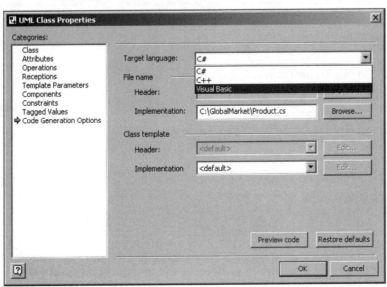

The **Target language** setting is interesting. The options are C#, C++, or VB. Since the basic architecture underlying VB and C++ isn't any different between Visual Studio .NET and Visual Studio 6, we can use the code generated to work in either tool. For comparison, here is the `Product` class in VB:

```
Public Class Product

   Public Name As String

   Public Price As Double

   Public Quantity As Long

   Private selects As System.Collections.ArrayList

   Public Function Order () As Boolean

   End Function

   Public Function Show () As Object

   End Function

End Class ' END CLASS DEFINITION Product
```

Even in the era of .NET, it's a handy feature to be able to use the documenting tools in the old architecture.

Another nice feature is the template generator. Click on the dropdown next to **Implementation** and select **ClassImpl1**. Then press the **Edit** button; we now have the template for generating the classes:

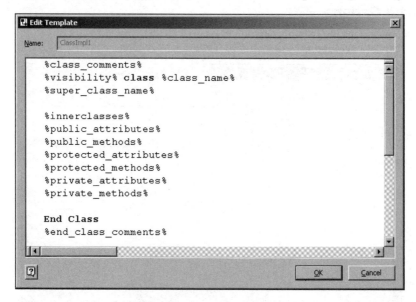

The best use for this is to insert standardized comments in the code that is generated. In fact, using the **UML | Code | Preferences** menu item, we can create and manage a number of code templates:

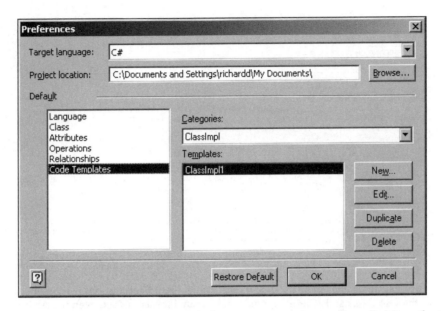

What's more, all of the macros in Visio – including custom macros – can be called from the templates. If we drop the %attrib_name% macro in the template, the actual name of the attribute in question will appear in the generated code. This gives us all sorts of linking and tying possibilities, to show the direct chain between the needs of the design, and our code.

Getting UML Class Diagrams out of Existing Code

The Visio plug-in will appear all over the place after installation – Excel, Visual Basic 6, everywhere. It's amazing. In Visual Studio .NET, however, we have to right-click on the tool panel and select Visio UML to get the Reverse Engineer button. This allows us to take well-formed C# code and make a Visio UML model with the coded classes all ready for us.

We need some code to reverse engineer – we used Dumawish Books from the Microsoft Visual Studio .Net\Enterprise Samples directory. You may need to install this if you haven't already done so, using the .msi file provided.

The Business Object directory has a project associated with it, and we can open it in Visual Studio .NET. After it is loaded, click on the project file, then the Reverse Engineer button. It will request a directory for saving the VSD file, and then generate the classes into UML components:

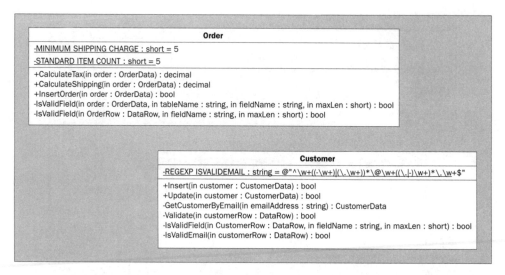

These are less usable for documentation than our hand-crafted diagrams, but inarguably more accurate. Of course, the Use Cases and other diagrams aren't created for us. In fact, even the static structure has to be generated by dragging the created classes onto the screen. The top-level items are well generated, however, and creation of implementation-level diagrams is much easier than starting from scratch.

When reverse engineering, we have the option of using an existing project, so as to save the coded classes into our documentation project, or adding the data layer to the business layer here in this project. In fact, Visual Studio even gives us access to this file as a Solution Item:

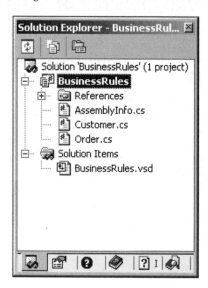

Summary

Documentation is never easy, but UML has the potential to sway even the most hardened programmers to the benefits of diagramming their applications. With its formulaic language, and simple methodology interaction, it can fit in with any design style, from the large paper-bound corporation to the small hack-and-slash code shop.

Visio and Visual Studio have made using UML with .NET projects as easy as writing the projects themselves. We've looked at the creation of the most popular and useful diagrams here. While we didn't discuss much about UML language itself, we've shown how simple diagramming can be, and how useful the integration is.

For more information about UML, may we suggest some of the following resources:

❑   http://www.uml.org/ – Object Management Group's UML web site

❑   *UML in a Nutshell* (O'Reilly, ISBN 1-56592-448-7)

❑   *UML Distilled*, second edition (Addison-Wesley, ISBN 0-201-65783-X)

Of course, anything by Jacobson, Booch, or Rumbaugh – the creators of the Unified Method and principal architects of UML – would be good, if dry, reading for anyone interested in the topic.

17

Enterprise Templates

Visual Studio has traditionally been a developer's tool, concentrating square on at the implementation of applications, their debugging, and their maintenance. With this latest incarnation (in conjunction with Microsoft's purchase of Visio and the advent of .NET), it has now become a tool that can accommodate the entire software development lifecycle as well. As we've seen in the last two chapters, there now exist facilities in the Enterprise Architect editions of Visual Studio .NET that support the modeling (analysis and design) of data that is to be used in an application along with an abstraction of the 'thought processes' and relationships between the objects that make it all work.

Modeling only takes it so far however. Development, especially at the large-scale, enterprise level, exists in a broad gray area between the analysis and design of an application and its development in a fashion consistent with guidelines written by the software architects (whose day-to-day involvement usually finishes as soon as the first line of code is written). The Enterprise Edition of VS.NET offers a way of narrowing that gray area with what are called Enterprise Templates (ETs). As the name suggests, these allow designers to define their design guidelines for developers more clearly than they have previously been able to.

In this chapter, we shall:

❑   Have a closer look at why Enterprise Templates are a 'good thing™'.

❑   Tour the Enterprise Templates that come with VS.NET and see how they work

❑   Investigate the XML-based Template Description Language, and the other components of a template

So, first things first – what's in this gray area that these ETs address and who are they really helping out?

Introducing the ET

The last decade saw the invention of a number of new models, architectures, and techniques for building applications, and some fundamental questions were asked of the application's design as well. The advent of COM, Java, and CORBA first gave designers a choice of platforms on which to place their applications. Then came the Internet, DCOM, .NET, and with them, the question of just how **distributed** an application should be and how capable it should be of propagating information across multifarious devices: desktops, mobile phones, tickertape, and the like.

Enterprise-level applications have been the most affected by each new change in Internet standards and technology, mostly because once the Web was established, they became the target and justification for the development of these standards. From a closed user base to the worldwide Internet, distributed applications must scale incredibly well, operating just as efficiently for a million people as for a few dozen. Most new web technologies can assist in one or several aspects of such an application. The most prevalent – XML – can be seen everywhere, in databases, Web Services, and as a bridge between incompatible operating systems and legacy applications, to name but a few. The gray area is not whether or not we should use XML and other enabling technologies when building an application; rather it's to what extent they should be used.

The Problem at Hand

Distributed applications are large problems that require multiple projects to solve; they frequently involve several development languages and dozens of platform services, developed by many people, possibly remotely and independently. Seventy percent of the development time for large apps is taken up with the design of the infrastructure. The emphasis is then on the developer to interpret that design as intended. Each begins with a clean slate and chooses which of the many components and UI elements to use, even whether to write their own. The software architects who analyze and design the application to begin with can recommend which components and elements to use in white papers, right down to naming conventions for methods and variables, but there is no guarantee that each project manager will interpret those instructions and develop their code in a consistent fashion. Some of the areas that may vary enormously include:

❑ The programming model to be used: ASP.NET \ Web Services, ATL Server \ Web Services, or .NET Remoting?

❑ Legacy system interoperability, message formatting and encoding, type-system fidelity, state management, or COM interoperability?

❑ The tradeoff between manageability, availability, performance, scalability, reliability, and security

❑ The structure of the application and the projects within

The same applies on a smaller scale between project managers and their development team – how to communicate the choices that should be made during the implementation of the application.

The Solution

White papers are a first step, but they rely on the development team to read, understand, and draw the same conclusions from them. Enterprise Templates take a further step toward the ideal hands-on approach where the design team are permanently hands-on in guiding the developers. While ETs can't solve every communication problem, or offer a clear-cut answer every time a developer has a choice to make, they can delineate a much narrower scope for decisions and speed up the development process as a result.

An Enterprise Template, then, allows the software architect to:

- predetermine the basic structure of a VS.NET solution – how many layers, how many tiers, which language to use, which components can be used, and which classes can be inherited from within a layer.

- customize the developer experience by restricting what VS.NET allows them to do.

- provide justifications as to why the template was constructed as it was and alert developers when something they are attempting breaks a rule of the template.

This template can be handed down to project managers who may choose to make further additions to the template – the addition of some base classes perhaps – before setting up source control for the project and assigning roles to the team. Developers can then take their assignments and develop solutions based on the guidance and rules built into the template.

Under the hood, an Enterprise Template is essentially a collection of three items:

- **A prototype file structure** to be copied into a new solution whenever one is created based on the template.

- **A policy file** written in a new XML dialect called Template Definition Language (TDL). This is where the rules governing the templated solution are defined. Note that each solution can have only one policy file, but that does not stop the file itself holding templates for several different projects.

- **A set of custom help messages** to be made available within the IDE. These work just like normal help pages, accessible through the Dynamic Help window as appropriate and the *F1* key.

The file structure and help messages are fairly self-explanatory, but the policy file is worth a longer look. It is this that governs the whole IDE and defines what you can and cannot add to your solution or project, be it an assembly, module, control, component, or reference, the properties that are read-only or not, and so on. Written in TDL, it manages this by dividing the user experience into a set of contexts – the application, one of its components, or other solution items – and defining rules for each one.

Actions occurring within a templated solution, such as when a new component is added, are validated against the policy file as they are performed. If an action (say, using a blacklisted component) fails this validation, a **policy reminder** is placed in the Task List, giving a description of the problem, where it occurs, and optionally detailing the specific area of policy that it violates.

A policy will cover every type of project that can be added to a templated solution. If say a new C# class library project is added to such a solution, VS.NET will read the template policy and if a setting there overrides the default for a class library, the IDE will reflect that. If the policy developer has done things properly, a related help topic will also be available detailing the changes.

> It's important to realize that a template will not *prevent* a developer entering whatever
> code they choose. If it recognizes that the developer has entered something that
> contravenes the policy, it will say so, but that's all. It's not a restriction on what is
> coded, but rather a guide for VS.NET to help the developer write according to a
> predefined plan.

We'll take a look at how a policy file is drawn up later when we investigate TDL in detail. For now
though, let's try out an example to get a feel of the basics.

Working with ETs in VS.NET

There are five predefined Enterprise Templates available in the Enterprise editions of VS.NET, and the
Enterprise Architect edition also provides a blank project for creating our own. These project types are
found under Other Projects | Enterprise Template Projects as shown below:

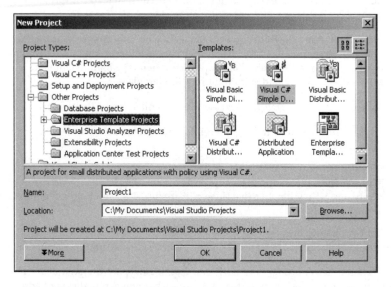

The prototype file structures for the five Distributed Application templates are all variations on the same
theme and all five use the same policy file, `policy.tdl`. The following sections briefly outline the
default files that these templates are created with.

The VB/VC# Simple Distributed Application Type

The **VB/VC# Simple Distributed Application** creates a traditional n-tier application split across seven class library projects, one for the data tier, two for the business tier, three for the front-end, and the last as an all-purpose utility set of classes and routines that any piece of the application may reference if it needs to. Each library is based in VB.NET or C# depending on which project you picked to start with and contains the standard set of files you would expect to see if you had added that type of class to a project under normal circumstances.

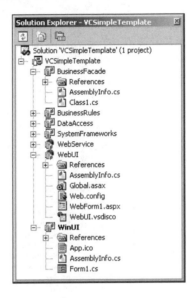

All seven libraries are contained within a single Enterprise Template project (ETP) folder (here called `VCSimpleTemplate`) so while it is easier to reason out the structure early on, the designer will have less control over it because there is only one overall layer – in a policy file the 'root node' is the ETP folder. Compare this with the next template which has more 'root nodes' allowing for a richer, less ambiguous policy file because the extra level of structure lets us define rules for more situations.

The VB/VC# Distributed Application Type

A bit more complex than the simple template we've just seen, the **VB/VC# Distributed Application**
project type maintains the same basic structure as we saw above, but each class library is now an ETP
folder containing a class library. This change of structure allows the developer to add extra projects to
each of the tiers as required and the designer to create specific rules for each tier as needed.

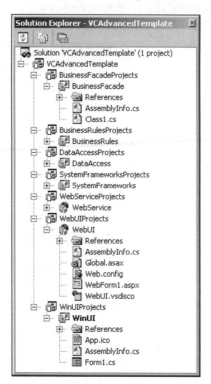

Note that ETP folders may contain projects written in any language, but the initial projects are all in the
language selected when the template was created. It is up to the policy writer to restrict what may or
may not be added to them (and indeed what the solution is called when created – here it would be
VCAdvancedTemplate). For example, the solution above contains only C# files to begin with, but the
policy file attached to it permits both C# and VB.NET projects (but not projects in other .NET
languages however) to be added to any of the ETP folders should we wish.

We'll look more closely at the user experience and the policy for this template in a few pages.

The Distributed Application Type

Last but not least, the **Distributed Application** project produces a language-agnostic structure of ETP folders only, to reflect the seven tiers of the application to be built, leaving architects and then developers to add the actual contents as they see fit, as long as they don't break policy.

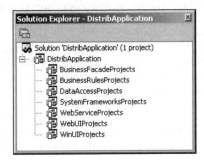

Layers, Tiers and Projects

If you're not familiar with the application structure that the templates generate, they are the end result of Microsoft's own experience with designing and building distributed applications over the last few years. The Duwamish and Fitch & Mather case studies supplied in the VS.NET help documentation are perfect examples of exactly this structure. As with all enterprise application structures, this one works around the n-tier model, advocating the separation of data access and persistence code from business logic, and from any presentation and layout code. This structure considers these tiers as sets of services divided up as follows:

Data Access and Persistence	`DataAccess`
Business Services	`BusinessFacade` and `BusinessRules`
Presentation Services	`WebServices`, `WebUI`, and `WinUI`

The seventh set of services, `SystemFrameworks`, acts as the backbone layer providing the central functionality for the whole application. Here we find classes and code that every other layer may reference, inherit from, and use. For example, this layer may contain an HTML page cache, a connection pooling service, or perhaps core data and business object classes that contain some basic functionality that every other business and data object must inherit.

The other six interact with each other as follows:

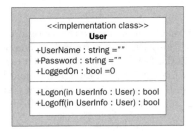

The easiest layer to determine on the server side is the Data Access layer which acts as the interface to a data source of some variety, fetching data from and sending data to it as required, perhaps using stored procedures and ADO.NET. Interacting in the main with the Data Access layer is the Business layer. This contains the actual business objects within the application, the constraints upon them, and how they may communicate with the Business Façade and Data Access layers. It may turn out that it is more efficient to encapsulate some business rules as stored procedures or triggers, but that will not really affect the purpose of this layer.

The Business Facade layer acts as an intermediary between the presentation services projects and the Business Rules tier, receiving input from users/clients and acting accordingly. This may mean interacting with the Business Rules tier to react to an event, gather or save data, or even going straight to the Data Access level to retrieve some data which doesn't require any additional processing before it is sent back to the client. As the name suggests, this façade exists as a layer over the business rules to hide their complexity and any changes to the rules from the presentation layer. The Web Services layer has a similar role to the Business Façade, but while the latter assumes that the client is on the same machine, the former provides an interface for a client that could be accessing it over a LAN or the Internet.

Finally, the Presentation layer, comprising WebUI and WinUI components, provides the user interface for the application. It could be windows- or web-based or both, but will regardless talk to the Business Facade layer, sometimes via Web Services, and will see no more of the application than this layer exposes.

The User Experience

For now, we're ignoring the policy file and contextual help for these project types, but we'll return to these after we've created a new project so we can see how the template affects what we can do with VS.NET. To this end, we'll now create a new solution using the C# Distributed Application template:

1. First of all, because this project generates web-based components, we must make sure that the local copy of Internet Explorer is not set to work offline and that IIS is up and running. VS.NET will tell you if this isn't the case and to remedy it, but it saves a little bother if we sort it out first.

2. Check that this is the case, and start up VS.NET. Create a new Visual C# Distributed Application project called **MyDistApp**. To remind you, you can find this in the New Project dialog box under **Other Projects | Enterprise Template Projects**.

3. Press **OK**, and you'll be asked where on your web server the WebUI and WebServices projects should be saved. Enter http://localhost/MyDistApp or something similar. It's at this point that VS.NET will complain if IIS or IE aren't running as noted earlier, but assuming they are, the wizard will then generate the skeleton file structure we saw earlier and we're off.

The Policy File attached to this project can be discovered by right-clicking the top-level **MyDistApp** ETP folder in Solution Explorer and clicking **Properties** from the context menu that appears. The name and location of the file can be found in the Policy File property. As it turns out, all the templates that come with VS.NET use the same policy file, DAP.tdl, although it should be noted that it does not apply the same rules to all the templates. We'll see exactly how and why it manages this as we dissect Template Definition Language in a minute, but for now, let's look at its effects.

As we've discussed, the aim of creating an Enterprise Template is to improve a developer's understanding of the designer's recommendations for building an application by removing some of the decisions that are required while implementing it. The immediate effect of the policy file is to reduce the number of items a developer has available for adding to the templated solution in VS.NET. Specifically, it restricts the number of language project types that can be added to a solution and the number of menu items and Toolbox controls that can be added to individual projects.

Restricting the Project Types

Right-click on any ETP folder and try to add a new project to it – firstly you'll notice that only empty language projects are available. VS.NET solutions are regarded by the policy as a large element with many subelements – ETP folders, projects, Toolbox items, and so on. A policy file can define elementsets that specify all the child elements a parent may have. In this case, an ETP folder element may only contain empty project elements and VS.NET reflects this by only displaying the allowed projects in the Add New Project dialog box. These constraints, which form part of the Template Definition Language, are defined by context. Hence, a different rule may apply when adding a new project to the WebUI layer rather than the WebService layer.

Restricting the Menu and Toolbox

Policy files also let us restrict or include the items that are offered in VS.NET's menus and Toolbox. For example, if you try to edit `Service1.asmx` in the WebServiceProjects layer, you'll find that only the Components, Clipboard Ring, and Pointer tabs of the Toolbox are available, whereas the Data and Windows Forms boxes are also available normally. Likewise, check out the Project menu; you'll see that the top three options are grayed out. VS.NET is reflecting the valid menu and toolbox contents when working within the web service layer as defined in `policy.tdl`.

Dynamic Help

Although it's not particularly obvious with the pre-defined templates, we can create a set of help files to display within the dynamic help window as developers select different elements within a templated solution. Even more usefully, we can create a whole new category for the window, aside from 'Help' or 'Samples' say, to really make it obvious when a specialized item is available.

Likewise, we can set up messages that will appear in the Task List window should the developer do something that breaks the rules in the policy file. For example, try adding the Shippers Maintenance project to the root MyDistApp ETP folder. Once it's added, you'll see a policy error appear in the task list window saying Policy Reminder: Project 'MyDistApp.etp' (Element etpDistributedApplicationFull) does not allow Project 'ShippersMaintenance.csproj' (Element projCSharpProject).

The Policy File

Up to this point, we've learned only what Enterprise Templates are for, who will benefit from their use and how developers might expect their IDE to be affected when using a templated project. Now we start getting our fingers dirty with the first step towards creating our own templates, by investigating the policy file and the XML dialect it's written in – Template Definition Language (TDL). Once we know how to structure our own policy files, it's only a matter of file handling to create a full template, so let's get to work.

The TDL Schema

Like any other modern dialect of XML, the structure of a document written in TDL is dictated by a schema against which any document is validated and checked for well-formedness. If a policy file does not obey the rules laid out in the schema, an error will be raised when it is attached to a project. Each TDL document must first identify the XML namespace for the schema as follows:

```
<TDL xmlns="http://www.microsoft.com/schema/EnterpriseTemplates/TDLSchema">
```

For easy reference, however, look in the `EnterpriseFrameworks\Schemas` subdirectory of the VS.NET program directory, and you'll find the schema there, under the name `TDLSchema.xml`. It is the ultimate reference for creating the correct structure within a policy file for your template. However, it does not govern the semantic intent of your policy file – that is up to you.

At top level, a TDL document is quite simple to understand. Under the root node, `<TDL>`, there are up to four child nodes:

```
<TDL>
    <ELEMENTS />
    <CATEGORIES />
    <DEFAULTSETTINGS />
    <FEATURES />
</TDL>
```

The only mandatory node of these four child nodes is `<DEFAULTSETTINGS>`, which, as you would expect, lets us specify a set of rules for the whole of a template project which apply unless overridden by rules specific to an element or set of elements of the project. The concept of scope – the domain over which a variable or other object is active – comes into play here. As we begin to divide our solution into a hierarchy of `<ELEMENTS>` and child elements, rules and constraints apply to an element, its children and other 'progeny'. We'll look more at this concept later on.

The other two nodes at the top level, `<CATEGORIES>` and `<FEATURES>`, allow us to group together pieces of the VS.NET IDE and our own code and components so we can more readily address them under a single name rather than having to repeatedly list them all.

Specifying Default Settings for the Template

At the template level, there are three mandatory behaviors and one optional set of constraints that can be specified inside the `<DEFAULTSETTINGS>` node of a policy file:

```
<DEFAULTSETTINGS>
    <DEFAULTACTION />
    <ORDER />
    <POLICYMODE />
    <CONSTRAINTS />
</DEFAULTSETTINGS>
```

The first mandatory node, `<DEFAULTACTION>`, determines whether or not 'unknown elements' – that is, project items, Toolbox or menu items regarded as part of a group (under the same Toolbox heading say, but not explicitly named in the `<ELEMENTSET>` defining that group) – should be considered part of the set by default. There are only two choices, `INCLUDE` or `EXCLUDE`. Members of an `<ELEMENTSET>` can be explicitly included or excluded as the policy requires.

Contrasting with `<DEFAULTACTION>`, the `<POLICYMODE>` node further defines how a templated project will react to unknown items in an `<ELEMENTSET>`. Its two possible values, `PERMISSIVE` and `RESTRICTIVE`, combine with the value of `<DEFAULTACTION>` as follows (according to MSDN anyway):

`<POLICYMODE>`	`<DEFAULTACTION>`	Resulting policy
PERMISSIVE	INCLUDE	Exclude only items explicitly excluded from an `<ELEMENTSET>`. Include everything else, whether recognized or not, and include their associated items.
RESTRICTIVE	INCLUDE	Include in the `<ELEMENTSET>` only those items explicitly included, together with their associated items. Exclude everything else.
PERMISSIVE	EXCLUDE	Exclude only items explicitly excluded from an `<ELEMENTSET>` together with their associated items. Include everything else, whether recognized or not, and include their associated items.
RESTRICTIVE	EXCLUDE	Include in the `<ELEMENTSET>` only those items explicitly included in the policy. Exclude everything else, even if it is associated with an included item.

The third mandatory node, `<ORDER>`, specifies in which order `INCLUDE` and `EXCLUDE` actions are evaluated when a policy is first applied to an element or `<ELEMENTSET>`. It takes either of the two values `INCLUDEEXCLUDE` or `EXCLUDEINCLUDE`. For example, if you wanted to define an `<ELEMENTSET>` as containing all bar one item of a group, you would first include the whole group (category) and then exclude the one item and the `<ORDER>` node, assuming it isn't overridden, would be given the value `INCLUDEEXCLUDE`. The alternative, `EXCLUDEINCLUDE`, would not make sense in this case, as excluding the single item first would accomplish nothing and the whole group would become part of the `<ELEMENTSET>`.

In `DAP.tdl`, the policy file for the Distributed Application Templates that comes with VS.NET, the defaults are:

```
<DEFAULTSETTINGS>
   <DEFAULTACTION>INCLUDE</DEFAULTACTION>
   <ORDER>EXCLUDEINCLUDE</ORDER>
   <POLICYMODE>PERMISSIVE</POLICYMODE>
</DEFAULTSETTINGS>
```

It's also possible to add some constraints to element properties, menus and the Toolbox for the entire project by adding to the optional `<CONSTRAINTS>` node here. We'll look at how to compose constraints a little later on.

Grouping Items into Categories

A handy shortcut to remember is that TDL allows us to group a number of elements under one category name and refer to that rather than having to list them all one by one. Look at this example:

```
<CATEGORIES>
  <CATEGORY>
    <ID>name for category</ID>
    <CATEGORYMEMBER>element name</CATEGORYMEMBER>
    ... more categorymember declarations ...
  </CATEGORY>
  ... more category definitions ...
</CATEGORIES>
```

We choose the category `<ID>` value ourselves, although for convenience the recommended convention is to prefix it with `cat` to distinguish such elements from menu items, projects, and so on. The value for each category member is the ID of an element declared elsewhere in your policy file.

Towards the end of `DAP.tdl` for example you'll find a number of categories defined that reflect groupings of items as you would find them in Visual Studio. The extract below for instance defines a category called `catCSCommonProjectItems`, which, as the comment suggests, groups all common C# project items under one roof for easy reference elsewhere:

```
<CATEGORIES>
..
<CATEGORY> <!-- Common Visual C# Project items -->
  <ID>catCSCommonProjectItems</ID>
  <CATEGORYMEMBER>codeClass</CATEGORYMEMBER>
  <CATEGORYMEMBER>projItemCSharpFile</CATEGORYMEMBER>
  <CATEGORYMEMBER>codeComponent</CATEGORYMEMBER>
  <CATEGORYMEMBER>codeInstallerClass</CATEGORYMEMBER>
  <CATEGORYMEMBER>codeGlobalApplicationClass</CATEGORYMEMBER>
</CATEGORY>
..
</CATEGORIES>
```

A complete set of categories to reflect elements as found in VS.NET can be found in `vside.tdl`.

Identifying VS.NET Menu and Toolbox Features

The `<FEATURES>` node under the root `<TDL>` node serves to establish which of the various menus, menu items, and pieces of the Toolbox in the VS.NET IDE have certain rules applied to them. The structure for this node separates out menu items from Toolbox items as follows:

```
<FEATURES>
  <MENUS>
    <MENU>
      <ID />
      <CMDID />
      <GUID />
    </MENU>
    ... more menu item declarations ...
  </MENUS>
  <TOOLBOXITEMS>
    <TOOLBOXITEM>
      <ID />
      <DESCRIPTOR />
```

```
        </TOOLBOXITEM>
        ... more toolboxitem declarations ...
     </TOOLBOXITEMS>
  </FEATURES>
```

Each `<menu>` element must be given an `<ID>` value by which it can be referred to elsewhere in the policy file, a unique command ID number in `<CMDID>`, and the GUID for the menu group of which it is a part (as found in `vside.tdl`). Similarly, every Toolbox item we want to declare also requires an ID for the policy file and a descriptor. Again, no need to worry if you've no idea what each of these values should be – they are all safely recorded in `vside.tdl`. Below, for instance, we've defined two menu items, Edit | Cut and Project | AddClass, and two Toolbox items, an HTML `<DIV>` tag and a WinForms label. Note that the HTML tag's descriptor is itself HTML, in escaped text to prevent angle brackets confusing the TDL structure.

```
<FEATURES>
  <MENUS>
    <MENU>
      <ID>menuEdit.Cut</ID>
      <CMDID>16</CMDID>
      <GUID>{5EFC7975-14BC-11CF-9B2B-00AA00573819}</GUID>
    </MENU>
    <MENU>
      <ID>menuProject.AddClass</ID>
      <CMDID>946</CMDID>
      <GUID>{5EFC7975-14BC-11CF-9B2B-00AA00573819}</GUID>
    </MENU>
  </MENUS>
  <TOOLBOXITEMS>
    <TOOLBOXITEM>
      <ID>tboxHTMLLabel</ID>
      <DESCRIPTOR>&lt;DIV style="DISPLAY:inline; WIDTH:70px;
        HEIGHT:15px" ms_positioning="FlowLayout"&gt;Label&lt;/DIV&gt;
      </DESCRIPTOR>
    </TOOLBOXITEM>
    <TOOLBOXITEM>
      <ID>tboxWinFormsLabel</ID>
      <DESCRIPTOR>System.Windows.Forms.Label</DESCRIPTOR>
    </TOOLBOXITEM>
  </TOOLBOXITEMS>
</FEATURES>
```

As we'll see in the next section, we can either hide or make available declared features directly as part of an `<ELEMENTSET>`, or we can associate them with a corresponding element using its `<FEATURELINKS>` node. Any rules on the element which make it unavailable to the developer will then make the associated items unavailable as well.

Defining Elements of the Project to Add Policy To

The last top-level node is `<ELEMENTS>`. It's in here that we declare each `<ELEMENT>` of the project and apply rules to them as appropriate. Going one level into an element declaration, the TDL syntax looks like this:

```
<ELEMENTS>
  <ELEMENT>
    <ID />
    <CONTEXT />
    <IDENTIFIERS />
    <<ELEMENTSET> />
    <CONSTRAINTS />
    <PROTOTYPES />
    <FEATURELINKS />
  </ELEMENT>
  ... more element declarations ...
</ELEMENTS>
```

The `<ID>` element is the only mandatory node in an element declaration and, like the other `<ID>` nodes we've encountered, assigns the element a name that will be used as a reference to it in the policy file. Once an element has an ID, it can be added to categories and element sets. For example, in order to create a policy for the C# distributed application template, the top-level ETP folder needs to be defined as the root element. So, in dap.tdl, its element definition has the following ID declaration:

```
<ID>etpDistributedApplicationFull</ID>
```

Be aware that your IDs may not contain any whitespace, parentheses, or the TDL keywords UNION, INTERSECT, or SUBTRACT. Microsoft has suggested a scheme for naming elements so that their actual nature (ETP folder, project, code, class, etc.) is easily identifiable but it's at our discretion whether or not we follow it of course. The details can be found in the help topic called Naming Conventions in Enterprise Templates.

Setting a Help Marker for an Element

The third piece of the template puzzle is the set of custom help documents a designer can create to guide the developer through their design and rules and justify why the template is built as it is. The `<CONTEXT>` node allows the designer to associate one or a number of keywords and attributes against an element that the template designer can link with one or a number of custom help files to aid the developer when dealing with this project element.

```
<ELEMENT>
  <ID> eltName </ID>
  <CONTEXT>
    <CTXTKEYWORD />
    ... more keyword declarations ...

    <CTXTATTRIBUTE>
      <NAME />
      <VALUE />
    </CTXTATTRIBUTE>
    ... more attribute declarations ...

  </CONTEXT>
  ...
</ELEMENT>
```

If you do choose to give an element a help context, you must provide at the very least one context keyword. These are the base terms on which VS.NET will search for information. If you specify two or more keywords, the search will OR them together. Context attributes meanwhile are written as a name-value pair and act as restrictions on the search results for the keywords, as if they were ANDed to the search for help.

For example in DAP.tdl, we see that the distributed application ETP folder is associated with two keywords and two attribute pairs. It's also worth noting the difference in connection between elements and keywords, and elements and attributes. Keywords are direct links to elements, but attributes tend to be more about what the element is part of or associated with.

```
<ELEMENT>
  <ID>etpDistributedApplicationFull</ID>
  <CONTEXT>
    <CTXTKEYWORD>DistributedApplication</CTXTKEYWORD>
    <CTXTKEYWORD>EnterpriseFrameworks</CTXTKEYWORD>
    <CTXTATTRIBUTE>
      <NAME>Product</NAME>
      <VALUE>VS</VALUE>
    </CTXTATTRIBUTE>
    <CTXTATTRIBUTE>
      <NAME>Solution</NAME>
      <VALUE>Active</VALUE>
    </CTXTATTRIBUTE>
  </CONTEXT>
  ...
</ELEMENT>
```

The next main section looks at how we set up the template's help files, but the net result will be that when a given element is selected by the developer, the keywords and attributes associated with it are looked up in a special context file against the help topics available to VS.NET. Matching results are then displayed in the Dynamic Help window.

Identifying Elements within Visual Studio

While the <ID> node allows us to make references to an element within the policy file, it's the <IDENTIFIERS> tag where we make the connection between the elements we're declaring and the actual part that they play in a solution. For example, we can define an element with the ID etpDistributedApplicationFull in our policy file but how does it intuit what we're referring to in the solution? Using one or a combination of <IDENTIFIER> tags, we can establish that the element refers to a type of project, a given file extension, a class that inherits from some other specified class, or even something in a Toolbox or menu item.

```
<IDENTIFIERS>
  <IDENTIFIER>
    <TYPE />
    <IDENTIFIERDATA>
      <NAME />
      <VALUE />
    </IDENTIFIERDATA>
    ... more indentifierdata here if needed ...
  </IDENTIFIER>
  ... more identifiers here if needed ...
</IDENTIFIERS>
```

In fact, an identifier can establish an element as one or a combination of six items using the <TYPE> node by giving the <TYPE>, <NAME> and <VALUE> items the appropriate value from those below:

❏ A project (TYPE = PROJECT) is usually identified by the global variable TDLELEMENTTYPE that we see how to set up later when building our prototype file structure. It is also possible however, to identify a project by its file extension, one of its properties, a GUID, or by a combination of all four. For example, the Distributed Application project is identified like so:

```
<IDENTIFIER>
  <TYPE>PROJECT</TYPE>
  <IDENTIFIERDATA>
    <NAME>GLOBAL:TDLELEMENTTYPE</NAME>
    <VALUE>DistributedApplicationFull</VALUE>
  </IDENTIFIERDATA>
</IDENTIFIER>
```

❏ Project item elements (TYPE = PROJECTITEM) act as catch-alls for all items of the same kind and can be identified only by a file extension. For example, a generic XSD Schema file:

```
<IDENTIFIER>
  <TYPE>PROJECTITEM</TYPE>
  <IDENTIFIERDATA>
    <NAME>FileExtension</NAME>
    <VALUE>.XSD</VALUE>
  </IDENTIFIERDATA>
</IDENTIFIER>
```

If you want to link an element to a specific file, you should identify the element as a code object.

❏ References to DLLs (TYPE = REFERENCE) can be made known by identiying the filename of the DLL, but you also have the option to make the reference to a specific version, stating major and minor version numbers of the DLL as well. This is a good example of when it's useful to use more than one <IDENTIFIERDATA> node.

```
<IDENTIFIER>
  <TYPE>REFERENCE</TYPE>
  <IDENTIFIERDATA>
    <NAME>FileName</NAME>
    <VALUE>System.Web.Services.dll</VALUE>
  </IDENTIFIERDATA>
  <IDENTIFIERDATA>
    <NAME>MajorVersion</NAME>
    <VALUE>2</VALUE>
  </IDENTIFIERDATA>
</IDENTIFIER>
```

❏ Code objects (TYPE = CODE) such as classes or components are most easily identified by listing the classes they inherit or the interfaces they implement. Alternatively, you can specify the kind of objects they are or a value for one of the object's attributes. For example, a web form inherits System.Web.UI.Page, so we can identify one as an element with:

```
<ID>codeWebForm</ID>
<IDENTIFIERS>
  <IDENTIFIER>
    <TYPE>CODE</TYPE>
    <IDENTIFIERDATA>
      <NAME>Inherits</NAME>
      <VALUE>System.Web.UI.Page</VALUE>
    </IDENTIFIERDATA>
  </IDENTIFIER>
</IDENTIFIERS>
```

Note that although TDL is almost completely case-insensitive when it comes to the values of the XML nodes, the one exception comes in the spelling of .NET Framework classnames like System.Web.UI.Page, which must be capitalized correctly.

❑ Code variables (TYPE = CODEVARIABLE) such as a control or other piece of code that would be treated as a variable within the code for a class can be identified either by their type name or the classes they inherit from. For example, the ASP AdRotator control is identified like so:

```
<ID>codeWebFormsAdRotator</ID>
<IDENTIFIERS>
  <IDENTIFIER>
    <TYPE>CODEVARIABLE</TYPE>
    <IDENTIFIERDATA>
      <NAME>TYPENAME</NAME>
      <VALUE>System.Web.UI.WebControls.AdRotator</VALUE>
    </IDENTIFIERDATA>
  </IDENTIFIER>
</IDENTIFIERS>
```

Again, be wary of the case-sensitive class names.

❑ Items from the HTML Toolbox (TYPE = HTMLELEMENT) are the easiest to identify. The name-value pair in the relevant IDENTIFIERDATA node should contain the values TAG and the name of the HTML element respectively. If you want to narrow this down further, you can specify additional pairs naming an attribute of the HTML tag and a value it should equal, as in this example:

```
<ID>codeHTMLTextField</ID>
<IDENTIFIERS>
  <IDENTIFIER>
    <TYPE>HTMLELEMENT</TYPE>
    <IDENTIFIERDATA>
      <NAME>TAG</NAME>
      <VALUE>Input</VALUE>
    </IDENTIFIERDATA>
    <IDENTIFIERDATA>
      <NAME>Attribute:type</NAME>
      <VALUE>text</VALUE>
    </IDENTIFIERDATA>
  </IDENTIFIER>
</IDENTIFIERS>
```

As you can tell from these examples, policy elements are often one type of thing rather than one specific instance of that type. For a full explicit list of the values the NAME node of the IDENTIFIERDATA tag can take, lookup the IDENTIFIERDATA (TDL) entry in the help files that come with Visual Studio.

Locating the Prototypes for an Element

While the <IDENTIFIER> node tells the policy how to spot an element in the solution explorer, the <PROTOTYPE> nodes inside an element declaration associate it with actual files or wizards on the hard drive. So it's here that we link the template's policy to its prototype structure that we've already created.

```
<PROTOTYPES>
  <PROTOTYPE>file location</PROTOTYPE>
  ... more prototype definitions here ...
</PROTOTYPES>
```

The file location value in question is an address relative to your VS.NET install directory that also incorporates the kind of element the prototype is built with. Invariably, it is either an ETP folder, or written in C#, VB.NET, or managed C++, and is stored in either the EnterpriseFrameworks, VC#, Vb7, or Vc7 folder under the root directory of your VS.NET installation. It is to a subfolder of these directories that the file location always points.

```
<PROTOTYPES>
  <PROTOTYPE>[EF]\Projects\CSharp Distributed Application\CSharp Distributed
Application.etp</PROTOTYPE>
  <PROTOTYPE>[EF]\Projects\Visual Basic Distributed Application\Visual Basic
Distributed Application.etp</PROTOTYPE>
  <PROTOTYPE>[EF]\Projects\Distributed Application\Distributed
Application.etp</PROTOTYPE>
</PROTOTYPES>
```

The example above shows the entries for the element representing a full distributed application template. Note that [EF] represents the EnterpriseFrameworks subdirectory off the VS.NET installation directory. The other abbreviations are [VB], [VC], and [VC#] for the other directories noted earlier. This example is also useful in that it illustrates a case where an element might have more than one actual prototype file – in this case, three. Thus, should any of the three projects be created, the policy will recognize them and treat them as the same element in the template (same ID, so same rules apply).

Associating an Element with a Menu Option or Toolbox Item

Having identified some or all the menu options and Toolbox items in VS.NET under the <FEATURES> node that we looked at earlier, we can now associate one or more of them with an element using its <FEATURELINKS> node. With this link established, should an element be excluded from an <ELEMENTSET>, the menu or Toolbox item will be excluded from the IDE as well. It's still possible to write the code for that particular element directly into the file of course, but for those designing a template for less experienced developers, this feature comes in very handy.

```
<FEATURELINKS>
  <MENULINKS>
    <MENULINK />
  </MENULINKS>
  <TOOLBOXLINKS>
    <TOOLBOXLINK />
```

```
      </TOOLBOXLINKS>
   </FEATURELINKS>
```

There is scope here for associating an element with both menu and Toolbox, but in VS.NET at least, the two are mutually exclusive. For example, in DAP.TDL, the HTMLPage element is linked to the **Add | New Item | HTML Page** menu option:

```
<ELEMENT>
   <ID>projItemHTMLPage</ID>
   .
   .
   .
   <FEATURELINKS>
      <MENULINKS>
         <MENULINK>menuProject.AddHTMLPage</MENULINK>
      </MENULINKS>
   </FEATURELINKS>
   .
   .
   .
</ELEMENT>
```

As we'll see in a minute, part of the <CONSTRAINTS> node for an element allows you to disable menu and Toolbox items as well, but using feature links is just a neater solution. If an element contains both, the <CONSTRAINTS> node will take precedence, but then again they *should* agree. Note that if a feature has no corresponding element (such as the **New Breakpoint** option in the **Debug** menu), using a constraint is the only solution.

The <ELEMENTSET> Node – What We Can and Can't Add

At the top of this section, we said that a policy file defines a solution as a hierarchy of elements. The <ELEMENTSET> node defines a group of child elements for the element we're defining. For example, if the element were a class library, then <ELEMENTSET> would by default include references to any DLLs, code files in any language, WinForms, components, controls, and so on. It's also by defining constraints inside this node, as well as in the main element node itself, that we can not only define rules for the element itself, but rules for other elements that are children of this particular element.

```
<ELEMENTSET>
   <DEFAULTACTION />
   <ORDER />
   <INCLUDE />
   ...more include declarations here ...
   <EXCLUDE>
   ... more exclude declarations here ...
   <CONSTRAINTS>
   <MEMBERCONSTRAINTS>
</ELEMENTSET>
```

By defining the contents of an <ELEMENTSET> explicitly, we can save a lot of developer time by removing decisions relating to what to use in their project (a class, a control, and so on). For example, once instantiated, the distributed application template only allows the seven ETP folders representing the seven layers of the application and HTML pages to sit directly under the root ETP folder. Try to add anything else to this folder in VS.NET, and either you won't be able to find it because the menu options are disabled, or you'll be told that you cannot load it into the project because the policy file doesn't allow it. Of course, this doesn't mean that you can't keep it there, simply that you're not supposed to. See the example in the *Dynamic Help* section earlier if you need proof!

```
<ELEMENT>
<ID>etpDistributedApplicationFull</ID>
.

.

.
<ELEMENTSET>
   <DEFAULTACTION>EXCLUDE</DEFAULTACTION>
   <ORDER>INCLUDEEXCLUDE</ORDER>
   <INCLUDE>etpBusinessFacade</INCLUDE>
   <INCLUDE>etpWebService</INCLUDE>
   <INCLUDE>etpBusinessRules</INCLUDE>
   <INCLUDE>etpDataAccess</INCLUDE>
   <INCLUDE>etpWebUI</INCLUDE>
   <INCLUDE>etpWinUI</INCLUDE>
   <INCLUDE>etpSystem</INCLUDE>
   <INCLUDE>projItemHTMLPage</INCLUDE>
</ELEMENTSET>>
</ELEMENT>
```

Defining the contents of a child <ELEMENTSET> is quite simple. The <DEFAULTACTION> and <ORDER> elements have exactly the same function as they do in the <DEFAULTSETTINGS> node except that they now refer only to the members of the <ELEMENTSET> in question and are not project-wide. Thus, they take precedence over what we have set for the project as a whole. To recap, you state in <DEFAULTACTION> either that you wish to INCLUDE every element that would normally be addable to the element and then explicitly exclude certain items, or you can EXCLUDE every element and start the list from scratch by including categories of and individual elements. Meanwhile the <ORDER> element states whether all the include nodes should be evaluated first followed by the exclude nodes (INCLUDEEXCLUDE) or vice versa (EXCLUDEINCLUDE). As we saw earlier, this can make a difference if for instance you want to include all the items in a category with the exception of one.

The <INCLUDE> and <EXCLUDE> nodes are also self-explanatory, allowing you to list exactly which elements you wish to include in or exclude from this <ELEMENTSET>. All six element types are valid here and any element can be included or excluded so long as it is defined elsewhere in the policy file.

The <CONSTRAINTS> and <MEMBERCONSTRAINTS> both impose restrictions on the VS.NET IDE with respect to the <ELEMENTSET> but at a slightly different scope. The former defines constraints that apply to all the members of the <ELEMENTSET> when created as a part of the parent element while the latter defines constraints that apply only to a specific member of that <ELEMENTSET>. Again, we'll cover the different scopes for constraints in the next section.

Constraints

Look closely at a policy file and you'll realize there are only two kinds of rules which you can create, namely:

- ❑ Which elements can form a part of another element, as defined in an <ELEMENTSET>
- ❑ Which elements and parts of the IDE should be accessible when a certain element is being used

We've just seen how to exact the first type of rule, and so the last part of our TDL walkthrough will concentrate on how to affect the VS.NET IDE using the <CONSTRAINTS> node that appears in several places around our policy file. Before we look at how the location of the constraints defines their scope, let's first look at their structure (which remains constant regardless of location in the file):

```
<CONSTRAINTS>
  <PROPERTYCONSTRAINTS />
  <MENUCONSTRAINTS />
  <TOOLBOXCONSTRAINTS />
</CONSTRAINTS>
```

The special case of the <MEMBERCONSTRAINTS> node in an <ELEMENTSET> declaration adds one extra piece of information to the constraints – the ID (as given in <ELEMENT>/<ID>) of the specific child element to set them against.

```
<MEMBERCONSTRAINTS>
  <ID />
  <PROPERTYCONSTRAINTS />
  <MENUCONSTRAINTS />
  <TOOLBOXCONSTRAINTS />
</MEMBERCONSTRAINTS />
```

Beyond that, the two nodes are written in exactly the same way.

It's possible to influence three things inside a constraints file:

- ❑ Which of the properties belonging to the element or <ELEMENTSET> the developer will have access to in the Properties window of the IDE, and what access they'll have to their values (PROPERTYCONSTRAINTS)
- ❑ Which menu options will be visible at any given time (MENUCONSTRAINTS)
- ❑ Which Toolbox items will be visible at any given time (TOOLBOXCONSTRAINTS)

The property restrictions have a different syntax to the menu and Toolbox, so we'll look at those in a bit and concentrate on the <PROPERTYCONSTRAINTS> node and its contents for now. Here's its skeleton structure:

```
<PROPERTYCONSTRAINTS>
  <PROPERTYCONSTRAINT>
    <NAME />
    <READONLY />
    <DEFAULT />
    <MINVALUE />
    <MAXVALUE />
```

```
        <LISTITEM />
        ... more list items here ...
      </PROPERTYCONSTRAINT>
      ... more property constraints here
  </PROPERTYCONSTRAINTS>
```

The first two child nodes, <NAME> and <READONLY>, are mandatory with the former giving the actual name of the element property we are concerned with and the latter defining whether or not the value of the property will be read only in the project (1 for yes, 0 for no) once we have set it here. The remaining four nodes meanwhile allow us to influence the value of the property in different ways. The <DEFAULT> node determines an initial value for the property while the <MINVALUE> and <MAXVALUE> nodes define a range of values that a property can take if the need arises.

For example, let's suppose we need to ensure that the thumbnail images in our application were no more than 125 pixels in width but no less than 50. We could create an element representing thumbnail images and add the following constraint:

```
<ELEMENT>
  <ID>codeWebFormsThumbnail</ID>
  ...
  <CONSTRAINTS>
    <PROPERTYCONSTRAINTS>
      <PROPERTYCONSTRAINT>
        <NAME>WIDTH</NAME>
        <READONLY>0</READONLY>
        <DEFAULT>100</DEFAULT>
        <MINVALUE>50</MINVALUE>
        <MAXVALUE>125</MAXVALUE>
      </PROPERTYCONSTRAINT>
    </PROPERTYCONSTRAINTS>
  </CONSTRAINTS>
</ELEMENT>
```

That takes care of it neatly. Every thumbnail will initially be 100 pixels wide, but the width property is not read-only, so it can be altered to any value in the range we've defined.

The decisions to make regarding menu options and Toolbox items are even simpler. In a nutshell, you can determine whether or not they are enabled and if they are visible:

```
<MENUCONSTRAINTS>
  <MENUCONSTRAINT>
    <ID />
    <ENABLED />
    <VISIBLE />
  </MENUCONSTRAINT>
  ... more menu constraints here ...
</MENUCONSTRAINTS>

<TOOLBOXCONSTRAINTS>
  <TOOLBOXCONSTRAINT>
    <ID />
    <ENABLED />
```

```
        <VISIBLE />
      </TOOLBOXCONSTRAINT>
      ... more Toolbox constraints here ...
    </TOOLBOXCONSTRAINTS>
  </CONSTRAINTS>
```

The semantics for both types of constraint are the same, so we'll treat them together. Both the ID node (containing the element ID for the item or option in question as defined under the <FEATURES> node) and the <ENABLED> node are mandatory if you choose to create a constraint. The latter node can take two values, 1 if the item or option is to be enabled in the IDE, and 0 if not. The optional <VISIBLE> node, as the name suggests, allows you to hide the item in question as well, using 1 for visible and 0 for hidden. Just make sure you don't hide something that is enabled.

```
<MENUCONSTRAINTS>
  <MENUCONSTRAINT>
    <ID>menuProject.AddUserControl</ID>
    <ENABLED>0</ENABLED>
  </MENUCONSTRAINT>
</MENUCONSTRAINTS>
```

And that's it for creating constraints. The only thing left to look at is how to determine the scope of a constraint and what that scope implies.

The Scope of a Constraint

In our tour through the various pieces of a policy file, we've had the opportunity to create constraints in four different places. With the help of surrounding elements, we can define six different scopes listed below in order of granularity, from most general to most specific. If two or more constraints at different scope levels contradict, then the one with the least general scope takes precedence.

❑   Default constraints are applied to the solution once it is created from the template and remain in effect until either the solution is closed or they are overridden by constraints with a smaller scope. They are defined in the <DEFAULTACTION>/<CONSTRAINTS> node.

❑   Default element constraints are attached to an element and apply whenever that element is in focus, either because it is being manipulated directly or because it is part of the <ELEMENTSET> of an element that is. For example, an HTML image would be in scope if either it or the web form in which it was placed were being altered. They are defined in the <ELEMENT>/<CONSTRAINTS> node.

❑   <ELEMENTSET> constraints are applicable to an element only when they are incorporated into a solution as part of another element – its 'parent' – as defined by the parent's <ELEMENTSET> node. They apply equally to all members of the <ELEMENTSET> and are defined in the <ELEMENTSET>/<CONSTRAINTS> node in the definition of the parent element.

❑   <ELEMENTSET> member constraints affect elements in the same way as <ELEMENTSET> constraints, but are specific to one particular child element in that <ELEMENTSET>. That is, the constraints will only apply when that specific element is used as a part of the named parent element. You can find these constraints defined in the <ELEMENTSET>/<MEMBERCONSTRAINTS> node of the parent element.

These last two scopes for a constraint apply only to an element's immediate children, as defined in the element's <ELEMENTSET>. However, if an <ELEMENTSET> contains no nodes other than <CONSTRAINTS> or <MEMBERCONSTRAINTS>, you can specify a set of constraints which will apply to a child element, grandchild element, great-grandchild element, etc. all the way down through the element hierarchy.

❑ Root/<ELEMENTSET> constraints apply whenever any element (regardless of immediate parent) that is contained within the parent element is in scope. You can find these defined in the <ELEMENTSET>/<CONSTRAINTS> node in the definition of the parent element where the members of the <ELEMENTSET> are not defined.

❑ Root/member constraints apply whenever a specific, named element (regardless of immediate parent) contained within the element whose <ELEMENTSET> this is, is in scope. You can find these defined in the <ELEMENTSET>/<MEMBERCONSTRAINTS> node in the definition of the parent element where the members of the <ELEMENTSET> are not defined.

Do remember that constraints apply only to identified elements, even if <DEFAULTSETTINGS>/<POLICYMODE> is set to PERMISSIVE. Unidentified (read: user-defined) elements will appear in menus, the Toolbox, and dialogs regardless of policy, so it's a good idea to exclude all items, and then only include those that you want to offer the developer, if you want to prevent their using 'hand-rolled' elements, so to speak. The VS.NET help section has a great example on using different scopes to refine a policy for the contents of a Windows form and I suggest you have a look at it to get a feel for the practical application of scope and constraint. The help topic is called Defining Default ELEMENT Constraints.

Writing Your Own Policy – Recap

Template Definition Language isn't all that difficult to understand and work with but with such a feature-rich IDE as that of VS.NET, it's obvious that grouping these features into manageable building blocks will be key to creating a useable policy file for an Enterprise Template. Fortunately the file vside.tdl provides us with a complete listing of all the elements in Visual Studio and its development environment together with a mirror mapping of those elements into the categories that exist in the IDE as well. So, although it's not a file to lose or alter, it's one we can copy and paste from with abandon.

The DAP.tdl file that holds the policy for the built-in templates we've been looking at is also very useful and you might well consider using a copy of this file for the first couple of templates you try to construct. It doesn't use any <CONSTRAINTS> nodes to restrict the IDE, but it does give a very good example of using an <ELEMENTSET> to restrict what can and cannot be added to an element.

If you're determined to start from scratch however, do remember to add the XML namespace declaration at the top of the policy file and use an XML editor that can validate your file against the TDL schema. You'll also find a good list of Tips for Authoring in Template Description Language in VS.NET help under that heading.

The Prototype File Structure

Now we have the know-how for building a policy file, we've got the trickiest part out of the way, and building a prototype file structure and writing custom help files are the most time-consuming tasks that remain. In the case of the former, it's actually putting that file structure into a place where Visual Studio will find it and then linking it into the policy file that takes the time when implementing a template. Of course, the most time-consuming task overall will be the design of the application's infrastructure and the template to fit it in the first place. Let's press on...

A Recipe for Success

There are three essential ingredients when creating a good prototype structure for your template. In sequential order, they are creating the files themselves, putting them in the right place, and advertising their presence to the policy file, VS.NET, and the user. None of this is rocket science, so we should be able to breeze through without problems.

Some Files

We're not limited to the type of file we can incorporate into our initial structure but it's worth noting that there are only a few file types that remember where all their children go themselves. These are the Enterprise Template Project files (.etp) and language project files (.csproj, .vcproj, or .vbproj) created as part of their respective projects. We've seen from our tour of the templates previously that the ETP folders are the containers of the file structure and can contain other ETP folders and project files, so the hierarchical structure of our design must incorporate only those. Any other files must be incorporated under the relevant project or ETP folder in this structure.

The easiest way to create the file structure for a template is to build a skeleton project in VS.NET and then 'convert' it into a proto-file structure for a template. Let's build up a structure for a classic 3-tier application (data, business, presentation) as an example. It's won't do anything amazing, but should demonstrate what we've learned nicely.

1. Start up VS.NET and create a new Enterprise Template Project. You'll find the wizard for this in the **New Project** dialog box under **Other Projects | Enterprise Template Projects | Enterprise Template Project**. Give it the name `Simple3TierApp`.

Add another ETP folder for the user interface. This template is fairly generic, so we'll not dictate what type of interface should be developed but we will provide for a Web Service (primarily because it illustrates the slightly different way these need to be handled).

2. This project will contain a C# class library for each of the data access and business rules tiers. Right-click the `Simple3TierApp` project in Solution Explorer, and select **Add | Add New Project**. Select the **Empty Project** template in the right hand pane, give it the name `DataTier` and click **OK**. Repeat the process to add another empty C# project called `BusinessTier`.

3. Right-click the `Simple3TierApp` project once more, and add a new Enterprise Template project called `UILayer`. Next, right-click the new ET project, and add a new C# Web Service project to it called `UIService`. Don't forget to make sure IIS is running on the machine where VS.NET will store the Web Service and that your local copy of Internet Explorer is not working offline before you do this.

You can add any type of project into the structure for your template, as long as your policy file agrees with it. At this stage it's a good idea to set any defaults, such as debug level, that you'd like to apply from the outset, and to add a reference to your policy file to the solution. You can do the latter by selecting the top ETP folder called `Simple3TierApp` in Solution Explorer (not the solution itself though), and setting the `Policy File` property to the location of your policy file. In terms of the project files, the structure should look like this:

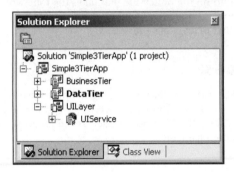

4. The `UIService.csproj` file, which belongs under `UILayer.etp` here, needs to be 'rescued' from the `Inetpub\wwwroot\UIService` folder along with the other files that make up the Web Service, and reunited with the rest of the template project. Close the `Simple3TierApp` solution in Visual Studio, and navigate to the `UIService` folder in Windows Explorer. Copy it over to the `Simple3TierApp\UILayer` subfolder of your `Visual Studio Projects` directory.

Note that this rescuing must be done for any web service or web-based projects we want to incorporate into our template, because VS.NET automatically creates their files on the local web server rather than with the rest of the solution.

5. One last optional step to prepare our structure for conversion: remove all files not strictly necessary for the template to work. They won't prevent the template from working if they are left in, but they will add to the size, which may be a factor you're concerned about.

Still in Windows Explorer with the `Visual Studio Projects\Simple3TierApp` folder open, you may remove the `.eto`, `.sln`, and `.suo` files. We don't need a solution file any more as one will be autogenerated when the rest of the files are copied into a new solution.

For each of the subdirectories under this folder, you may remove the `.eto` file, and the `bin` and `obj` folders.

Our template files are now ready for 'conversion'.

Finding a Suitable Location

The next step is to store these new files where Visual Studio will be able to find and clone them when a new project is created based on this template. There isn't really one specific place to put them as one of the founding ideas behind ETs is that they can be shared and used directly from a central location, but by default, they are spread over several directories, most of them under the `EnterpriseFrameworks` subfolder. Should you download any templates from the Internet for example, here's where each file should go once installed:

File Type	Location of the VS.NET Installation Folder
Policy file (`.tdl`)	`EnterpriseFrameworks\Policy`
Project Files and Directories	`EnterpriseFrameworks\Projects`
`.vsdir` file	`EnterpriseFrameworks\Proxyprojects`
`Content.xml` (The custom help index file)	`Common7\IDE\HTML\XMLLinks\1033`
Custom help topic files	User-defined location given in `context.xml`

Any templates that are used centrally will of course be in a location made known to developers who use the project. We'll work on the `.vsdir` file in the next section, but let's get our wannabe template structure in position first.

1. Copy and paste at your `Visual Studio Projects\Simple3TierApp` folder into `...\EnterpriseFrameworks\Projects`.

The first thing to do is remove the GUIDs to the language projects from the Enterprise Template project files.

2. Open `Simple3TierApp.etp` for editing. In each reference to the language project file, you'll find a `<GUIDPROJECTID>` node. Delete them both, save and close the file. Repeat this for the GUID in `UILayer.etp`.

All the project files except for one won't notice the change in location, the offender being `UILayer.etp`. This will still be set as if the Web Service it contains is located on your local web server. Before we go any further we have to fix this.

3. Navigate to the `Simple3TierApp\UILayer` folder of your newly relocated template, and open the file `UILayer.etp` for editing.

Every `.etp` file in Visual Studio is written in XML against a schema in the `EnterpriseFrameworks\Schemas` folder called `ProjectSchema.xsd`. We won't go into the semantics of each node as we did with Template Definition Language; it's enough to note that it allows you to define some information local to that project and some global to VS if the project is open in Solution Explorer. For our part, we need to connect our Web Service to the `UILayer` ETP folder in Solution Explorer (by adding a `View` on `Project Explorer`) and to tell VS.NET that when the template is opened it will need to prompt the user for a URL to which it will clone the files.

4. Edit the `<Views>\<ProjectExplorer>` node so that it reads as follows:

```
<Views>
  <ProjectExplorer>
    <File>UIService/UIService.csproj</File>
  </ProjectExplorer>
</Views>
```

5. Edit the `<References>\<Reference>` node so that reads as follows:

```
<References>
  <Reference>
    <File>UIService/UIService.csproj</File>
    <RequiresURL>1</RequiresURL>
  </Reference>
</References>
```

The `<RequiresURL>` node can be set to 0 if you don't want a prompt for the save location of the Web Service to appear. Again, don't disable the prompt unless you're sure that every developer will have a local web server – having a Web Service project that is always unavailable is unlikely to make you any friends in the development team!

Some Advertising

With your basic file structure set up and located in the right place, your final task is to get it talking to a policy file and to Visual Studio. After all, there's little point in leaving your work somewhere no one can find it.

Linking Files to our Policy

If you had a browse through the `UILayer.etp` file while editing it, you'll have noticed a global variable for the policy file this project adheres to at the bottom of the file.

```
<GLOBALENTRY>
  <NAME>TDLFILE</NAME>
  <VALUE>apolicyfile.TDL</VALUE>
</GLOBALENTRY>
```

If you attached a policy file to your solution back in Step 3, this file will be the one named here. Now this establishes the link to the policy file but until we identify each of our projects as an element the policy has information about it won't do us much good. Recall that in our look through TDL we learned that the standard way to identify an item as a specific project was with the `TDLELEMENTTYPE` global variable. It's in these `.etp` and `.xxproj` files that we declare this global variable for the policy to tag onto.

1. For each `.etp` file in our `Simple3TierApp` file structure, add a new `<GLOBALENTRY>` node to the `<GLOBALS>` section of the file like so:

```
<GLOBALENTRY>
  <NAME>TDLELEMENTTYPE</NAME>
  <VALUE>elementId</VALUE>
</GLOBALENTRY>
```

where `elementID` corresponds to the value of the `<ID>` node of the appropriate element for the project in the policy file – `etpUITier` or `etpSimple3TierApp` for example.

If you need to declare your language projects as elements in a policy file, you've also to declare a global variable in their `.xxproj` files. However, their layout varies between language as follows:

Language	Additions to Make

C# (`.csproj` files)	Add a new `<CSHARP>/<UserProperties>` node to the end of the file:
	
	`<VisualStudioProject>`
	  `<CSHARP>`
	  ...rest of file
	    `<UserProperties TDLFILE = "apolicyfile.TDL" />`
	    `<UserProperties TDLELEMENTTYPE = "elementId" />`
	  `</CSHARP>`
	`</VisualStudioProject>`

VB.NET (`.vbproj` files)	Add a new `<VisualBasic>/<UserProperties>` node to the end of the file:
	
	`<VisualStudioProject>`
	  `<VisualBasic>`
	  ...rest of file
	    `<UserProperties TDLFILE = "apolicyfile.TDL" />`
	    `<UserProperties TDLELEMENTTYPE = "elementId" />`
	  `</VisualBasic>`
	`</VisualStudioProject>`

Visual C++ (`.vcproj` files)	Add a new `<GLOBAL>` node to `<GLOBALS>` section of the file:
	
	`<GLOBALS>`
	  `<GLOBAL NAME="TDLFILE" VALUE="apolicyfile.TDL" />`
	  `<GLOBAL NAME="TDLELEMENTTYPE" VALUE="elementId" />`
	`</GLOBALS>`

Again, in all three instances above, `elementID` denotes the value of the `<ID>` node for the appropriate element for the project in the policy file.

2. Bearing this in mind, we can amend the `.csproj` files for the `BusinessTier`, `DataTier` and `UIService` projects accordingly.

That's the policy file in sync with the prototype structure. Now we just have to tell Visual Studio where to find the template files.

Creating a .vsdir File for the Template

Your connection from template to IDE is a `.vsdir` file to be created and stored in the `EnterpriseFrameworks\ProxyProjects` folders. With this file, you can add the template into the New Project dialog box that we initiate all our projects from. Like the other templates, it will be found in the **Other Projects | Enterprise Template Projects** folder of that box when we are done.

If you open up a `.vsdir` file, say `ProxyProjects.vsdir`, you'll find a number of entries for different projects to be added to the new project dialog box. In this case, you'll find two: one for the language-neutral distributed application template and one for the empty Enterprise Template we've used to create our own template. Each entry sits on one line of text and consists of nine fields separated by a bar '|' character and no spaces. In order from left to right, these fields contain:

❑ The **path name** of the tempate project, language project, or wizard the entry relates to, relative to the location of this `.vsdir` file.

❑ A **GUID** for a product (such as VB.NET) that contains required resources for the project. Third-party templates generally don't need one because they should carry all they need with them, but for one created locally, the GUID the built-in templates use is `{AE77B8D0-6BDC-11d2-B354-0000F81F0C06}`.

❑ The **name of the project** we'll see in the Add New Project dialog box under its icon.

❑ The **sort priority** of the wizard. Determines how far up the list of projects this project will come. An integer value of 1 is the highest, decreasing through 2, 3, 4, etc.

❑ A **longer description** of the project that will appear in the new project dialog box when the project is initially selected.

❑ **An absolute path or GUID** of the DLL/EXE file containing the icon to be used for the project. This icon is mandatory, so you'll have to create one if you haven't already done so.

❑ The **resource number of the project's icon** inside the DLL/EXE file identified in the previous field.

❑ A **set of flags** determining how the project will be initialized.

❑ A **default name for an instance of the template** if a developer decides to create one and doesn't name it before initializing it. If one is not given, the IDE will use 'Project*x*', where *x* is the next available integer.

Of these nine, only the first GUID field, the name to go under the project's icon, and the project icon's resource number are optional. You do have to use 0 as a placeholder however, should you decide not to specify them. You can also use a `#ResID` number that corresponds to a resource in the project's DLL file in place of actual text for fields 3, 5, and 9. The value for the flags field should be the sum of the decimal values of all the options below that you want to have effect.

Flag name	Decimal value	Description
VSDIRFLAG_NonLocalTemplate	1	Use non-local user interface behavior and save mechanisms.
VSDIRFLAG_BlankSolution	2	Create a blank (empty) solution. Do not create a project.
VSDIRFLAG_DisableBrowseButton	4	Disable the Browse button for this project or item.
VSDIRFLAG_DontAddDefExtension	8	Do not append a default extension to the name provided for the item. (This setting is not invalid for projects.)

Flag name	Decimal value	Description
VSDIRFLAG_DisableLocationField	32	Disable the location field for this project or item.
VSDIRFLAG_DontInitNameField	4096	Do not initialize the name field for this project or item with a valid name.
VSDIRFLAG_DisableNameField	8192	Disable the name field for this project or item.

The easiest way to build our own .vsdir file is to copy another one and simply change the fields for our own purposes, which is what we'll do for our Simple3TierApp template.

1. Navigate to vsnet_installdir\EnterpriseFrameworks\ProxyProjects in Windows Explorer, and create a copy of ProxyProjects.vsdir in that directory. Call it simple3tierapp.vsdir.

2. Open simple3tierapp.vsdir in an editor and remove the entry for the Enterprise Template project.

3. Change the other entry to:

```
..\Projects\Simple3TierApp\simple3tierapp.etp|
{AE77B8D0-6BDC-11d2-B354-0000F81F0C06}|
Simple 3 Tier Application|15|A basic template for demo purposes|
{AE77B8D0-6BDC-11d2-B354-0000F81F0C06}|124|0|SimpleProject
```

The five italicized fields are the ones changed from their original values. Don't forget that this entry should all be on one line; it's been split across four here so it's easier to read.

4. Save the file and test it by opening Visual Studio and trying to create a new project. If all is well, you'll see our prototype readily available along with the other templates:

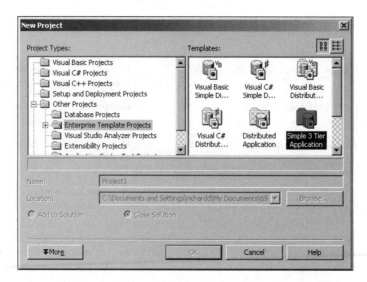

At this point, if this were all we wanted to specify for our policy file and prototype file structure, we could distribute the template for testing with an installer that places all files into the locations given in the table in the earlier section *Finding a Suitable Location*. All that remains are is help files that we decide to provide to explain how our template works.

Custom Help Files

The contents of the help files you create to assist developers in using your template are entirely up to you, but the way to link them into your template remains the same.

❑ Create and write your help files. They need only be HTML files, possibly all linked to the same CSS file to add a bit of consistency. Initially they may just be empty placeholder files until you get time to write them in full.

❑ Create a context-linking file that associates keywords and attributes with the relevant help page.

❑ In the policy file, associate the same keywords and attributes with the appropriate elements by adding a <CONTEXT> node to the definition of the elements.

We'll skip the trivial step of creating the HTML files and go straight to building our link file.

Creating a Context File

True to the nature of .NET, the link file between elements and help files is written in XML. You'll find an example file called context.xml in *installdir*\Common7\IDE \HTML\XMLLinks\1033 and it's here that you will have to save your finished file again. Taking a look inside the file, within the root <DynamicHelp> node are several <LINKGROUP> nodes like this:

```
<LINKGROUP ID="GettingStarted" Title="Getting Started" Priority="300">
 <GLYPH Expanded="vs:/ctxhelp_show.gif" Collapsed="vs:/ctxhelp_hide.gif"/>
</LINKGROUP>
```

These <LINKGROUP> definitions represent the groupings of help topics you can see in the Dynamic Help window in VS.NET. The one above, for instance, defines the Getting Started header initiative. What are missing from the file however are any references to help files. These we must add inside a <Context> node also under the root node. A skeleton for our context file then looks like this:

```
<?xml version='1.0' encoding="utf-8" ?>
<DynamicHelp xmlns="http://microsoft.com/vstudio/tbd/vsdh.xsd">
  <LINKGROUP>
    <GLYPH />
  </LINKGROUP>
  ... more link group definitions ...

  <Context>
    <Keywords />
    <Attributes />
    <Links />
  </Context>
  ... more keyword to file links ...
</DynamicHelp>
```

<LINKGROUP> has several attributes. ID is the internal name for the group that we'll use when placing our help files within the group. Title is the name of the group we'll see in the dynamic help window in VS.NET and Priority sets where you'll find the group amongst the others. A value of 1 will see it at the top of the help window and greater values will see it further down. Its only child node, <Glyph>, represents the icon used for the group. You may either give it two forms, one for the help group being expanded and the other for the help group being collapsed, as above, or define a static icon which remains the same regardless. For example:

```
<GLYPH Static="vs:/ctxhelp.gif">
```

Making the Links

If you recall from our discussion on TDL, the context node of an element looks like this:

```
<CONTEXT>
  <CTXTKEYWORD>Simple3TierApp</CTXTKEYWORD>
  <CTXTKEYWORD>Template</CTXTKEYWORD>
  <CTXTATTRIBUTE>
    <NAME>Product</NAME>
    <VALUE>VS</VALUE>
  </CTXTATTRIBUTE>
  <CTXTATTRIBUTE>
    <NAME>DevLang</NAME>
    <VALUE>CS</VALUE>
  </CTXTATTRIBUTE>
</CONTEXT>
```

It defines a set of keywords and attributes that VS will search for in the context file when the element whose context this is, is in scope. The context node in the help link file works in much the same way, except that in this case it is associating a number of help files with keywords and attributes.

```
<Context>
  <Keywords>
    <KItem Name="Simple3TierApp" />
    <KItem Name="BusinessTier" />
  </Keywords>
  <Attributes>
    <AItem Name="DevLang" Value="CS" />
  </Attributes>
  <Links>
    <LItem URL="c:\help\businesstier.htm" LinkGroup="GettingStarted">
      Intro to the Business Tier
    </LItem>
  </Links>
</Context>
```

The `<KItem>` nodes correspond to the `<CTXTKEYWORD>`s in the policy file and the `<AItem>`s to the `<CTXTATTRIBUTE>`s. When an element is selected, VS will scan through your context file for `<Context>` nodes where one or more of the `<KItem>`s matches those keywords associated with that element and make a list. If there are attributes assocaited with the elements as well, VS will scan the newly made list of keyword-matching contexts for those which also match one or more attributes, removing those that do not. The remaining list is displayed as a list of HTML links where the target URL is given in the `LItem` URL property and the link text is the value of the `LItem` node. Each link is sorted first by the `Priority` of the `<LINKGROUP>` and then alphabetically under the linkgroup by the `LItem`'s LinkGroup attribute:

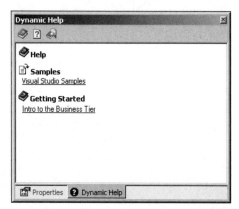

When you've created your context file, save it back in the *installdir*\Common7\IDE \HTML\XMLLinks\1033 directory. Note that it doesn't have to be called `context.xml`. Visual Studio will scan this directory for any XML help link files and use them all ordered by `<LINKGROUP>` as necessary.

Summary

In this chapter, we've investigated a fairly impressive new addition in the VS.NET Enterprise Edition – the Enterprise Template, or ET. This concept represents a first attempt on Microsoft's part to bridge the communication divide between designers and developers, and also perhaps to encourage the reuse of best practices by enforcing them. They are designed to allow a designer to create a prototype project that reduces the choices developers have to make when interpreting the design of a solution.

We've seen how a template can affect the user experience and also how to build and connect the three component parts – file structure, policy file, and custom help files – and built our own small template in the process. These templates are a great invention and even in this first incarnation, they are quite powerful, but only as intrusive as an application's developers require them to be; a very fine balancing trick and one pulled off very well.

18
Epilogue

We wrote this book for a certain breed of programmer: a programmer who needs to get the job done; not necessarily a guru of some specific topic, more of the jack-of-all-trades programmer, as comfortable in Java as they are in VB – perhaps even the company's network guy as well. In aiming at such a person, we've attempted to achieve certain goals.

Firstly, the book had to be, well, 'effective'. We didn't want to overload it with excessive theory, but nor did we want our readers to have to traipse through too much practical work. We wanted a reasonable blend of the two; theory interspersed with relevant and quick-to-grasp sample code. Moreover, we wanted to achieve this aim without making the book so long-winded that it would take too long to read through, nor so light that it would not provide a truly useful and long-lasting reference for the programmer as they continue their computing career.

Secondly, we wanted to have the book available as soon as possible. At the time of writing this conclusion, Bill Gates and Anders Hejlsberg have only just introduced the release Visual Studio .NET package to the world stage. We wanted to give our fellow programmers a boost at the critical moment of first getting to grips with this sprawling and powerful tool.

Naturally, we all hope that you, the reader, feel that we have succeeded in these goals, and that you will take the time to communicate with us your thoughts, suggestions, compliments, and even – dare we say it – criticisms. We've built this book with the programmer in mind, and we hope that, as professional working programmers ourselves rather than full time authors, we have managed to hit the mark – please feel free to let us know whether or not you would agree!

Enhancing the Experience

In this book, we've focused on the core components of the Visual Studio .NET platform – and as I've said many times already, it's a package that encompasses a great deal of the programming domain, from design right through to final deployment. Nevertheless, there are still areas where extra capabilities are required, and VS.NET's extensible nature will surely mean that we see plenty of useful and sophisticated 'expansion packs' coming onto the scene. In this section, I've described just two of those that are already around.

Microsoft SQL Server 2000 Web Services Toolkit

The Microsoft® SQL Server™ 2000 Web Services Toolkit includes tools, code, samples, whitepapers for building XML Web Services and Web applications with SQL Server 2000. This toolkit enables developers to easily create XML Web services via SQLXML 3.0.

SQLXML 3.0 extends the built-in XML capabilities of SQL Server 2000 with technology to create XML Web services from SQL Server stored procedures or server-side XML templates. SQLXML 3.0 also includes extensions to the .NET Framework that provide SQLXML access to the languages supported by Visual Studio .NET, including C# and Visual Basic .NET.

Even if XML Web Services aren't very important to you, it's worth downloading this toolset anyway. The whitepapers alone make it worth your while, in particular the Word version of the ADO.NET Primer, which is almost as good as David's *ASPToday* article on the same topic:

http://www.asptoday.com/content/articles/20011019.asp

Unless you are a registered subscriber to ASP Today you will need to buy the article to read it.

Microsoft BizTalk Server 2002 Toolkit for Microsoft .NET

With this toolkit, we can build complete BizTalk projects using Visual Studio .NET and orchestrate ASP.NET XML Web Services, even those that we created outside of BizTalk environments originally. The BizTalk Server Toolkit includes:

❑   Two samples that demonstrate how to use XML Web Services and BizTalk Orchestration

❑   Five samples that demonstrate how to write AICs, preprocessors, and access the Interchange, Configuration, and Tracking object models with Visual Studio .NET

❑   Samples written in both C# and VB .NET

❑   A BizTalk Server 2002 sample that has been migrated to Visual Studio .NET

❑   Comprehensive help file containing information about using Visual Studio .NET and BizTalk Server together – a must for anyone trying to make money with this combination.

This toolkit is essential if Web Services are likely to play a major role in your future. *If Professional ASP.NET Web Services* is already on your bookshelf, and BizTalk 2002 server is something you're keen to have a further look at, drop everything and get this. It is an absolute must for Web Service developers because BizTalk orchestration will add genuine scalability to your Web Service efforts – don't try to do it alone, folks! Although fairly early software, this toolkit is very useable.

User Groups

Many user groups are independently run volunteer efforts that meet on a regular basis to discuss and share information on a variety of computing topics. Joining a developer group is a great way to meet with peers and learn how to get the most out of your developer tools and resources. David and I were blown away when we found an invaluable user group in our own hometown of Columbus, Ohio (run by InDepth Technology), and we've found it to be very active and a great deal of fun. Microsoft maintains a list of local user groups at:

http://msdn.microsoft.com/usergroups/find.asp.

Since the final launch, an international users group coalition has formed that will bring nationally recognized speakers, resources, and Microsoft assistance to user groups throughout the world. It a tried and tested model, and right now it looks like becoming the most expansive user group effort ever made by Microsoft.

Postlude

Thanks for reading all the way through to the conclusion. If, however, you started here, please now go on to read the rest of the book! Either way, I hope that you feel as myself and David, and the other authors who've helped on the book: Visual Studio .NET – while not perfect – is a huge step in the right direction and will really improve the lives of Microsoft developers.

We've made a lot of points throughout this book, and covered a great deal of ground. We should probably use this final chapter to sum up, but can we do this in a half page? Well, we can only try!

- ❑ **Design your applications**. The architect tools don't have to be used to their full potential, but do use them to some extent. Learn UML and ORM; you'll find it truly worth the outlay. Use Visio to properly think through the app before coding begins. Change control is reduced somewhere in the order of 400% if the app is fully reviewed at the design stage.

- ❑ **Think like an enterprise architect, act like a RAD developer**. There just isn't any excuse to write customer-facing applications with ASP right on top of SQL without a middle tier anymore. It is just too easy to write components.

- ❑ **Broaden your horizons**. Web forms. Windows forms. XML Web Services. SOAP message transfer. Stored procedures. Mobile Web Applications. The world is your oyster, and thanks to VS.NET, the learning curve isn't all that steep any more. Use this book as the launch pad, then go, go, go.

- ❑ **Test**. The debugging tools now work very well – use them. Application Center Test is a great tool that you'd be foolish to ignore. Web Services can be tested through ASP.NET, unlike most other development tools. Put out software that works, using the .NET stamp.

- ❑ **Be flexible**. At press time, 22 languages ran on .NET. Don't think that because you have always used VB that no other language will suit. Different languages do different things well. Look around – there might be something better out there.

Index

A Guide to the Index

The index is arranged hierarchically, in alphabetical order, with symbols preceding the letter A. Most second-level entries and many third-level entries also occur as first-level entries. This is to ensure that users will find the information they require however they choose to search for it.

wrox

Programmer to Programmer™

Registration Code: 6969M2O0HZ21E502

Wrox writes books for you. Any suggestions, or ideas about how you want information given in your ideal book will be studied by our team. Your comments are always valued at Wrox.

Free phone in USA 800-USE-WROX
Fax (312) 893 8001

UK Tel.: (0121) 687 4100   Fax: (0121) 687 4101

Effective Visual Studio .NET – Registration Card

Name _____

Address _____

_____

_____

City _____ State/Region _____

Country _____ Postcode/Zip _____

E-Mail _____

Occupation _____

How did you hear about this book?

❏ Book review (name) _____

❏ Advertisement (name) _____

❏ Recommendation _____

❏ Catalog _____

❏ Other _____

Where did you buy this book?

❏ Bookstore (name) _____ City _____

❏ Computer store (name) _____

❏ Mail order _____

❏ Other _____

What influenced you in the purchase of this book?

❏ Cover Design   ❏ Contents   ❏ Other (please specify):

How did you rate the overall content of this book?

❏ Excellent   ❏ Good   ❏ Average   ❏ Poor

What did you find most useful about this book? _____

_____

What did you find least useful about this book? _____

_____

Please add any additional comments. _____

_____

_____

What other subjects will you buy a computer book on soon?

_____

What is the best computer book you have used this year?

_____

Note: This information will only be used to keep you updated about new Wrox Press titles and will not be used for any other purpose or passed to any other third party.

wrox

Programmer to Programmer™

Note: If you post the bounce back card below in the UK, please send it to:

Wrox Press Limited, Arden House, 1102 Warwick Road,
Acocks Green, Birmingham B27 6HB. UK.

Computer Book Publishers